The Special-Needs Collection

CHILDREN
with VISUAL
IMPAIRMENTS

A Parents' Guide

Edited by M. Cay Holbrook, Ph.D.

WOODBINE HOUSE • 1996

Cover illustration: Elizabeth Wolf
Illustration of the eye, p. 22, reprinted with permission of Prevent Blindness America. Copyright © 1995.

Library of Congress Cataloging-in-Publication Data

Children with visual impairments : a parents' guide / edited by
M. Cay Holbrook.
    p. cm.
    Includes bibliographical references and index.
    ISBN 0-933149-36-0
    1. Visually handicapped children. 2. Children, Blind. 3. Parents of handi-
capped children. I. Holbrook, M. Cay, 1955-
    HV1596.3.C55 1995
    649'.1511—dc20   95-25645
                                              CIP

Manufactured in the United States of America

10 9 8 7 6 5

Table of Contents

Acknowledgements

Many people have helped make this book happen. The chapter authors were each excited about the book from the very beginning and carried that excitement through till the end. I received support and encouragement from Susan Stokes and the other staff at Woodbine House, who persisted and showed great patience and commitment to this project.

Thanks to Wayne Peternel, who compiled much of the resource list and chapter readings, and to the preschool consultants at the Arkansas School for the Blind, Janie Humphries, Joan Rabjohn, Cindy Lester, and Bette Parker, for their consistent support of this project through arranging parent interviews and taking pictures and reading draft after draft of text. Thanks to Bob Brasher, Pat Smith, Mary Hendricks, Darick Wright, Debbie Cearley, Tom Smith, Bonnie Smith, Calvin Churchwell, Judy Jewell, Carolyn Nash, Jo Ellen Croft, Luanne Ewald, LeAnn Nannen, Christy Reese, Kathy Brown, and Ronnie Hallsell for providing valuable information, and to Alan Koenig for his unique gift of troubleshooting computer problems and his encouragement throughout this project.

My most heartfelt gratitude goes to the parents of children with whom I have worked throughout the years, especially to the Suttons, the Lewises, the Lanhams, the Faulkners, and many others who allowed me to participate in a precious part of their lives. I have learned so much more from these wonderful families than I have taught them.

Finally, I must thank my siblings who have generously allowed me to participate in the parenting of six delightful nieces and nephews, David and Carter, Carol, Katherine, Joe, and Sam. Through these children, I have learned that teachers have in their care the most precious of all resources. Thank you Jane and Scott, Corley and Sandy. And to my parents, Carl and Sara Holbrook, thanks for allowing me, during the final days of this project, to retreat back to a home where there is always pound cake and homemade peach ice cream waiting along with the support that parents provide to their children, no matter how much they "grow up."

Introduction

M. Cay Holbrook, Ph.D.

In my eighteen years of working in the field of visual impairments, I have had the opportunity to get to know many families. I have discovered that all parents, regardless of their age, experience with other children, educational background, or place of residence, want information and support on issues relating to their child's visual impairment. They have questions about the cause of their child's visual impairment and whether it will get worse. They have concerns about how their child with a visual impairment will affect their family. They wonder if they could and should be doing more to maximize their child's independence. And on top of everything else, they may be struggling to cope with very intense feelings about their child's diagnosis.

This book is intended to help parents of children with visual impairments begin to get a handle on these common types of concerns. It was written by a team of professionals and parents, each of whom is an expert on a different aspect of caring for children with visual impairments. Much of the information in the book is slanted toward the concerns of parents of younger children (birth to age five), but a great deal of information should also be valuable to parents of school-aged or older children. We have included information that we hope will be helpful to children with a wide range of visual impairments—from children with "low vision" to those who are totally blind. We also address the concerns of parents whose children have one or more other disabilities in addition to a visual impairment.

It is our hope that parents will benefit from the information in this book and that it might be a starting point for gathering information and becoming informed advocates. Not everything included in this book will apply to all children; likewise, not all available information is included within these pages. *Children with Visual Impairments* is intended to serve as a beginning point. Some parents will read this book before they read anything else, while others will already have a wealth of knowledge and information before reading it. In any case, by the time your child reaches school age you will probably feel that you have enough information to fill a library of books!

The following chapters in this book will help point you in the right direction:

- Chapter 1 addresses very basic information about the nature of visual impairments, how the degree of visual impairment is assessed, and the impact of visual impairment on the life of a child and a family.

- Chapter 2 focuses on medical aspects, including the most common causes of visual impairments and how they are treated. This chapter was written by a team consisting of an optometrist and an ophthalmologist, combining the best of information from both professionals.

- Chapter 3, written by a parent, addresses the process of accepting your child's disabilities from diagnosis through childhood. Chapter 4 provides information about child development, and how development typically differs for children with a visual impairment. Chapter 5 discusses the impact of a visual impairment on day-to-day activities and offers suggestions for working on daily living skills at home.

- Chapter 6 focuses on how having a child who is visually impaired can complicate and enrich family life, while Chapter 7 is devoted to encouraging positive self-esteem for your child throughout his life.

- Chapter 8 contains an overview of special education issues, including what you can expect in early intervention and school-age programs, and Chapter 9 gives a brief overview of legal issues related to education, discrimination, accessibility, and other areas.

- Chapter 10 offers information about reading options for individuals with visual impairments and about helping your child develop the skills to be a good reader, which you can do starting in infancy. Chapter 11 discusses orientation and mobility skills—the skills that enable a child with visual impairments to know where he is in his environment and to travel independently from one place to another.

- Chapter 12 provides information relevant to children who have other disabilities in addition to visual impairments, focusing on differences in development and how developmental problems can be minimized.

- Chapter 13 takes us on a trip to the future and provides some insight into what educational, social, travel, self-help, and other issues your child might face in the years to come.

Finally, there are additional resources (lists of organizations, schools, and publications, and a glossary) at the back of the book to help you continue your quest for more knowledge about visual impairments and about services and resources that can help your child.

In this age of political correctness, a few notes about word usage are in order. First, we used the personal pronouns "he" and "she" alternately by chapter. We didn't want to imply that all children with a visual impairment are either boys or girls, and constantly using "he/she" and "his/her" can become very cumbersome. Second, we chose to use the term "visual impairment" rather than such variations as "visual disabilities" or "visual handicaps." Visual impairment is a generic term that is widely used and accepted to refer to all levels of vision loss.

Gathering information that will help you and your child is an on-going process that will probably never end. You are beginning a journey that will take you through a lifetime of successes and failures. The more prepared you are and the more prepared your child is, the more successful you will be at weathering the storms that might come. This book and others like it will help you gather needed information. Over time, however, you will become the person who best knows your own child's strengths and abilities. Knowing this will add to your confidence, and your confidence will add to your ability to stand up for your child and for what you know is right for him.

Chapter One

◄○►

What Is
Visual Impairment?

M. Cay Holbrook, Ph.D.*

Most people believe that they know the answer to the question "What is visual impairment?" Maybe this is because blindness
is one of the few disabilities that we can simulate. From the time
we are children, we play games that involve wearing a blindfold.
We close our eyes and believe that this is "what it is like" to be
blind. In reality, however, visual impairments are seldom like this.
Most children and adults who are considered visually impaired
have some useable vision. In fact, even children who are considered blind often have some visual perception of light and dark that
will assist them as they learn about their world.

This chapter will give you a basic understanding of the great
variability in visual impairments. It introduces and explains some
of the terminology used to describe different types and degrees of
visual impairment. It also explains how a visual impairment is diagnosed and provides an idea of what the future may hold for your
child.

Throughout this chapter and this book you will find general information about children who have visual impairments. Some of
this information and some of the suggestions may be useful for you
right now. Other information may not be useful to you now, but
may help you in the future. Still other information may seem as if

---

* M. Cay Holbrook is currently Associate Professor of Education at The
University of Arkansas at Little Rock. She has worked with children who
have visual impairments in South Carolina, Georgia, Louisiana, and Florida.
She received her Ph.D. in special education from Florida State University.

it is just not applicable to your child. This is to be expected. Children with visual impairments, like all children, are individuals, first

and foremost. There is no one accurate picture of what "the child with a visual impairment" is like. Remember that you are now and will always be the best judge of your child's needs, abilities, and weaknesses. This book can give you a general idea of what to expect for your child, but only your child can show you his true capabilities.

What Is Visual Impairment?

In general, the term *visual impairment* can refer to any condition in which eyesight cannot be corrected to what is considered "normal." In this book, the term is used to refer to a loss of vision that makes it difficult or impossible to complete daily tasks without specialized adaptations. This visual impairment is often due to a loss of *visual acuity.* That is, the eye is not able to see objects as clearly— to make out as much detail—as usual. Visual impairments may also be due to a loss of *visual field*—the total area that can be seen without moving the eyes or head. A child with a visual field loss may or may not be able to see objects clearly within his smaller field of vision.

There are three underlying reasons for impairment of vision. First, there may be damage to one or more parts of the eye essential to vision. This damage may interfere with the way the eye receives or processes visual information. Second, the eyeball may be proportioned incorrectly (have different dimensions than usual), making it harder to focus on objects. And third, the part of the brain that processes visual information may not work properly. The eye may be perfectly normal, but the brain is not able to analyze and interpret visual information so that the child can see. Chapter

2 discusses the most common conditions that cause these problems with the eye or the brain.

A visual impairment may be present at birth, or it may develop during infancy or childhood. Some visual impairments get worse over time, some stay about the same, and a few may even get better. Some children have "fluctuating vision"—or visual functioning that is different at different times of the day. (See below.)

The same eye condition can sometimes affect two children's vision very differently. One may have a slight vision loss, while the other has a more significant loss. Chapter 2 will give you some specific information about various eye conditions and typical effects of the conditions. You must remember, however, that every child is unique. Your child's vision may be very different from that of another child with the same condition. Your ophthalmologist or optometrist will be the best source of information about the nature and extent of your child's visual impairment.

The Diagnosis of a Visual Impairment

Sometimes visual impairments are detected at birth, before the baby leaves the hospital. Other times, parents may be the first to notice that something is not quite right with their child's eyes. They may notice that their baby doesn't watch them as they walk across the room. Maybe his eyes are crossed or he seems startled when someone picks him up without talking to him first. No matter how strong a parent's suspicions are, however, the diagnosis of a visual impairment is not "official" until an eye care professional confirms that there is a significant loss of visual acuity or field. This section introduces the professionals who may evaluate your child's sight and explains how they determine if your child has a significant loss of vision.

Professionals Qualified to Make a Diagnosis

Two different professionals are qualified to measure your child's vision and determine whether he has a visual impairment. The first is an *ophthalmologist,* a medical doctor who has specialized training in diagnosing and treating diseases and conditions of the eye. When an ophthalmologist's name is written, the letters M.D. follow it, because he or she is a medical doctor. This doctor is qualified to prescribe medications, perform surgery on the eye, and ad-

dress medical problems relating to eyes. He or she can also measure visual acuity and visual fields and prescribe eye glasses.

The other professional who can evaluate vision is an *optometrist*.
The optometrist is a "doctor of optometry" (O.D.), who spent four
years in optometry school, but is not a medical doctor. This eye
care professional is qualified to measure visual acuity and visual
fields and to prescribe eye glasses.

Either an ophthalmologist or optometrist can make the initial
determination of whether your child has a visual impairment. Both
are qualified to prescribe corrective lenses and should be able to
discuss your child's visual impairment with you. If, however, your
child needs medical attention because of his eye condition, it is advisable for him to be under the care of an ophthalmologist. Chapter
2 discusses some additional considerations to keep in mind when
choosing an eye care professional for long-term care of your child's
visual impairment.

How Vision Is Measured

To understand how visual impairments are diagnosed, you
need to understand how vision is measured. Most of us have had
our vision checked at one time or another, but what does it really
mean if we are told that our vision is 20/20 (or worse)?

Measuring Acuity. The phrase "20/20 vision" is a measurement of how well someone is able to read a chart that contains letters and/or numbers of different sizes. The most common chart
used by eye care professionals has a large E at the top and is sometimes called the "E Chart," but its official name is the "Snellen
Chart." Visual acuity (how clearly you see) is determined by the
size of letters that you can read and the distance at which you can
read them. The typical testing distance is 20 feet from the chart,
because at 20 feet your eye is relaxed; the lens of your eye is in its
natural position instead of trying to focus (or *accommodate*).

People with normal visual acuity can clearly read 3/8" letters or
numbers at a distance of 20 feet. They are said to have 20/20 vision
because at 20 feet from the chart they see what a normally sighted
person sees at 20 feet. When someone's visual acuity is worse than
normal, the second number will be larger than 20. Someone with
20/80 vision, for example, sees at 20 feet what a normally sighted
person sees at 80 feet. Someone with 20/600 vision sees at 20 feet
what a normally sighted person sees at 600 feet. When someone's

acuity is better than normal, the second number will be smaller than 20. For instance, someone with 20/15 vision sees at 20 feet what a normally sighted person sees at 15 feet. (Note: to convert the Snellen Notation used in the United States to Metric Notation, divide both the top and the bottom numbers by 3.25—for example, 20/200 equals 6/60 in Metric Notation.)

You should note the use of the phrase *normally sighted.* There is no such thing as "perfect" sight. A visual acuity of 20/20 only indicates that the person, while sitting in the eye doctor's office, was able to read certain letters on a chart. This acuity measurement does not carry with it a judgment of how someone uses the information that his eyes are gathering.

Naturally, the Snellen Chart is only used to measure visual acuity in those who are able to read letters and numbers. For young children and nonreaders, there are other ways that visual acuity can be measured. One of the most common is through a test known as the *Lighthouse Flash Card Test for Children.* This test works the same way as the Snellen Chart except that there are bold line drawings of a circle, an apple, a house, and a square instead of letters and numbers. Even very young preschoolers can identify these shapes (especially after a little practice), so acuity can be measured at a very young age. Approximate visual acuities can also be obtained by using toys and household objects of various sizes and determining the child's ability to see the objects at various distances. If the child wears glasses, acuity is measured both with and without glasses.

It is very difficult or impossible to determine an accurate acuity for infants or for children with communication difficulties. One way to attempt to determine approximate visual acuities is through *Preferential Looking.* A doctor using this technique shows two cards to the child at the same time. One card has black and white stripes, and the other has a large gray area. The doctor watches the child to determine whether he fixates (focuses) on the striped card, which is presumed to be more interesting for him to look at. The doctor continues to present cards with stripes that are smaller and closer together until the child no longer focuses on them. This gives a general idea of visual acuity until a more accurate measurement can be made.

The eye doctor will measure acuity in each eye and in both eyes working together. It is possible to have a visual acuity of 20/20 in one eye, and 20/40 in the other eye, and still see with an acuity

of 20/20 with both eyes together. As the eye doctor measures your child's visual acuity, he or she will give you information on the visual acuity of each eye and also a visual acuity of both eyes working together.

Measuring Visual Field. The eye doctor may also conduct an assessment of your child's visual field. This assessment will help your doctor determine how much of the space around him your child can see without moving his eyes or head. Visual field is expressed in degrees. "Normal" visual fields are obstructed by facial features such as the nose and eyebrows, but are approximately 160 to 170 degrees horizontally.

Testing your child's visual field may be difficult because in order to get accurate results, your child must keep his head straight and still and focus his eyes for an extended period of time on a spot directly in front of him. As you might guess, small children are rarely able to do this! Instead, your doctor may ask you or someone else to help do a less precise but more dependable assessment. You will sit on a chair or on the floor with your child in your lap and the doctor sitting right in front of you. Usually, the doctor holds an interesting toy or object and draws your child's attention to him while you slowly bring a toy, bright object, or penlight from in back of your child to in front of him. By watching your child's eyes, the doctor will be able to see when your child's gaze shifts to something new coming into his visual field. You will repeat this procedure several times, bringing the toy into your child's visual field at different locations—sometimes from above, sometimes from the sides, sometimes from below.

If you participate in the assessment process, you may find that you are aware of shifts in your child's gaze as he uses his peripheral vision and throughout the day. For example, as your child is sitting at the kitchen table eating lunch, his gaze may shift as the family cat walks by. He is demonstrating an awareness of movement outside his central vision.

When your child gets older and is able to sit still for longer periods of time, your doctor will probably want to conduct a more sophisticated assessment of your child's visual field. Until then, informal assessments provide very useful information.

Sometimes eye doctors use abbreviations to describe a child's visual impairment. Listed in the Glossary are the most common abbreviations that are used in eye reports from ophthalmologists and optometrists. You should also not hesitate to ask questions if your child's eye doctor uses terminology you do not understand. The professionals working with you should be willing to explain anything that you do not understand. In the same vein, let professionals know that you *do* understand what they are trying to explain and that they can give you more complicated information. You will have to set the tone for your interactions with professionals. See Chapter 2 for more information on dealing with eye care professionals.

Degrees of Vision Loss

After your child's visual acuity and visual field have been measured, the ophthalmologist or optometrist will be able to tell you: 1) whether your child has a visual impairment, and if so, 2) how significant it is.

If your child has a visual impairment, you may find that additional labels are used to describe the amount of vision he has. In fact, there have been many debates over labels and terminology to be used when referring to individuals with impaired vision. In part, this debate continues because of a need or desire to use terminology which accurately reflects the person's visual ability, but also because of an unfortunate sensitivity over the use of the words "blind" and "blindness." Historically, the word "blind" has not been used positively in our society. No one sitting at the ballpark would mistake the angry cry, "What? Are you blind, ump?" with a compliment of the umpire's officiating skills. Likewise, someone who is said to "blindly follow his peers" is pegged as a person with little independence and poor judgement. But truly, the word blind is accurate when describing significant loss of vision and does not carry with it a judgement of a person's worth or his ability. We must be diligent in our insistence that there is no shame attached to the word blind.

Still, in order to accurately describe individuals with different degrees of vision loss, additional terms may be used. For instance, individuals who have vision which can be used to read print (either regular print or large print) may be referred to as being *"partially sighted"* or having *"low vision."* You will probably also hear the term *legal blindness.* This term does not mean that the child is totally blind. This term has a specific definition. It is: "a visual acuity of 20/200 or less in the better eye after correction and/or a visual field of no greater than 20 degrees." In other words, even with glasses or contacts on, this person would see at 20 feet what a normally sighted person sees at 200 feet, and/or would have a visual field of no greater than 20 degrees.

There are children whose vision is so limited that it cannot be expressed in 20/XX terms. These children are not able to see any of the letters on the eye chart as they sit or stand 20 feet away. The first thing an eye doctor will probably do is try to test the child closer than 20 feet away from the chart. If this is the case, the top number of the acuity measurement will indicate the distance at which the testing is done. The bottom number still indicates what the child is able to see at that distance. You may see an acuity like 10/200 or 5/200. Theoretically, these acuity measurements can be converted into more standard acuities (for example, 10/200 can be converted to 20/400; 5/200 to 20/800). As mentioned below, however, these numbers often don't tell us much about how a child uses his vision and so are not as valuable as an examination of his functional vision.

There are some children whose acuity cannot be measured using the eye chart at all. In these cases, the eye doctor may try alternative methods for testing vision. Here are some terms that might be used:

Counts Fingers (or CF) at _____ feet (or inches)

This simply means that the doctor holds up his fingers and asks the child to count them (or for very young children, to point at them or touch them) and takes note of the distance at which the child is able to do this.

Hand Movement (or HM) at ____ feet (or inches)

This measurement indicates the distance at which the child can recognize the movement of a hand in front of his eyes.

Light Projection

This term refers to the ability to tell where light is coming from and can be tested by asking the child to point to the light coming from the window or an open door.

Light Perception

This term refers to the ability to tell the presence or absence of light (whether the light is on or off) without being able to tell where the light is coming from.

As you can see, there are many terms to describe different visual abilities. Rarely do we assume that a child has absolutely no vision, unless his eyes have been *enucleated* (removed) for some reason. If the child has some level of visual ability, it may be used for important tasks such as orientation and mobility and daily living skills.

It is difficult to understand what is referred to as *"total blindness."* The most clever explanation I have ever heard came from an adult whose vision in one eye had been destroyed by a severed optic nerve. In other words, the nerve that carries impulses from the eye to the brain was completely cut and no information was being transmitted from that eye to his brain. He was asked several times, "What do you see with that eye? Is it just black?" His answer was, "I see with this eye what you see with your nose—nothing." This was an amusing way to express an extremely difficult concept.

Some services or benefits are only available to individuals with a measured acuity of a certain level or less. Often this level is 20/200. For this reason, you may hear about legal blindness a lot. Maybe you will hear it because a camp offers summer scholarships for children with a visual acuity of no greater than 20/200. Or maybe you might need your eye doctor to sign a form certifying that your child's visual acuity is no greater than 20/200 so that you can get books on cassette tape or in braille from the Library of Congress/Library for the Blind and Physically Handicapped.

Some school districts have a visual acuity level which must be documented prior to a child being admitted into a special education program. More commonly, though, school districts consider each child individually to determine eligibility for special education services. A child would be eligible if it is determined that his visual impairment has had or will have an impact on his learning.

Although it is important to know what your child's visual acuity or visual field is, you must remember that 20/200 (or any measurement) is not a magic number. What is much more important is *how* your child uses the vision he has to accomplish daily tasks at home and in the community. Your child has his own unique abilities and needs, strengths and weaknesses. Learning about the general characteristics of children with visual impairments, as well as your child's particular eye condition, can be useful and helpful. It is most important, however, that your child be allowed to develop in his own way without preconceived expectations based on what is considered "typical."

Your Child's Functional Vision

Sometimes two children who have the same visual acuity have different abilities to use their vision to accomplish everyday activities. One six-year-old with 20/400 vision may be able to walk independently to the corner bus stop, while another child with the same visual acuity may not. One twelve-year-old with 20/600 vision might effectively use his vision to examine maps in his social studies book, while another student with the same visual acuity might struggle with the same task. To help you and the adults who interact with your child know how well your child uses his vision to function in his world, he should be given a functional vision assessment. This assessment should be conducted by a teacher who has special training in the area of visual impairments.

There are many different types of functional vision assessments. In general, however, information about how your child uses his vision will be gathered by observing him in a variety of settings. The person conducting the assessment should observe your child during inside and outside activities, during structured activities (such as calendar time at preschool) and unstructured activities (such as play time when your child is deciding what activities to do and how to accomplish tasks). The functional vision assessment should yield such information as:

- How well does your child use his eyes to scan across the environment to locate something or someone?
- What lighting is best for your child? Does your child easily move from a light room into a dark room (or from dark to light) without visual difficulties? Although it is a common belief that children with decreased vision require more or brighter lights, this is not always true. Children with albinism, for example, are often bothered by bright lights.
- What size objects is your child able to identify at what distance?
- Does your child get tired easily when trying to accomplish visual tasks such as reading, writing, coloring, and looking at pictures?
- What natural compensations does your child use when he is having difficulty accomplishing a task? Does he squint, place the object closer to him, tilt his head?
- What postures and positions are best for your child? Does he need to have toys, food, etc. presented to him on the right? on the left?
- What does your child enjoy looking at? Bright lights? Colorful toys? Objects with black and white patterns?
- How does your child use his vision to move around? Can he avoid large objects by using sight alone, or does he need to touch them?

By gathering this type of information, the vision specialist can help you create a safe environment for your child that is stimulating and visually interesting for him. Even if your child has very little vision, he can be taught to move safely and efficiently throughout his world.

Some states require that every child with a visual impairment have a functional vision assessment to be eligible for special education. Some states do not require one. Even if your state does not require that your child be given a functional vision assessment, however, your child's vision teacher should do one to learn how best to arrange his environment. By examining how well your child uses his vision, his teachers will be able to begin teaching him strategies to use it more efficiently. The goal is not to improve visual acuity, but to encourage your child to maximize the use of his vision.

Even before your child has a functional vision assessment, you may be able to recognize situations in which he can use vision to

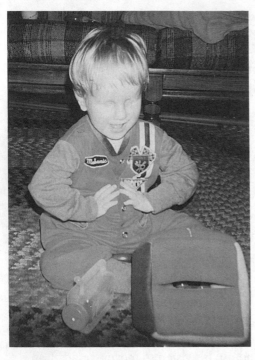

gather information, and situations in which he will find his other senses more useful. It is important that you begin to communicate how your child functions visually with people who work with him. For example, let the Sunday School teacher know that your child will enjoy looking at the brightly colored illustrations in the Sunday School book, but will not be able to color in the faint lines of the workbook. Or, tell the babysitter that she needs to say something when she enters or leaves a room so that your child will know where she is. The more time you spend caring for, playing with, and observing your child, the more you will understand how he is able to use his vision for daily activities.

Fluctuating Vision

Not all children who have a visual impairment have fluctuating vision, but it is important to recognize if your child does. Fluctuating vision may be due to factors such as changes in lighting, familiarity and complexity of the task, fatigue, and/or characteristics of some medical conditions. If your child's vision is fluctuating, you may notice that he is able to accomplish a visual task more easily at some times than others. You may see him get frustrated or angry, or he may rub his eyes or complain of headaches. By watching your child carefully, you will begin to notice which factors affect his ability to use his vision. You will also be better able to help control these factors wherever your child is—at home, at school, at church, or other places.

A rheostat control on lights in your house can allow you to alter the illumination to meet your child's needs, even if those needs change throughout the day. Encouraging your child to close his eyes and rest for a few minutes between activities may help with fatigue. Likewise, helping your child learn to wait patiently when he moves from sunlight into a darker inside room (or from an inside room into the sun) while his eyes adjust to the change may be useful. Your child may learn how to compensate for these changes himself; but then again, he may not. By teaching him some of these "tricks," you help him to be safer and more efficient. Just as importantly, you also show him that making these kinds of adaptations are a normal part of his life and completely accepted, even though they may take a little more time.

Is My Child the Only One?

It is likely that before the diagnosis of your child's visual impairment you had little or no experience with vision loss. You may have known *adults* with a visual impairment, as blindness is most common in those over 65 years old. You probably didn't know parents of a *child* with visual impairments, however. Even now you may not yet have met other families with children with visual impairments. It may feel as if your child is the only child who is visually impaired, and that your family is the only one with questions and concerns about visual impairments.

Although your child is *not* the only one with a visual impairment, there are legitimate reasons for you to feel somewhat isolated. Blindness or visual impairment is considered a "low incidence disability" among children. This means that compared to other disabilities, visual impairments occur in fewer numbers. Approximately one-tenth of a percent of the children in the United States are visually impaired. In other words, 1 in 1000 children have a visual impairment. Of these children, approximately 80 to 85 percent have some useable vision. Although estimates about the number of children with visual impairments may vary according to definitions used, it is clear that the number is relatively small.

To help you cope with feelings you may have of being alone, here are some initial suggestions.

- Realize that being a good parent of a child with a visual impairment is very similar to being a good parent of a child without disabilities. Your child needs your love, your sup-

port, and your consistency: the same things that are
needed by any child.

- Trust yourself. There will be times when you would love
  to call a neighbor, friend, or relative and ask, "What did *you*
  do when your child. . . ." Feel comfortable asking those
  questions, even when the issues revolve around vision loss.
  But don't think that you must wait for solutions from others. Trust yourself, your instincts, and your own solutions.
- Look for support. There are a number of resources you can
  use for support. Family and friends can provide a special
  kind of help; let them know when you need them. There
  are many groups of parents of children with visual impairments (at the local, state, and national levels). Some are
  listed in the Resource Guide at the back of this book.
  Medical and educational professionals in the area of visual
  impairment can also provide support, including helping
  you find resources to answer your specific questions. More
  specific information about the need for and availability of
  support can be found in Chapter 3 and throughout this
  book.
- Look for your child's unique talents, and try to understand
  that visual impairment is only one of your child's characteristics. Perhaps your child is very affectionate or has a
  great sense of humor. Maybe he is mischievous or adven-
  turous or creative. By focusing on all of your child's characteristics, you will begin to realize that in many ways your
  parenting challenges parallel those faced by all parents.

When a Visual Impairment
Is Not the Only Problem

It is estimated that up to 50 or 60 percent of children with visual impairments also have other disabilities. They may, for example, also have a hearing impairment, mental retardation, or cerebral
palsy.

One reason that visual impairments so often go hand in hand
with other disabilities is that more and more premature babies are
surviving, due to improved medical technology. As Chapter 2 explains, prematurity can lead to problems such as bleeding in the
brain or loss of oxygen to the brain. These complications can not
only damage the visual system, but also parts of the brain that gov-

ern movement, hearing, or thinking. Other causes of visual impairment, such as viruses or maternal infections like rubella, can also damage more than one part of the brain, leading to multiple disabilities.

If your child has two or more disabilities, there is a good chance he will be considered "multiply handicapped." Schools often label children multiply handicapped if they have two or more disabilities which each make it more difficult for them to learn in a regular classroom setting.

If your child has multiple disabilities, it will be especially important to pay close attention to his particular strengths, weaknesses, needs, and abilities. The combination of your child's disabilities will be unique to your child. You will need to gather information from a wide variety of sources and learn to apply the information to your unique situation. There will be many professionals who will be able to help you, but you will become the first and most important expert on your child. See Chapter 12 for information on some of the most important issues associated with children with visual impairments and other disabilities.

What about Future Children?

The decision to have children is a highly personal decision for all parents. Parents must take many factors into account, including financial, home, and lifestyle considerations. Parents may also weigh the impact that a new baby will have on other children in the family. Parents of children with disabilities have a couple of special considerations on top of these other concerns. When trying to decide whether to have additional children, these parents need to think about the time and money they have available, since children with disabilities often take more of both.

Perhaps the biggest concern for many parents of children with any disability is that future children may also have a disability. Many eye conditions which result in visual impairments are genetic, meaning that they are passed on by one or both parents. Chapter 2 contains information about specific eye conditions and whether or not they are considered genetic.

There is a great deal that we do not understand about genes and passing on traits from generation to generation, but there is also a great deal that we do understand. Parents who want to know their chances of having another child with the same visual impairment can consult a geneticist or genetic counselor. These professionals usually cannot tell you with any certainty whether your next child will have a visual impairment. Instead, the probability will be expressed in terms like "you have a 1 in 4 chance that your next child will have a similar visual impairment," or "you have a 50–50 chance that future children will have this same condition."

Parents in the process of making this decision may receive unasked-for advice from family members, friends, and total strangers. Consider the example of a young mother who was grocery shopping with her son Tony, who was blind. The cashier, noticing that the mother was pregnant, pointed to Tony and asked, "Aren't you afraid that your baby will be like him?" The mother replied, "I'd have a dozen if I knew they would all have Tony's sense of humor and easy-going personality!"

In contrast, a thoughtful father expressed well his family's decision *not* to have additional children: "We've decided to keep our family small so that we will have the time and energy to do all of those special family activities we have been looking forward to."

Remember that this decision is an important one, but only you can know what is best for your family. By gathering all the information possible, including genetic information, you will be able to make a more knowledgeable decision.

Your Child's Future

As a parent, you are naturally concerned about your child's future. You are also naturally worried about the effect that your child's visual impairment will have on his future. At this point, it is probably impossible for anyone to predict exactly how your child's visual impairment will affect his life. But it may reassure you to know that with each passing year the quality of life is generally improving for *all* people with disabilities.

We have come a long way from the days when people who were blind were placed in institutions or hidden from sight. Your child will have opportunities that were only dreamed about even a generation ago. For example, the printed word has become increasingly accessible to blind children since the invention of braille in the nineteenth century. There are computers with speech output that can "read" printed matter aloud, as well as braille printers that can be attached to word processors.

There are new devices as well as tried-and-true techniques for orientation and mobility that can enable your child to move about independently in his environment. And in 1990, a promising new law—the Americans with Disabilities Act—was passed to prohibit discrimination against people with disabilities in a number of areas. As a result, your child will be able to become more a part of his community than ever before. He will grow up knowing that employers cannot discriminate against him simply because he has a visual impairment, and that public buildings have braille labels on their elevators and restaurants have braille menus.

The challenge for you as parents is to make sure that your child receives the training and services he needs to become as independent as possible. The following chapters of this book should help to point you in the right direction.

Conclusion

If you have just learned that your child has a visual impairment, your questions and concerns may be overwhelming. Bear in mind, however, that you don't have to learn everything about your child's condition at once. Over time, you will meet others—parents, teachers, doctors—who can help answer your questions, offer advice about caring for your child, and refer you to helpful resources. Gradually, as you get to know your child, you will realize that some information is relevant to your child, and some is not, and you will get better at separating the important information from the unimportant. Like other parents, you will learn the best ways to take care of your child's needs, play with him, and enjoy his company. More importantly, you will learn that despite your child's visual impairment, he is really much more like other children than different.

With time, your early focus on your child's visual impairment will shift so that it is no longer your overriding concern. As difficult as it may be to believe today, there *will* come a day when your family's situation will seem manageable again and you and your child will be able to get on with your lives.

Parent Statements

As soon as I found out my son had a visual impairment I got on the phone. I called everyone I could. I would ask people to send me information and sometimes it would take weeks to get it. After a few calls I realized that I was the only one in a hurry.

—◄o►—

Before Kevin was born, I had never met one blind person.

—◄o►—

We have to keep this all in perspective. Michael is healthy and happy. His visual impairment will have an impact on his life but it won't ruin it.

—◄o►—

Sometimes I just sit and close my eyes to try to understand what it is like.

—◄o►—

The best thing to happen to us was linking up with a blind adult almost from the very beginning. He has helped all of us so much. We have a sense of what Sarah's life will be like in the future.

—◄○►—

I never really noticed before how much I use my vision during the course of the day. Now I think about it all the time.

—◄○►—

I've spent so much time just trying to find out very basic things. I've been to the library, I've spent hours on the phone, I've even gone to a conference. Every time I get more information I feel better and more powerful.

—◄○►—

I refused prenatal testing during my first pregnancy, but I had CVS done the second time around. Once burnt, twice shy, I guess.

—◄○►—

The first blind person I had any personal contact with was the man who tuned the pianos at my college. There was also one blind student, who used a dog guide, and lived in my dorm. She was very outgoing and self-confident, and everyone knew her and her dog. Up until then, I had hardly even *seen* anyone with a significant visual impairment out in public. I guess this was partially because visual impairments are relatively rare, but also because community inclusion was not as common as it is today.

—◄○►—

I never realized how uncommon visual impairments are. I sometimes think it would be a lot easier to find out information and get support if my child had a more common disability.

—◄○►—

I called the School for the Blind and they were able to help me immediately even though my child was only a few months old.

—◄○►—

When I first found out about Heather's blindness, I tried to get all kinds of books and magazine articles and anything else I could read about blindness. A friend of mine even ran a computer check at the library and came up with lots of good information.

We laugh so much more than we cry these days!

Chapter Two

-◄O►-

Medical Issues, Treatments, and Professionals

Steven Stiles, O.D., and Robert Knox, M.D.*

Most children with visual impairments are just as healthy as other children. They are no more likely to catch routine childhood illnesses, develop allergies, or need to visit the pediatrician than any other child. They do, however, need specialized medical care to diagnose and treat their eye condition. Consequently, you may find yourself spending more time in doctors' offices than you would otherwise. You will also need to spend more time learning about selected medical issues in order to understand your child's condition and feel comfortable talking to doctors about it.

This chapter provides the basic information you need to get started talking with your ophthalmologist or optometrist. It explains how the eye ordinarily works, as well as the most common eye conditions that can cause visual impairments in children. It also covers important considerations in choosing and working with eye care professionals and gives you an idea of what to expect during a complete eye examination. Over the months and years, it will, of course, be important for you to focus more on the issues di-

---

* Dr. Stiles graduated from Southern College of Optometry and is currently in private practice in Fort Smith, Arkansas. He has a special interest in the needs of individuals with low vision.

   Dr. Knox graduated from The University of Texas Medical Branch and is currently in private practice in Fort Smith, Arkansas with the Ophthalmology Clinic, Inc.

rectly related to your child. But at least in the beginning, a basic knowledge of general ophthalmology and medical terms will help boost your confidence in dealing with eye care professionals.

Basic Anatomy of the Eye

When you talk with your child's eye care specialist, you may hear references to different parts of the eye as they relate to your child's visual impairment. Nobody expects you to have a complete medical knowledge of the eye. However, a general understanding of the parts of the eye and how they work is essential to understanding your child's visual impairment.

The eye is small, but complex. It contains many of the tiniest parts of the body, and the way it works is still not completely understood. Knowledge about the parts of the eye and their function, however, has greatly increased during the past century. The parts of the eye have been assigned to three different groups, based on the role they play in vision. These groups are known as the optical system, the nervous system, and the eye movement system. This section explains how these three systems work together to enable us to see.

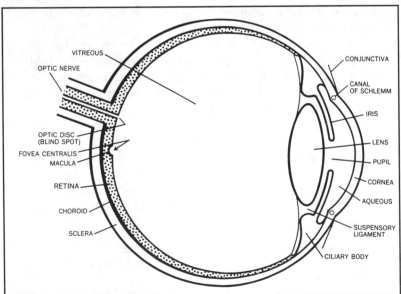

Reprinted with permission by Prevent Blindness America. Copyright © 1995.

You may want to refer to the drawing of the eye on page 22 as the different parts of the eye are described.

The Eye's Optical System

Perhaps you have heard the eye referred to as a light receptor organ. This means that the eye receives light rays, which are then interpreted by the brain. The optical system is the part of the eye which receives the light rays and focuses them before they are relayed to the brain. The optical system consists of the following parts of the eye:

The **cornea** is the clear dome on the front of the eye. To function properly, the cornea needs to be smooth, evenly curved, and clear so that light can pass through it. The cornea is the only part of the eye that can currently be transplanted.

The **anterior chamber** is the space between the cornea and the iris. It is filled with fluid called **aqueous.**

The **iris** is the colored part of the eye. The amount of pigment in the iris may vary from minimal in the light blue eye to densely pigmented in the dark brown eye. The function of the iris is to regulate the amount of light that enters the eye. A healthy or normal iris is circular and controls the size of the pupil, which looks like a black dot in the center of the eye, but is really a hole created by the doughnut-like shape of the iris. The iris allows the **pupil** to contract or expand (get smaller or larger) and thus let the correct amount of light into the eye.

Behind the iris is the **lens** of the eye, sometimes called the crystalline lens. The lens must be clear so that light will pass through it. The lens changes shape, getting fatter or thinner in order to help focus the light on the back of the eye. This focusing ability of the eye is called *accommodation.* Children have the maximum ability to accommodate for near reading or activities at a close distance. This is why some children can hold reading materials very close to their eyes without fatigue. The ability to accommodate diminishes with age.

The back of the eye consists of three main layers. The outer layer (covering the outside of the eye) is called the **sclera**. It is the white part of the eye, and extends from the back of the eye to the cornea. It helps the eye maintain its shape. The second layer is called the **choroid**. It is rich in blood vessels which carry nourishment to the eye. The final, inner layer is known as the retina. The

retina consists of millions of specialized cells which serve as light receptors. The signal initiated in these light receptors is then transported to the brain via the optic nerve.

The Eye's Nerve System

As explained above, the retina consists of millions of light receptors. There are two types of light receptors: cones and rods.

The cones are located in the center of the retina, in an area on the retina called the **macula.** Thus, the cones are sometimes referred to as central or macular receptors. The cones enable us to see detail and color. They are what enable us to see details for reading.

The rods are primarily responsible for peripheral, or "side," vision, and are therefore sometimes referred to as peripheral receptors. They also enable us to see movement and to see in dimmer light.

The nature and severity of many visual impairments is determined by which of the two types of retinal receptors is affected (damaged or non-functional) and to what extent. Unfortunately, it is currently impossible to repair retinal receptors or optic nerve fibers once they have been damaged or failed to function.

The **optic nerve,** which consists of millions of nerve fibers, carries the message from the light receptors to the area of the brain associated with vision.

The Eye's Movement System

Each eye's movement system consists of six muscles connected to the outside of the eye. These muscles, called the *extraocular* muscles, allow the eyes to aim, search, follow, converge (come together), diverge, and fixate. When these muscles align properly, the eyes can then fuse their separate images into one single three-dimensional image. This is what allows *depth perception* (binocular vision).

How We See

The process of seeing begins when the movement system directs the eyes to aim at and fixate on something in the environment. The optical system then focuses the image in much the same way that a camera focuses an image on film. First, light rays reflected from an object enter the eye through the smooth, clear, curved cornea. The cornea begins the process of bending the light rays so that they will focus correctly on the back of the retina. The light rays than pass through the pupil and hit the lens. The muscles in the iris surrounding the pupil expand and contract so that the correct amount of light is available. The lens then finely tunes the light rays so that they form clear images where they strike the retina. Light rays striking the receptors of the retina are converted into nerve impulses by photochemical reaction. The nerve impulses are next carried to the brain via the optic nerve. Finally, the brain "develops" and interprets the image that was projected on the retina. When we perceive this interpreted image, we are doing what is commonly known as "seeing."

Causes of Visual Impairment

Because so many parts of the eye and brain must work closely together in order for us to see well, there are many ways that vision can be impaired.

In children, there are a variety of reasons that one or more parts of the visual system may be damaged or may malfunction. In general, however, visual impairments are due to one of three broad causes:

1) structural impairments, or damage to one or more parts of the eye;
2) refractive errors, or an inability of the eye to sharply focus images on the back of the retina; or
3) cortical visual impairments, which are due to damage to the part of the brain that interprets visual information.

The section below describes the most common types of eye conditions that result from these broad causes. The descriptions are fairly basic; so, for additional information about your child's particular visual impairment, contact your family doctor or refer to one of the references listed in the Reading List at the back of this book.

Structural Impairments

When a child has a structural impairment, one or more parts of the eye's optical, movement, or nerve system is poorly developed, damaged, or does not function properly. Structural impairments may occur before birth or after birth. When they occur before birth, it may be because the baby has inherited a condition that causes structural impairments, or because something happened to disrupt the normal development of the visual system. After birth, structural damage may be caused by injury to the eye, disease, inherited conditions, or a variety of other causes. Regardless of when the damage occurred, the key is to identify the vision problem as soon as possible and promptly take steps to minimize its impact on your child's growth and learning.

Cataracts

A cataract is a cloudiness of the crystalline lens of the eye. Since light cannot pass normally through the cataract, it obscures vision. The effect on vision may vary from no detectable visual impairment to a severe loss of vision. In severe cases, the child may only be able to detect light from dark. Some types of cataracts progressively worsen, while others remain unchanged throughout life. Cataracts may be found in only one eye (unilateral) or in both eyes (bilateral). In children, cataracts may be present at birth.

Cataracts vary in size and severity. Since the early months and years in childhood are critical in learning, prompt assessment and diagnosis are very important.

There are many causes of cataracts in children. They may be inherited, or they may result from an infection to the mother during pregnancy. They may also occur as part of a disease or syndrome that affects many parts of a child's body. Marfan syndrome, Turner syndrome, Cri du chat syndrome, Crouzon syndrome, Apert syndrome, Lowe syndrome, Down syndrome, osteogenesis imperfecta, and juvenile rheumatoid arthritis are examples of conditions associated with cataracts.

The definitive treatment involves surgically removing cataracts from the eyes. Cataracts that are sufficiently cloudy to obscure vision require prompt attention. Often surgery is needed within the first three months of life so that vision can develop properly. Cataract surgery in children is performed under general anesthesia, either on an outpatient or inpatient basis, depending on the child's overall health and age. Young infants are often kept in the hospital for an overnight stay; rarely is a more prolonged stay necessary. The operation is not usually painful.

Surgically removing the crystalline lens results in what doctors refer to as *aphakia* (an eye with no lens). Without a lens, the eye can no longer focus on its own. Consequently, your child will need either contact lenses or glasses to provide a clear image to the retina. Cataract surgery is usually very successful for all ages. If your child's eye is otherwise healthy, she could possibly develop normal vision after the operation. Usually children become quite farsighted immediately after the operation and need strong corrective lenses. The farsightedness is corrected with one contact lens if only one eye underwent cataract surgery and with two contact lenses or eyeglasses if both eyes had surgery. The amount of farsightedness frequently decreases over several years as the child's eye grows, reaching normal adult size near puberty. As your child's eye grows, she will require frequent changes in her prescription for corrective lenses. Once her eyes have stopped growing, she may be able to have artificial lenses (intraocular lenses) permanently implanted. Your doctor might even suggest implanting lenses earlier.

Sometimes children who have had cataracts have trouble learning to use vision in one eye or both eyes. If so, your doctor may prescribe the use of an eye patch, as described in the section on Amblyopia, below. The road to maximal visual development following cataract removal requires long-term follow-up and much dedication. Be sure to follow your doctor's advice and schedule routine visits to make sure your child's visual development continues to progress.

Glaucoma

Glaucoma is a condition in which the pressure from fluid inside the anterior chamber of the eye is too high. If the condition is not promptly detected and treated, the excessive pressure can irreversibly damage the optic nerve. This nerve damage results in loss of peripheral (side) vision initially, and central vision if the damage continues.

If glaucoma is treated before severe nerve damage results, there can still be lasting visual impairments. Since the outer wall of an infant's eye is very elastic, continued high pressures cause the wall to stretch and the eye to enlarge. (Only in infancy does the eye actually enlarge due to glaucoma; once enlarged, the eye usually remains large even after surgery.) The effects of glaucoma result in high degrees of nearsightedness and astigmatism. (See "Refractive Errors," below.) As the eye enlarges, the cornea may also become stretched, which can lead to clouding and scarring of the cornea. Glaucoma in infants is usually not painful.

To prevent or minimize damage to the eye and the optic nerve, your child's doctor will try to decrease the pressure inside the eye. Sometimes prescription eye drops or oral medications may decrease the pressure. Usually, however, surgery is necessary. The surgery opens the "drainage channels" in the front chamber of the eye, allowing the fluid to drain out more readily. This operation is usually very successful in decreasing the pressure. As in cataract surgery, the glaucoma surgery is performed under general anesthesia on an outpatient or inpatient basis. When glaucoma occurs in infancy, surgery alone may control the pressure for life. Continued follow-up and monitoring of the intraocular pressure, however, is very important.

The degree of visual impairment resulting from glaucoma varies from no visual impairment to complete blindness. The amount of impairment depends on the age of onset of glaucoma, how soon the condition is diagnosed and treated, how well the condition responds to the treatment, and how severely the pressure is increased. Once the pressure is controlled, glaucoma usually does not cause further damage. Often, children need glasses to improve visual acuity which has been impaired by enlargement of the eyes. Many children also require patching treatment for amblyopia, as described below.

In approximately 1 out of 10,000 children born, glaucoma occurs in infancy and early childhood as an isolated inherited disorder. Glaucoma may also be associated with other conditions that affect the eyes or other parts of the body. These conditions include Sturge-Weber syndrome, aniridia, Lowe syndrome, neurofibromatosis, Marfan syndrome, Stickler syndrome, Rubinstein-Taybi syndrome, Trisomy 13, mucopolysaccharidosis, and retinopathy of prematurity.

Amblyopia

Amblyopia is a term derived from the Greek work for "dullness of vision." Colloquially, you may hear it called "lazy eye." Amlyopia refers to the visual impairment that results when a child suppresses the image from one eye. It is important to note that amblyopia is *not* a turning or wandering eye, but may result from an eye that turns or wanders.

Ordinarily, the visual system continues to develop until a child is about nine years old. Sometimes, however, something interferes with normal visual development in one or both eyes. This most often happens: 1) when one eye has better acuity than the other (due to a refractive error, cataracts, corneal scarring, droopy eye lid, or tumor); 2) when one eye is crossed or turned due to strabismus (See "Strabismus," below). To prevent blurred or double vision using both eyes, the child's brain may selectively ignore vision in one eye. Over a period of time, this can result in a permanent visual loss in the unused eye. Vision loss may range from mild to severe, but not total blindness.

If amblyopia is detected and treated before the visual system has reached maturity (approximately age nine), the visual loss may be reversible. Just as the eye can become "lazy" with suppression or with a poorly focused image, so too can it regain vision with proper treatment.

The first step in treating amblyopia is generally to determine why the child isn't using one eye and to treat any underlying vision problem in that eye. For example, if one eye has a droopy eyelid, cataracts, or a large refractive error, these conditions would be treated first. Treatment for amblyopia itself consists of forcing your child to use the "lazy" eye. This is commonly done by covering the stronger eye with a patch. This patch may need to be worn for anywhere from a few months to over a year. Glasses are often also necessary to provide the eyes with a well-focused image. Early detection and treatment are essential, as the younger the child, the more rapidly her eyes respond to treatment.

Patching an eye is sometimes uncomfortable for children. It feels very different to see with only the "lazy" eye, and some children may protest. It is very important that you realize that the number one factor in the success of eye patching is to keep the patch on the eye as prescribed by the doctor. You will need to be diligent in your efforts to help your child keep the patch on. Think of ways to reinforce or reward your child for keeping the patch on. These rewards should have nothing to do with the patch. In other words, allowing her to take the patch off for a reward is not a good idea. Instead, you might suggest a trip to the library for story hour or a visit to a favorite aunt. Remember, the best time for this treatment is early in your child's life. Damage to the eye caused by failure to wear the patch will likely be permanent.

Strabismus

Strabismus is a general term for misaligned ("crossed") eyes. One or both eyes may turn inward (esotropia) or turn outward (exotropia), or the gaze of one eye may be higher than the other (hypertropia). Strabismus may become apparent within a child's first year of life, or may suddenly appear several years later. Strabismus is one of the most common eye conditions among children.

Treatment for strabismus depends on its cause. Sometimes children who are farsighted cross their eyes as they focus to see more clearly. Glasses that correct the farsightedness often also cure the strabismus. Other times strabismus results from paralysis of the extraocular muscles of the movement system, which creates an imbalance in the muscles' strength. Sometimes children are born with esotropia (congenital esotropia). In these instances, the cause of strabismus is not known. In congenital esotropia, surgery is necessary to correct the misalignment. The operation is performed under general anesthesia on an outpatient basis. About 70 percent of the time, one surgical procedure is enough to "fix" the misalignment. Additional surgery can be performed months or years later if further straightening is needed to improve binocular vision or the appearance of the eyes.

If strabismus is not promptly treated, your child may ignore or suppress the vision in one eye to avoid double vision. As discussed above, this can prevent the suppressed eye from developing normal vision (amblyopia). Your child will also have reduced binocular ("3–D") vision if her eyes are not properly aligned. (Children with congenital esotropia may still have reduced binocular vision even with surgery.) Because the crucial period for the development of the visual system is approximately in the first ten years of life, strabismus should be treated as early as possible. This can maximize your child's development of binocular vision and minimize the risk of amblyopia.

Retinopathy of Prematurity

Retinopathy of prematurity (ROP) is a condition that can cause vision loss or blindness in infants born prematurely. As the name implies, it is caused by damage to the retina.

Ordinarily, the blood vessels of the retina complete their growth at the baby's approximate due date (9 months gestation). Premature infants are thus born before the retinal blood vessels have completed their growth. As the vessels continue to grow after a premature baby's birth, abnormal vessels, as well as scar tissue, can form inside the eye. In extreme cases, the retina may become scarred, distorted, or detached (separated from the back of the eye). This causes visual impairment ranging from a mild decrease in acuity to total loss of vision. Usually, however, ROP spontaneously improves before the retina is severely damaged.

The more premature an infant is and the less she weighs at birth, the greater the risk of developing ROP. Infants who weigh at least 2500 grams (5 pounds, 8 ounces) are usually not at risk. Infants born at 28 weeks of gestation or earlier or with a birth weight of 1250–1500 grams or less (approximately 2 pounds, 12 ounces to 3 pounds, 5 ounces) have the greatest risk of developing ROP. One study found that 66 percent of infants who weighed 1250 grams or less at birth and 82 percent of infants who weighed 1000 grams or less (approximately 2 pounds, 3 ounces) developed some degree of ROP. Premature infants who are given oxygen treatment for respiratory problems are thought to be at increased risk for ROP.

Several types of treatment can often prevent ROP from reaching its most severe stages. Cryotherapy (freezing therapy) and laser therapy can be used to decrease the abnormal growth of blood vessels. The point at which either of these treatments is recommended is termed *threshold disease*. If a child's retinas have already become detached, complicated surgical procedures are necessary to try to reattach the retinas. If the retina is totally detached, surgery is much less likely to be successful and a significant visual impairment is more likely.

Children with ROP usually require long-term eye care. Although some children have normal visual acuity, amblyopia and significant refractive errors, including nearsightedness, farsightedness, and astigmatism, are common. Total blindness with no light perception may also occur. Strabismus and glaucoma may also develop and require additional treatment.

Nystagmus

Nystagmus is a rhythmic oscillation or "jiggling" of the eyes which cannot be controlled by the child. Most often, the eyes move back and forth, but they may also move up and down, in a rotary or bobbing fashion, or in a combination of these movements. Nystagmus is usually present in both eyes, but can also occur in one eye. Nystagmus may occur alone, or it may accompany another vision problem such as congenital cataracts, albinism, a neurological condition, or an abnormality of the cornea.

Although congenital nystagmus generally does not appear to make objects move, visual acuity is reduced. In children with congenital nystagmus, distance vision may be limited to 20/40 to 20/400. Often, however, children with nystagmus find a head position or eye position which diminishes the intensity of the nystagmus. This head position, called the "null point," is strongly preferred by the child, as it gives her the best possible visual acuity. Sometimes this position or posture is so extreme that surgery to alter the alignment of the eyes and thus move the null point over may be beneficial. This type of operation usually succeeds in moving the null point, but does not eliminate the nystagmus. Frequently, nystagmus is dampened when a child focuses on a near object. Therefore, your child's vision when reading may be much better than her vision for distant objects. Some parents report that their child's nystagmus gets worse when her eyes are tired.

There is no generally accepted treatment for nystagmus. Special prescription prism lenses, however, may improve visual efficiency and comfort if your child is able to reduce the nystagmus by turning her head. The prisms would not necessarily be prescribed for full-time wear, but would be worn during specific activities. The doctor should also determine whether your child has nearsightedness, farsightedness, or astigmatism that could be improved with glasses. Attempts to decrease the intensity of the nystagmus through eye muscle surgery or by injecting botulinum toxins (poisons) around the eyes have been investigated with varying levels of success. These treatments are generally considered to be of questionable benefit. Your child's ophthalmologist can give you more information about the possible risks and benefits of these controversial treatments.

Albinism

Albinism is an inherited condition which causes decreased pigment either in the skin, hair, and eyes, or in the eyes alone. The lack of pigment in the front of the eye (iris) is most noticeable and leads to a very light blue color of iris. The lack of pigment allows the red reflex to shine through the iris tissue as well as the pupil, giving the iris a "pink" appearance. Albinism is present at birth and does not become worse over time. Approximately 1 in 20,000 children is born with the condition.

Children with albinism have incompletely formed (hypoplastic) maculas—the central portion of the retina which provides the sharpest vision. They also have nystagmus and often have refractive errors (see below). As a result, they have reduced visual acuity.

With corrective lenses, visual acuity usually measures around 20/100 to 20/200, although it may be as good as 20/40.

Because their eyes lack pigment to block or absorb light, children with albinism may be very sensitive to the light (photophobic). Tinted glasses or contact lenses can relieve sensitivity to light, and proper prescription lenses or low vision aids can help maximize vision.

Optic Nerve Atrophy

The optic nerve consists of approximately one million fibers which transmit signals from the retina to the brain. If fibers are damaged, they may die and atrophy (waste away). When fibers atrophy, transmission of information from the eye to the brain is impaired. The resulting visual impairment can range from minimal loss of acuity or visual field to total blindness.

Optic atrophy can result from a variety of disorders, including hydrocephalus, glaucoma, retinitis pigmentosa, or from trauma. How significantly vision is affected will depend on the severity of the damage. Depending on the cause of the atrophy, your child's vision may or may not continue to worsen. If possible, treatment is directed at the specific cause in an attempt to prevent further damage to the nerve. For example, if the damage is due to hydrocephalus, treatment involves treating the pressure around the brain; if the damage is due to glaucoma, treatment involves reducing the pressure in the eyes.

Refractive Errors

Refraction refers to the process by which the cornea and lens of the eye bend light rays so they are focused on the retina. For the light rays to be sharply focused, the eyeball must be the right length, the lens must have appropriate power, and the cornea must have the right shape. If any of these parts of the eye is *not* properly proportioned, then visual acuity is reduced. This type of visual impairment is known as a refractive error. Common varieties of refractive errors include nearsightedness, farsightedness, and astigmatism.

Refractive errors, especially nearsightedness, continue to change (usually for the worse) as a child grows. Usually, however, they do not change as much after the teenage years or early adulthood. Some refractive errors are inherited, or passed down from parent to child. There are also some specific eye conditions that may result in extreme refractive errors. These conditions include retinopathy of prematurity, aphakia, glaucoma, and microphthalmia.

Glasses can often compensate for refractive errors, improving vision at least to some degree when they are worn. Contact lenses may also be an option when your child is mature enough to handle the responsibility, or if she has had a lens removed during cataract surgery. See the discussion on "Corrective Lenses and Their Limitations" below for more information.

Myopia (Nearsightedness)

In myopia (nearsightedness), the cornea is excessively curved, the lens is too strong, or the eye is elongated. As a result, images of distant objects are not focused precisely *on* the retina, but in front of it. This makes them appear blurry. Usually, children with myopia can see nearer objects more clearly.

Myopia is quite common. It affects about 2 percent of children by age 6 and 10 percent by age 10. By age 20, approximately 20 percent of young adults have myopia.

The degree of myopia is measured with a unit called the *diopter*, which corresponds with the 20/XX formula explained in Chapter 1. The higher the bottom number in the fraction, the greater a child's myopia. A child with 20/100 vision, for example, sees an object 20 feet away as well as someone with normal vision would see it from a distance of 100 feet. A child with 20/600 vision sees at 20 feet as well as someone with normal vision sees at 600 feet. If your child is unable to see the largest test symbol (which could be a letter, number, picture, or shape) on the regular chart at twenty feet, the examiner will test at a closer distance and note the distance at which your child is able to see it. For instance, 6/400 would indicate that your child could identify a 20/400 size symbol at six feet. Similarly, 2/400 would mean that your child needed the 20/400 symbol to be placed at two feet before she could identify it.

Myopia may appear alone, or in combination with other eye conditions. Premature infants with retinopathy of prematurity, for instance, are more likely to have high (significant) refractive errors, including high myopia and/or high anisometropia (see below).

Hyperopia (Farsightedness)

Hyperopia (farsightedness) occurs when the cornea is relatively flat, the eye is not as long as normal, or the focusing power of the eye is too weak. Consequently, objects are focused at a point behind the eye's retina. As a result, the child must strain excessively to focus, especially on nearby objects. Children with relatively mild hyperopia, however, often can see both distant and near objects clearly. This is because children have a tremendous ability to increase the focusing power of their eyes and thereby "focus" objects on the retina. Children with a high degree of hyperopia generally cannot do this, though, and need glasses to see a clear, single image. Glasses are also needed if a child crosses her eyes when attempting to focus to keep them aligned.

The degree of hyperopia is expressed in diopters, as with myopia. The greater the number of diopters in the prescription for corrective lenses, the more farsighted a child is.

Anisometropia

Usually a child's two eyes are very close in refractive power. Occasionally, however, there is a significant difference between the refractive power of each eye. For example, one eye may be nearsighted, while the other is farsighted. This disparity in refractive power is known as anisometropia.

Because the eyes may appear normal and straight when a child has anisometropia, the condition may go undetected. This can result in amblyopia and below normal "3–D vision" (stereoacuity) if the brain selectively ignores the image from one eye. Providing glasses to correct any significant difference between the eyes and treating the amblyopia as soon as possible can maximize a child's potential for clear, 3–D vision.

Astigmatism

In astigmatism, the shape of the cornea is not quite right, so light rays passing through it are not properly focused. Most often, the cornea is steeper (more curved) in one meridian (that is, vertically), than it is in the horizontal meridian. Consequently, each meridian has a different focusing power. Both near and far objects may appear blurry to a child with astigmatism, depending on the severity of the astigmatism. Astigmatism often appears in combination with nearsightedness or farsightedness.

Cortical Visual Impairment

In contrast to a structural impairment or refractive error, a cortical visual impairment ("cortical blindness") is not caused by any abnormality of the eyes. Instead, it results from damage within the brain, often within the visual cortex of the brain. (Hence the term "cortical.") This damage prevents the child from adequately receiving or interpreting messages from the eyes, even though the eyes may be quite capable of gathering visual information. This damage may result in a decrease in visual acuity or possibly total blindness. Causes of cortical visual impairment range from insufficient oxygen to the brain at birth or during heart surgery, to hydrocephalus, stroke, or trauma.

Children with cortical visual impairment *often* have other disabilities such as cerebral palsy, seizure disorders, mental retardation, or hydrocephalus. This is because the same injury that damages the brain's visual center can also cause other damage that results in cognitive, motor, or other impairments. When cortical visual impairment occurs alone, it is often as the result of *anoxia* (no oxygen) or *hypoxia* (insufficient oxygen) during the birth process.

There is no medical treatment for cortical visual impairment. It is important, however, to rule out any ocular abnormality, such as cataracts or retinal or optic nerve abnormalities, which may contribute to the vision loss. Glasses should also be prescribed if your child has a significant refractive error in addition to cortical visual impairment. Cortical visual impairments do not usually worsen over the years. Occasionally, vision improves spontaneously over a period of months or years. In these instances, however, vision usually remains impaired to some degree.

Searching for the Cause of Your Child's Impairment

Knowing the cause of your child's visual impairment is obviously very important in knowing how to treat it. Obviously, the treatments for structural problems such as glaucoma and cataracts are very different from treatments for refractive errors. And diagnosing and treating problems as early as possible is often vital to preventing further visual impairment or total blindness.

In this day and age, it is unusual that the cause for a child's visual impairment cannot be determined. Usually some explanation can be given as to the most likely cause for a visual loss. Although it is beyond the scope of this book to cover every possible cause of visual impairments, rest assured that eye care professionals are trained to recognize and diagnose many more conditions than are described here. If, for some reason, you have been told that the cause of your child's visual impairment is not known, it may be helpful to seek a second opinion.

Choosing an Eye Care Professional

Chapter 1 introduced the ophthalmologist and the optometrist—the eye care professionals most often involved in diagnosing and treating visual impairments. As you may remember, the areas of expertise of these professionals overlap somewhat. But they also have special and unique areas of expertise. For this reason, many parents find that the most effective and beneficial approach to vision care is a team approach, using the services of both ophthalmology and optometry.

Using the team approach, your child would see an ophthalmologist for diagnosis and treatment of a visual loss with an underlying medical problem. For example, your child would need to see an ophthalmologist for surgical treatment of glaucoma or cataracts, and for medical follow-up of these conditions. Depending on the laws in your state, your child may also need to see the ophthalmologist for prescriptions she needs related to her visual impairment.

Using the team approach, your child would see an optometrist for treatment of refractive errors (or she could see the ophthalmologist). She would also see the optometrist for special treatment if she has "low vision." Many optometrists specialize in evaluating and treating children with low vision, prescribing specific low vision devices which may help the child live and perform up to her potential. These optometrists are often called low vision specialists or low vision consultants. Low vision specialists may be in practice by themselves, or may be associated with a larger clinic, low vision center, teaching institution, or child development center.

Low vision specialists prescribe, fit, adjust, and train patients to use low vision optical devices such as special magnifying glasses,

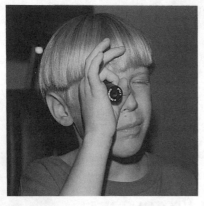

special glasses for reading or distance vision, permanent or temporary "prism" lenses, or telescopic devices which are used to spot things at a distance (for example, a telescopic device your child could use to find a street sign or a house number). In addition, many new, high-tech devices are now available for use with computers in reading or even spotting objects at a distance. New technology is continually being developed.

If you are not sure whether your child should see an ophthalmologist or an optometrist, you may wish to ask whether the ophthalmologist or optometrist you are considering works with the other as a team.

Here are some suggestions to help you choose among the eye care professionals in your community:

- *Check the qualifications of the doctor.* Has he had special training in working with very young children? (Pediatric ophthalmologists are specially trained to work with young children and are interested in their unique conditions.) Has he had experience working with children who are visually impaired? Does he have a particular specialty, such as diseases of the retina? If your child has other disabilities, has he worked with other children with multiple disabilities? Is he involved in professional activities such as attending special conferences related to visual impairments? Has he published papers which you might read? If you think your child might benefit from low vision devices, does he have experience and a special interest in working with patients with low vision?

- *Consider carefully the geographic location of your doctor's office.* The location of your primary eye care professional will be important, especially if your child has an eye condition that should be closely monitored. While you may consult closely with eye care professionals at a distance, it is a good idea to have someone locally available to call in case of an emergency. Long trips to the doctor can also be burdensome, especially if your child's condition could be followed just as well by a local professional.

- *Talk with the doctor.* Tell him your concerns and questions about your child's eye condition. Note how he responds to you. Does he speak in medical jargon, or is he willing to explain things in language you can understand? Is he patronizing, or does he treat you like a respected member of your child's health care team? Make sure that you are comfortable with your interactions. There may be times when you and your doctor must discuss difficult issues and make difficult decisions about your child's care. It is very important to trust your doctor and be able to talk to him about the most sensitive issues.

- *Consider how your child responds to the doctor.* You will want to make sure that your child is comfortable with the doctor. You must also realize, however, that a visit to the eye doctor may not always be pleasant for your child so she may sometimes react negatively. An understanding eye doctor will try to alleviate this difficulty as much as possible.

In searching for an eye care specialist, it is a good idea to ask friends, family members, your pediatrician, or others in your community for recommendations. Especially good sources of recommendations are local groups for parents of children with visual impairments. If you have difficulty locating an appropriate ophthalmologist, optometrist, or low vision specialist, you may contact The American Optometric Association or The American Academy of Ophthalmology. Addresses for these associations can be found in the Resource Guide at the back of this book.

What to Expect at an Eye Examination

Over the years, your child will have eye examinations for many different reasons: to monitor eye health, measure refractive errors, and, if she has a progressive disease, to monitor vision. In addition, low vision devices may need to be changed or prescribed to meet the changing needs of a growing child. It is beyond the scope of this chapter to describe every possible test and procedure that might be done on your child. Instead, this section explains in a general way what often happens at a complete eye examination. Your child may have some of these procedures done at some visits, but not others; she may or may not ever have them all performed on

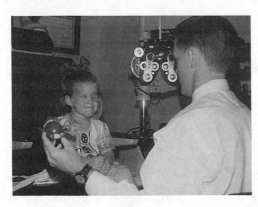

the same visit. Knowing how and why particular procedures are done, however, may help you and your child be more knowledgeable participants in the examination.

A complete eye examination is done by either an ophthalmologist or optometrist. Sometimes it is difficult to examine the eyes of infants and small children, as they cannot respond the way that adults can respond. A patient doctor will spend time with your child, trying to obtain the best information possible. Rarely, it may be necessary to medicate your child to sedate her or even to give a general anesthesia in order to fully evaluate her eyes.

Especially during early exams, the doctor will begin by getting a complete history from you. He will especially want to know about other family members with similar eye disorders. Since the growth of the eye begins very early in fetal development, the doctor will probably ask questions about events during pregnancy. For instance, he may ask which medications the mother took or whether she had any infections. The more specifically you can answer the doctor's questions, the more quickly an accurate diagnosis and plan for treatment can be made.

After discussing your child's and family's history, the doctor will measure visual acuity. As discussed in Chapter 1, the method he uses will depend on your child's age and her ability and willingness to respond. Testing of pupils, external facial appearance, and motility/muscle balance is then performed. The doctor will dilate (widen) your child's pupils with eye drops in order to examine the inner structures of the eyes (lens, retina, optic nerve) and to make it easier to measure refraction. Your child's refractive error can be measured precisely by holding different lenses in front of her eye and measuring the eye's reflex with a special hand-held instrument. No input is required from the child; therefore, even a day-old infant can be assessed for the need for glasses! The retina and nerve are examined with hand-held and head-mounted lights, as well as with special hand-held lenses.

A visit to the ophthalmologist or optometrist can give you valuable information. Listed below are some of the results you might expect from the doctor's exam:

1. Practical information concerning the size of materials your child is able to see. This will help you choose appropriate toys and books. It may also help you know how best to modify your child's preschool classroom or your own home.
2. The best type of lighting for your child, especially if her eye condition is associated with difficulty in seeing in either dim or bright lighting.
3. A prescription for the best corrective lenses for your child. The doctor will also prescribe medication, if necessary.
4. A complete understanding of your child's visual condition, visual history, and prognosis, in both technical and layman's terms. Having this is important not only for your knowledge of your child's impairment, but also in case you change doctors and another eye care professional becomes involved. Understanding all this information will also be helpful for sharing information with other professionals, especially school professionals and vision specialists.
5. Information about any secondary eye conditions your child has. Some eye conditions such as retinopathy of prematurity carry with them the danger that some other optical difficulty will develop as a result of the first or primary eye condition. Sometimes your doctor will let you know that your child should be followed closely and that warning signs should be carefully monitored. Sometimes your doctor might indicate that your child's physical activity should be limited. A thorough knowledge of your doctor's recommendations will be essential to help you monitor your child's visual difficulties.

Something you should *not* expect from your doctor is educational or rehabilitational recommendations. Eye care professionals are rarely qualified to make these recommendations. Decisions to teach braille, for example, should *not* be made by the ophthalmologist or optometrist based on what he finds during his eye exam. These types of recommendations are best made by vision specialists, O&M instructors, and rehabilitation teachers.

Preparing for an Eye Exam

Unfortunately, a trip to the eye doctor may not always be pleasant for your child. As positive and encouraging as your eye care professional may be, your child will be asked to perform tasks during the exam that may be difficult for her. She will be required to respond, not just once but many times, to questions about what she can see. She may not understand what the "correct" response is and may become frustrated because she is not able to do as she is asked. In addition, an eye exam is time-consuming, and your child may become bored. Listed below are some suggestions that may help make visits to the eye doctor a little more pleasant:

- Contact the doctor's office before your visit to find out if there are forms to complete or specific questions that the doctor may want to ask you. By completing forms in advance and being prepared for your doctor's questions, you can limit the time your child must be at the doctor's office.
- Be careful not to communicate any negative emotions you may feel about the examination to your child. Pay attention to the way that you talk about the eye doctor's office. Your child will reflect your attitude. Even if you think that your child is not paying attention to the conversation between you and your spouse, you may find that she acts more on your attitudes than you expect. It is important,

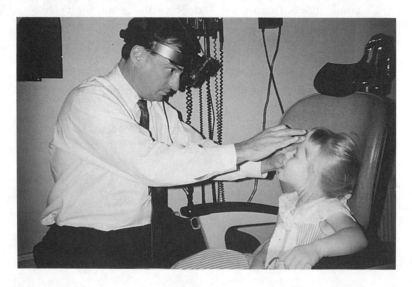

then, to talk positively, in a matter-of-fact manner about trips to the eye doctor.

- As your child becomes older, discuss the procedures at the eye doctor's office in more detail. When your child is curious about her eye condition or about any part of the examination, be sure to answer her questions as completely as possible and encourage her to ask more questions when she is ready.
- Bring some of your child's favorite toys, books, or tapes with you to the examination. Even though the eye doctor may have toys in the waiting room, there may be familiar play things that will make your child feel more comfortable and help to pass the time.
- Help to make a trip to the eye doctor something to look forward to by planning a treat after the appointment. This does not need to be an elaborate special event. A walk around the park or a visit to the ice cream parlor would be a pleasant reward for the work that your child has done at the doctor's office. It is a good idea to have several treats in mind and let your child select the one she would like. Your child does not have the choice of going to the eye doctor or not. By giving her a choice of what to do after her visit to the doctor, you allow her to have some control of the situation.

Besides preparing your child for a visit to the eye doctor, you may also want to prepare yourself so that you can help the doctor, yourself, and your child get the maximum benefit from an exam. Following are some suggestions to help you become a more effective participant:

- Be observant. Watch your child's behavior. For example, how does she handle toys? What kinds of head positions does she use when looking at objects? You may be the best "examiner," and your observations will be important. This is especially true during a functional vision assessment, as discussed in Chapter 1. It will also be helpful information, however, during a clinical examination (during testing performed by the doctor). Be sure to communicate your observations to your child's doctor.
- Ask questions. It is your right to have your questions answered in a clear, understanding, nonjudgemental way. However, some parents find it difficult to know the ques-

tions to ask. It may be helpful to make a list of questions before you go to the doctor. The more prepared you are, the more likely it is that your doctor will be able to give you the information you want and need. If you think of questions after you leave the doctor's office, do not hesitate to write or call your doctor for additional information. A caring doctor will be sympathetic to your needs and will welcome an open discussion.

- Provide stimulation to your child. Some people believe that children who are visually impaired do not need visually interesting environments. Nothing could be further from the truth. Most children with visual impairments do have some vision that they can use. Maybe they see light and shadows, or maybe they see colors. Regardless, it is important to provide your child with toys and room decorations that are visually motivating. If your child is used to examining things visually as well as tactually, she will be more prepared to respond to questions from her eye doctor.

- Be positive. Encourage your child to explore her world. Reinforce her exploration through vision, touch, and hearing.

- Put things in perspective. Remember that 20/40, 20/200, or any visual acuity is not a magic number. Base your expectations on your child's abilities, not clinical numbers. Make sure that the doctor does the same—that he actually looks at what your child can do, without making assumptions that she's in every respects like a "typical" kid with 20/200 vision. Not all children adapt to visual impairment the same way, although most adapt very well.

- Keep good records of your child's eye exams or know the names of doctors who have seen your child so you can readily obtain records. Keep copies of reports, records of medications taken, and information about your child's operations so that you can readily answers doctors' questions. This is especially important if you child sees many different doctors.

- Help your doctor. Most doctors would welcome your help if your child is having trouble with the eye examination. You will know how to help your child in ways that the doctor may not know. Especially if your child is misbehaving or is struggling or seems upset by the process, feel free to offer your help.

Corrective Lenses and Their Limitations

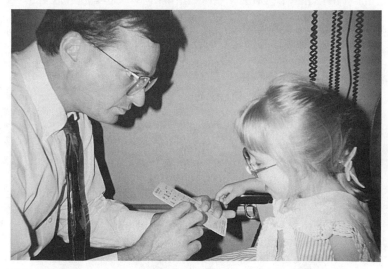

Eyeglasses and contact lenses do not normally "correct" far-sightedness, nearsightedness, or astigmatism. Instead, they actually compensate for these refractive errors by allowing a clear optical image to be focused on the retina. When the glasses or contacts are removed, the child is still farsighted, nearsighted, or astigmatic. The glasses or contacts do not permanently "fix" the refractive error. Normally, eyeglasses or contacts can only compensate for refractive errors. They cannot compensate for physical damage to the eye due to other causes, such as optic atrophy, glaucoma, or corneal scars.

Corrective lenses work by refocusing images so that they fall *on* the retina, rather than in front of, or behind it. They are ground to very precise curves based on the degree and type of refractive error your child has. The lens's total power is made up of a combination of the powers of the curves on the front and back surfaces of the lenses, and on the lens's thickness. A lens that compensates for nearsightedness is thinner in the center and thicker at the edges (concave). A lens that compensates for farsightedness is thicker in the center and thinner at the edges (convex). Generally, the higher the prescription, the thicker the lenses.

Parents frequently wonder why lenses can't be made stronger and stronger so that every child can have better vision or 20/20 vision. The purpose of prescription lenses is to compensate for the child's refractive error only and thus focus incoming images on the retina. There may be other factors limiting vision—such as glaucoma, optic atrophy, or amblyopia—that cannot be corrected simply with glasses or contact lenses. Any additional lens power would only over-compensate for the exact refractive error. It would not help visual acuity, because it would cause the image not to be focused on the retina.

Reading glasses for children with low vision are one exception to the rule that extra strong lenses are generally not helpful. Special higher-powered low vision reading glasses may be prescribed specifically to allow a child to read at a closer distance. These types of glasses magnify, rather than correct for refractive error.

Many parents wonder where they should go to have their child's glasses made. There are several different options, including the "one-hour" optical centers available in many communities. Although these may be fine for some prescriptions, some prescriptions are more complicated than others and require more extensive work. You should check with the ophthalmologist or optometrist who prescribed the glasses to find out the best place to get your child's glasses. Often your eye doctor can recommend a specific *optician*, the technician who grinds lenses to make glasses. An optician is not qualified to prescribe glasses, but once the prescription is written by an optometrist or ophthalmologist, he or she can make your child's glasses so they have the proper correction.

Conclusion

The importance of proper eye care for your child with visual impairments cannot be overstated. Neither can the importance of your involvement in decisions related to your child's eye care. As the expert on how your child uses her vision on a daily basis, you play a crucial role in ensuring that she gets the medical treatment that will help her maximize her vision. Understanding your child's eye condition will help you find the best medical care for your child and will help you, along with your child's medical and educational team, make the best decisions for your child's future.

Parent Statements

I will always be greatful to our ophthalmologist. When he told me that he suspected that Ryan was blind, he said that they would do everything that they could medically but that I needed to be strong and see that Ryan got the services he needed. Then he gave me the card of another parent of a blind child in our town. Some people might not have liked our doctor's abrupt style but he really started me out on the right foot.

◄o►

One doctor told us it wasn't fair to our baby to have any expectations of him. We should just take him home and love him.

◄o►

Once I drove for three hours to get to an ophthalmologist in another city. He was with my child for about ten minutes and seemed too busy to answer my questions.

◄o►

I suspected something was wrong with Tom's eyes very early but it took a long time to get a final diagnosis. During the time of uncertainty I went a little crazy. I was always trying to get Tom to look at things, jiggling toys in front of his eyes and turning the lights on and off.

◄o►

My child's vision specialist goes to our eye appointments with us. It helps me so much to have someone else thinking of questions. Sometimes she thinks of things I would never think about.

◄o►

My daughter hates to go to the ophthalmologist's office. We need to go for checkups every four or five months and it is so difficult that I begin dreading the trip about a month in advance.

◄o►

I took my four-year-old to the eye doctor recently. While we were there, Bobby wouldn't answer any questions and when the doctor asked if he could see something he said he couldn't even when I knew that he could. I was so embarrassed, and I didn't know what to do. Should I take Bobby out of the office and punish him or should I tell the doctor he was not answering the questions right? I just sat there and was miserable.

—◄○►—

I have noticed that if I bring my child's vision specialist with us to an eye exam, the doctor mostly talks to her, not to me. I become invisible.

—◄○►—

Because of her age, the doctors were unable to tell us how well Maggie could see.

—◄○►—

I think our doctor has horrible "people skills." When he was explaining Justin's visual impairment to us he was so matter-of- fact. The whole time I thought "our world is falling apart and this doctor doesn't even care!" He wasn't at all sensitive to our feelings.

—◄○►—

Our ophthalmologist is great! He's funny and he has so many neat toys in his office that Christy loves to play with. He is really good with her but he is also good to us. We feel that there is no question too basic and he really takes his time with us. We feel very fortunate to have found him.

Chapter Three

◄❍►

Adjusting to Your Child's Visual Impairment

Janice Herring*

As you prepared for the birth of your child, you probably had your own ideas about what your child would be like. You may have imagined a little girl with her mother's smile, or a little boy with his father's red hair. A visual impairment probably did not enter this picture. When the diagnosis was made, whether at birth or sometime later, you undoubtedly experienced a variety of very strong emotions. Some parents refer to being "devastated"; some to being "confused." Many parents say, "I didn't believe it at first," or "I didn't want to believe it." All of these emotions are perfectly normal. Many parents have wrestled with these very same feelings en route to adjusting to their child's visual impairment. But that doesn't mean that coping with these emotions is easy or that you will be able to adjust overnight. Coming to terms with your child's visual impairment will be a many-stage process that could take months or years to complete.

This chapter provides information about various aspects of the adjustment process. It discusses common emotions, as well as suggestions for working through these emotions. Suggestions are also given to help you understand and cope with the changes and differences in your family's life.

---

* Janice Herring is the mother of two. She has been a teacher for nine years. Her son, Casey, who has a severe visual impairment, was the inspiration for her decision to return to college and work toward certification to teach students who are visually impaired. She is now a vision specialist for the Fayetteville Public Schools in Fayetteville, Arkansas.

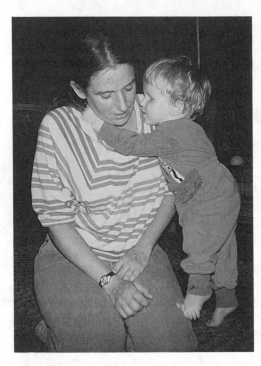

As you read this chapter, remember that everybody is unique and may react differently to similar emotions and experiences. One parent may want to talk with many people and gather information from a variety of sources. Another may prefer to discuss his thoughts and concerns only with close family members. There is no "best" way to adjust to your child's disability. You should let your personality dictate your own "best" way to cope with your emotions.

Getting the News

My son, Casey, was born five years ago. For the first four months of his life, I had no idea that anything was wrong. Then, one afternoon when I was rocking him to sleep, I noticed that his eyes seemed to be bouncing up and down. I watched him closely for a couple of days while the occasional bounce turned into a constant one.

When I took Casey to the pediatrician, he said he wasn't sure what the problem was. He instructed me to see a pediatric ophthalmologist. As luck would have it, a big ophthalmological convention was going on at the time and all of our local eye doctors were out of town. To wait even a few days seemed like torture to me and my husband, Rick. We began to contact ophthalmologists in nearby towns. Finally, we located one about sixty miles away. He agreed to see Casey the next day.

After the doctor had examined Casey's eyes, he said that he couldn't find anything wrong and that we should contact a neurologist. Our pediatrician set up an appointment and the tests began.

After a multitude of tests and four nerve-wracking months, we were referred to an ophthalmologist at the Arkansas Children's Hospital. He told us that Casey had a serious vision problem. In fact, this doctor said that we should contact our state residential School for the Blind, since our only option would be to send Casey there. At the age of eight months, our son was fitted for glasses.

On the ride home that day, I remember feeling relieved that Casey did not have a brain tumor. I was devastated, however, by the diagnosis of a visual impairment. Thus started the process of accepting my son's disability.

Regardless of how and when *you* heard the news, it was probably a bitter pill to swallow. While some parents hear the news from an eye doctor who is sensitive and willing to spend enough time to answer questions, others receive the news in a matter-of-fact way that might appear cruel. You will probably never forget how, when, and where you found out about your child's disability.

Since you are reading this book, you already know about your child's visual impairment. You have already experienced the initial feelings associated with the diagnosis. It is therefore impossible for you to go back in time to handle your earliest feelings differently. You may not, however, have worked through all of your feelings completely. Or you may think you have overcome one emotion only to have it return several months or years later. You might also be interested in helping other parents as they receive this news. You might want to volunteer at your ophthalmologist's office or Children's Hospital to be a resource for parents who are just hearing about their child's visual impairment. Sharing information about what you found helpful and harmful in "getting the news" might help doctors, nurses, and other professionals be more sensitive to the needs of parents. In any case, it can help to learn what feelings are common and how others have successfully dealt with them.

Your Emotions

Being told that your child has a disability is one of the most emotional experiences anyone can go through. It's not something that you can plan for, and you certainly cannot plan what your reaction should be. There are no "right" and "wrong" emotions. Most parents have many of the emotions described below, although not necessarily in the same order. Other parents may have only a few of these emotions, or have different emotions altogether. It is also perfectly normal for husband and wife to experience different emotions, of different intensities, at different stages than one another. Whatever you feel is normal for you. Regardless of the particular emotions you have, however, acknowledging what you are feeling is often the first step to being able to cope constructively. Denying your emotions will only prolong the adjustment process.

Grief

After the initial shock of their child's diagnosis, many parents say that they begin to feel very sad. This grief has sometimes been equated with the grief that is felt at the loss of a loved one or a cherished dream. Parents of children with a visual impairment may feel as if they have lost the dream of a "normal" child—a child who might excel in sports, share their fondness for Impressionistic art, or become a hiking companion. This is not to say that parents do not love and appreciate their child, but rather that it pains them to realize that their life will be very different than they imagined.

Grief is the first emotion I recall having after learning of Casey's impairment. I could not imagine how we could possibly cope with a child who could not see well. I was sure he'd never ride a bike, play ball, or drive a car. I was sad to think that people were going to judge Casey based on his blindness. In my mind, I couldn't imagine that he would ever be able to go to school—any school—or even to be a part of our family. Today, now that so many things have changed, it is hard for me to believe that everything seemed so horrible. I really had no perspective of what his life would be like, however. I believed that our happy life would surely end.

Eventually, my husband helped me to see that this grieving wasn't very productive and that we had to get on with our lives. It was silly for me to spend so much time looking at all the things Casey would never do. I was limiting him before I even had any idea of what he would be able to do. Gradually, I began trying to focus on Casey rather than on his disability and found that he could do things I'd never even imagined he could.

At first, I was actually surprised at some of the very basic things that Casey could do. This may have been because I had had little experience with children with disabilities. My limited experience had, however, included spending some time with a child who had multiple severe disabilities. I guess because of this I was surprised that Casey could recognize us, walk, talk, and feed himself. I watched with fascination as he began to develop his own little personality. I learned that he was not the child we had expected, but he is a great child with hopes and dreams and likes and dislikes of his own. Rather than limiting his accomplishments, I now play a wait-and-see game while encouraging him to try a variety of activities.

Even so, at times I still experience flashes of grief. It pains me to see Casey struggle to accomplish something that would be so much easier to do if he could see, or I worry when he misses something because of his vision loss. For example, recently he attended a play during Vacation Bible School. The play had lots of visually funny things (motions made by the characters or their facial expressions). Even though Casey was in the front row, I could tell that he was confused or puzzled when the other children laughed. Sitting across the room from him, I realized that there will be things throughout his life that Casey will miss. Even though I am now convinced that he will live a full, productive, enjoyable life, I can't help feeling sad about the things that he may miss.

Guilt

Historically, blindness has been associated with guilt in many ways. In old books and movies, for instance, you may find references to someone being "struck blind" because of something bad he or she did. These days, this notion seems very outdated. Many parents, however, still try to fix the blame for their child's visual impairment on someone or something. Often, they may worry that their child's disability is a direct result of something that they did before their child was born. Mothers might say, "If only I had been more careful about what I ate when I was pregnant," or "I shouldn't have tried to lift those boxes of books." Fathers might say, "I shouldn't have painted the nursery when my wife was pregnant," or "I should have helped out more with the housekeeping." Both parents may feel as if they must have done *something* to be singled out for this bad fortune. Most children, after all, do not have visual impairments, so there has to be some reason why their child does, right?

It is very natural to want an explanation for your child's disability. Your child's ophthalmologist may be able to help you understand the true cause of your child's visual impairment. Sometimes, however, the cause may never be known. In most cases, however, there is absolutely nothing you could have done that would have prevented your child's visual impairment. Do not torture yourself with "might have beens" and "if onlys." You *know* you would never have deliberately done anything that you could have foreseen would result in your child being born with a visual impairment.

Fear and Anxiety

It is easy to fall prey to fear and anxiety when you have a child with a visual impairment. You may worry about the future and what it holds for your child. Can your child possibly lead a fulfilled life with little or no vision? What if his vision gets worse? You may worry about your child's safety at home and in the community. Will you have to watch him every minute of every day to make sure he isn't injured by some unseen hazard?

My biggest worry was about Casey's quality of life. How would people react to Casey? Would they give him the time he needs to respond to them? Would he have any friends? Would he date? Would he get married? I wondered whether Casey would feel confident in his abilities, or see (as we had) only the things he couldn't do. Seeing him grow and develop has helped me overcome much of my fear. With the mastery of each new skill comes confidence. Although Casey often does things differently or at a different pace than sighted children, the possibilities are endless.

Fears about safety are something that can be difficult to let go of completely. You may feel that you cannot encourage independence because obstacles in the environment may hurt him. Your fears may be reinforced by others who encourage you to watch your child closely and to shelter or protect him. Of course, it is important to make sure that your child is safe. But it is also important to encourage him to be as independent as possible, allowing him to freely explore the world around him. It may help to remember that all children get minor cuts and scrapes. Letting your child experience the feeling of independence is one of the most important things that you, as a parent, can do.

As your child begins to show you that he wants more independence, try to find small ways that you can encourage him and yet still feel comfortable. Make sure that your child's room is organized so that he can find toys, games, and books he might want. This might mean building or purchasing bookcases that are low to the ground and stackable plastic containers to store a variety of small toys. You will want to take special care to see that there are no eye-level hazards such as corners of coffee tables or half-opened doors.

"Toddler-proofing" your home may take a little extra effort. You may want to take a look at your house from your child's point of view by getting on your hands and knees and checking for obstacles that might be in his way. Don't be afraid to make changes in your home such as rearranging the furniture or carpeting the floor. If you do make changes, however, be sure to point them out to your child and then watch him carefully as he gets used to the new arrangements. See Chapter 11 for more information on boosting your child's mobility.

As you encourage your child to increase his independence, you will see the many successes that he will have. This will help both you and your child become more confident and more willing to try new things.

Resentment

It is not uncommon to feel that you are the only person in the world facing this kind of misfortune. As a result, you may resent other families and their seemingly carefree lives. Or you may resent the insensitive remarks that people make without even realizing they are wounding you. Your child might also be a target for resentment if you blame him for all the changes he brings to your life.

When Casey was an infant, I resented the fact that I could no longer take a leisurely trip to the grocery store. Casey hated to go to the grocery store. We didn't know it at the time, but the bright lights hurt his eyes. The building itself had a strange sound to it. He could tell there was a bustle all around him, yet could distinguish little from it. This combination of sights and sounds was, I'm sure, a frightening experience. Consequently, he would scream from the time we entered the store until the time we left. We must have made quite a sight: a baby wearing glasses and screaming at the top of his lungs, his five-year-old sister being dragged along, and a very irritable mother flinging groceries into the cart as fast as possible.

Obviously, a trip to the store had to be well planned and thought out. I often hired a sitter or left Casey at home with Rick. Fortunately, he can now tolerate the store. But any outside activities have to be seriously thought about, as we now know that he is photophobic and sunlight hurts his eyes. We try to plan activities for the early evening hours so he will feel comfortable. Going out in the daytime is often unavoidable, though, because so much time must be scheduled around doctor appointments or therapy sessions. Needless to say, it is difficult not to resent all these changes to our life.

Resentment, although a perfectly natural reaction to having a child with a visual impairment, cannot be allowed to dominate your life. Otherwise, it can rob you of the ability to see opportunities for joy and happiness.

Denial

Denial is very common and can take many forms. Sometimes denial is destructive—for example, when parents refuse to believe something or do something, and end up doing their child more harm than good. Parents might deny that there is a diagnosis of visual impairment or ignore what they have been told about how this will affect their child's development. They may think, "My child is just a baby; why can't we leave well enough alone? I want to enjoy my baby." Or they might think, "How can these teachers know that my child will have a developmental delay? They don't know my child." As a consequence, they might not participate in an early intervention program that would benefit their child.

Denial can also be productive at times. Naturally, it is important to recognize the realistic difficulties your child will have. But this doesn't mean that you have to believe, without question, everything that doctors or other professionals tell you. I think back to the day our ophthalmologist told us that our only option was to send Casey to the School for the Blind. My refusal to accept this doctor's advice may have been denial, but it was productive denial.

In the long run, living at home with a loving and supportive family has benefitted Casey far more than living alone in the School for the Blind ever could have.

Sometimes it can be difficult, if not impossible, to know the difference between productive denial and destructive denial. Just remember that the more information you have about your child and the more interaction you have with professionals you *trust*, the more realistic you will be able to be about your child.

Anger

You may have anger—lots and lots of it. Anger because your spouse or other children or family and friends are not reacting like you are. Anger at the way you were given or not given information. Anger at the way people stare or the things they say, or don't say. Anger at God, or Fate, or whatever you believe in for letting this happen.

Although anger is normal and understandable, it is not very productive. Anger probably hurts you a lot worse than it hurts anyone else, and it rarely makes anything better.

You will know how you best handle anger. Some people take their mother's advice and "count to ten" before saying anything; others walk away from difficult situations. Some people find that a strenuous aerobics class at their local gym helps, while others draw comfort from a peaceful retreat. Whatever method you use, taking care of your anger can help relieve stress and give you the ability to focus your energies on activities that will be useful to you and your child.

How to Adjust

Take Your Time

Finding out that your child has a visual impairment is a true crisis. As with any crisis, your first instinct may be to *do* something—anything—about it. Should you look for a doctor who can "fix" your child's eyes? Do you need to rush out and buy him a cane? What about early intervention?

Even though you might feel as if you have no time to lose in solving all of your child's problems, take your time. You are in no state to make major decisions while you are still reeling from the di-

agnosis. Until you have addressed and begun to control your initial emotions, you can't be sure that you are thinking things through rationally.

You need to get in touch with your feelings in whatever way seems natural to you. Parents who are talkative by nature may find that it helps to talk about their feelings with their spouse, another parent, or a professional counselor. More reticent parents might want to keep a journal or log on to CompuServe's Disability Forum, America On-Line's Disability Bulletin Board, or a similar database to share their feelings more privately. You might want to do something physical like jogging or chopping wood while you ponder your feelings, or you may feel more comfortable sitting or lying down. My husband and I had slightly different coping styles when Casey's vision loss was first diagnosed. I wanted to take charge of the situation, to gather all the information I could, to read all the books, and to talk to many different people. Rick, on the other hand, took more of a wait-and-see attitude. This was, in fact, the way we had handled other difficult issues. We respected each other's differences, realizing that we complemented one another's styles.

While you are sorting out your emotions, don't let anyone or anything rush you. Don't feel as if you should be over your grief, for example, because your spouse seems to have moved on. Also, don't allow yourself to be rushed by others' needs. For instance, don't feel as if you need to hurry through the adjustment process because your spouse needs you to be strong or because you need to put up a brave front when your parents come for a visit. If you don't work through your feelings in the beginning, you will only have to do it later.

If at all possible, consider letting some outside responsibilities slide while you adjust to the differences in your life. Put off painting the house, ignore the laundry for a while, or let the dandelions take over your garden if you find that taking care of these chores prevents you from focusing on your feelings. Nobody is going to fault you for taking a breather from your daily routine while you put your life back together.

Finally, don't be surprised if coping with your feelings develops into an ongoing process. Although your emotions will probably be the most intense and varied immediately after your child's diagnosis, you will need to work through some emotions over and over again during the course of your child's life. I was reminded of this fact just the other week when I took my children to the zoo. Before Casey was born, my husband and I had often made such visits. Recently, however, going to the zoo has lost some of its appeal because we know the sun hurts his eyes and he can't see much, anyway. On this day, however, I pushed away all my doubts and fears and just took them.

In the two hours we were at the zoo, my daughter, Amy, flitted from cage to cage, looking at all the animals, reading the animal names, and thoroughly enjoying herself. Casey, on the other hand, had to be guided from cage to cage and told what each animal was doing, and was limited to seeing animals close to the edge of their cages. During our stay there, I ran the whole gamut of emotions. I felt grief that he missed so much, fear that he would feel badly about himself for missing it, resentment that other children could see all of the animals, and depression that I couldn't "fix" things for him so he could enjoy all the animals. These negative feelings, however, gradually subsided as I began to share his pleasure at watching the animals he could see and feel proud of his commitment to peering into every cage—even those where I know he saw nothing. Later, on the trip home, there was the intense joy of hearing him ask when we could go back to the zoo!

When I think about the day at the zoo, I have to think positively. Even though I worried and fretted, it was a successful day.
By addressing my emotions and taking Casey to the zoo, I gave him
an experience he might otherwise not have had. Best of all, I
learned something about my child—he likes the zoo!

Get to Know Your Child

Despite what you may have heard, parents do not always bond
instantaneously with their child at birth. They have to get to know
him as a person—not just as a squalling little creature who eats,
sleeps, and produces an unending stream of dirty diapers. Parents
of babies without vision impairments gradually get to know their
child by learning what he likes and dislikes, what he does easily
and what he does with more difficulty, what interests him and
what he is indifferent to.

For parents of children with visual impairments, the process
can and should be the same. Sometimes, however, parents have
more trouble seeing their child for the child he is—because they
see the disability first. Actually, seeing the disability is easy to do
because a visual impairment is generally something you *can* see by
looking at your child. The more you let your child do independently, however, the more you will be able to see the wide variety of abilities he has. Spend time with him—get to know his
interests. By doing so you will allow him to show you who he really
is.

Gather Information

Unless you are very fortunate, you will not simply be given all
the information you need to make intelligent decisions about your
child's and family's needs. You will need to find ways to gather information about your child's visual impairment and the educational, therapeutic, and medical services that can help him. Good
sources of information on visual impairments include:

- Books and magazines such as those listed in the Resource
  Guide, as well as pamphlets and other publications distrib-
  uted by the organizations in the Resource Guide;
- Other parents you meet through support groups such as
  those described under "Develop a Support System," or par-

ents of children enrolled in the same educational or therapeutic programs as your child. Not only can these parents
give you firsthand information about services and schools
in your community, but they can also share information
about coping with emotional issues.

- Professionals who work with your child. Your child's doctors can answer questions about your child's eye condition
  in general (cause, effects on vision, prevalence, treatment), as well as questions about how the condition affects your child in particular (degree of vision loss,
  prognosis). Teachers and therapists can provide information about how your child's eye condition might affect his
  ability to learn and develop (whether specific areas of development might be delayed, whether your child will be
  able to read print, whether he may need a mobility aid).
  Don't be afraid to ask them about anything you might be
  wondering about, or to ask them to explain something in
  simpler terms.
- Workshops relating to visual impairments given by schools,
  state agencies, professional organizations, parent groups,
  etc.
- Children and young adults with visual impairments similar
  to your child's. It can be helpful simply to observe these
  young people to see how they are able to function. You
  might also wish to ask them questions about practical or
  emotional issues related to growing up with a vision loss.
  You may be able to arrange a meeting through your child's
  vision specialist or a parent support group.

Part of educating yourself is knowing what services are available for your child. As Chapter 8 explains, early intervention is essential to make sure your child learns and grows as well and as
quickly as possible. There are many people who can help you decide what services your child needs. An outreach consultant from
your state's school for the blind, the Department of Human Services, Division for Blind Services, the local school district, the education cooperative in your area, your child's pediatrician, and his
ophthalmologist all may be able to direct you to services. In addition, other parents can often offer good advice about specific programs or therapists in your community. Don't be afraid to ask
questions, get second opinions, and evaluate the advice you are
given based on your knowledge of your child. Weigh your options

and make your decisions wisely. No one else will ever want as much for, or care as much about, your child as you do. Once you have the knowledge, you can make things happen for him.

Develop a Support System

When most parents have a question or concern about their child, advice and support are easy to come by. They can ask friends, family members, or neighbors for advice on dealing with their baby's teething pain, or switching from a bottle to a cup, or choosing toys appropriate for their child's age, or just about any concern related to child rearing. They can choose almost any pediatrician in the phone book, and be assured that the doctor will know how to care for almost any medical problem their child is likely to have. And they can find an understanding ear almost anywhere when they want to commiserate about the stresses of parenting.

When you have a child with a visual impairment, you cannot always rely on the usual avenues of support. Although family and friends may wish to be supportive, they may not know how to give you the help you need at first. Medical and other professionals may be at a loss to explain your child's vision or developmental problems. And other parents' concerns may seem irrelevant or even petty to you. Consequently, you may feel very isolated, depressed, and stressed out.

Fortunately, there are many good sources of support for families of children with visual impairments. The key is knowing how to find them. The following sections describe resources that you may want to use as links in your support system.

Other Parents

Difficult as it may be to fathom, there *are* other people who understand exactly what you have gone through, as well as your worries about the future. Although they may not live on your block or even in your town, there are other parents in the same boat as you are who can give you many different kinds of support. Other parents of children with visual impairments can, first of all, offer a sympathetic ear if you simply want to pour out your feelings about your child. They can help you realize that you are not the only person dealing with the obstacles that face you and your child. And they can help you find ways around these obstacles. For example, they can give you tips on working with the school system to get the services your child needs to be as independent as possible. Or they can recommend an ophthalmologist who is really good with children.

You can find other parents through your child's early intervention or preschool program, in the ophthalmologist's waiting room, or by asking the doctor if he has any other patients with your child's condition or a similar condition, etc.

Support Groups. Perhaps the easiest way to meet other parents is through a support group for parents of children with visual impairments or other disabilities. Support groups run the gamut from loosely structured groups of parents who meet in one another's homes to chat, snack, and play with the kids to more formal organizations with elected officers, guest speakers, newsletters, and dues.

There are several national organizations that have local or state chapters in many communities. The National Association for Parents of the Visually Impaired (NAPVI) is an organization by and for parents which is committed to providing support to the parents of children with visual impairments. The national organization provides information through workshops and publications to help parents meet the unique needs of their children with visual impairments. Local chapters provide support and information by offering workshops, holding family picnics, providing braille classes for parents, and so forth.

Another national organization is the National Organization of Parents of Blind Children, a division of the National Federation of the Blind (NFB). It, too, was founded by and for parents of children with visual impairments. It publishes a newsletter called *Future Reflections*, which includes many interesting and informative articles by parents and children. The addresses for these organizations can be found in the Resource Guide.

You might also find it useful to join a group for parents of children with a variety of disabilities. I belong to one such local organization and have found that all of the parents, regardless of their child's disability, have had or are experiencing the same emotions I have dealt with. They worry about their children's education, social life, self-esteem, medical bills, and all the other things that concern me and my husband. Perhaps more importantly, they also share exciting success stories. The report that someone's child has taken his first step can send the whole group into a round of applause that only we can understand.

If you feel squeamish about opening up to a roomful of strangers, don't worry. Nobody in a support group is going to force you to talk. But listening could do you a world of good. Remember: help is out there. It is yours for the asking.

Professionals

In your quest for services for your child, you will encounter innumerable doctors, therapists, teachers, and other professionals. Some will have a good understanding of your child's needs, others you will learn to steer clear of; some will give you questionable advice, and others you will trust unquestioningly. As you learn which professionals are which, you will also learn which could become a valuable part of your support network.

Different professionals can support you in different ways. Some might be willing to write letters or make phone calls on your child's behalf—for instance, to persuade your insurance company that a particular service should be covered, or to convince the school system that your child needs a certain therapy. Others might go the extra mile to find the answer to a question that is troubling you, or refer you to a person or organization that might help. Still others may be able to solve a problem that you have been unable to resolve on your own.

If the first professional you approach cannot give you the support you need, keep looking. I learned this lesson in trying to find an explanation for Casey's odd behaviors. Besides going berserk in the grocery store, Casey would scream if he got anything gooey (like mashed potatoes) on his hands. He wouldn't let anyone do anything with his hands. In fact, he began to keep them in his pocket to avoid contact. He would sleep only with his favorite blanket, wrapped up inside it like a tamale. He couldn't tolerate sweaters, and wore only cotton shirts. He went two winters in a row without a coat because he couldn't stand to wear it. A hat was, of course, out of the question. The list goes on and on.

The first occupational therapist we took Casey to said that he was just stubborn and independent. We couldn't disagree with either of those claims, but we knew there was more to it. The second occupational therapist hit the bull's eye. She told us that Casey was tactually defensive. Much of our frustration was relieved just knowing what the problem was and that someone was eager to help him overcome it. Now, after a year of sensory integrated occupational therapy, we can't even believe the difference in Casey's behavior.

To get good, caring professionals on your support team, you need only ask for their help. Although it is possible they may say they are too busy, more likely than not they will be happy to help.

Family and Friends

Your family and friends can also become an essential part of your support system. They can

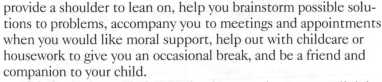

provide a shoulder to lean on, help you brainstorm possible solutions to problems, accompany you to meetings and appointments when you would like moral support, help out with childcare or housework to give you an occasional break, and be a friend and companion to your child.

My family has rallied around to become the strongest link in my support system. I share my emotions with them and they share their emotions with me. My mother in particular has been wonderful about including Casey in her thoughts and concerns. She takes special effort when buying birthday or Christmas gifts to find something for him with interesting tactual or auditory features. She also lets me know about relevant workshops in her city (about an hour away from me) that I might like to attend. Together, my extended family has become strong enough to deal with almost any obstacle.

I have found that there is one big difference between asking for support from family and friends and asking for it from others. Generally, you cannot expect family and friends to give you much support until they have come to terms with their own feelings about your child's diagnosis. For this reason, the next sections cover strategies for helping family and friends adjust.

Reaching Out to Your Family

When a child with a disability is born into a family, it is not only the parents who experience the pain. Siblings, grandparents, aunts, uncles, cousins, and countless others are also affected. They may experience some or all of the same emotions you are feeling. Consequently, it is imperative that you give them as much information as they seem to need about your child and his vision impairment. Don't dwell on the negative, however. Let them know that you don't want them to pity your child, and that you expect them to treat him as much like the other children in the family as possible.

In the beginning, family members may seem reluctant to interact with your child. This could be because they are afraid they might say the "wrong thing" or look "silly." Or they could be afraid that your child is more fragile than usual and they could hurt him. You can help family members through much of this initial reluctance. Let them know that your child likes to do the same kinds of things as other children. Point out, for example, that your child likes to swing or be read to. Point out things about each family member that your child might like. "Oh, Aunt Mary, that sweater is such a nice bright color. I think Casey will like it." Or, "The last time you were here you bounced Janie on your lap. She liked it so much she talked about it all through dinner." Everyone likes to know when they are doing the "right thing." Be sure that you give everyone the reinforcement they need to feel comfortable around your child.

Grandparents

It can be especially hard for grandparents to cope with the news of your child's vision loss. They may not only grieve for the loss of their "perfect" grandchild, but they are probably also anxious about the pain that you, their child, might be going through. Also, since they are older, they grew up in a time when having a disability was considered more of a stigma and opportunities for a fulfilling life were much fewer.

Feelings like these can be hard on you and your parents. Obviously, you do not want such emotions to come between your child and his grandparents. The support and love of grandparents is invaluable for children. Grandparents can provide an adoring kind of love that parents rarely can, since they are primarily responsible for discipline and setting limits. Because of the close relationship that grandparents usually have, it can be especially hurtful if they do not understand or cope with your child's vision loss.

You are not responsible for your parents' feelings in the situation, and, of course, your number one concern is your child. However, by working hard to make sure your parents are included in your family and are comfortable with your child, you will increase the possibility that your child will benefit from the unique advantages that grandparents can offer. Below are a few suggestions that might help:

- Share your reading material about your child's vision loss with your parents—you might pass this book along to them.
- Discuss what you have read.
- Ask your parents for parenting advice. While this can be hard even in the best of circumstances, it will point out that you have the same questions about your child as they had about you.
- Share your child's accomplishments as well as difficulties.
- Try to create an atmosphere in which you can share your feelings with your parents and they can share theirs with you.

Brothers and Sisters

Your other children will, of course, need to cope with their feelings about their brother's or sister's visual impairment. Unless they are old enough to understand the diagnosis when you receive it, however, they will probably learn about their sibling's differences in bits and pieces over the years, rather than all at once. For this reason, helping siblings adjust is discussed along with other family life issues in Chapter 6.

Your Friends

Having a child with a visual impairment can profoundly affect old friendships. Some friends may stay away because they don't know what to say or do, or think that you are too busy with doctor and therapy appointments to see them. Or they may treat you differently because they feel sorry for you or feel apologetic about their own relatively good fortune. For your part, you may give friends the message that you want to be left alone. Perhaps you cut phone calls short or repeatedly refuse offers of help because you think they can't possibly understand your new life or because you can't bear to hear them talk about all the "normal" things their children are doing.

I experienced a variety of reactions from friends. One friend I had was very uncomfortable around Casey. She seemed on edge whenever we visited her and seemed to be afraid that Casey would knock something down or hurt himself. Not surprisingly, we seldom see each other anymore. When we do get together, I leave Casey home. Another friend is very interested in our trials and tribulations, and I share everything with her. Still another loves Casey dearly, but seems to deny the extent of his visual problems. I try to deal with each friend individually and give them what they need: opportunities to get to know Casey, information provided in a slow, as-they-need-it manner, or time to adjust.

If you are interested in keeping a particular friend, I think it is important to jointly cultivate whatever mutual interests brought you together in the first place. If you used to swap gardening tips or talk sports before your child was born, you should continue to do so. Your child is only a part of your life. You shouldn't let his visual impairment consume every bit of your energy and conversations. Keep in mind, too, that your friends may have concerns about their own children. Nobody wants to be around someone who is so obsessed with their life that they can't talk about anything else.

Conclusion

In the four and a half years since Casey was diagnosed as visually impaired, our lives have changed in ways we could never have imagined. Our family is learning to be patient, dedicated, and to assert ourselves when need be. We've had experiences no family should have to endure: encounters with interns at the children's hospital (who can never see in Casey's eyes what the doctor wants them to), with rude people who stare and make odd comments in front of Casey (as though he also has a hearing impairment), with day care workers who sat Casey in a high chair while the other children played (so he wouldn't get hurt), with a pediatrician who told me at Casey's thirty-month check-up that Casey would probably bump into things.

Along with the negative experiences, we have also had many positive ones. Perhaps most importantly, Casey is teaching us to appreciate the little things we used to take for granted: the rumble of an eighteen-wheeler passing, the picnic possibilities of a cool, cloudy day, and the thrill of listening to our gerbil make scratching noises. We stand on the curb and watch the trash men empty our garbage cans. We hug trees and walk in the rain. We hunt laboriously for dandelions in the park. And occasionally, much to my husband's dismay, we jump on the bed.

We still don't know all the things Casey won't be able to do, but we do know some of the things he can do. First and foremost, he can bring joy and love and hope into the hearts of his family. Casey is truly a very special child. I'm sure your child is, too.

Parent Statements

When the ophthalmologist told us that David was blind, he said that we would want to put him in an institution. He said that they could take care of him there. I was so angry, but at the time I didn't know if I was angry at the doctor or at the situation.

-◄o►-

While I was still in the hospital after Tony was born, the pediatrician told me that he was blind, but it didn't sink in. I really believed that all I had to do was to get him home and then he would be okay.

—◄o►—

I really didn't have much trouble with the initial news that John Henry has a visual impairment. I know he can see some things so it really didn't have a big impact on me that he would have trouble in other areas. But the thing that really got to me was seeing him in his first pair of glasses. He was so tiny and the glasses seemed so big. I started to cry. Thank heavens the doctor stepped in and gave my son some encouragement while I composed myself.

—◄o►—

After a few tries of going to the store or to church, I just stopped. I couldn't stand how people looked at my baby (or at me). Now I see my parents, my husband's parents, and every once in a while a neighbor. It's a lot less stressful this way.

—◄o►—

I never thought this would happen to me.

—◄o►—

Hearing about Franny's blindness was the worst moment of my life.

—◄o►—

I get so annoyed at the strangers who ask what's wrong with my baby's eyes. Sometimes I just say she's sleeping and try to be polite. At other times I growl something and walk off. What's wrong with people anyway?

—◄o►—

After my son was born, I just kept on going back over the events of my pregnancy, wondering if there was something I could have done differently to prevent this from happening. I felt very guilty.

—◄o►—

This sounds crazy but I spent several days when Amy was about six months old worrying about whether or not she would go to the senior prom.

—◄o►—

Tony is a double miracle. He was almost three months premature and had some severe medical problems. But he lived—that's one miracle. And even though the doctors thought that he would be totally blind, he has some light perception. That's the second miracle.

—◄o►—

We have had to be patient and go at David's pace.

—◄o►—

Some people just want to feel sorry for Brian.

—◄o►—

My biggest pet peeve is people who stare. Don't just stare at my child. Come and talk to me. I am proud of him and I can talk about him all day long.

—◄o►—

My wife and I have difficulty communicating with each other about our child. She is probably farther along than I am so I always feel guilty about what I am thinking.

—◄o►—

I don't think my husband and I have been on the same wavelength since our daughter was born. It seems like one of us is always up, while the other is down. Sometimes I think he's being unrealistically optimistic, and sometimes he thinks the same of me.

—◄o►—

Right now I just try to treat Jessica as normally as possible. I try not to make too many exceptions for her. I especially try to make sure that Jessica knows I expect the same things from her that I expect from her sister.

━◄○►━

I hate it when people say "I know exactly how you feel." I know they are just trying to be nice but I don't think anybody understands unless they've been through this.

━◄○►━

I think I've started to trust my instincts more. I'm beginning to believe that if I think there is something wrong, there probably is.

Chapter Four

Your Child's Development

Kay Alicyn Ferrell, Ph.D.*

Most child care books include lists or charts of the skills that children are "supposed" to be learning and doing at particular ages. You have probably scanned these charts, wondering where your child fits in. Perhaps you have been concerned that your child seems to be lagging behind in certain skills. Or you may have been puzzled because your child has picked up some of the later skills without first learning the early skills. These types of reactions are common among parents of children with visual impairments. Although all children with visual impairments grow and learn, or *develop*, the pattern and rate of their development is often different from other children's.

Unfortunately, health and education professionals have not studied the development of children with visual impairments as thoroughly as that of children without disabilities. In fact, we know very little about the development of children with visual impairments. To make predictions about development even more difficult, every child with a visual impairment is a unique individual, born with her own unique traits into a unique environment. Some are precocious, and seem to be older and more advanced than their friends without disabilities. Others make much slower progress, and every new behavior learned becomes a cause for celebration.

* Kay Ferrell is currently Professor of Education at The University of Northern Colorado. She is well known for her work and research in preschool services and development of infants and toddlers who are blind or visually impaired. She is the author of various publications, including *Reach Out and Teach*, a program for parents.

The point is, even the "experts" do not know what makes the difference among children with visual impairments—why some sail through life effortlessly, while others seem to take two steps backward before taking one step forward. We *think* we know where and why some of the problems arise. We think we can help parents work around these problems. But we don't have all the answers.

This chapter will look at what is known and unknown about the development of children with visual impairments. You will find some things that are true for your child, and some things that could not be further from the truth. Hopefully, this chapter will help you to enjoy your child as an individual, to recognize what she does best and where your help is needed, and to make the most of her educational opportunities.

What Is Development?

When educators talk about "development," they mean the process by which children grow physically and mentally and learn increasingly complex skills. It includes mastery of skills such as making sense of the environment, communicating with others, making purposeful movements, caring for oneself, reading and doing math, and figuring out a bus schedule. It is, in short, the process that enables a child to change from a tiny, helpless newborn to an adult who is capable of looking after most, if not all, of her own needs.

There is tremendous variability in human development. Some children make faster than expected progress in all areas of learning, and others make slower progress. Some progress quickly in some areas, but have more difficulty in others. Usually, however, children who are developing normally tend to follow approximately the same timetable in learning skills. That is, most children acquire skills in the same sequence at about the same age. For example, children without disabilities usually learn to roll over by the time they are about three or four months of age, and then learn to sit up at about six to eight months. They begin to babble at about six to eight months, and then learn to say "mama" sometime around twelve to fourteen months of age.

Developmental Areas

During the course of development, children learn many different types of skills and behaviors. Child development experts usually group related skills into six general areas or domains of growth: cognitive, communication, motor, self-help, sensory, and social. In each of these areas, there are certain important skills, or *milestones*, that children are expected to acquire as they develop into more capable individuals. For example, standing alone is a milestone in motor development and smiling is a milestone in social development.

The domains are interrelated. That is, growth in one area usually affects growth in other areas. For example, a child who has learned to take turns with others when communicating will also develop social skills such as sharing and working with other children in play. In spite of this, there are many children with really good abilities in one domain and poor abilities in another, as well as children whose progress in one developmental area seems to hamper their progress in another area, at least temporarily. A child who is having difficulty with motor skills, for example, would have more difficulty working on self-help skills such as dressing or feeding herself. Development is a dynamic, constantly changing process.

Understanding how skills are categorized into developmental areas is important if your child will be receiving early intervention or special education services. Before beginning school, your child will likely be evaluated in each of these developmental areas, since these areas help us to organize our thinking about how children grow and learn. Developmental areas also help us to identify strengths that can be used when children need help. For instance, a child who is especially good at social interactions might benefit from being placed in a play situation to work on motor skills or cognitive skills. The child's strengths in social interaction would help her develop abilities in her weaker areas (motor and cognitive skills).

Cognitive development involves acquiring the ability to think, reason, and problem solve. Babies pick up the building blocks for these more advanced skills by manipulating toys and other things in their environment. For example, babies learn such concepts as *object permanence*—that things continue to exist even when they can no longer be seen, heard, or touched. They also learn *object constancy*—that objects that look different can still be the same thing. (An egg is an egg whether it is fried or boiled; our puppy, Smokey, is still our puppy whether he is curled up by the fire or running after the ball in the backyard.) In addition, they learn that their own actions can make something happen (*cause and effect*); and that objects can be organized according to characteristics such as color, size, group, function, etc. (*categorization*). These baby concepts lead to memorization and abstract thinking and help the young child understand how the world works and how her own actions can influence what happens.

Communication development enables the child to understand what is being communicated to her by others (*receptive language* skills), and also to make others understand her wants or needs (*expressive language* skills). Communication does not just involve speech, but also gestures, body language, reading and writing, crying, even whining. In addition, it can include the use of communication boards (laptop devices containing pictures or words that the user points to) or sophisticated electronic equipment that produces synthesized speech.

Motor development allows the child to move around in, and act upon, her world by controlling the muscles of her body. Motor skills are usually divided into two basic types: gross motor skills and fine motor skills. Gross motor skills involve large muscles such as those in the arms, legs, and abdomen. Examples of these skills include reaching, walking, and sitting up. Fine motor skills involve small muscles such as those in the hands and face. Examples of fine motor skills include grasping a crayon, fastening buttons, smiling, and moving the eyes.

Motor development follows four general principles: 1) It moves from head to toe, so that you expect a baby to be able to hold her head steady before you expect her to sit, and you expect the baby to sit before she can walk. 2) Control over large muscles occurs before control over small muscles, so that you expect a baby to play patty-cake before you expect the baby to tie shoes or print her name. 3) Muscle control moves from inner body to outer body, so that babies are not able to control arm and leg muscles until they have achieved control over abdominal muscles. 4) Motor development moves from simple movement to complex movement, so babies first swipe and pat objects before they are able to manipulate, poke, push, and pull objects. The development of all children—with or without disabilities—follows these same four principles.

Self-help development involves learning skills that enable a child to take care of herself and gradually become less and less dependent on adults for meeting her needs. For young children, this means learning to eat, dress, bathe, and use the toilet. While self-help skills may seem relatively unimportant compared to walking and talking, they are especially critical because they help children develop self-confidence and an understanding of their own abilities.

Sensory development involves learning to recognize and use the information that is being gathered by all of our senses: touch, vision, hearing, smell, and taste. Sensory development is not always viewed as a separate developmental domain. It is usually considered part of cognitive development. This is because we typically measure how our senses have developed by the way that we use the information received through them, which is a part of our thinking and reasoning process. But however you look at sensory development, learning to make the most of *all* the senses is extremely important. As explained in the section called "Developmental Hurdles," when a sense such as vision fails to develop properly, a child's entire course of development can be altered.

Social development occurs as children learn to interact with their parents, family members, other adults, and other children. Babies begin life as very self-centered little beings; gradually they learn to build relationships, to seek out others, and to care about how others feel. During the preschool years, your child will learn some critical early social skills, such as taking turns and sharing with others. Social development is an important prerequisite for entering school.

Differences in Your Child's Development

Specialists in the education of children with visual impairments have thought for a long time that children with visual impairments follow the same sequence of development as children without disabilities, although perhaps at a different rate. Lately, however, these specialists have begun to rethink this idea. They now believe that children with visual impairments follow a *different* sequence of development. These differences may occur because visual impairments interact with development in such a way that the usual behaviors are learned in a different order.

Much of the research on children with visual impairments compares them to children without disabilities. In such comparisons, children with visual impairments almost invariably seem behind their peers. But why shouldn't they? Think about how much ba-

bies who don't have visual impairments use their vision. It is a constant source of information and sensory input. Recent research suggests that infants use their vision to enhance their understanding of the world long before they can demonstrate what they are thinking. Some studies, for example, have shown that five-month-olds, when shown pictures of various people, recognize their mothers not only from a black-and-white photograph, but even from a black line drawing! To do this, they must make the transition from real experience (from real moms in real color, who touch and talk and smell), to abstract concepts (to two-dimensional *representations* of moms, in black and white, who don't *do* anything). Those babies have so many visual experiences of their mothers stored in their memories that they can make the connection to a visual experience that is unlike the real thing—and at five months of age!

Now think about what that experience is like for infants with visual impairments. First of all, depending on the degree of impairment, their visual images of their parents might not be constant—they might only be able to see Mom's or Dad's face when it is a few inches away. Or, the image they see at six inches away might be much clearer than when Mom or Dad is three feet away. Their visual image of Mom and Dad is changing constantly, depending on where their parents are and how much light is in the room. Instead of storing *one* image in memory, they have to store *several*. Eventually their brains will merge these images, and they will understand that these images belong to Mom or Dad. But it is certainly a much more difficult process.

It would be nice if the other senses could substitute for vision—if they could provide the same type of information that helps babies to learn and form concepts about their world and if they could do so as frequently as vision. Unfortunately, they do not. What they do is provide a different set of experiences, which may or may not be confirmed by visual experiences. When a baby with normal vision plays with a squeeze toy, for example, she primarily uses vision, even though hearing and touch also provide sensory information. A baby who has a visual impairment, however, primarily uses hearing and touch, and only secondarily (if at all) uses vision. The difference occurs when that squeeze toy is held by someone else. The infant with regular vision can see the toy and recognize it as what she was playing with before; her vision helps to connect new experiences to what has occurred in the past. The infant with visual impairment cannot make such easy connections. The toy doesn't look the same, because it is further away; the toy is not being held by the baby, so there is no memory of what the object feels like; and the sound may be similar, but not quite the same because the toy is not as close as it was before. Children with visual impairments do learn how to put all of these bits of sensory information together, but the process takes longer without reliable visual input.

Another way visual impairments typically slow development is by making it harder for children to learn from experience, without their parents doing anything out of the ordinary to teach them. This is called *incidental learning.* You cannot assume that incidental learning occurs for children with visual impairments, because if they have not *seen* something happen, they don't necessarily *know* it happened.

To understand this problem, consider the family pet. Children with normal vision see a cat's mouth open when it meows or spits, so they can connect the sound to the cat. When they pet the kitty, they feel the soft fur and see the cat's entire body simultaneously. When Dad tells the cat to stop scratching the couch, they look at Dad, see that he is looking at the cat, and follow his gaze over to where the cat is pawing at the couch.

The experience is different for children with visual impairments. They have no way of knowing what that meow, growl, or purr is. They can pinpoint *where* the sound is coming from, but they cannot see *what* it is coming from. When the cat remains still long enough, they can feel its soft fur, but they can only feel one part of the cat at a time. They can't see that the cat has a head with ears, a body, four legs, four paws with claws, and a tail. When Dad yells at the cat, they cannot be sure what he is yelling at, or why. And if they get scratched, the paw comes out of and returns to nowhere. Children with visual impairments can still learn the concept of cat, but if they rely on incidental learning, it will take quite a while to put this jumble of isolated experiences together.

One teacher talks about the Good Fairy Syndrome—how, for children with visual impairments, objects and people seem to come out of and disappear into a secret world. Children need to learn the totality of actions: that clothes come out of a chest of drawers, or that toys do not get back into the toy chest by themselves, or that a banana has to be peeled to get to the edible part. Again, this is something that children with visual impairments can and do learn, but unlike other children, they need deliberate teaching to do so.

Because learning *is* more difficult without the clues provided by sight, it makes sense that children with visual impairments do not develop either at the same rate or in the same sequence as children without disabilities. They have much more to learn. For these reasons, comparisons to normal development are not really relevant for children with visual impairments. In other words, what is considered a delay for other children may not be a delay for your child—it may, in fact, be normal.

Developmental Milestones

Even though your child's development may differ somewhat from the norm, this does not mean that you shouldn't have expectations for her development. If you do not expect your child to be able to do something, the chances are good that you will not try to teach her *how* to do it. If you do not teach her, then she has no chance to learn. Or if you teach your child but do not give her a chance to practice it, she may not learn it correctly. What this means is that your expectations—your belief in your child's abilities, or your ideas of what people who are blind can and cannot do—have a lot to do with your child's development.

To help you set reasonable expectations, Table 1 suggests some developmental milestones that are important for your child's development. This list may look different from other developmental checklists you have seen. It includes skills that are important to children with visual impairments, but which are not necessarily important to children without disabilities. The age ranges are estimates, since we are not yet certain exactly when children with visual impairments learn these behaviors. Your child may do certain skills earlier and others later. This table should help you understand what you and your child are working toward.

Table 1
Developmental Milestones for Infants with Visual Impairments

Developmental Area	Birth–12 months	13–24 months	25–36 months
Cognitive	• Imitates sounds, gestures, or actions • Shows displeasure at loss of toy or object • Demonstrates object permanence • Begins to demonstrate cause and effect or means-end behaviors	• Imitates use of toy • Points to body parts • Demonstrates memory (e.g., sings a song) • Uses objects as tools • Uses trial and error	• Matches objects • Remembers past events • Begins to sort objects by size, color, texture, and shape • Tells use of objects
Communication	• Smiles • Makes eye or face contact • Babbles • Laughs • Says first word • Understands "no" • Responds to own name	• Uses gestures (points, waves) • Uses 2-word sentences • Follows simple directions • Names familiar objects and people	• Uses first person pronouns (I, me) • Asks questions • Understands some prepositions (on, next to, on top of) • Begins to use imagination
Gross Motor (large muscles)	• Controls head (holds upright when being held or when lying on tummy) • Rolls over • Sits • Crawls	• Pulls to stand • Walks • Climbs into adult-size chairs • Rolls, then throws balls	• Walks up and down stairs • Begins to run • Begins to jump • Balances on one foot

Developmental Area	Birth–12 months	13–24 months	25–36 months
Fine Motor (small muscles)	• Brings hands together • Grasps objects • Reaches for toys (either visually or auditorially) • Searches for a dropped toy • Explores objects (pats, pokes, hits together)	• Releases objects on purpose • Uses pincer grasp (thumb and index finger) • Scribbles • Puts objects inside containers • Completes simple form board puzzles • Turns pages of books • Uses wrist rotation (turns doorknobs, jar lids, etc.)	• Stacks objects • Copies geometric figures (either tactually or visually) • Strings beads • Sorts objects by size and texture
Self-Help	• Eats with spoon • Holds and drinks from bottle • Eats some finger foods	• Drinks from cup • Removes some clothing independently • Indicates toilet needs • Anticipates some daily routines	• Puts on some clothing independently • Puts toys away • Partially or fully toilet trained
Sensory	• Focuses on and follows objects • Turns to sound • Explores objects by touch	• Identifies hot and cold • Identifies familiar sounds • Identifies familiar odors • Recognizes objects by touch • Explores objects or surfaces with feet	• Recognizes places or activities by odors or sounds • "Tracks" braille (follows along in book or on label) • Identifies textures
Social	• Makes eye or face contact • Smiles • Recognizes parents and family members • Reaches for familiar person • Cries when parent leaves	• Plays interactive games with adults • Hugs • Repeats actions that others laugh at • Imitates household activities (feeding baby, sweeping, etc.)–fantasy play • Plays independently	• Plays interactively with peers • Shows signs of ownership • Asks for help • Pretends

Developmental Hurdles

Although we still have a lot to learn about developmental ages and sequences, we can identify some areas that seem to be more difficult for children with visual impairments. These areas are described in the sections below. Bear in mind, however, that visual impairment has a very individualized impact on a child's development. Your child may have relatively few problems in some of these areas, or she may have a great deal of difficulty in most. For strategies to help your child over these hurdles, see the section on "Helping Your Child's Development" at the end of this chapter.

Cognitive Hurdles

As Chapter 12 explains, some children with visual impairments have mental retardation and therefore encounter more difficulties than usual in learning. Visual impairments, however, do not cause mental retardation. As in the general population, most children with visual impairments have at least average intelligence, while some are intellectually gifted. A visual impairment in and of itself does not affect *what* a child is able to learn cognitively. It does, however, affect *how* children learn, as the section on "Differences in Your Child's Development" discusses. As a result, children with visual impairments often have trouble with several areas of cognitive development, including parts to whole learning, categorization, and object permanence.

Parts to Whole Learning. While most people see the whole
object first, and then explore the little parts, children with visual
impairments are limited to what they can see or feel at any one
time. They have to construct a whole image or idea for something
they will never experience as whole. It is like putting a puzzle together without seeing the photograph on the box. This may not
seem like much of a problem, given the size of infant toys, but as
your child grows, she will begin to explore toys and objects that are
larger and more complex. And what about that pet kitty? Since
your child can only feel one body part at a time, the image of the
kitty in your child's mind could be entirely different from yours.
This does not mean that learning is impossible—only that it needs
to be structured, so that you are sure that your child is getting all
the information, and getting it in the right order.

Imagine that you want to show your child her brother's new
wagon. You might first let her sit in the wagon and explore the bottom and sides with her hands and feet. As soon as you feel that she
is comfortable with the inside of the wagon, you will want to encourage her to feel the outside of the wagon and the wheels. You
can do this first while she is sitting in the wagon and then you'll
want to take her out of the wagon to continue exploring the outside. As you do this, place her hand on the inside (or seat) of the
wagon to remind her that she was sitting inside the wagon just minutes before. Finally, show her the handle and demonstrate that as
you walk with the handle in your hand, the wagon follows you.
Now you're ready to go! Help your child place a favorite toy or
stuffed animal in the wagon and then let her pull it a short distance and check to make sure the toy has "followed her" in the
wagon.

Your child will also enjoy sitting in the wagon and being pulled
by you. As you pull her, talk to her, so that she can feel the movement of the wagon and hear your voice in front of her. A word of
caution: as you are about to begin to pull her in the wagon, make
sure you warn her and tell her to hold on. While her brother may
see you prepare to pull the wagon and grasp the sides of the
wagon, your child with a visual impairment will not have the visual
cues to prepare herself.

Categorization. Categorization is a way of ordering or sorting
people and objects that most children begin doing actively when
they are older than three years. Children begin by sorting objects
by physical attributes, such as color and shape. Later they sort by

group ("foods"), function ("things that you eat with"), and association ("things you need for a trip"). By categorizing things, we begin to organize our thinking so that we can be successful in learning new things and building on existing concepts and knowledge. This cognitive skill is difficult for children with visual impairments because they cannot see the similarities and differences among the objects in their environment. You can help your child learn to categorize by verbally pointing out similarities and differences and showing her the tactual qualities as well. For example, the first time your child encounters a motorcycle, point out that it has two wheels and a seat like a bicycle but it has a key to start it and it sounds more like a car.

Object Permanence. Object permanence is the concept that something continues to exist even when you can no longer see, hear, touch, or otherwise perceive it with your senses. For example, a teddy bear still exists when it is stashed out of sight in the toy box; the vacuum cleaner still exists when it is turned off and put in the closet. If a child does not understand object permanence, everything is new to him each time it is presented; there is no continuity from time to time or object to object. Mastering this concept is a little more difficult for children with visual impairment, because they cannot rely on their vision to inform them about what happens to things. Even the toys they throw disappear, from their perspective. When they drop something, the only way they know it still exists is if they are able to touch or hear it. Yet babies with visual impairment seem to develop "people permanence" fairly easily. They know Mommy and Daddy, and they know that their parents will return even if they "disappear" momentarily. You can help your child develop object permanence by helping her feel around for dropped objects and by using the same words for objects consistently.

Social Hurdles

Social development is important for all children, including children with visual impairments. Just as with children without disabilities, some children with visual impairments have an easier time picking up social skills than others. Some children are just naturally more outgoing and at ease in social situations. There are, however, some common problems encountered by children with visual impairments. For example, preschoolers with visual impair-

ments often have a hard time initiating interactions with other children, choosing social activities, and playing alongside peers. You can help your child by arranging opportunities for your child to play and interact with other children on a regular basis.

Attachment. Attachment is the process by which infants and parents learn to care for and love one another and form a human bond. It is important because it provides security and assists in emotional development. This process can be slower in babies with a visual impairment, primarily because they often do not seem to cuddle like other babies. In fact, they may respond to being picked up by stiffening their bodies, arching their backs, and crying. Their message seems to be that they want to be left alone. In reality, however, they may merely have been surprised when they were picked up, and therefore responded by acting frightened. Remember: babies with visual impairments are not always able to watch people approaching them, and you can't be sure they can hear or understand the sound of approaching footsteps.

Babies with visual impairments do attach to their parents, and they do cuddle. But they need some preparation before sudden moves. Try touching and talking to your baby first, giving her time to adjust, before wrenching her from the comfort and security of her crib or infant seat. Although your baby may give different signals, with patience and understanding you can learn to read them and to respond to them with love.

Communication Hurdles

Vocal and verbal imitation are usually not problems for children with visual impairments—they very quickly learn verbal play like repetitive nursery rhymes and songs and it becomes a source of pleasure for them and their parents. There are, however, other aspects of communication that children with visual impairments typically have trouble with. First, communication can be difficult when there is little visual feedback. Children with visual impairments may not make eye contact, so it is hard to tell whether they are paying attention to what someone is doing or saying, and it is hard for them to know if someone is paying attention to them. Without the cues from others' facial expressions (the raised eyebrow or the smile), children with visual impairments may also have trouble understanding when it is their turn to speak. You can help by practicing turn-taking with your baby, even in early infancy—imitate your baby's sounds, then wait and give her a chance to respond, then repeat your imitation again.

Another aspect of communication that may be difficult for your child is nonverbal gestures such as waving, pointing, or nodding. If your child cannot observe these gestures being used by others, she will not automatically learn how to make them. Teach your baby about these simple, but meaningful gestures that will add to everyone's understanding. It will be most effective if you use naturally occurring events to teach your child about nonverbal gestures. For example, when you are playing with your child and she smiles, you might tell her that you like it when she smiles and that it lets you know that she is happy or pleased.

Motor Hurdles

Although a visual impairment does not affect a child's ability to use her muscles, it does affect the way she learns to use them. One reason is that many of the motor skills children learn are acquired by watching someone else do things, imitating them, and then repeating them over and over again. This means your child will not automatically pick up skills such as crawling, walking, skipping, and jumping the way other children do.

Another reason visual impairments can affect the development of motor skills is that if a child can't see an attractive toy or mobile, he won't be as motivated to try to touch or grasp it. In addition, children who can't see where they're moving are likely to be reluctant to explore their environment.

Fine Motor Skills. You would think that babies with visual impairments would just naturally use their hands, because so much information is available that way. But remember that they have not had the same visual experiences—they may not be able to watch their hands, or see their hands contact and manipulate objects, or watch what other people do with their hands. You can show your child what to do—whether it's eating or stacking or scribbling—by using a hand-over-hand technique.

Your child's fine motor skills may also be delayed if she does not like lying on her tummy or crawling, as is the case with some babies with visual impairments. This is because a baby's hand grasp tends to become more mature when she bears weight on her hands and shifts weight from one hand to the other. If your child does not get these experiences, she will probably have difficulties in eating finger foods and playing with objects. Other than showing your baby how to do these things with her hands, the next best thing is to make sure she gets lots of gross motor activity. Good activities for encouraging movement include: playing with a variety of toys that require your child to use her hands in different ways; patty cake; ball play; rolling a wheelbarrow; making obstacles courses that encourage climbing, scooting, etc.

Locomotion. Moving independently from place to place (locomotion) seems to be one of the most difficult skills for children with visual impairment. For children without visual impairment, the motivation to move comes, first, from watching others move and then from seeing something desirable that is just out of reach. Children with visual impairment do not have these experiences. Consequently, they are usually at least slightly delayed in skills such as crawling and walking. Children with visual impairment can be shown how to move (using that same hand-over-hand technique, even if it means you have to get down on the floor!). You can also use other sensory cues (your voice, the sound of a favorite toy) to help your child understand that something is "out there" and worth going after. See Chapter 11 for more suggestions about helping your child with locomotion.

Sensory Hurdles

According to some researchers, vision is usually involved in 90 percent of the learning that takes place in early development. But the way your child learns about the world is going to be different. To a greater or lesser degree, your child will have to rely instead on her senses of smell, touch, hearing, and taste for information. As mentioned above, this will make it harder for your child to learn because she cannot watch and imitate what others are doing, and may make her less motivated to learn if she cannot see enticing objects in her environment. It will also make it harder for her to learn about objects and people in her environment through intersensory coordination.

Intersensory Coordination. Intersensory coordination is the process of taking information obtained through one sensory system and using it in another. It involves figuring out how the information obtained through one sense is related to the information obtained through another sense. For example, a young child might hear a siren and figure out that the noise goes with the big red fire engine that just sped by. Vision plays an important role in intersensory coordination, because it seems to blend the other senses automatically. Vision, because it is always present, can take all the separate pieces of sensory information and pull them together into a whole.

In the absence of vision, this process is much harder, because the other pieces of sensory information do not come in on a constant basis. Toys sometimes make sounds, but they may sound different across the room than they do close up, and may stop making sounds if batteries or wind-up mechanisms run down. Toys can be touched and smelled, but only if they are within reach. Babies with visual impairments eventually develop intersensory coordination, but until they do, it is probably a good idea not to overload or bombard them with sensory stimuli. Give your child one sensory input at a time—let her touch an object before squeezing it to make noise, and let her touch food before you give her a taste of it. At the same time you are presenting a new object to you child, be sure to explain what you're showing her: "Feel the fuzzy bear. Listen to the pretty music the bear makes. . . ." As mentioned in the section on Object Permanence, be sure to use the same words in describing objects at first, so that your child does not become confused.

Helping Your Child's Development

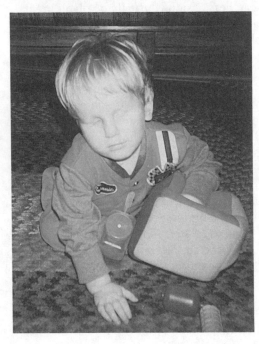

One of the best ways you can help your child's development is to get some help yourself. As Chapter 8 explains, there are laws that entitle your family to early intervention and special education services. These services are intended to help maximize your child's development.

Be sure that the services you receive are what you want—they should never feel burdensome or intrusive. And because children with visual impairments send different signals and experience the world differently, insist that your services include a professional who is knowledgeable about blindness and visual impairments (a vision teacher or an orientation and mobility instructor). These professionals have been trained to understand how children with visual impairments experience things and to help them learn. Perhaps most importantly, they have also been trained to see the possibilities for people with visual impairments and not the limitations—just as you will see the possibilities, as you watch your child grow and learn.

Besides getting professional help for your child's developmental problems, there are also ways you can help her learn. Some general principles include:

- Experience the world from your child's point of view. This might mean getting down on the floor and learning to crawl all over again, or it might mean closing your eyes before you try to hold and drink from a cup. The point is that you want to get an idea of what you are asking your child to do before you ask her to do it. It might not be as easy as it seems!

- Create opportunities when the opportunities do not create themselves. Although we are still learning about how babies with visual impairments develop, one thing is certain: They will not learn what they have not experienced. Since you cannot rely on incidental learning, you have to *make* opportunities for learning. If you drop an egg on the floor, your toddler can help clean it up, while you talk about eggs and compare *this* egg to the eggs he had for breakfast. Seize the time!

- Make your child a do-er instead of a done-to-er. Help your child to learn on her own, instead of always doing things for her. By allowing her to accomplish things on her own, you are sending a clear message to her that you not only *expect* her to do things on her own, but you also trust her to accomplish them correctly. While your child is very young, it will be important for her to experience success often as she tries new things. As she grows, however, it will be just as important for you to know that some of the things she tries to do will be difficult. You must encourage her to work through her frustration. It will be well worth it as she grows into an independent and capable young adult.

- Give enough time. Give enough time for your child to learn a skill, and then give enough time to practice it. This may mean you have to change your schedule a bit, but it will help make your child a do-er.

- Help make connections. It is difficult to apply what you have learned in the past to a new experience (*generalize*) if you are unable to see the similarities in the situations. You help make connections when you relate the broken egg on the floor to breakfast. You help make connections, too, when you point out that the wheels on the car are circles, and serve your child mashed, baked, scalloped, and diced potatoes instead of only French fries.

- Use co-active movements. Hand-over-hand or *co-active* movements are great for showing your child what your expectations are, especially when introducing a new skill.

- Use concrete (real) objects and experiences. It will be easier for your child to understand the concept of the *real* object before asking her to understand a representation of that object. The family cat is a better learning tool than a stuffed animal.

- Beware the fairy godmother. Help your child to understand the totality of actions, instead of thinking that things just happen. Make sure that she knows that the apple juice doesn't just "appear" in her cup at breakfast— that *you* open the refrigerator door, pick up the juice bottle, pour the juice into her cup, and set the cup on the table.
- Use touch. Your touch means a lot to your child. Sometimes a touch on the shoulder can be just the reassurance your child needs to plod ahead!
- Use language that is rich in description. You do not have to talk *at* your child all day long, but when you do talk, try to be as informative as possible. Explain what is going on, or why everyone is laughing. Tell her about colors and textures and the weather.
- Be consistent in the names you use. It can be confusing if you talk about your baby's overalls one minute, and then refer to them as pants the next minute. Try to use the same words for objects and events until your baby is old enough that you can point out similarities and differences and can help her make connections for what seems obvious to you.
- Use your child's name. A child with a visual impairment cannot see the facial expressions or body language that tell her she is the one being spoken to. Especially if there are other adults or children in the room, speak to your child (and everyone else) by name.
- Point out visual features. If your child has some vision, it may help her sort out what she is seeing if you draw her attention to various visual characteristics of objects. Point out that her toy is bright yellow or that her patent leather shoes are shiny. "See" and "look" are appropriate terms to use, even if you think your child is totally blind.
- Point out the sensory qualities of people, objects, and events. If you walk past a bakery, comment on the wonderful smells coming through the door. Your baby will smell it, too, but will not necessarily know what it means unless you tell her. Point out that Aunt Sara always smells like

flowers and Uncle Dan has hairy arms. Show her that grass feels and smells different from carpeting.

- Make no assumptions. You can never be sure your child has witnessed events that you have, and you can never be sure that she understands them in quite the same way. Do not assume that learning has occurred—check it out, probe, ask questions. Exposure does not mean absorption.
- Encourage interactions with people and places. It can be difficult for children with visual impairments to take risks in social situations because they do not have the same clues available. For example, they cannot read body language to tell if they would be welcome into a group. Help your child to feel comfortable with adult family members, and, if necessary, show her how to play with her peers. In new places, help your child explore the surroundings and feel comfortable in them.
- Encourage socially appropriate behaviors. Children with visual impairments may not be able to make eye contact, but they can turn their head toward someone who is speaking to them. "Please" and "thank you" are appreciated in any youngster. As your child grows older, you may also have to explain which habits are appropriate in public and which are not.
- Remember that eye function can vary. Children with visual impairments are affected by different lighting conditions, different times of day, and even different weather patterns. Their behavior may not be consistent, and they may have legitimate reasons for it. Be patient if your child comfortably completes visual tasks one day and seems frustrated by them the next.
- Use your voice to convey meaning. The volume and tone of your voice can tell your child a lot about your current state of mind—whether you are angry, sad, happy, exasperated, or thrilled. This will be another clue that your child can use in social situations.
- Relate directions to body parts. Whenever possible, give directions by referring to positions in relation to your child's body parts. Instead of saying, "You dropped your rattle on the floor," say "Your rattle is on the floor next to your foot." As your child grows, her orientation to the world will

occur in terms of her body—in back, in front, next to, on the side, left, right, etc.

- Challenge your child. No one knows what makes the differences among children, and with today's technology, no one knows what the possibilities are for your child's future. Try to create experiences that will help your child make connections and reach a better understanding of the world, and to seek out her own opportunities for learning.

Conclusion

As a parent, you have probably already realized how fascinating it is to watch your child as she learns new things. Day by day, week by week, you watch as your child develops her own strengths and discovers her unique likes and dislikes. Still, you likely have some concerns about your child's development. This is only natural—all parents do.

Your child with visual impairments will need your help in providing many opportunities to explore her world. These experiences will help your child develop skills and understanding in the cognitive, communication, motor, self-help, sensory, and social domains. By encouraging this development when your child is young, you are helping your child establish a firm foundation for learning later in life.

Parent Statements

I know Jason has delays—I just keep expecting them to go away. I wonder what I have done wrong that he still has these delays.

◄o►

I always thought I would be the expert on my child. Now I have to rely on all these outsiders—teachers, therapists, psychologists—the list goes on and on. I should be the boss—not them.

◄o►

Don't feel sorry for my child. Just be proud of her accomplishments.

◄o►

We are learning something new every day.

—◄o►—

My friend's baby is the same age as Josh, and she's way ahead of him. When I'm depressed, I don't want to visit them. But then I look at how far Josh has come!

—◄o►—

I talk to Katie a lot—I try to explain everything I'm doing, even though I know she doesn't really understand yet. Some day she will.

—◄o►—

The early intervention team told us that Marty's motor development might be delayed because she doesn't reach out for things since she can't see them. We bought all kinds of toys that make noises so that she will have something to reach out for, but she is really interested in people and will be more likely to reach out to someone than to a toy.

—◄o►—

With Billy, it seems like he takes two steps backward before he makes any progress.

—◄o►—

The therapists in the early intervention program have been really helpful in helping me understand the areas in which my daughter excels, as well as the areas in which she is lagging behind.

—◄o►—

With my first baby, I didn't have to do anything—she just did everything on her own! Now, with my blind baby, I can't take anything for granted. I have to show him how to do things, like crawling, and how to get food from the table to his mouth. But then he seems to know what to do. He just needs to know what's expected.

—◄o►—

I get very defensive when people point out what Carrie isn't doing yet.

—◄o►—

It frustrates me that my baby never does as well when his development is being assessed as he does when he's with me at home. But I guess what matters in the long run is that he *is* making progress, even if he doesn't demonstrate that progress to his therapists and teachers.

—◄o►—

It's amazing how far Diandre has come, and how far we as his parents have come!

Chapter 5

❤

Daily Life

Beth Langley, M.S.*

When your child has a visual impairment, day-to-day activities must still go on. Family members need to sleep, prepare and eat meals, dress appropriately for the events of the day, do chores, run errands, and take time to relax and have fun. In the beginning, your child will need a great deal of help to participate in these activities, just as any child would. As he grows older, however, you can expect him to learn self-help, social, and other skills that will enable him to become more and more independent.

How your child learns to master his daily routine will be similar in many ways to how any other child does. He will, however, need to learn unique and creative ways of taking part in daily activities in order to compensate for his lack of vision. For instance, he may learn to recognize his favorite sweater by the way it feels, or figure out that if he always puts his teddy bear on the table next to his bed, it will be there when he wants it at night. As he learns about his environment, your child may discover many of these unique adaptations himself. As a parent, you may also sometimes have to show him the way, or present him challenges to overcome and experiences and opportunities from which to learn. The earlier in life you begin giving your child these experiences and challenges, the more likely he is to grow up to be an active and capable adult.

This chapter covers issues that you will face daily as you interact with your child at home and in the community. Many hints,

---

* Beth Langley is currently an educational diagnostician for Pinellas County Schools, Florida. She is well known for her expertise is working with children with disabilities, and has had extensive hands-on experiences with children with multiple disabilities, including visual impairments.

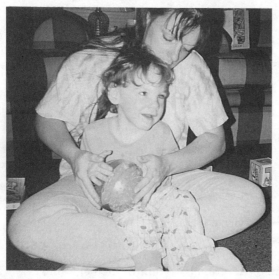

tips, and strategies accumulated from personal experiences, as well as methods and techniques proven to be effective with children with visual impairments, will be shared. If these ideas work for you, so much the better. If they do not, do not hesitate to develop your own unique methods for helping your child learn to adapt to his daily routine. The ideas in this chapter should serve only as a springboard to discovering your own special set of coping mechanisms.

Sensory Development the Natural Way

Every parent wants to provide his child optimal experiences for learning and growing. When your child has a visual impairment, you may hear that optimal experiences for him are those that emphasize sensory development. By emphasizing sensory development, the theory goes, you help your child learn strategies that will enable him to compensate for his impairment and get along in his surroundings. He will learn to rely on his hearing to recognize the voices of friends and relatives. He will learn that different smells mean that Mom is cooking dinner, that the dog has just had a bath, or that Uncle Fred, who smokes a pipe, has come to visit.

While you may be tempted to bombard your child with multiple sensory experiences to make sure he learns as much as possible as quickly as possible, this can be a mistake. Overloading your child with nonfunctional and meaningless sights, sounds, textures, and smells can be just as damaging as a complete void of sensory information. For example, while driving down a country lane, you might think it is a good idea to keep a running commentary going: "We're driving down the road; it's a little gravel road. We're passing a barn and a farmhouse and some cows, and now let me roll down your window—can you smell the fresh-cut grass?" As you can see, it would be difficult to keep such a commentary going, and your child would receive so much information that it would become meaningless. It will probably be more meaningful for your child if you choose specific things to work on. For example, on this particular trip in the country, you could choose to focus on learning about cows.

Sensory input will only be effective if the context, situation, and setting is meaningful to your child. Regardless of what professionals may recommend or what "sensory activities" designed to "stimulate" your child's development you may read about, the first question you should ask is whether a specific recommendation will give your child a more functional way to control or adjust to his environment. For example, using a black light might increase contrast and therefore allow your child to use visual information more effectively. This can hardly be called a "functional" adaptation, however, since black lights are not widely available for daily activities.

"Stimulating" should not take the form of "doing to the child," but of allowing him to actively explore, control, and make accommodations in a naturally occurring setting or play opportunity. That is, you should not try to devise different isolated ways to "stimulate" sensory development. Instead, look for ways to involve your child in sensory experiences that occur naturally. In particular, help your child learn to use sights, smells, sounds, surface changes, and textures to serve as cues for: 1) alerting him to dangerous situations; 2) comforting him; 3) helping him make appropriate choices or decisions; 4) controlling the environment; 5) orienting him in space; or 6) guiding him to move safely in his environment.

If a particular sensory experience will not immediately fulfill one of the six functions described above, then it may not serve a useful purpose for your child. For example, letting your child explore his towel and applying well-paced pressure to various body parts as you dry him after a bath will help him develop tactile discrimination and the beginnings of space-body awareness needed for orientation. Indiscriminately rubbing him with squares of velvet, terry cloth, or silk, on the other hand, provides a much less valuable experience. A younger child can begin to anticipate activities associated with specific smells. For example, the smell of powder may cue him he is about to have his diaper changed, soap bubbles signify it is bath time, and the smell of toast means breakfast is finally ready. Calling your child's attention to the oven buzzer or microwave beeper helps him orient to and navigate his way into the kitchen for mealtime and alerts him to prepare for eating. In contrast, ringing bells or shaking noisemakers around your child is much less likely to help him adapt to his environment and may, in fact, confuse him.

Table 1 provides examples of natural sensory cues and potential meanings associated with each cue.

TABLE 1
Natural Environmental Cues

Natural Cue	Associated Event/Location
Mom's perfume Dad's shaving lotion	Informs child who is approaching
Music from clock radio	Time to get up
Bib on/off	I'm going to eat/I'm finished
Bath water running	Time for bath
Smell of powder	Time for diaper change
Sound of battery-operated toothbrush	Time to have teeth brushed
Hand on bannister	I'm going up/down stairs
Tile/rug	I'm in the kitchen/family room
Sound of radio/TV	My toys are near
Blender	Time to eat
Keys	Time to go for a ride
Book	I get to sit with Dad
Toilet flushing	That's the bathroom
Coffee, meals cooking	That's the kitchen
Warmth from sunshine	That's a window
Pulling on sweater, coat, or snowsuit	Time to go outside/playground
Sound of bike horn	I'm going to ride my trike
Sliding doors opening	I'm at the grocery store

Moisture, splashing water,
  sounds of voices, smell of
  chlorine, swim ring
	Time to go swimming

Leather shoes	Time to go to church
Crinkly paper	I'm at the doctor's

A Word about Tactile Stimulation

When children with visual impairments are hesitant to touch and explore different types of textures, they are frequently labeled "tactilely defensive." Often, however, this label is misapplied. If your child is reluctant to experience touch sensations, it is more likely because his sensory system is trying to protect him from dangerous or unpleasant experiences. To some degree, everybody's sensory system does this. Most people are hesitant to touch unknown substances or objects or substances which are associated with unpleasant events and experiences. This is a survival technique intended to help the system recognize danger and to regulate sensory input that is too intense.

All babies and young children are more likely to have these primitive, protective responses to touch and other sensations. This is because their sensory system is immature. Immature touch systems respond best to pressure, weightbearing, and hard, firm textures, and resist light touch at all costs. Providing sensory input from soft materials such as fur, silk, or velvet, or from light stroking may not only disorganize a child's behavior, but cause a great deal of emotional stress.

It is all right for your child to be somewhat tentative when touching something for the first time. He also has a right to refuse to touch particular textures or to have certain tactile experiences. For example, he should not be forced to participate in playdough, finger painting, or gluing activities. Children, particularly those with visual impairments, learn most efficiently when they have some control over the amount of incoming sensory information. Your child should be offered encouragement and frequent opportunities to participate, without imposed judgement or expectations, and should be allowed to decide for himself when to participate. Once your child knows what to expect and can trust that an experience is predictable, he will often accept new objects, textures, and substances and integrate them into his play and sensory repertoire.

Occasionally, tactile defensiveness does pose a real problem for children with visual impairments. Sometimes a child's resistance to touch interferes significantly with everyday routines or contributes to delays in development. In these instances, a highly trained professional such as a pediatric occupational therapist with sensory integration training or certification can help. See Chapter 8 for more information on occupational therapy.

Mealtimes

Mealtime can be the single most frustrating time for both your child and your family. Mealtime can be hurried and noisy and messy. Parents often spend their time trying to teach feeding skills and table manners while their children vigorously resist their efforts. What could be a relaxing time for families to get together and review their day often turns into a battleground.

Many children with visual impairments master eating skills with little difficulty. Others may be quite delayed in learning to eat. How your child reacts to eating will depend on how well he uses his senses to accomplish daily tasks, his general temperament, whether specific eating experiences and textures are introduced at the right time, and, most importantly, your attitudes, emotions, and consistency.

Feeding during Infancy

Babies with visual impairments follow the same developmental feeding milestones as sighted babies. You should therefore follow general feeding guidelines when selecting and offering different textures of foods.

In feeding your child, it is important to remember the Good Fairy Syndrome discussed in Chapter 4. That is, that children with visual impairments have trouble realizing that objects (including food) don't just appear from thin air. To avoid this misconception, it will be important for you to signal your child (by talking to him or allowing him to put his hand on your wrist) before placing a spoonful of food in his mouth.

Children with visual impairments usually manage pureed foods as well as sighted infants do. Most feeding difficulties coincide with the introduction of cereals and foods with more consistency and texture. One reason is that babies with visual impairments often do not spend as much time exploring a broad array of textures with their mouths. You can help your child in this area by gently guiding him to place his hands in his mouth, and by giving him a variety of teethers. Later, giving him foods such as hard pretzels, strips of hard cheeses, frozen vegetables, and graham crackers can accustom him to different textures. The most difficult textures for children with visual impairments are those without a definite consistency, such as jello, and those with mixed textures, such as casseroles and beef stew.

When you introduce your baby to unfamiliar foods, he may react by coughing, sputtering, mild choking, and spitting. These are typical reactions from *all* infants. If you have not experienced these reactions with other children, however, you may be alarmed and think that your child is struggling because of his visual impairment. As with other infants, you should calmly continue to offer the offending food while supplementing your child's nutrition with acceptable foods. Your child may require a longer period of time to adjust to new foods, but he will most likely get used to the new textures with experience and warm encouragement. Sometimes children with significant oral motor problems just cannot seem to adapt to new foods. In these instances, a pediatric occupational therapist or speech therapist with specialization in treating oral motor difficulties can help.

If your child has feeding difficulties, he should always be encouraged to stay with the family during mealtime, even if only to play in his high chair or infant or booster seat while the family eats. Your child needs to learn that, regardless of his behavior, your family still expects him to participate as a family member during family events.

Poor Appetite

Poor appetite can be another obstacle to overcome with children with visual impairments. While every child is different, poor appetite is often due to the oral motor problems discussed in the previous section. Other common causes include too little activity and meals served too closely together. One mother was surprised when her child brought a note home after the first day of school asking her to send snacks for her child, as she was still hungry after lunch. Typically, this child refused to eat more than a few bites at any meal. The mother admitted, however, that her daughter spent most of her days at home listening to tapes or lying on the sofa and listening to television with her siblings. Another child ate heartily at lunch once his class switched to the last lunch period, allowing nearly seven hours between meals.

If your child has a fairly inactive daily life, offering several "little meals" throughout the day, rather than the traditional breakfast, lunch, and dinner may entice him to eat. Also consider whether your child finds his meals tasty enough to eat. While each child has his own preferences, children with visual impairments often prefer spicy foods over sweet ones. Many children have highly developed taste cells and acquire a preference for specific types and brands of foods, refusing the same food of another brand. A child might, for example, eat only McDonald's™ french fries, Mrs. Baird's™ bread, Oreo™ cookies, and Birds Eye™ orange juice.

If your child is not getting sufficient calories, either because he is a "picky" eater or because his metabolism is high, ask your pediatrician to refer you to a nutritionist. The nutritionist can recommend simple ways of providing a higher calorie consumption, including adding Instant Breakfast™ to your child's milk or cereal, offering fruit and yogurt milkshakes, and blending peanut butter, wheat germ, mayonnaise, butter, or oil into foods your child will eat.

Finger Feeding

As mentioned above, many children with visual impairments are hesitant to touch and handle unfamiliar objects, including foods. This hesitancy often delays finger feeding, a critical step in the acquisition of self-feeding skills. Finger feeding aids in the development of fine motor skills. It also helps teach and reinforce *scanning techniques*—searching for food on a tray or plate.

Even though tactile sensitivities may delay finger feeding, you should still introduce your child to finger feeding at the usual age (about six months). To help your child make the transition to finger feeding, try letting him hold his hand over yours while you place bites in his mouth. Some children may require most of the food to be fed to them and then can be encouraged to feed themselves the last couple of bites. Or you might offer the first bite directly to your child's mouth to encourage him to pick up the rest and finger feed. If you can identify one specific favorite food that lends itself to finger feeding, it may help to allow him to perfect his skills with that food before moving on to others. One parent decided that if the child was motivated to open his mouth when his favorite food was offered, he should be motivated to hold it and feed himself. After only two short sessions in which his parents placed the cookie in his hand and quickly guided it to his mouth, the boy began to hold a broader variety of finger foods.

Whatever your child's age, it is important to remember that most individuals have a few foods that they would rather not eat. When your child rejects only certain foods, his "message" should be honored.

Managing Utensils

Although most children with a severe visual impairment learn to feed themselves as well as sighted children do, other children have difficulty learning the process. One reason is that some children with visual impairments have not developed wrist control or sufficient supination of the forearm (turning the arm so that the palm of the hand faces up). Sighted children automatically develop these skills as they turn over toys to visually explore all surfaces. In addition, a child may be less motivated to seek out and discriminate foods on his plate if he has tactile defensiveness. And without the benefit of sight, it can be harder to realize that food is there and to learn the process of taking food from a container of some nature.

Your child can begin building the motor skills he needs to manage utensils even when he is just drinking from a bottle. Encouraging him to help hold his bottle, and, when appropriate, hold his own bottle is a good start. A number of devices which help an infant hold onto his bottle are on the market. There are also specially designed covers that are brightly colored and patterned and encourage a child to use his residual visual abilities as he drinks.

Before your child can attempt to scoop with a spoon, he must have sufficient sensitivity to know whether the spoon is loaded or check it out with his other hand. One way to accustom your child to the feel of scooping is to work from behind, guiding him hand over hand to bring his spoon firmly into contact with the dish at an angle. This approach will encourage him to turn his hand in the appropriate direction to scoop. It also sends a message to his large muscles as to what they are supposed to do and provides a cue as to exactly where his plate is on the surface. A transition step that may help your child learn to scoop is for him to actually pick up appropriate foods and place them on the spoon or the fork.

When your child is ready to spoon feed, buy a dish or bowl with high edges so that food will not slide off the plate as he scoops. You might also consider buying a specially notched plate to help your child know where to find and to replace the eating utensils on his plate. These types of bowls and plates are readily available in discount, toy, and child specialty stores. To stabilize the plate or bowl during scooping, place it on a mat of some type of non-skid material such as Dycem™ or use a suction-cup base.

Utensils that are designed for any child are often more appropriate than utensils designed especially for children with disabilities. Spoons and forks which make grasping easier can be found in the youth department of discount and toy stores. Even musical plates and spoons/forks are commercially available. These can add to your child's motivation and help him locate his utensils. Remember, whenever possible your child should use items that do not set him apart from other children his age. Creativity and ingenuity, as well as brainstorming, may be necessary to construct or modify utensils for your child's needs and still be aesthetically pleasing. The need for adapted eating utensils must be continually reevaluated and new eating utensils must be considered as your child grows older and either becomes more independent or continues to need assistance of some nature. An occupational therapist can help modify utensils and work on problems holding them if your child is having difficulties.

To learn what is on his plate and where to locate it, teach your child to explore his plate with his nondominant hand (the one he does not use to hold utensils). When he is older, you can teach him to look for foods based on the positions of a clock. For example, his peas are at two o'clock and his meat is at six o'clock. At first, it may help if your child uses his nondominant hand to lightly touch the plate or food as a reference point to know where to put his spoon or fork.

When your child is learning to drink from a cup, always encourage him to search for and pick up his cup from the surface so that he knows where it belongs. If you hand the cup to your child, he may attempt to replace it on the "invisible shelf" and consequently drop it in midair. You can encourage your child to tilt the cup sufficiently to drain the last drops of liquid by giving him a cup that plays music once it is empty. Other cups play music once the cup is lifted from the surface. These provide a great auditory clue that you have picked up the cup and will hand it to him for a drink. When introducing cup drinking, explore all avenues to evaluate which cups are best for your child.

Mealtime Preparation

Helping with meal preparation can be both educational and enjoyable for your child. It gives him opportunities to assume responsibility and to interact socially, and exposes him to a myriad of concepts, textures, and cognitive and motor experiences. For example, your child practices memory and classification skills as he recalls the location of the milk, the napkins, and the silverware. When he helps to set the table, an older preschooler builds directionality and spatial orientation skills and learns about one-to-one correspondence (each family member gets one knife, one fork, one spoon). A young child can fill glasses with ice from a container strategically placed to avoid a mess if a few cubes are dropped or can help remove lids from the milk or plastic containers. Throwing away empty cans and boxes provides practice in orientation and mobility skills. "Guessing" what is being prepared or which food was in each empty container builds inferential reasoning abilities and promotes language development. Finally, helping in the preparation of the family meal may motivate your child to try different foods and to view mealtimes as a fun part of the day.

Dressing

Dressing an infant or toddler is much the same as dressing any child. As with many other aspects of daily life, however, it is a good idea to provide cues to let your child know what is about to happen. For example, if you always dress and undress your baby in the same place (perhaps on a terry cloth changing pad), he can begin to anticipate when it is time to get his clothes changed. It is also a good idea to talk with him about what is happening, while it is happening.

Instructional Strategies for Dressing

You can lay the groundwork for teaching your child to dress or undress himself when he is quite young by teaching him the names for clothing and body parts. One way to help him learn these labels is to be consistent in the order that you take off and put on clothing. Consistency will also help your child learn to anticipate and assist with the next step. Even a toddler can begin to help by lifting his bottom during a diaper change if he knows what is coming next. To help your child anticipate actions, always give him a cue by tugging gently on the clothing article prior to its removal and than pause to see whether your child will lift his arms or hold out his foot.

Once your child has the motor skills to begin learning to take off or put on clothing articles on his own, there are several points to keep in mind. First, be sure that he has a stable sitting base, either on the floor or on a sturdy chair, low to the floor, and with support to the back or sides. Second, dress and undress your child from in front of him. Although dressing him from behind may teach him more normal movements, he will feel more secure with you in front of him and you will be better able to communicate with him.

There is no one best procedure or order for what to teach. Removing unlaced or opened shoes and socks are often the first skills mastered, however. In teaching this skill, as in teaching any skill, it is important to make sure that your child feels successful early on. To ensure success in removing socks, be sure they fit very loosely! Cross your child's leg over his other leg to bring the foot closer to his hands. First, let your child simply pull his sock from his toes once you have pulled it over his heel. Gradually increase the number of steps your child must do. For instance, when he is ready, show your child how to hook his thumb into the cuff of his sock to pull it off. Similarly, when you are teaching your child to remove a pull-off shirt, begin with the last step first. Once the shirt is over his face, have him pull it the remaining way. Later, teach your child to grab the back of his shirt near his shoulders and pull it over his head.

Watch your child for preferences in getting dressed and undressed. For example, it is easier for some blind children to first push their arms into the shirt sleeves of a pull-over shirt, raise them, and then tug the shirt over the head. Be patient and systematic. A word of advice to working mothers and fathers. Teaching your child to dress and undress is best done at bedtime, when the pressures of time do not exist! If you are in a hurry, it is better to help your child than to frustrate him and risk confusion and error.

Dressing: Clothing Selection

Clothing selection involves two phases: 1) selecting and purchasing appropriate clothing for your child to wear, and 2) choosing (or having your child choose) appropriate clothing to wear on any given day. Clearly, if your child is to succeed in choosing clothing to wear, his wardrobe must first be stocked with clothes that he can match himself and easily put on and take off.

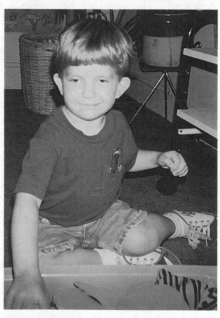

In buying clothing for your child, you should take into account his age, level of vision, tactile skills, and motor skills, as well as your family's and child's preferences. In general, however, there are several considerations to keep in mind. For young children just beginning to dress and undress themselves, or for children with poor motor control, it is important to buy clothing that fits loosely but still looks appropriate. The looser the clothing, the easier and less stressful it will be for you and your child to pull it on, up, and over. In particular, the neck openings should always be sufficiently loose or flexible enough to allow your child's head through easily and smoothly. If a tight shirt becomes "stuck" while you are pulling it over your child's face, he may become fearful and protest about all pull-over shirts in the future.

Clothing items made with Velcro closures or magnetic snaps may be a good choice at first, since they are easier than zippers or buttons for young children. But remember that you want your child to be able to wear all types of clothes, so buttons and zippers will eventually be important to learn about.

Clothing in the bright fluorescent colors so popular among children today can be a good choice for children with some vision because they can more easily distinguish the clothing item from their surroundings. It is also easier for children to distinguish their clothing from other family members' if it is brightly colored, especially when made with puffy, shiny, or sequined textures.

When your child is ready to match his own clothing, there are several strategies you can try. Again, you can provide your child with clothing items that he can discriminate by touch—clothing decorated with puff or slick paints (available at most craft stores), rhinestones, "jewels," or other textures. You can then teach your child, for example, that the shirt with the rhinestones only matches the stretchy stirrup pants. You can also buy clothing that can be mixed and matched so your child can put together an outfit acceptable to the most conservative person.

When your child is ready to put on and take off his shoes, you can substitute brightly colored, fluorescent shoelaces to encourage use of vision. One helpful technique for children who are beginning to lace their own shoes is to coat one half of the shoelace with one color of puff paint or the new fluorescent colored glues and the other half with a different color. Using matching colors of paint to encircle the shoe eyelets will help your child discriminate the eyelet and to correctly lace his shoes by matching the lace to the same colored eyelet. If your child has no vision, try using a slick paint on one side and a textured paint on the other instead of different colors. Elastic shoelaces may also be used so the shoes can be simply pulled on and off.

Presenting a Neat Appearance

It will be just as important for your child to have clothes that match, zippers zipped, and tags tucked in as it is for any child. However, your child may not realize this on his own because he cannot see that other people have clothes that match, zippers that are zipped, and tags that are tucked in. The best way to teach your child about the importance of these things is to mention them to him over and over as you work with him on daily routines. When you are helping him dress in the morning, you might say, "You're wearing your blue shorts today. Let's put on the blue striped shirt since it matches your shorts. You'll need matching socks, too." Letting your child help as you pack a small suitcase with clothes for an overnight stay at grandmother's house can be a fun time to talk about matching clothes.

As you leave your house in the morning (or any time), talk with your child about checking to make sure his zippers are zipped, buttons are buttoned, tags are tucked in before he is *ready to go*. Remember, even children without visual impairments do not learn about these things quickly. All children need repeated exposure (verbal or visual) to understand their importance.

Grooming and Hygiene

Bath Time

Some children with visual impairments are initially afraid to sit inside the tub. If your child is afraid of the "unknown," it may help to allow him to sit on the side of the tub with just his feet inside or to have him sit next to the tub and splash or pour water. Slowly and gently, but firmly, you should encourage him to put more of his body in the water. Depending on your child, this process may take one  bathtime, or it may take weeks or months. Simply providing him with a secure surrounding may also help eliminate his fear of the "wide open spaces" of the bathtub. An infant can be eased into the tub in a plastic infant seat. A toddler can be "grounded" in any of the bathframes commercially available. For a larger toddler or a preschooler, plastic laundry baskets are an inexpensive solution for holding the child while he plays in the tub.

To make the tub a safe environment, consider using one of the many different faucet covers, especially if your child likes to "swim" in the bathtub. These covers, which are available in a variety of shapes, colors, and themes, help protect little heads from being scraped during play and the child from being burned. You may also want to use adhesive stickers on the bottom of the tub to prevent slipping. If you use bar soap, be sure to select a brightly colored bar or one which contrasts well with the surrounding tile and surface areas in the bathroom. To help your child distinguish his towels, they should have a significantly different texture or have a wild stripe or pattern, if your child has some vision. You might also consider sewing a pocket into your child's towel so he can store his washcloth there and easily find it.

Most children love bathtime, so it is a natural time to foster independence and teach a variety of skills. Encouraging your child to reach for, splash, and hold toys and bathmitts builds motor, cognitive, and tactile integration abilities. Letting your child wear a sponge or terry cloth bathmitt in the shape of an animal or favorite character is an enticing way to get him to cooperate with bathing. Talking to your child about body parts he is "washing" is a natural way to increase body awareness and function: "John, you are washing your feet; they help you run." Gently trickling water over your child's head with a strainer or a sprinkling water toy or guiding him to do the same will help prepare him for having his hair washed and rinsed.

Brushing Teeth

While many children with visual impairments enjoy the sensation of having their teeth brushed, just as many find it a noxious activity. In particular, children who are sensitive to other types of touch are extremely hypersensitive to brushing their teeth. Often, however, these children will accept deep pressure inside their mouths. Consequently, they may not mind having their teeth "brushed" with a warm washcloth rubbed over their gums and teeth. Gradually, they may tolerate the firm rubber surface of a Nuk™ or Sassy™ toothbrush, which is part of a stage system. Next, you can try a small finger brush placed on your finger. Simply using an electric or battery operated toothbrush may also persuade your child to cooperate.

As soon as your child can accept the different textures inside his mouth, encourage him to hold the brush on his own. To entice your child to brush his teeth on his own, you might try a toothbrush with a musical handle. Older children can be motivated to brush their teeth with toothbrush bases with popular characters who say familiar phrases and encourage the child to brush while they talk. Reach™ toothbrush company makes a toothbrush that glows in the dark, which can be a great source of motivation for both brushing teeth and using residual vision.

As your child becomes more capable, help him learn to place the toothpaste on his brush. Letting him help select his own toothpaste is the first step in the process. A flavored toothpaste, for example, may make him more eager to brush. Be sure your child has the motor abilities to handle the applicator he selects. Many pump-type dispensers are too complicated for a young child to manipulate with one hand. Show your child how to remove the top and to place it in the same location so that he can easily find it (usually the soap dish attached to the wall is a good place). The flip-top lids on some toothpaste tubes eliminate the need for more refined motor skills *and* the search for a lost cap. Show your child how to extend his index finger, third finger, or thumb on the bristles so he can tell where to place the toothpaste and know when he has applied enough paste.

Toilet Training

Toilet training is another area of difficulty for children with visual impairments. Still, how you go about training your child will be very similar to toilet training any child.

Signs of readiness for toilet training are the same for children with visual impairments as they are for other children. They include the ability to pull pants up and down, staying dry throughout a nap, the ability to understand simple directions and to communicate the need to use the potty, and knowing when their diaper needs changing.

Once your toddler seems ready, you can begin by reading one or more of the many good children's story books designed to prepare a child for toilet training. Your child can also begin helping to dispose of his diaper. In addition, give your child repeated supervised opportunities to explore all components of the toilet, including flushing.

Once your child has grasped what toilet training is about, get
him a small potty. It will be very important that your child feel safe
and secure during early toilet training. The small potty will ensure
that he has a stable base of support and will not cause any gravita-
tional insecurities, as the large toilet might. (Even when he is
ready to sit on the "big potty," it will help to support his feet in
some way.) Let him sit on the potty while Mom and Dad carry out
grooming routines in the bathroom so he can become accustomed
to his potty. Later, gently encourage him to sit, even for a few sec-
onds, at regular intervals throughout the day, and then reward him
with hugs and praise for at least trying. You may want to help your
child understand that there is an end to the process by setting a
timer to go off after several minutes, after which you let him get
up, regardless of success, and reward him with hugs for sitting and
trying.

Some children benefit from listening to songs about toileting
while they sit. The song lets the child know what activity is coming up and reinforces him for sitting. Other children enjoy "training" a favorite doll or stuffed animal. Often the best method is
simply to be consistent in offering encouragement and opportunities without pressure over time. If your child is successful, let him
help dispose of the waste and flush the toilet, if he seems to enjoy
it.

One word of caution: never leave your child on the potty for
longer than five or ten minutes and always supervise him in the beginning. He needs to know that you are there to support him. Also,
if left with too much idle time, your child may engage in eye-pok-
ing or other types of "mannerisms." (See below.)

Bedtime Routines

Many children with significant visual impairment have sleep
difficulties due to confusion between day and night. There are several theories as to why this might be. Some children may have no
light-dark contrast to signal time of day. Other children may be passive the majority of the day, and may not be tired and ready for
sleep at bedtime. They may therefore stay awake most of the evening and then sleep during the day to compensate for lack of sleep.
At night, they are not tired, and the cycle repeats itself.

The most practical solution to sleep pattern difficulties is to establish a consistent daily routine. An essential part of this routine

is to keep your child active during the day. It is also helpful to develop an evening bedtime routine and stick to it, regardless of the setting. There will always be times when your child sleeps away from home—at the babysitter's, in hotels or motels, in the hospital, at relatives' homes. Thus, the actual activities and physical actions included in your child's routine are more important than the bed or room. Your child's nighttime routine will necessarily vary as your child grows older, to match his chronological as well as developmental needs. When your child is an infant, simply rocking and singing a specific song, sung at no other time except when putting him down for the evening (for the first or last time!), may be all that is needed.

As your child grows older, you can allow him to sleep with a stuffed animal which plays a brief song while you gradually dim the light. Older children enjoy a favorite nighttime poem, story, or phrase. One child loved Dr. Seuss's *One Fish, Two Fish, Red Fish, Blue Fish.* When his mother began to read the last page—which began "Today is done; today was fun"—he would turn over and hug his pillow, ready to settle for the night. Eventually, reading the entire book was not necessary. Reciting the last page was sufficient to signal bedtime.

When your child balks at going to bed, even after his routine, it is critical that both parents react the same way to ensure that your child remains in bed, or at least in his room. First, make sure that toys or other items which might invite play are stored out of sight. When your child becomes sleepy during the day and wants to rest because of fatigue from lack of sleep the previous night, it is essential that he *not* be allowed to do so. If sleep is allowed, do not permit more than ten to fifteen minutes of rest within a two-hour framework. Walking your child, playing with him, or offering a snack may distract him. Coping with a cranky, miserable, screaming child is a very difficult task. It will, however, be well worth the misery and effort to ensure a peaceful night of sleep in the long run. While some children have a will of iron, most get the message within at least one to two weeks.

One clever mother initiated her own plan of attack when her deaf-blind youngster refused to sleep at night, playing into the early morning hours. When he began to curl up on his favorite chair in the middle of the day, his mother commented on his need for sleep. She led him into his room to change into his pajamas, then into the bathroom to brush his teeth, the same sequence followed prior to putting him to bed for the evening. Brushing teeth was definitely a non-preferred activity for this youngster, and subsequently, a natural negative reinforcer. He quickly learned that sleeping in the daytime was not worth the work or aggravation of having his clothes changed and teeth brushed. After being awake all day, he was too tired to play at bedtime and began to sleep most of the evening. Over a two-week period, his sleep patterns became more appropriate.

Household Responsibilities

Your child with visual impairments can and should reap the same benefits from doing chores as any other child. He can gain self-esteem from being a useful, participating member of the family, build cognitive, motor, and sensory skills, and become increasingly independent. By pitching in and doing his share, he can also contribute to family harmony. After all, if he is excused from chores and his siblings are not, there are bound to be cries of "That's not fair!"

A good place to start is by giving your child responsibility for his own items and room. For example, your child can take his dirty clothes to the laundry hamper. He can help identify and put away his own laundry by searching for specific sizes or for easily identifiable features such as puffy paint textures, loops on pants, metal clips on the end of suspenders on painter's pants, or bows or lace on socks. To provide cues as to where clothing items belong, you might stick a sample of that clothing on the outside of a drawer (for example, put a small piece of denim on his jeans drawer). You could also suspend one sample of an item from the shelf above the place where similar items should be hung in the closet.

As your child grows older, you should expect him to participate in household chores that are within his capabilities. For example, filling the dog's water dish, pouring dry pet food, transferring silverware from the dishwasher to the utensil drawer, emptying his own trash can, or taking dirty dishes to the sink are all activities that may be suitable for a preschooler.

Recycling is a great activity for involving your child in both home and community responsibilities, and an excellent means for teaching and reinforcing concepts, motor skills, tactile skills, and classification. Having your child help separate paper, cans, bottles, and glass into the appropriate containers offers opportunities to reinforce memory skills, discrimination, and concepts such as heavy, light, smooth, rough, big, little, empty, full, in, out, over, beside, right, left, etc. Auditory localization skills (being able to listen to something and locate it) can be integrated with classification as your child sorts plastic, glass, and aluminum containers.

With practice, you will learn how to take advantage of readily available and natural situations to enhance your child's development. In time, helping your child develop sensory, motor, and social skills will become spontaneous and routine.

Do's and Don't's of Daily Care

The suggestions about daily care in the sections above are intended to be just that—*suggestions*. The way that you deal with daily care routines will depend largely on your own family's schedule, routine, and priorities. Below are some general strategies that may help you in figuring out how best to manage daily care routines.

- Be patient and persistent. Sometimes it may feel as if the task of teaching your child to feed himself, dress himself, etc. is too difficult. He won't achieve independence in self-care, however, unless you insist that he try.
- Feel free to get advice from friends, relatives, and professionals. However, you also need to learn to trust yourself and your instincts since you will be the major influence on your child's success in learning self-care routines.
- Talk to your child about what you are doing whenever you are working on daily care routines. When he is very young, you might say, "Let's take off your t-shirt now." As he gets older, this becomes "It's time to take off your t-shirt. Why don't you help me by holding up your arms?" Still later, you might say, "Go ahead and take off that dirty t-shirt. Let me know if you need help."
- Don't assume that your child *can't* do something just because you don't think you could do it if you had a visual impairment. Go ahead and try difficult tasks; your child will probably surprise you.
- Don't be too quick to rescue your child in difficult situations. Working through the situation will probably help him become a better problem solver. When he does need

help, try to provide the least amount of assistance possible—for instance, start him out, but let him finish the task.
- Make sure that during each activity your child feels at
least a little success. Provide lots of hugs and praise for the
tasks he does accomplish.

Behavior Management

Some parents are reluctant to discipline their child with visual
impairments. They may feel that the vision loss is to blame for
their child's misbehavior or fear what others will say about being
too hard on their "poor little blind child." However, your child
needs to be held to the same behavior standards as any child. Fail-
ing to discipline your child may mean that he will grow up without
rules or limits and that he may consequently be unpleasant to be
around.

Consistency is the key to behavior management with all children. Make sure that your child knows the rules, as well as the rewards for following the rules and consequences for not following
them. The same techniques for disciplining any child should work
with your child. Make sure, however, that the rewards you use are
truly reinforcing to your child. For example, stars or smiley faces on
a chart may be meaningless to your child if he can't see them, but
he may find scratch and sniff stickers quite rewarding.

Mannerisms

Mannerisms, sometimes called blindisms, are a behavior parents are often interested in changing. Mannerisms consist of repetitive, seemingly purposeless, body movements. Typical mannerisms
include head weaving, flicking fingers before the eyes, flipping objects against the fingers, rocking, flapping the arms in space, light-
gazing, and eye poking or rubbing. Although not considered a
mannerism, the characteristic head drop associated with severely
limited vision can be just as frustrating for parents.

There are a number of reasons mannerisms should be discouraged or prevented. Most obviously is that these behaviors are not
socially acceptable. Mannerisms make your child appear even more
different from "normal" children. The more mannerisms your child
engages in, the less he can interact with his environment. This
translates into decreased attention to what is going on around him

and fewer meaningful experiences. Another reason for preventing mannerisms is the physical damage that behaviors such as eye rubbing or poking can cause.

The degree, frequency, and intensity of mannerisms is often influenced by stress, cognitive abilities, and amount of residual vision. Mannerisms are more common in children who are under stress and in children with mental retardation. It is important to determine why a child engages in a mannerism so that both the origin of the behavior and the behavior itself may be addressed. By treating the underlying cause of the mannerism, the mannerism itself can often be minimized.

Some mannerisms may evolve out of a need for vestibular, proprioceptive, or visual input. (Vestibular input provides information about balance; proprioceptive input provides information about position of the child's body or body parts in space.) For example, one researcher found that the most frequent eye pokers are children with retinal disorders. Among the most persistent eye-pokers are children whose eye disorders stem from rubella. The poking creates phosphenes, chemically triggered constellations of light, which provide some form of visual sensation even for blind children. Other children who eye-poke enjoy the pressure and proprioceptive feedback they receive from doing so. Mannerisms in general may be more common in children who are passive and who enjoy little physical activity.

To nip a mannerism in the bud, give your child consistent verbal feedback at the first hint of the behavior. A simple verbal cue such as "You are flapping" or "You are head weaving" may help your child realize what he is doing. If you ignore the behavior, an occasional mannerism may become a habit that your child engages in unconsciously or when particularly excited.

Physical therapy designed to strengthen the neck and back muscles can help to minimize head drop and mannerisms such as head weaving and rocking that are vestibular based. You can learn to incorporate the specific techniques used by the physical therapist in everyday handling and play routines.

Another strategy that may reduce the frequency and intensity of mannerisms is to figure out what sensory information—visual, vestibular, proprioceptive—your child craves. Then offer him this sensory information through alternative, more acceptable means. For example, a child who likes to rock or spin may enjoy opportunities to swing, spin in tire swings, rock on equipment designed for that purpose, or play on Sit N' Spins™ . Giving your child toys, especially manipulatives, that provide him with the same type of sensory input as his mannerism does is often a good solution. For example, textured wrist bands, "funky" textured jewelry, miniature trolls, and wrist-worn video game watches can be effective in reducing inappropriate movements of fingers and hands. Even children with no useful vision enjoy the noises made by hand-held videos or watches. Other toys than can provide socially acceptable alternatives to mannerisms include small party favors such as "crickets" or holiday noisemakers that are intended to be "flicked" and plastic toys designed to be twisted into various shapes or knocked together. When giving your child one of these alternatives, quietly point out the mannerism, as described above, and suggest he try playing with the toy instead.

As your child becomes older and social acceptance is more important to him, he will probably begin to control his mannerisms on his own. If not, your child's vision teacher or orientation and mobility instructor can help devise a plan for eliminating them.

Your Child in the Community

Daily life does not just go on in the home. Your family and your child also have a life in the community. Like any other child, your child needs to accompany his family on trips to the grocery store or the post office, on visits to the playground or the zoo, on walks around the block or through the woods. Also like any other child, your child needs to feel as if he is a welcome, participating member of the community. He needs to feel as if he has the freedom to enjoy

and learn from community activities without constantly worrying about what others are thinking or saying about him.

As a parent, you do not have much control over how community members react initially to seeing your child. But you do have control over how you deal with others' reactions and how you teach your child to deal with them. In fact, how you choose to react to the attitudes and reactions of others will determine the extent and opportunities for acceptance and integration into the community. Reacting with anger or embarrassment will teach your child to be angry or embarrassed in similar situations. It is far better to show your child understanding while brainstorming ways to handle such questions and reactions.

You are the most natural role model for both your child and the community, as your child is likely to be with you in many more situations and contexts than with anyone else. In addition, you may be the first and only individual in whom your child has total trust for quite a while. Therefore, you are in the best position to help him understand how to behave in the community.

Handling Questions, Comments, and Stares

Almost everyone's attention is attracted to the unusual. Without realizing what we are doing, we focus on the difference out of curiosity. Then, just as quickly, we decide how to react to the novel information. Children of all ages are naturally curious about a child with a difference.

Many factors influence how a nondisabled child reacts to a child with a disability. These include the chronological age of the child and how much previous experience he has had with children with disabilities. Reactions from children range from a child who watches intently but without judgement, to a child who forthrightly asks, "Can he see?" to a child who is so totally overwhelmed that he sees only the disability and none of the child. It is also not unusual to see the parent of the sighted child cringe in embarrassment or even become angry with their child at the slightest suggestion that he will ask about your child or point and stare.

It is important for you to know how to respond to all of these situations in the most positive way possible to demonstrate appropriate ways to interact with your child and to educate others whenever possible. The most important lesson you can teach is that your child is competent and independent; the vision problem just happens to create a need for doing things a different way.

As the parent of a child with a visual impairment, you will need to adopt a variety of strategies useful for dealing with the general public and their reactions to your child. It is helpful to react based on a quick analysis of how much information you think the questioning individual will appreciate. People who ask direct questions are generally truly interested in your child and want to know the most appropriate way to interact. For example, a Sunday School teacher who asks if your child can see bright colors may actually be asking the question in order to determine how to best plan your child's involvement in next week's lesson. You might say, "Yes, he can see some bright colors and he sees them best when there is lots of light in the room." People who give the impression that they are awed by your child and have no means of establishing contact simply need an example to sensitize them to your child's needs and competence. Cuing your child to say hello, extend his hand, or help with some simple task such as helping to take groceries from the cart or holding the door open demonstrates that your child is like other children, just inconvenienced by his loss of vision.

Occasionally, you will run into people who are truly embarrassed or say things that are really hurtful. These people need more education than you can provide in a brief encounter. Your main concern is your child. The best thing to do is to remove yourself quickly from the hurtful situation. Then, in a calm manner (which will probably be difficult since you will also be hurt), explain that some people are hurtful because they do not understand and that it has nothing to do with your child—it is just a bad reflection on that person.

Trying to change attitudes is one of the most difficult jobs you can undertake. The primary task is to try to make people realistic and open-minded and to change harmful stereotypes. Some people automatically look at a child with severe visual impairments as a "poor little thing." They may view your child as totally helpless and pitiable rather than as a productive and contributing member of society. Or they may believe that your child can be "healed." These well-meaning people need to be assured that everything possible is being done for your child and that "healing" takes many forms. For example, let them know that your child is learning important adaptive skills that will enable him to be independent and productive. You should acknowledge their interest because, typically, they have your child's best interests at heart.

Inevitably, you will encounter some of these well-meaning people who say something to you that really makes your blood boil. Be prepared for statements such as "God must have had a special purpose in mind for your child when he chose him to be born blind." Again, removing yourself from the situation as quickly as possible can help, but you might also want to have a "pre-recorded message" that you can say in these situations. For instance, you could try saying "I'm sure that is what you believe, but I have different beliefs, and since we don't agree it will be better for us not to discuss this."

Feel free to share your anger and frustration with your child's vision specialist and with sympathetic family and friends. You will receive lots of support and maybe some useful suggestions for handling such situations in the future.

In general, you should openly and frankly model how you want others to address and interact with your child. The key is to encourage his independence and competence in everything you do or say. By showing others your standards and expectations, you are providing the most direct avenue for integration and acceptance. In addition, you are modeling for your child how to deal with unwanted attention. As he grows, you will want to show him how to refuse help politely and to express his independence assertively. You can help by encouraging him to talk through early problem situations.

Social Acceptance

Children with disabilities often have to "earn" their way into the community in a way that nondisabled children do not. Because they are often perceived as different, they have to prove that they can function in society. If they can convince others that they are competent, *then* they will be treated as if they are competent. This will, in turn, help them feel like accepted members of the community.

Regardless of your child's age or abilities, there is one variable that most obviously affects how others perceive him and decide what may be within his capabilities. That is his behavior. A ten-year-old child who is allowed to rock and bounce an eggplant in a vegetable basket during church is perceived as a severely limited child even though he may be quite capable of reasoning and decision making. In contrast, a child who participates appropriately in church activities is perceived as being alert and competent, even though his cognitive abilities may be far more impaired than the other child's. One child is pitied, the other admired because of the choices the parents have made about how to manage their child in public. This underscores the importance of making sure your child understands the rules and is disciplined appropriately when he does not follow them.

Community Learning

To an adult, a trip to the grocery store or the dry cleaner's is just another errand to complete as quickly as possible. To your child, however, that same chore is a wonderful opportunity to exercise his independence and learn about the world around him. Simply allowing your child to reach into the refrigerated section at the grocery store and lift out the milk or pull his choice of cereal from the shelf tells your child (and the observing public) that he is just as capable as any child. Letting your child decide which of two frozen vegetables or which flavor of ice cream to buy tells him that you trust and value his judgement.

The grocery store also provides a myriad of opportunities to teach and reinforce concepts critical to mobility and orientation, as well as pre-braille and other preschool learning activities. Involving your child in selecting and handling grocery items helps with motor skill development, language acquisition, classification and reasoning skills, and understanding concepts. You can work on concepts by asking your child to reach up, find something on the bottom shelf, select the bigger bottle or the smaller box, and use two hands to carry the milk, and by commenting that an item is "cold" or "heavy." Your child's classification abilities are enhanced as he builds a repertoire of associations with specific smells and temperatures as he passes through the household cleaning aids, pet foods, seafood, florist, bakery, and frozen food sections at the grocery store. At the checkout counter, you can further encourage your child to classify by asking for his help in putting all the cans on the conveyor belt, or all the boxed items, all the cold items, all the beverages, all the fruits, or all the vegetables.

Health Care Settings

Behaving appropriately in a grocery store, restaurant, post office, library, or laundromat is one thing. But maintaining appropriate behavior when you are frightened or confused is something else again. *Most* children (and even some parents) occasionally forget how they should behave when a nurse is drawing their blood or a dentist is drilling their teeth.

To make visits to the doctor or dentist as bearable as possible, prepare your child and the health care personnel. Inform everyone who will be interacting with your child about the functional nature of his vision—whether he is able to see light or has some perception of objects and the environment. Just as important is to explain that they should tell your child before they touch him and let him explore any equipment before they use it with him. If your child needs to sit or lie on an examining table, let him first feel the table and its height. Otherwise, he may be frightened if he is suddenly lifted into the air and placed on the table.

If your child is old enough to be concerned about being in medical facilities, it may help to let him explore the office and equipment before any painful or frightening procedures may be necessary. You can often arrange a visit to establish a friendly rapport with the doctor at a time when your child is not ill or in need of critical care.

Sometimes it is possible to help prepare your child at home for upcoming medical or dental procedures. For example, many blind children are easily terrorized by a blood pressure cuff. To desensitize and prepare your child, you might give him many opportunities to wear inflatable arm floats (swim fluegals) when he plays or swims in the pool. While the pressure is not the same, children are not as panicked if they have had some simulation of the experience and know they will be okay afterwards. Similarly, using an electric or battery operated toothbrush is often helpful in preparing your child for his first visit with the dentist.

Conclusion

Encouraging a child's independence is one of the most difficult responsibilities a parent has. When your child has a visual impairment, helping him achieve independence may not only be more challenging but emotionally draining for both you and your child. Every child with a visual impairment, however, can learn skills and behaviors that will help him move further down the road to independence. True, you will likely have to make small adjustments in attitude and in your child's environment that would not be necessary if your child did not have a visual impairment. With planning, consistency, and creativity, however, you can not only foster independence, but also self-esteem, acceptance, and competence in all aspects of your child's life.

Parent Statements

Patience, patience, patience!

—◄o►—

I tried and tried to teach Mary how to tie her shoes. When I was about to give up, I realized that I had to teach her differently than I taught my other children. She is still having trouble but it is getting better.

—◄o►—

My child's preschool teacher gives us suggestions of activities to do at home and when we are sitting talking to her it all sounds so simple. When we get home it is anything but simple!

—◄o►—

I taught my daughter to eat finger food by using Cheerios because they stick to her fingers once her fingers are wet. She can't drop them.

—◄o►—

I once heard of a restaurant which was catering a dinner to which several blind individuals had been invited. The head waiter asked if he should put out plastic glasses. That made me so mad, but it also made me determined that my child would learn how to feed himself really well.

—◄o►—

Brushing teeth was a real problem at first. I think Carol didn't like the feel of the toothbrush or the taste of the toothpaste.

◄o►

I know that I should let Molly do more for herself and every morning I wake up telling myself that this will be the day I will back off a little bit. But it is so hard—we are always in a hurry to get somewhere or I watch her struggling to put on her socks and I just give in. Most of the time it is just easier to do it myself.

◄o►

Eric will only eat two things—macaroni and cheese and oatmeal. I have tried and tried to get him to eat something else but he just screams and spits it out. I'd give anything to be able to take him to McDonald's for a "Happy Meal."

◄o►

Ashley has trouble with anything different. She won't play with playdough and doesn't like to touch anything that feels different. She doesn't even like soft fabrics like velvet. It makes it very difficult to do anything new.

◄o►

I try to tell Andy I am going to pick him up before I do. I talk to him as I am walking up to him. I don't want him to be scared.

◄o►

It seems like everything takes so much more time.

◄o►

Sometimes you have to make choices. You can't do everything.

Chapter Six

◄○►

Family Life

Ruth and Craig Bolinger*

When parents first learn that their child has a visual impairment, their chief concern is often *how will this disability affect my child?* They may spend every waking moment thinking or talking about their child's visual impairment, skimming through medical books and magazines, and looking into educational programs or medical treatments, just trying to fathom all the ways that their child's life will be different than expected.

Sooner or later, however, parents realize that their child's visual impairment touches the lives of everyone in the family—it is not just their child's life that will be different. They begin agonizing over a new concern: *how will this disability affect my family?* Will her special needs consume all our time and energy until we have no time for our own interests? Will she be more of a burden than a friend to our other children? Is there any hope that we can still have a "normal" family life?

The answers to these questions depend largely on you, the parent. If you are determined that your family have the most "normal" life possible, then you will probably develop the coping skills and attitudes needed to meet the challenges that face you. Other family members will also learn effective methods of coping by following your example.

Of course, you won't learn how to cope with your child's differences overnight. And en route to learning how to handle them,

---

* Craig and Ruth Bolinger and their son, Jesse, live on a farm in Southwest Iowa, where they raise corn and soybeans. Craig and Ruth also both work for the United States Postal Service as rural mail carriers. They enjoy gardening, the great outdoors, and each other.

your family is bound to run into stresses and strains that other families don't have to deal with. To help reduce your learning time, this chapter discusses typical attitudes of family members that can hurt or help the adjustment process. It also points out some common problem areas that families of children with visual impairments often face over the years, and suggests some solutions that may work for your family.

Your Role as a Parent

All parents have the same basic responsibilities. They must see that their families are provided with food, shelter, health care, clothing, education, and love. This is a tall order for any parent. But when you have a child with a visual impairment, looking after these basic needs can seem incredibly challenging. To begin with, money may be tight because meeting the everyday and special needs of a child with a visual impairment is expensive. Two costs that add up very quickly are loss of income from missed days of work, and health insurance co-payments and deductibles. And health insurance often does not even pay for eye glasses, vision aids, and assistive technology such as computers, reading machines, and closed circuit televisions. Adapted equipment like interactive toys, descriptive videotapes, and audio cassette tapes can also take a toll on the check book. In addition, child care may be more costly if your child requires additional staffing and monitoring. The list of potential expenses goes on and on.

The time you can devote to your family's needs is just as likely to be in short supply as money. Dealing with the "hows" is the most time-consuming part of raising a child with a visual impairment. Everyday tasks—breast feeding, diapering, bathing, feeding—become "hows." How do you accomplish these tasks for a child with a visual impairment, and how do you present them to your child so that she will learn and grow from the experience? How do you make sure that a specific experience will not frighten, harm, or humiliate your child? And, how do you plan your days and your life so that you can navigate the "hows" without wearing yourself out? To add to your stress, you know that if you lose control and become frustrated, your child will, too.

Other energy zappers are connected with your child's medical and educational needs. If you are checking out a possible educational placement or activity for your child, you may make one or two trial runs to determine if this activity is right for your child. Once your child is in an educational placement, you may need to devote large chunks of time to following up on therapists' recommendations. You will likely spend hours in doctor's offices, hospitals, and evaluation centers, not to mention traveling to and from appointments. If your child is eligible for a government benefit such as Supplemental Security Income (or you want to find out if she is), endless hours may be wasted waiting, filling out forms, and untangling red tape.

On top of everything else is the feeling that maybe you don't have what it takes to raise a child with a visual impairment. Maybe you don't have the skills, knowledge, patience, sensitivity, or some other special ingredient needed to bring up a child who can't see the way other children do.

Many parents doubt their ability to handle the practical and emotional aspects of raising a child with a visual impairment. In fact, it is not unusual to wish that your child would just go away and take all your child care problems with her. These feelings, although normal, usually diminish as you learn ways to make your responsibilities more manageable. With time and experience, most parents gain the self-confidence they need to effectively lead their family. And, as mentioned earlier, being a good leader is extremely important, because other family members will rely on you to demonstrate how to adjust to your child with a visual impairment. To help you make the adjustment process as smooth as possible, the sections below discuss some common obstacles parents must overcome before they feel good about themselves as parents.

Being a Good Enough Parent

There are a multitude of reasons you may feel intimidated or inadequate at the prospect of raising a child who can't see. It would be impossible to list them all, but here are some of the big ones:

First, you might feel as if it is up to the experts to make decisions about your child and that what you want to have happen is of little importance. Since you might not know what the doctors, educators, or therapists are talking about, you may feel you cannot help yourself or your child. In dealing with all these experts, you may also feel that you have little or no privacy or control in making parental or family decisions. Often, they have access to personal in-

formation about you, your child, and your family because it is in your child's records.

Second, you may feel as if it is hard enough figuring out how to parent your child without having to do it on center stage. Often, you may feel as if people are staring. Sometimes the way your child looks and acts will draw the undesirable attention of others. At the restaurant, for example, your child may make just a tad bit more of a mess than the average child, or do some eye rubbing or rocking, or get a little loud when requesting information about what is going on around her. Even though *you* may think that your child looks, acts, and behaves like a "normal" child, just one disapproving or judgmental stare can suddenly make you realize that others do not. Having to respond to your child's behavior like a "perfect" parent when you know others are watching can be difficult or impossible at times.

The keys to dealing with these and other feelings about being an inadequate parent are basically the same as those offered in Chapter 3 for coping with your feelings about your child's disability: seek information and support.

Having accurate, up-to-date, and complete information about your child's visual impairment in general, and how it affects her specifically, can help you feel more in control when it comes to decisions about her care and future. You can at least agree or disagree knowledgeably with professionals' recommendations, and possibly begin to offer some recommendations of your own. You will also feel more assured that you are doing what is right for your child. (See Chapter 3 for tips on getting the information you need.)

As a parent, you can also restrict, or keep tabs on, others' access to information about your family, if you feel as if your privacy is being invaded. Always read, sign, and date any release of information forms for doctors, educators, etc. you are asked to fill out. If you are not given a copy, ask for one. Remember that all information that you share may be made available to your child in the future, or may be available to your child's future employers or to professionals making decisions about assistance programs. If you have already given out information about yourself or your child, find out where this information is stored, who has access to it, and what happens to the file when your child is no longer being served. (See Chapter 9 for information on the confidentiality of educational records.)

Other parents who have had the same or similar experience can be a tremendous source of information *and* support. You can meet others who seem calm, collected, and in charge. You may gain a new perspective on how seemingly ordinary people like yourself have managed many of the dilemmas you may encounter. You will receive practical tips on handling specific problems related to caring for a child with a visual disability. Eventually you will find that by reading, talking with other parents, and attending workshops and special training events for parents, you will feel that you are doing what you need to do.

Finding others like yourself is sometimes not an easy task. Chapter 3 gives some suggestions. Additional ways you might try to locate other parents include:

1. Contact your state department of education. Someone there should be able to guide you to a consultant or department that works with blind or visually impaired children. Once you reach the right department, the staff people should have a good idea of whom you might contact.
2. Contact the state agency that serves adults with visual impairments (usually through the vocational rehabilitation agency). Although these agencies are not geared toward helping children or their families, a counselor there may be able to put you in touch with other parents or with an adult with a visual impairment who could answer some of your questions.

One point that is often difficult for new parents to accept is that you don't have to do it all alone to be a good parent. Good parents know it isn't a sign of weakness to accept help; it's just common sense. Although your family and friends may not know much about raising a child with a visual impairment, they do have skills, life experiences, and resources that can help you and your family. Consider taking them up on their offer if they say, "I can watch the other kids while you take Jeffrey to the doctor," or "Let me check your oil and tires for you, since I know you'll be on the road more," or "I know a teacher who might know what to do about this; should I ask her?" If you don't feel you need the help at the moment, try to leave the door open for future offers of help. Let them know how glad you are that they offered their help, and that you will be sure to call on them in the future.

In the end, remember that *you* are the ultimate judge of what makes a good enough parent for your child. Family, friends, and people in the community may have different expectations for you. But you have different responsibilities than most of these people could even dream about. You have to perform a balancing act that most people never have to learn about, let alone do. You alone know what kind of parenting your child really needs to thrive. Embrace every successful moment! Rejoice every time you realize what mistakes not to repeat! Give yourself a pat on the back when you understand that being a parent means being a person first!

Managing Your Money

Although money isn't what makes the world go around, it *is* what helps you meet your responsibility to your child. There are times when money seems to drive every decision you make, and if you are short on funds, you may feel as if you are shortchanging your child with visual impairments, and other family members as well. Perhaps you don't have enough money to send your child to a camp that would help her acquire new skills or confidence. Or computer equipment, braillers, and other hardware may be so costly that to have a system at home to match the one used at school may be out of the question. Then again, you may pour so much money into caring for your child with visual impairments that little is left over to give other children what they need or want. Your other children may have to wear hand-me-downs or forego music lessons or Little League, and it may have been years since you were able to afford a family vacation.

The decision to ask for financial assistance is up to you, of course. But you should be aware that there are human service, family support, and special assistance programs available to help families of children with special needs. These programs may offer financial support through cash subsidies or payments, or may offer vouchers that can be exchanged for products such as formula, diapers, toys, or transportation. Eligibility criteria for programs vary, but you should have the opportunity to explain why your child's needs are important and why you need money or services to meet and maintain those needs. Be aware that you may have to provide detailed financial information or release information that documents your income level and family circumstances.

One specific source of help is your local Lions Club. The Lions Club has charged itself with supporting programs for the blind and often will assist a family or individual. Other parents or your child's doctors or educators may be able to refer you to other community, county, regional, or state programs that offer financial assistance.

Managing Your Time

For some parents, budgeting time is an even bigger problem than budgeting money. Especially if both parents work, you may find there are never enough hours to accomplish what you really *must* do, let alone spend "quality" time with your spouse and children. By the end of the day you may be so frazzled that you have no energy left for socializing or even for asking your kids how their day went.

One strategy that may help you gain a little time is to take a hard look at everything you do for your child with visual impairments. You may be giving her a larger share of your time than she actually needs. You may be doing things for her that she can and should do for herself, or you may be putting all of her needs ahead of your other children's. If so, you are making ineffective use of your time. You may also be robbing your child with visual impairments of the chance to become more independent and breeding resentment among your other children.

Overprotection. To divide your time equitably, you must decide which of your child's special needs really need your attention. Be open to comments from others about what you are doing on behalf of your child. If you start to hear that you are being too protective or such a good verbal interpreter that you are making it hard for your child to be independent, pay attention. Although you may not agree with these comments at first, it is time to stand back and assess the situation. Are you hearing these remarks from an individual who only sees your child in one isolated environment? For example, are you hearing this from a teacher who only sees your child in a classroom where she has oriented herself so well to the routine and environment that she gives the illusion that she could be ex-

tremely independent anywhere? Or are you hearing this from an
O&M instructor who has worked with your child for several years
in many different environments?

There are many sleepless and tear-filled nights when parents
lay their heads down at night. They see visions of what could happen if their child tried to walk alone from one end of town to the
other; visions of their child getting cut off from the group she is
with; visions of her being left alone at the side of the dance floor.
These visions are normal and are part of your apprehension about
facing new and emotionally difficult situations. The fact is, however, overprotecting your child will do more harm than good in the
long run. You will deprive other family members (and yourself) of
the time they need from you. You will disable your child more in
the eyes of others if you treat her as if she is more helpless than
she is. And you will not be able to "let go" when she is ready to be
independent at every stage of her development.

One strategy that might help you overcome your fears and your
natural instinct to protect your child is to have a trusted friend,
neighbor, or relative take your child to activities. Since other people never seem to do things just the way you do, there is a greater
chance that your child may actually get to do a few things for herself. Get feedback from day care staff or teachers on all the things
your child accomplished for herself while you were away. Each
time your child makes progress toward learning a skill, realize that
all the little pieces do add up to independence.

Overinvolvement. Even if you are not overprotecting your
child with visual impairment, you may still be devoting too much
time to her if you try to spend every spare minute working with her
on therapeutic or educational activities. If your child is involved in
an early intervention or therapy program, the number of skills that
you "need" to work on with your child may seem overwhelming.

It may help to get a list of goals and activities from each and
every professional working with your child. Have each professional
look at all the other professionals' lists. Ask for suggestions of activities that will help you work on more than one goal at once, or for
ways to incorporate suggested activities into your daily routine. If
simply having time to interact with your child is *the* problem, then
you may want to ask your child's day care provider or respite care
worker to work on some of the therapy goals. Grandparents, older
siblings, and other family members may be able to work on selected activities as well. You should not feel that you personally

have to follow through on every goal and objective that every vision specialist, preschool teacher, physical therapist, or occupational therapist thinks should be done. Delegation may not win you the war, but it will win you a great deal of battles.

It *is* important for your child to learn to be as independent as possible. But there is a limit to how much your child can learn in a day, and a limit to how much time you can spend teaching and still be effective. Remember, both you and your child need a break from teaching now and then.

Once you have a clear idea of what you should and should not be doing for your child with a visual impairment, plan ahead. You know which activities happen on a daily basis, and which happen weekly, monthly, or quarterly. Note these events on a calendar, together with estimates of how long you expect them to take. If you aren't sure, ask. For instance, ask a new therapist, "How long does an average appointment last?" and ask your doctor, "Will this treatment require any future follow-up visits, and if so how many and for how long?" There will still be times when the unexpected disrupts your schedule. For example, the doctor may cancel an appointment, your child may balk at going to an appointment, or you may have a day when you think, "I really cannot deal with this now." But if you know basically what you will be doing on a given day and for how long, you will be less likely to try to squeeze more into a day than you can.

Defining Who You Are

As this book emphasizes, your child is a person first, and only secondarily a person who happens to have a visual impairment. The same is true for you. Although you may spend a large portion of your time doing things as the parent of a child with visual impairments, you, too, are a person. Parents of children with visual impairments sometimes lose sight of this and forget that they are many-fac-

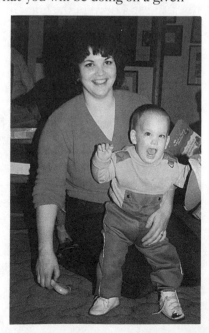

eted individuals with more to offer than parenting skills. They may be so busy looking after their family's needs that they neglect their own needs to develop talents and interests and to grow as a person. As a result, they may feel as if they have been unfairly pigeonholed and even resent their child for "forcing" them into the role of perennial parent. These attitudes naturally make it harder for you to accept your child and set a good example for the rest of the family.

The tendency to think of yourself only as a parent is sometimes related to how others treat you. Many people who will play a big role in your child's development, including doctors, nurses, teachers, and human service agency personnel, will only see you in your parent role. They do not have the opportunity to see the rest of you. Generally, these people work with many different families, and can only guess what you are like. An easy solution is to gradually share more information about yourself—your likes, dislikes, hobbies, experiences, what you do for a living.

Actually, changing how others see you is the easy part. The hard part is looking at yourself and reflecting on who you are and what you want as a person. This can be especially difficult when you think about all the unknowns the future holds for your child and how these unknowns also affect your future. In fact, thinking about yourself as separate from your child may physically hurt you if you are still deep in the grieving process. But time away from your child can actually do both of you good. Pursuing activities that you enjoy and do well enhances your feelings of self-worth as a person, and makes it easier for you to accept occasional "failures" as a parent. So, while you are budgeting your time, make sure you occasionally schedule some time to do something that is important to you—whether it is taking classes, working on your tennis game, going fishing, or attending the symphony. Just take separation from your child in steps that you are comfortable with.

One early step you can take to prepare yourself and your child for separation is to have someone else watch her while you do something around the house or yard for a half-hour or so. You will be accessible if there is an emergency, but will have some privacy. Taking a nap, soaking in the tub, or watching a half-hour TV program may be a good place to start. Soon you will be able to be apart for an hour or two. Only you will know when you feel comfortable leaving your child completely under someone else's supervision.

Your Marriage

Just as having a child with a visual impairment can affect you as an individual, it can also affect you and your spouse (or significant other) as a couple. The stress of coping with the diagnosis and the challenges that come with it can leave you little time for one another. At times, one or both of you may be short-tempered, distracted, or upset. You may be too worried about money or the future to care much about your spouse's personal problems. Sex may seem like something you should forget about, because how can you possibly enjoy it when this awful thing has happened to your child?

Believe it or not, your child is not in control of your relationship. You are! You had a relationship with your spouse before any children entered the picture. This relationship may have been founded on mutual attraction, shared interests, faith, or any of a number of things. Having a child with a visual impairment may change the nature of your relationship somewhat, but it doesn't have to damage its foundation. Below are some suggestions to help you keep your marriage on an even keel.

Share Your Emotions

Remember the grief cycle? It can bog down the best of relationships. If you or your partner are grieving, you may not be able to make decisions together. For example, you may not be able to agree about surgeries, educational or medical recommendations, having a care provider in your home, or any number of important issues. This sort of impasse can affect every aspect of your family life. In the end, coping with this emotional crisis may either bring you and your spouse closer than you have ever been before or it may drive you apart. How your relationship is affected depends a great deal on your ability to be open about your feelings with one another.

Sometimes one spouse (often the husband) feels he must be "strong" for the sake of the other. This is a mistake. First, the "strong" partner must publicly deny his real feelings, and therefore may not work through his grief as quickly as he would otherwise— or at all. Second, the grieving spouse may mistakenly conclude that her spouse doesn't really care about what has happened to their child, or doesn't grasp the seriousness of the diagnosis. This can make her feel lonely and resentful.

If you share your emotions, you will often find that you and your spouse have or have had the very same worries. At worst, this discovery can help dispel some of your loneliness or your thoughts that you must be "crazy" to feel this way. At best, the two of you may jointly be able to come up with a constructive way of ironing out your concerns. You might also find that you are needlessly worrying about something. For instance, you may believe that your spouse must blame you for your child's visual impairment when the thought has never even crossed his mind.

Of course, if you and your spouse are not used to sharing your innermost thoughts and feelings, having a child with a visual impairment will not magically loosen your tongues. In fact, sharing the jumble of feelings you have about your child may sometimes seem impossible because feelings are so hard to put into words. As a start, you might try giving your partner a few examples of things that make you feel low and then ask if these things affect him the same way. If they do not, it is important not to be judgmental—to act as if there is something wrong with him for seeing things differently than you do. If he does feel the same way, then you will both be aware of situations that can throw you back into the grief cycle.

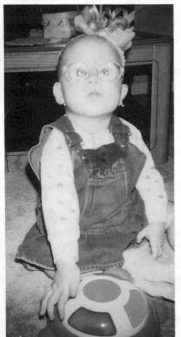

You may be able to help each other get back on track by being supportive and understanding during these times.

Learn about Your Child Together

Often one person in the couple ends up doing most of the reading, the searching, and the leg work needed to find out more about their child's condition. This may be because one spouse has more time, or because family members, friends, or professionals seem to expect it. If only one of you is actively involved in looking at this new situation, however, you may be isolating your best ally. You both need to keep current on information about your child's visual impairment as well as what doctors, teachers, and therapists are saying. Otherwise, one of you may end up making most of the decisions about your child's ongoing care, treatment, and future. This can be an awesome responsibility, and you may resent your spouse for saddling you with it—especially if he seems not to recognize the additional responsibilities you have taken on. If you and your spouse are used to sharing child-rearing responsibilities, it can upset your family's structure.

Just because one parent may be going to more of the doctor visits or educational meetings does not mean that the other parent has to be excluded from the decision-making process. The parent who attends these events can share information with the other parent afterwards, and together you can make any important decisions. Then you can get back to the professionals with your joint decision. If conflicts consistently develop because one parent is always having to make spur-of-the-moment decisions, then something is wrong. One or both of you are not communicating effectively. You need to look at why these decisions are having to be made quickly and with little input from both of you.

Divide Responsibilities Fairly

Before your child with visual impairments was diagnosed, you and your spouse may each have routinely taken care of specific chores or responsibilities. You will likely need to re-think those responsibilities now. Visits to doctors or therapists and meetings with early intervention or school staff can be very time consuming, so you will have to discuss who is going to do what and how these new responsibilities will affect both of you. It is quite possible that both of you will have to give up something you enjoy or miss work to take care of these responsibilities. It is also possible that the bulk of the child care will fall primarily on the unemployed spouse, or the one who has the most understanding boss or the most sick days.

If your job situations require that one of you take care of most of your child's special needs, be careful that that person does not become overburdened. Ideally, the other spouse should take on some of the other person's old responsibilities, so that the division of labor remains about the same. For example, if you no longer have time to do the grocery shopping on Wednesdays because you must take your child to early intervention, perhaps your spouse can do the shopping some evening. It is simply not fair if one spouse must make all the sacrifices. The overburdened spouse may "burn out" fast, or end up resenting the other spouse or the child with visual impairments. It may be little consolation now, but eventually things will develop into a new sense of normalcy for both of you.

Take Time to Be a Couple

As tempting as it may be at first, you shouldn't make your child the center of every activity you do alone and as a couple. Everyone needs to take an occasional break from the demands of parenthood, just as they need an occasional vacation from work. You and your spouse need time off to recharge your emotional energies and regain your perspective on life with your child. You also need time alone so you can reconnect as a couple.

Sometimes it is not possible to physically get away from your child. But you can still set aside some time in the evening to watch a video, eat a special meal, or simply have a conversation about something other than visual impairments. To buy time for this date, you may have to put off doing the chores you usually do after your child is in bed, but the boost to your mental health should be well worth it.

In the beginning, you may feel very anxious at the thought of leaving your child alone with someone else. Like any parent, though, you will likely feel more comfortable if you can leave him with someone you know well. If you have used a babysitter for other children in your family, you may therefore want to hire him or her to look after your child with a visual impairment, too. If the sitter is willing to try, you can gradually teach her what she needs to know. Review strategies that you have found helpful yourself when your child becomes upset. Help the sitter understand why and how to talk to your child. Make sure you leave clear, written directions about anything out of the ordinary, as well as where you can be reached.

If you have never hired a sitter, then locating one can be a challenge (even if your child does not have a visual impairment). Start by asking friends or neighbors that you trust for names of possible sitters. Or, if you have located a parents' group, ask other parents in the group if they know of good child care people. You might also check with your child's teachers. Often they will know about individuals that other families hire for babysitting. Finally, you could call a high school counselor or post a notice at a nearby college describing the kind of person you are looking for.

Respite care is another option, especially if your child has multiple disabilities or you have a great deal of difficulty getting out of the house. Respite care is provided by paid or volunteer child care workers who will come into your home for an hour or two—or even several days—to watch your child so you can have a break. Respite care workers receive training in general child care skills, as well as in specific skills, if needed, so that they can safely care for children with disabilities. Sometimes respite care is a free service; other times fees are charged on a sliding scale based on your income. A local hospital, public health agency, community action agency, ARC, or your child's teacher may know whom to contact about respite care in your community.

Single-Parent Families

No one travels a more stressful road than the single parent. The news you have learned about your child is one more thing that makes you say "HELP!" to your support system, if you have one, or pat yourself on the back and say, "Here I go again," if you don't. There is no "tag team" of support for you to tell "It's your turn" or ask, "Will you please sit and tell her about *Sesame Street* today?" You may also have to communicate with an ex-spouse or ex-lover you do not really want to contact. Or you may have to deal with memories and feelings related to an old relationship that you don't feel you can cope with on top of everything else.

If you have joint custody of your child, you may have no choice as to whether you must tell your child's other parent about the diagnosis. Check with legal counsel. Otherwise, you will have to decide when and if to share the news. If you do share it, ask point blank whether your child's other parent wants to be involved in her support or not.

If your child's other parent really wants to be involved, try laying out some ground rules before you have to go anywhere together or with your child. Examples of rules might be: Each of you must let the other know who they are bringing with them to doctor visits or educational meetings; or, you must mutually agree on what information about your family to share with professionals. You can, again, seek legal counsel for this framework to make sure the rules apply to both of you.

Be aware that your child's other parent will need to work through the same emotions as you. This will be an additional complication when you meet to hand off children for visits. You should try to keep the other parent's emotional state in mind when you share information that he may find as upsetting as you did. Just handing him a report will not do the trick. You may have to offer to discuss the results of a developmental evaluation or medical report with him if he has any questions.

If there is someone new in your ex-mate's life, he or she could see your crisis over your child as a ploy or a challenge to re-establish your relationship. One way around this problem is to ask that notices about appointments with therapists, doctors, etc. be sent directly from the service provider. This way, you are not the messenger. If there is even a remote chance that this new person could become part of your child's life, you may want to educate this person about your child's diagnosis. You might also consider bringing him or her onto the team of people who is looking for answers and providing support for you and your child. This would mean that there is one more concerned person looking after, teaching, and nurturing your child.

If your child's other parent does not want to be part of your support system, it may be a wise choice to secure sole medical, payor, and educational decision rights. This way you and others will not have to seek out the absent parent whenever a decision needs to be made. The best place to seek counsel on these issues in general is from an attorney who specializes in disability-related issues. If you are looking for protection under a specific educational program, the teachers who work with your child should be able to give you information on rules and laws that you can share with your attorney. Likewise, you can get specific information on payment of Social Security benefits from the Social Security Administration. You should also tell the professionals who work with your child that you are the only parent involved in your child's life. Explain any financial, physical, or time limitations you have that you would like them to keep in mind when setting up plans or programs for your child.

Sometimes single parents stay away from parent groups because they think it will be hard to listen to parents who have spouses or partners talk about how difficult it is to balance everything. Don't let this keep you from making contacts! Just be sure to let others know that you are a single parent and what it means to be the only person responsible for all aspects of a child's needs. Chances are you will find enough understanding and advice to make it worth your while.

Family Life

All families grow and change over time. How they grow and change depends a lot on need, circumstances, and family or community influences. For example, changes may occur because one parent starts or stops working, or because the family moves into a new school district. But change also depends on 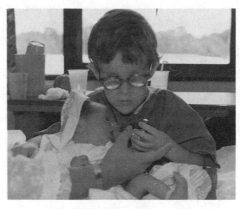 the parents, who are the leaders of their families. Children and extended family members will generally follow the parents' example in coping with change.

Having a child with a visual impairment is a new circumstance that will undoubtedly change your family. Do not assume, however, that these changes will necessarily be for the worse. You and your family have the same strengths and weaknesses now as you had before you heard your child's diagnosis. In addition, there are many new resources (professionals, organizations, other parents) that can support your strengths and give you information or assistance for working on the weaknesses. Remember, too, that as the leader of your family, you can do a lot to help your family cope.

For your family, the real challenge will be to grow and change because you are a family, not because one of your family members has a visual impairment. That is, you cannot allow your family's foundation to rest on the fact that you have a child with a visual impairment. Despite her special needs, your child is, after all, just one part of the family. She should not be the focus of all attention and activities.

Being your family's leader will not always be easy. And it may be especially difficult in the beginning. While you are still learning how to cope with your child's diagnosis and special needs, you will also have to be showing other family members how to adapt. Indeed, the expression "changing a flat tire on a van while you are driving down the road" could have been coined to describe the experience. You might have a bumpy ride until you can figure out how to get all the people riding in the van to work together with you to keep the van moving down the road. The next sections offer suggestions to help you do just that.

Dealing with Siblings' Emotions

It is not just the adults in the family who will need to work through their emotions about your child with a visual impairment. Brothers and sisters will also be profoundly affected—if not right away, then as they grow in understanding and maturity. Like you, they will have feelings about their sibling's disability ranging from anger and resentment to anxiety and grief. They will also have feelings about the way their sibling's visual impairment affects their lives. For example, they may be resentful if Mom or Dad has to skip a ball game because of a doctor's appointment, or angry at being corrected for "pointing at things without talking again." In addition, they will have feelings about their feelings. They may, for instance, feel guilty about resenting the extra time you spend with their sibling.

You and your other children need to understand that all of these feelings are perfectly normal and nothing to be ashamed of. You also should expect that your other children may need to work through some emotions over and over again, just as you do. Something that may really help your children is for them to see you (or another adult) act as upset as they feel. In other words, you can show your children some tears. This can be overdone, though, so be careful if your children have never seen you scared or upset before. To help you recognize your children's emotional states and guide them through the adjustment process, this section outlines emotions that siblings typically feel at different ages.

Preschool. Preschool-aged brothers and sisters are often completely unaware that there is anything different about their sibling with a visual impairment. Consequently, they have a hard time understanding why their sibling needs more of Mom and Dad's time, and may feel frustrated when their needs are not met. Preschoolers tend to mimic behaviors they see, and therefore may imitate blind mannerisms such as rocking and eye rubbing. Through mimicking, they can also learn positive ways of interacting with their sibling. For example, by observing their parents, they can learn how to describe what they see or how to use sighted guide techniques.

Elementary School Age (5–12). By age five, brothers and sisters are well aware of differences in their sibling with a visual impairment. Children of this age are notorious for their desire for sameness. They poke fun at anyone or anything that is different. Even though they may grasp what it means to have a visual impairment, they may lash out with an unkind comment about how their sibling looks or acts.

On the other hand, children of this age can also be quite protective and loyal. If someone else embarrasses or makes fun of their sibling, they are likely to defend her.

Adolescence. Teenagers understand that if something like vision loss happened to their brother or sister, it can also happen to them. This is a good age to think about genetic counseling, because it can help them understand why this happened to their sibling and whether it could happen to them or any children they might have.

Teenagers are very critical of anything and everything. Disgust with *any* family member is as common as acne and to be expected. They are also very conscious of everyone's role within the family and will quickly pick up on any inequities in how they are treated. Although their sibling with a visual impairment may not be the intended target, she can become the excuse for any frustration or anxiety they may be feeling.

Since conformity is very important to teenagers, they may sometimes be embarrassed by the mere fact that they have a brother or sister who is different. They may be embarrassed by their sibling's behavior, her dependence, or her use of special equipment such as a cane or braille writer. Discussing your teenager's embarrassment with her may help, especially if you can help her understand the reasons for behavior problems or dependence, and the need for adapted equipment.

No matter how well you think your children are coping with this new situation, you should watch for signs of too much stress. These might include an illness that is hard to explain, poor schoolwork from a good student, nightmares in a good sleeper, and loss of interest in play. If you notice any of these signs, talk to your child and try to find out what is bothering her. If talking the situation through does not clear up the problem, you may want to contact a professional who is experienced in counseling children. Ask for recommendations from a doctor, teacher, or therapist, or someone at a support organization or your church.

Teaching Siblings about Visual Impairments

As mentioned above, young children really might not see their brother or sister as being different until someone points it out to them. Children are not born with responses and opinions. When the time comes to teach siblings about your child's visual impairment, you can therefore give them the attitudes, opinions, and responses you want them to have. You can give them information that will help them be themselves while supporting what your family believes in.

Explaining a visual impairment to children is even more difficult than explaining it to adults. Somehow you need to come up with the words to explain not only the diagnosis, but also what this means for their brother or sister, for them, and the family.

If your children are quite young, you may need to begin by explaining what vision is. You might tell them that vision or sight is one way that we learn about the world; taste, smell, and hearing are other ways. We use vision to see how things work and to take in information about what is happening around us. When something happens to vision, we miss out on information that we would normally get from using our eyes. You might also mention some of the terms (good and bad) they may hear to describe their sibling: handicapped, disabled, blind, low vision, visually impaired, four-eyes, blind baby.

Most parents start with simple statements such as "Your brother doesn't see like you do." Your children's questions will naturally follow.

In answering questions, keep your children's age and level of understanding in mind. Young children (ages two to six) want concrete answers. They want to know about what they can see and feel. Older children will have more abstract questions. They can think about things they can't see. Carefully listen to your child's questions, then try to answer only what the child is asking. Don't give too much information at one time. Afterwards, let your child think about what you have said.

Your children may ask a question more than once. They might not understand everything you tell them about the diagnosis or what is or will be happening with their sibling. They may understand better if you answer in a different way.

It may help your children if you show or draw them a picture. Point to their body rather than yours when you talk, as they see their brother or sister as a child, not an adult. Acting things out can be helpful no matter how old your children are. For example, you might have your children close their eyes and have someone guide them using sighted guide technique so they can see what it is like.

There are visual acuity kits that can be purchased or borrowed that may help your children understand visual impairments better. These devices are put on like glasses or goggles and actually simulate how people see with different acuity levels or vision conditions. Your child's vision specialist may be able to help you find a kit. In addition, the American Foundation for the Blind has videos available which give good explanations of how children with visual impairments see and don't see.

You should approach demonstrations of this nature with some caution. Otherwise, your children might get the idea that all people who have a vision loss see (or don't see) like their sibling does. It is important that your children understand the variety of types of visual impairments so they can understand why the public at large is often confused about people with visual impairments.

Inevitably, your children will ask why their sibling has a visual impairment. If you don't know, it is all right to say that no one knows. Either way, tell your children that it is no one's fault that their brother or sister will not see like they do.

An important part of teaching your children is to dispel the myths they will hear about blindness or visual impairment. They may be told, for example, that blind children hear better than other children because their hearing compensates for their vision loss. Or they may hear that it's such a shame that such a pretty baby will never be able to run and play like other children, or that she's a judgment on your family.

To help your children (with and without visual impairments) separate fact from fiction, teach them to clarify. This is a skill they can learn even as preschoolers. Clarifying means teaching your children to say, "I am not sure that I understand what you mean." It means saying this if the children have *any* question in their mind about what the person talking to them really means. It is important to explain to your children that some adults may think that this is disrespectful because children do not question adults in our society. So, you should explain to your children that manners are an important component of this approach.

Once your children are sure they understand what is being said, teach them to come to you or the nearest adult they know and tell that person what has been said and by whom. Make sure you get the whole story from your child and then fill in the gaps or provide correct information as needed. Try not to make the person who gave your child the information sound like they did something wrong or that they are out of touch, or your child may lose trust in that person. As a parent, you can then go back to the source of misinformation and provide the correct information.

Sometimes parents choose to involve their other children in activities that may help them learn first-hand about their sibling's impairment or special treatment. For example, they may take siblings on trips to the doctor, the hospital, school, therapy, or evaluations. If you are thinking of involving your children in such activities, remember that you may have to discuss information you may not be comfortable sharing in front of your children.

If you do include siblings on trips to see professionals, make sure they know what is expected of them. Tell them how to behave. Explain what their brother or sister will be doing and why. If you are not sure what will be happening or have never been a good "rule setter," let the office staff tell your children the ground rules. ("We walk and are good listeners when we are in the office.") Such experiences can often satisfy your children's curiosity about the "special" treatment their sibling gets. Children get bored very easily. Once they figure out that their brother or sister would rather have stayed home to play, they often decide that the whole thing is no big deal.

If you ever feel as if you cannot help your children understand what is going on with their sibling with visual impairments and how that will affect them, let someone know that you need ideas or assistance. Sometimes a doctor, teacher, or counselor can talk to your children and help them understand the situation. Having them explain to you and your children that you all will need to keep doing the same things you have always done, plus a few new things, may be all it takes to get the under- standing and cooperation you need.

Giving Siblings the Support and Attention They Need

All parents who have more than one child need to make an effort to ensure that each of their children feels special. They don't want to send the message that they love one child more than another or that one child's problems are more important than another's. The same holds true for parents who have a child with a visual impairment. When you need to spend more time with one child than another, however, this message of specialness can be harder to get across to the "normal" siblings.

There are two approaches you can use to ensure that your chil- dren's emotional needs are not neglected. The first is to read every- thing you can get your hands on about sibling relationships in families like yours. There have been volumes written on this sub- ject, and some of the best are included in the Reading List at the back of this book. The second is to seek out a sibling workshop, or a counselor who can help you get a group of kids together who are experiencing similar situations in their homes.

When brothers and sisters with and without disabilities get to- gether to talk, they can reach a better understanding of why they feel the way they do about one another and their family situation. If you can understand the value of talking to other parents who have been where you are now, then you can appreciate how your children might benefit from a similar experience.

If there are no sibling groups in your community, you may be able to persuade a counselor at a church, school, or community mental health program to put one together. You may have to volunteer to help out.

Once you have located or devised a sibling group, you may have to make this a mandatory activity for your children. At least in the beginning, your children will probably not jump up and down with joy at the prospect of talking about subjects that make all kids uncomfortable.

Encouraging Positive Sibling Interactions

Sometimes parents expect that their children will get along better than usual because one of them has a visual impairment. Usually, however, they have the same problems that all brothers and sisters have, plus a few more. This is not to say that the problems are insurmountable. Often, just knowing what to expect can help you nip problems in the bud. Siblings of children with visual impairments can and do enjoy one another's company. They often share common interests and grow up to have strong, loving relationships.

As in any other family, the more your children know and care about each other, the more they will also know how to push all the right buttons when they want to get under each other's skin. Be assured that if one of your children has something that the other wants, the fact that one of them can't see won't prevent a battle from ensuing! Usually, there is nothing special about fights in families with a child with a visual impairment. Your child with a visual impairment is *not* more fragile than her siblings (unless she has additional physical disabilities such as cerebral palsy), and therefore does not need you to step in to defend her. If she is the target of verbal insults related to her visual impairment, however, it is important to let your other children know that such name calling is *not* acceptable.

You will have to remember that much of the bickering, teasing, and crying are part of any normal sibling relationship. If you don't believe this, it may help to do a reality check by spending time with other families that do not include a child with a disability.

Occasionally, conflicts may progress beyond normal sibling rivalry. Your child with visual impairments may seem to be at the root of all frustrations, or your other children may always claim that "it's all her fault." In this situation, you need to talk to the child who is upset. Find out whether she is feeling temporary frustration and resentment about one particular situation, or whether she is blaming her sibling with a visual impairment for all her worldly problems. If your child is really only frustrated about one aspect of living with a sibling with a disability, you may be able to solve the problem once you know it exists. For example, your son might be angry that he can't play on a community football team because you take your daughter to therapy at the same time the team practices. You might be able to change your daughter's appointment times or find another parent who would be willing to drive your son to football practice.

If your children's displeasure with one another is more pervasive, you will need to take another approach. A guided conversation between the siblings may help them understand each other better. Just because they are brother or sister does not mean they have ever really shared how they feel and why they feel this way. You may want to seek guidance from someone experienced in sibling relationships. Perhaps a school counselor, minister, or close family friend may be able to lend a listening ear.

As in any family, all of your children should be encouraged to pursue their own interests and own friendships. But it is also important for everyone to occasionally do something as a family. Choosing outings and activities the whole family can enjoy is very important. While going to a movie might not be very enjoyable for your child with a visual impairment, a picnic in a park with swings, slides, and monkey bars may be just the thing for everyone.

Deciding that Family Means Three

One of the most difficult decisions for any couple is how many children to have. Now that you are experiencing parenting with a twist, your decision may be influenced by what has happened to your child, your finances, and your lifestyle.

It can be difficult to admit to yourselves that your child's visual impairment influenced your decision not to have additional children. Answering the inevitable questions that friends, family members, and your child herself have about your choice can be equally painful. A frequently asked question will be, "Was it because of the vision loss?" Anticipating this question will give you and your spouse time to agree upon an answer that does not rob you of your privacy. Most importantly, coming to believe that you have made a responsible choice for your family and yourselves can help you feel comfortable and secure about this decision.

Getting Counseling

Although this chapter offers some solutions to problems families often face, there is no guarantee that they will work for your family. Families are as different as the people in them, and something that doesn't trouble one family at all could be a major stumbling block for another. If, for any reason, one or more of your family members simply cannot adapt to the changes in family life, don't hesitate to seek individual or family counseling.

As the leader of your family, it is especially important that you not let your feelings interfere too much with normal family life. Like many parents, you might eventually want to seek counseling for the chronic grief that can go along with having a child with a disability. This is the kind of grief that lies dormant for a while, only to resurface when you least expect it. It's the kind of grief that gets you when you think, "He won't be able to play catch," or "She won't be able to tell whether she has a pink or a blue dress on." It's the kind that makes tears come to your eyes when you see a girl half your child's age riding down the street on a bike, when your child can't even cross the street. Or when you see a child pointing to something—anything—or when people "Shhh" you in a movie because you are describing everything that is happening on the screen. Getting counseling for yourself is a good way to start seeing the high points (sometimes it takes someone else to point them out).

You may want to consider counseling for your family as a whole if there seems to be no balance in your family life, if constant crisis seems to be the norm, or if every day at least one family member seems to be depressed, resentful, or nonresponsive. If possible, visit a counselor who has experience working with families who have children with special needs. You might pick someone out of the phone book and ask about their background when you call to make an appointment, or ask for recommendations from a parent group or your child's doctor or teacher. If your child is receiving services through an early intervention program or through an agency that serves children with visual impairments, there may also be a social worker or other counselor on staff who is available to do family counseling.

Conclusion

No one is ever totally prepared for being a parent. All parents need to learn how to take care of *their* children, not just the generic children described in child care books or classes. At least in the beginning, there is always a certain amount of trial-and-error learning and on-the-job training.

Like other parents, you will gradually learn how best to care for your children simply by caring for them. Because you have a child with visual impairments, however, there will also be a team of professionals you can turn to for advice. These professionals are there to help you reach your goals for your child and your family, not to take over. With a little time, a little practice, and a little patience, there is no reason you can't be just as much in control of your family's life as any other parent is. You should be able to provide a secure environment that all of your children will thrive in and learn from.

Parent Statements

It is so hard to find activities for our whole family. My children are years apart in age and have very different interests. Add to that Maria's visual impairment and our choices become very limited.

◄◦►

Sometimes I just get so tired.

◄◦►

I know my children love each other but sometimes I wish they were a little more tolerant of each other.

◄◦►

The first time my husband and I went out alone together was when Meridith was three years old. A friend came over and basically made us go out to dinner.

—◄○►—

My husband and I don't have much of life outside of work and our home. I don't think we've been out to see a movie in two years. Usually, we're too tired to even rent a video. I'm hoping this will change as the kids get older.

—◄○►—

Sometimes I think my other children get short-changed. Derrick needs so much of our time and attention.

—◄○►—

Right now, our other daughter is too young to notice anything different about her sister. We're hoping that she'll just take the differences in stride, since she's never known her sister any other way.

—◄○►—

We started a braille class for parents. We would meet once a week and the purpose of the class was to learn braille but it turned into so much more. I couldn't believe how much support we all gave each other. At Christmas we brailled the gift tags for the presents under the tree. It was great for our children to figure out which presents were theirs!

—◄○►—

I've never been much of a "joiner," so it's hard for me to go to parent group meetings.

—◄○►—

I try to make sure other parents are comfortable with my child. I don't want him to be left out of birthday parties or spend-the-night parties.

—◄○►—

I didn't feel up to going to a parent group until my daughter was seven or eight months old. It took me that long to feel like I was ready to talk about things with strangers.

◄o►

I always want to do everything by myself. It's so hard for me to ask for help.

◄o►

We used to get a babysitter and go out with friends every once in a while but ever since T.J. was born I have been reluctant to give that responsibility to anyone. I just don't think I could enjoy myself—I'd be too worried about him.

◄o►

I couldn't do it without my mother. She has been great. She always loved Jimmy, from the moment he was born. His blindness just doesn't matter to her.

Chapter Seven

◄◦►

Nurturing Your Child's Self-Esteem

Dean W. Tuttle, Ph.D., and
Naomi R. Tuttle, B.S.N.*

Welcome to Holland

I am often asked to describe the experience of raising a child with a disability—to try to help people who have not shared that unique experience to understand it, to imagine how it would feel. It's like this. . . . . .

When you're going to have a baby, it's like planning a fabulous vacation trip—to Italy. You buy a bunch of guide books and make your wonderful plans. The Coliseum. The Michelangelo David. The gondolas in Venice. You may learn some handy phrases in Italian. It's all very exciting.

---

* Dean Tuttle has a distinguished career spanning 35 years. He has been a classroom teacher of mathematics and science, an itinerant vision specialist, a principal at a residential school for the blind, and a professor of special education at The University of Northern Colorado. He has published over 34 publications, including the book *Self-esteem and Adjusting with Blindness*. Currently he is a consultant with Hadley School for the Blind in Winnetka, Illinois.

Naomi Tuttle received a BSN and RN from Cornell University. She is currently a teacher for Hadley School for the Blind and has been instrumental in the development of courses. She has co-presented workshops for parents and professionals on adjusting to a vision loss and has co-authored the revision of *Self-esteem and Adjusting with Blindness*.

After months of eager anticipation, the day finally arrives. You pack your bags and off you go. Several hours later, the plane lands. The stewardess comes in and says, "Welcome to Holland."

"*HOLLAND?!?*" you say. "What do you mean Holland?? I signed up for Italy! I'm supposed to be in Italy. All my life I dreamed of going to Italy."

But there's been a change in the fight plan. They've landed in Holland and there you must stay.

The important thing is that they haven't taken you to a horrible, disgusting, filthy place, full of pestilence, famine, and disease. It's just a different place.

So you must go out and buy new guide books. And you must learn a whole new language. And you will meet a whole new group of people you would never have met.

It's just a *different* place. It's slower-paced than Italy, less flashy than Italy. But after you've been there for a while and you catch your breath, you look around . . . . and you begin to notice that Holland has windmills . . . . and Holland has tulips. Holland even has Rembrandts.

But everyone you know is busy coming and going from Italy . . . and they're all bragging about what a wonderful time they had there. And for the rest of your life, you will say "Yes, that's where I was supposed to go. That's what I had planned."

And the pain of that will never, ever, ever, ever go away . . . because the loss of that dream is a very, very significant loss.

But . . . if you spend your life mourning the fact that you didn't get to Italy, you may never be free to enjoy the very special, the very lovely things . . . about Holland.

(© 1987 by Emily Perl Kingsley. Printed with permission of the author. All rights reserved.)

The story above is often reprinted as an illustration of what it is like to come to terms with having a child with a disability. Indeed, you probably identified with the expectations that the parents had in the beginning—expectations of going to Italy, of having a healthy, "normal" baby as all their friends had. You may also have identified with the shock and denial that strike when you learn you are not in Italy, but in some unknown, unexpected place.

But you, the parent, aren't the only one living in Holland, so to speak. Your child will spend his entire life there, while other children take off for Italy and other flashier destinations. Your child, too, will need to come to terms with the fact that he is different from others in some ways.

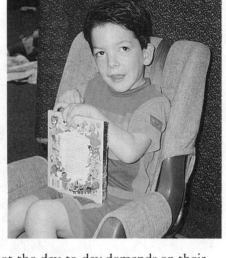

As a parent, you have a great deal of influence over how your child comes to view himself. This is important, because how your child views himself is intimately connected with his self-esteem, or feelings of self-worth. Healthy self-esteem is an essential ingredient for your child's sense of well-being.

People with high self-esteem feel competent to meet the day-to-day demands on their lives. Therefore, they feel as if they have control over themselves and their lives. Rather than waiting helplessly or passively to see how events will turn out, they take active steps to influence the events. They feel good enough about themselves to set high goals, and they have the persistence to keep trying in spite of disappointing setbacks. They are able to make decisions for themselves and to live with the consequences of those decisions.

Children with visual impairments are just as capable of developing high self-esteem as other children. Because of their vision loss, however, they may encounter more than the usual number of obstacles on the road to self-esteem. Many, if not most of these obstacles, are thrown in their way by others. For example, your child may not be included in the neighborhood game of hide-and-seek. The other children may not mean to be insensitive, but may not understand that your child would enjoy participating in their fun. Also, some parents tend to want to do things for their child with a visual impairment because it often seems easier, quicker, and more efficient. But this prevents their child from learning to do things independently and from experiencing success for himself. Parents may overprotect their child to shield him from making mistakes, from experiencing failures, or from encountering danger. But once again, this inhibits the child's ability to learn and grow from the types of experiences that other children have. Further blows to developing self-esteem can come from unthinking or ignorant remarks made in the child's presence.

Obviously, parents cannot (and should not) intercept every passing comment that might bruise their child's self-esteem. But they can nurture feelings of self-worth in their child. These feelings will help him feel comfortable and secure with himself and his abilities regardless of others' opinions. This chapter describes specific steps that you can take to increase your child's self-esteem.

Nurturing Your Child's Self-Esteem

Developing good self-esteem is a life-long task, and can be plagued by many setbacks. Experiences or events that cause your child to question his self-worth can occur at any time, forcing him to work through his feelings about himself once again. The groundwork for healthy self-esteem, however, is laid during the early years. Young children depend almost exclusively on feedback from others in forming conclusions about their own self-worth. Your child's self-esteem will tend to rise and fall with what people say and do and how these words and actions are interpreted. As he grows and matures, however, he will increasingly rely on his own judgements of success and worth for his sense of self-esteem.

As a parent, you are in the ideal position to shape your child's self-perceptions in a positive way. You can help him begin to find meaning and purpose to his life, establish a strong set of personal standards and values, and begin setting goals for himself. In so doing, you can pave the way for him to become a mature adult, capable of objectively judging his own strengths and weaknesses.

The Life-Long Adjusting Process

Because of the ever-changing demands in your child's life, he will continue to strive toward self-acceptance and self-esteem all of his life. Although some days will be better than others, you can help your child by understanding that he will continue to struggle from time to time with a variety of issues related to his visual impairment. He may, for example, need to think through and respond to unexpected difficulties or to demeaning stereotypes about individuals with visual impairments.

Your child may not experience all of the emotions described below when he encounters a problem or crisis stemming from impaired vision. However, when he becomes uncharacteristically angry, moody, or withdrawn, you may want to consider the possibility that he is wrestling with another personal predicament.

Trauma. From time to time, your child may experience the sting of being different. This may be caused by the need to use adaptive techniques that are not used by his classmates: low vision devices, slate and stylus, or a talking calculator. For the teenager, the trauma may occur when his friends obtain their learner permits to drive.

Another type of trauma results from encounters with the social stigma of blindness within the community. Many insensitive remarks are rooted in the false notions that people with visual impairments are helpless, unthinking, and unfeeling. One horrified mother tells of an encounter at a theme party with an elderly gentleman who patted her five-year-old on the head and said, "Bless his poor heart. I just want to cry when I see children like him."

Shock and Denial. After your child has experienced a trauma similar to the one described above, he may be stunned or numb. Or he may simply deny that it ever happened, unable and unwilling to talk about it. Feelings of unreality, detachment, and disbelief are common during this phase. Within reason, both shock and denial are normal and healthy parts of the adjusting process. Shock and denial allow your child to buy time to sort things out before dealing with the consequences of the trauma. Your role as a parent during this phase is to provide continuing emotional support and let some time pass.

Mourning and Withdrawal. As the numbness fades, your child may express feelings of sadness. You will want to allow (and even encourage) him to vent his frustrations concerning the painful encounter. This is usually a time of self-pity, when your child will withdraw from family and friends—a lonely time. Along with the feelings of sadness, there may be expressions of anger and hostility. Try not to become defensive if you just happen to be around when your child lashes out at the closest person around. Your child is reacting to a difficult situation, not directing his anger at you personally. You need to be a good listener, to try to understand your child's point of view, and above all, to give him an extra dose of tender loving care.

Succumbing and Depression. Your child may then begin to verbalize, one by one, the activities or relationships he feels he has lost or cannot achieve. Frequently, your child's perceptions of in

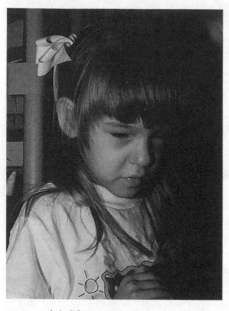

abilities or losses are not grounded in fact. It is a good idea to help him sort fact from fiction. For example, he may conclude, after being teased on the playground, "I will never have another friend in my whole life." Or, as a teenager, he may say, "If I can't drive, I can't date." This is the "I can't" phase. Before your child gets too depressed, try to help him by establishing some short-term goals that are easily attainable. For instance, if he is worried about making friends, invite one child over to play a game with him, or to accompany your family to McDonald's.

Reassessment and Reaffirmation. Sooner or later, your child will get tired of feeling sorry for himself and he will want to get on with his life. This is often a time to re-examine the meaning of life and prioritize the things considered most important. "It's more important that I get my work done with pride than it is to be embarrassed about using my slate and stylus in public." "It's more important to develop friendships than it is to drive." Since your child will be searching for affirmation as a person of value and worth, you will want to provide approving and confirming feedback.

Coping and Mobilization. Once your child's desire to live life to the fullest and as normally as possible reawakens, he will be ready to learn additional techniques and strategies for coping with life's demands. Your child will be more willing to identify himself as "different" with respect to his vision, freeing himself to learn and use the adaptive skills and devices essential for a productive, satisfying life.

Also during this phase, your child will begin to mobilize to use the available resources in the country, in the community, and within himself. Help him develop a system for obtaining and organizing information about service agencies, specialized programs, companies that sell adapted materials and equipment, and consumer groups, and teach him how to access these resources. Your child's vision specialist can help with this task.

Self-Acceptance and Self-Esteem. With the confidence that competence brings, your child will begin to develop or regain self-esteem as a person of dignity and worth. Rather than seeing himself as a visually impaired person, he will see himself as a person with many characteristics and traits, only one of which is related to his impaired vision. As much as possible, you should structure situations that will encourage and reinforce these positive perceptions. Your goal is to help him to become comfortable with himself—to like himself. It will be worth all of the effort when your child has acquired or regained self-acceptance and self-esteem.

Acceptance of others is based on self-acceptance. Your child will find it very difficult to appreciate and accept others until he has first learned to appreciate and accept himself.

Your child's journey toward healthy self-esteem will be facilitated by a warm and caring home, by genuine acceptance, and by a freedom to express thoughts and feelings no matter how strange they may seem. His self-esteem will fluctuate from day to day, depending on his experiences of the moment. Do not be surprised or alarmed when your child periodically cycles back through some or all of the emotions described above.

Guidelines for Fostering Self-Esteem

The suggestions below should help you foster healthy self-esteem in your child. Admittedly, it is impossible to stick to all of the guidelines all of the time. But if you can follow most of these recommendations most of the time, you will be doing your child and yourself a great service.

1. Don't neglect your own self-acceptance and self-esteem. Studies have shown that children are more likely to grow up with high self-esteem if their parents have high self-esteem. The reason is easy to understand. Unless you have some self-acceptance and self-esteem yourself, you will find it very difficult to accept and support your child. If you doubt your own abilities to make good decisions, you are less likely to trust your child to make decisions for himself.

   Unfortunately, having a child with a visual impairment can be a serious threat to many parents' self-esteem. At first, parents may lack the knowledge and coping skills es-

sential for handling the new situation. They may feel overwhelmed by the emotional, physical, and financial stresses of raising a child with a disability, and may doubt their ability to manage. In addition, if they feel as if they have to rearrange their lives around their child's needs, they may feel as if their opportunities for personal growth have been stifled.

Chapters 3 and 6 describe some of the feelings and attitudes that can negatively color your outlook on life when you have a child with a visual impairment. The suggestions in these chapters may help you begin to regain what self-esteem you may have lost so that you can better support your child.

2. Treat your child as a child first; focus on the child, not the visual impairment or other disabilities. Your child needs to know that you see him primarily as a child—your child—with the same basic needs of love, acceptance, and feelings of worth as everyone else. If you don't, you risk making your child feel separated from the family emotionally or physically, and he will become increasingly isolated and lonely. As you interact with your child, talk about experiences, friends, and emotions that he has in common with other children. He feels the cold snow on his nose, devours pizza, and likes to be hugged. Don't deny the fact that he has a visual impairment, but emphasize that this is only one of his many attributes. He is also five feet tall, has brown hair, and is a good trombone player.

3. Accept and respect your child's way of perceiving the world. Just because your child cannot see the things you can see does not make his interpretation of experiences any less real or valid than yours. The sound of a cardinal singing or his teacher's encouraging tone of voice can be just as thrilling for your child as the flash of red feathers or gleam of a smile is for a sighted child.

Don't point out what he cannot do. For example, don't tell him it's a shame he can't see the colored fall leaves. Instead, emphasize the different shapes of the leaves and the crunching sound they make as he walks through them. Encourage him to use the senses he can—for instance, by identifying what's cooking for supper by the smells and sounds in the kitchen.

4. Emphasize what your child can do while maintaining a realistic perspective about possible limitations. This means finding a middle ground between setting expectations that are too low and expectations that are too high. To reduce discouragement and frustration, you will want to help him establish goals that are not too high. On the other hand, you do not want to set your sights too low, or your child will not be challenged to grow and you will foster helplessness. For example, if you don't really expect your child to learn to use a knife and fork, you may let him give up after only a few attempts, rather than searching for another way to teach him. The end results of both overly low and overly high expectations are the same: your child's self-esteem suffers and his feelings of worthlessness increase.

   Goals that can be achieved with effort and ingenuity will give your child a sense of accomplishment, a desire to keep on trying new activities, and a boost to his self-esteem. It is important for you as his parent to help him find his strengths and capitalize on them.

5. Speak clearly, without relying on facial expressions and body language to convey meaning. If necessary, and with your child's permission, you may need to manipulate his body to show him what you want him to do. Children who do not have visual impairments pick up cues indicating approval and encouragement from smiles, winks, and other body language of others. Children with visual impairments need to rely more on the spoken word and tone of voice to feel included in interactions with family members and peers.

   Keep conversations with your child as natural as possible. There is no need to avoid visually oriented words such as "look" and "see," as they are also part of your child's vocabulary.

6. Encourage your child to do things independently. As his parent, you might be tempted to protect him from all danger, physical or emotional. Your motive may be a genuine

desire to shield him from failure. However, it is impossible to shield him throughout life and it is important to allow him to experience difficulty while you are around to support and encourage him. He also learns that failure to accomplish something does not mean he is a failure. He can learn the joy of finally accomplishing a task by himself after repeated attempts, trying harder, and perhaps adapting his method of attack.

Do not rush to help your child at the first sign of difficulty. If he seems to be struggling, especially with a new task, ask him if he needs help, rather than assuming that you need to step in and help. Although it may be quicker to dress him each day, this conveys a subtle message that he is not as capable as his peers who can put on their own clothes. Until he can perform a task successfully, it is far better to break up the task into smaller, achievable steps and to allow more time to finish. Praise his accomplishments and compare his achievements today with what he could do a month ago, not with what his sighted peers can do.

7. Praise your child for genuine accomplishments and tasks well done. Praise encourages him to keep on trying a task that is initially difficult for him. Praise him when he completes a task even if it is not done perfectly, but done to the best of his ability. A child is never to young to understand that he is a source of joy to Mom and Dad.

Try to avoid false praise for achievements that are ordinary or routine. Phoney, excessive flattery can have two possible consequences: the child's self-esteem might be unrealistically inflated, or a more mature child might perceive it as a demeaning and devaluating attitude toward blindness.

8. Do not accept blindness as an excuse for unacceptable behavior. Your child needs to understand and keep to the same behavioral standards as any other child. Avoiding discipline because your child has a disability is likely to damage his self-esteem. When a child knows he has done wrong, he expects his parents to respond appropriately. In addition, siblings and peers are quick to pick up on subtle differences in behavior standards and may resent your child if he is allowed to get away with behavior they are not.

9. Be honest with your child about his appearance and behavior. When his appearance or behavior is not socially acceptable, let him know in a tactful, caring way. You will need to serve as your child's mirror, letting him know when his clothes don't match, hair looks uncombed, or fly is unzipped. Help your child to keep current with clothing fads and hair styles so that it is easier for him to be a part of his peer group. Be sure also to teach socially acceptable behavior: how to shake hands when greeting an adult or how to face someone when in conversation. When your child is comfortable and confident with his appearance and social behaviors, he will be comfortable and confident when interacting with others.

10. Give frank and accurate answers to your child's questions about how his visual impairment will affect his life. As he grows up, your child, like every child, will wonder about careers, sex, relationships, and so forth. And like every child, he has a right to know what possibilities lie ahead of him so he can plan realistically for the future. All children are naturally curious, and if your child is unable to get satisfactory answers from his parents, he will seek answers from his peers. This can lead to faulty, distorted, or prejudicial information which would undermine your child's self-esteem even more.

   If you don't know the answer to a question, admit it. Then make an honest attempt to find someone who does know the answer. There are a number of resources that can help. On the local level, your child's vision specialist or the rehabilitation teacher who works out of the state department of rehabilitation services would be more than happy to answer your questions. On the national level, such organizations as the American Foundation for the Blind, the National Association for Parents of the Visually Impaired, the American Council of the Blind, and the National Federation of the Blind all have knowledgeable people available to assist you.

11. Encourage your child to be involved in community activities. Active participation in school activities, club programs, sports, and other group activities will help him feel like an accepted part of the community. This leads to two important outcomes. In the first place, your child will gain a

sense of belonging to a group. Fulfilling the need to belong is fundamental to healthy self-esteem. Second, peer interactions within these groups provide your child with many more opportunities to practice and reinforce his emerging social skills. Such opportunities to socialize outside the home may be just as important as school work for your child. For this reason, every effort should be made to mainstream your child into youth programs in the community outside of school hours.

12. Be aware of your feelings and attitudes toward blindness and be careful not to inadvertently communicate negative attitudes. As parents learn to cope with the demands of raising a child with a visual impairment, it is normal for them to feel a wide range of emotions. Some of these emotions will be positive—pride in their child's accomplishments; admiration at the way their child handles challenges; the warmth of a hug from the loving arms of your child; pleasure in his spark and spontaneity; gratitude for support services.

Other emotions will inevitably be negative. At times, for example, you may resent your child for taking up so much of your attention and energy. You may find yourself blaming him because you no longer have time to socialize with friends or pursue your interests and hobbies. Some parents may even blame their child's disability for all the problems in the family, from money woes to sibling rivalry.

Whether or not negative feelings about your child's disability are justified, it is important not to communicate them to your child. If your child senses negative or hostile messages from you, he may conclude that he is bad because he is blind or he is unwanted because he is a burden. Respond to your child as a person, not to his visual impairment, and your child can avoid associating negative values with his visual impairment.

13. Help your child develop a healthy sense of humor. The ability to laugh at yourself, at your mistakes or blunders, or at the absurdities of life helps to relieve stress and boost self-esteem. Like any child, your child will learn to laugh from the example of others around him. He may, however, need some explanations. When Dad breaks into laughter as he is heading out the door for a meeting and discovers he has on one brown and one black shoe, the situation will need to be described for your child. The absurdity of a little cat keeping a large dog at bay with one swipe of his paw is funny, but not to your child until someone interprets the absurdity for him. Although these explanations take time, they will help your child develop a healthy perspective of himself and life.

    One note of caution: when modeling a sense of humor for your child, steer clear of humor that depends on sarcastic or caustic remarks. For example, if your child knocks over a glass of milk at the dinner table, don't say something like "For a blind person, you're doing just fine." Remarks that are intended to be funny but are really put-downs are damaging to the self-esteem of the one who is the brunt of the joke.

14. Don't make your child the focal point of the family. Although your child may sometimes need more attention and help than other members of the family, he needs to understand that family life cannot always revolve around him. Like every child, he must learn that other people have needs and desires, too, and that these needs and desires will sometimes take precedence over his. If he does not learn these lessons, he will be in for a huge blow to his self-esteem when he enters the real world of school and work. In the real world, everyone competes as an equal. Everyone is expected to take turns, wait in lines, share, and pull their own weight; so your child may as well learn to do these things within the family.

Conclusion

Most parents share similar dreams for their children. They want their children to be happy. They want their children to have rewarding, fulfilling lives. And they want their children to grow up to be capable, independent adults. How much you can do to help these dreams come true for *your* child depends on many factors. Some of these factors—such as the extent and nature of your child's disabilities and how they affect his ability to learn—are out of your control. But other factors are very much under your influence. One of the most important factors you can influence is whether your child has the self-esteem to enable him to keep striving for success even when he is occasionally confronted with overwhelming odds.

Building self-esteem in your child is not a difficult job, but it is an ongoing job. As this chapter explains, almost any interaction you have with your child can either lead to higher or lower self-esteem. The key is to become aware of how your actions and attitudes can affect your child's perceptions of himself. With the right kinds of support from you, your child can develop healthy self-esteem and look forward to a rich, rewarding, and satisfying life.

Bibliography

Hartman, D. and Asbell, B. *White Coat, White Cane.* Chicago: Playboy Press, 1978.

Henderson, L.T. *The Opening Doors: My Child's First Eight Years without Sight.* New York: John Day, 1954.

Hocken, S. *Emma and I.* New York: Dutton, 1978.

Kemper, R.G. *An Elephant's Ballet: One Man's Successful Struggle with Sudden Blindness.* New York: Seaburg, 1977.

Krents, H. *To Race the Wind.* New York: G.P. Putnam, 1972.

Lunt, L. *If You Make a Noise I Can't See.* London: Gollancz, 1965.

Mehta, V. *Daddyji.* New York: Farrar, Straus, Giroux, 1972.

Resnick, R. *Sun and Shadow.* New York: Atheneum, 1975.

Sperber, A. *Out of Sight: Ten Stories of Victory over Blindness.* Boston: Little, Brown, 1976.

Sullivan, T. and Gill, D. *If You Could See What I Hear.* New York: Harper & Row, 1975.

Tuttle, D.W. *Self-esteem and Adjusting with Blindness.* Springfield, IL: Charles C. Thomas, 1995.

Ulrich, S. *Elizabeth.* Ann Arbor: University of Michigan Press, 1972.

West, E. "My Child Is Blind, Thoughts on Family Life." *Exceptional Parent*,
11: 9–12 (1981).

Parent Statements

I want to protect my child from all those people who say hurtful
things.

—◄◦►—

My child's grandparents love him unconditionally. Sometimes I
think that they spoil him, but it is really wonderful.

—◄◦►—

I think the way I react to blindness will make a difference in how
my child feels about himself.

—◄◦►—

I feel sure we will be able to take care of Joey's physical needs but
I worry about his self-esteem. I have less control over that.

—◄◦►—

The more independent Patty is, the better she will feel about herself.

—◄◦►—

As Vicki grows up she will need to know successful blind people
who can model their independence and their self-esteem.

—◄◦►—

My son, my daughter (who is blind), and I were shopping at a local
mall recently. I had just taken them to get new haircuts at a shop
in the mall and as we were walking back to the car my son said
"Daddy, why are all those people staring at us?" Well, I took a deep
breath and was about to explain that maybe they had never seen
anyone who was blind when my daughter put her hand up to her
head and said, "They probably like my new hairdo!" What a great
self-concept!

—◄◦►—

It's hard to think about working on self-esteem when we have so many other problems to address.

David's brother is very accepting of David. That's got to help him feel good about himself.

Chapter 8

◄○►

Early Intervention and Special Education

Bob Brasher, M.S., and
M. Cay Holbrook, Ph.D.*

Children with visual impairments run the gamut of intellectual abilities and interests. Some may become accountants, psychologists, teachers, computer programmers, or other types of college-educated professionals. Others may complete regular or vocational high school programs and go on to satisfying white- or blue-collar jobs. Still others may benefit from a "functional" rather than an "academic" program and may require some degree of assistance to live independently as adults. Regardless of intellectual abilities, however, most children with visual impairments need some extra help to succeed in school. This is because of the challenges that visual impairments (and sometimes additional disabilities) pose to learning.

Many children with visual impairments begin receiving educational support in infancy to help them learn to cope with our visually oriented world and to prepare them for formal education programs. Others may not be enrolled in a formal educational program until the preschool years or later.

* Bob Brasher is currently director of Educational Services for the Visually Impaired, the outreach program of the Arkansas School for the Blind, and the Arkansas Department of Education, Special Education. He supervises vision consultants throughout the state of Arkansas, oversees materials production and distribution of textbooks to public school students, and provides technical assistance to parents and teachers.

See Chapter 1 for biographical information about M. Cay Holbrook.

Some parents are fortunate enough to receive help early. They then become aware of their child's educational needs and ways to meet those needs right from the start. Other parents may be at a loss as to what to do before they are able to hook up with professionals who can help. This chapter is designed to minimize the time you flounder so that you can get your child the help she needs as soon as possible.

What Kinds of Help Are Available?

As Chapter 9 explains, a very important federal law guarantees children with visual impairment the right to special educational help, if necessary. Part B of Public Law 101–467 (the Individuals with Disabilities Education Act—"IDEA") mandates educational help for children with disabilities aged three and over, while Part H of the IDEA provides for educational assistance for children birth to two years of age. If your child is three years of age or over and qualifies for assistance under IDEA, she will receive what is known as "special education." If she is under three years of age, she will receive "early intervention." Both special education and early intervention are available to your child at no cost to you, the parent. As the sections below point out, early intervention and special education services are basically the same, no matter what they are called. However, there may be some differences in how often and where the services are provided.

What Is Special Education?

There are many reasons that special education can be considered "special." The main reason, however, is that special education programs are tailor-made to fit the unique learning strengths and needs of the individual child. Teaching rates and styles, instructional materials, and educational goals are all designed to fit the child's specific learning abilities. This is in contrast to "regular" education programs, where teachers teach many children the same subjects using the same methods and materials.

A major goal of special education is to teach children the skills and knowledge that they need to become as independent as possible. For this reason, special education programs are not limited to traditional "academic" subjects such as reading and math. They also include special therapeutic and other services intended to help children overcome difficulties in all areas of development. For example, special education can help a child improve mobility or communication skills.

By law, a child's special education program must include all the special services, or "related services," she needs to benefit from her educational program. These services are provided by one or more professionals trained in working with children with special needs. For children with visual impairments, special education services may include instruction from a vision specialist, orientation and mobility training, speech/language therapy, occupational therapy, physical therapy, or psychological services. As discussed later in this chapter, special education and related services may be provided in a variety of educational settings. For example, a child might receive special education services within a regular classroom or within a classroom of only children with visual impairments, or in many other classroom settings. Where a child receives services depends on how and where she learns best.

What Is Early Intervention?

Early intervention can be thought of as special education for children two years old or younger. It consists of special instruction or therapy designed to help infants and toddlers with special needs improve their developmental skills. This intervention is intended to optimize a child's abilities and build a foundation for further learning. Just as in special education programs,  the therapeutic and educational services a child receives are tailored to meet her unique learning needs. Educational services for infants with visual impairments often include instruction and support from a vision specialist; physical, occupational, or speech/language therapy; or counseling services for your family.

It has been estimated that 80 percent of learning occurs through vision. A sighted child learns about the world through observation of the people, places, and things around her. She watches her mother salt her food, so she picks up the salt shaker and imitates the motion. She sees Daddy come into the living room and wipe his dirty shoes on the mat, so she tries to do the same thing. Sighted children use their vision to begin learning about the world from the day they are born.

Children with visual impairments also begin learning about their world from the day they are born. A visual impairment limits the learning, however, by limiting opportunities to benefit from experiences that are farther away than the child can reach, or that do not make noise. Children can and do learn effectively by using their senses of touch, hearing, smell, and taste. The sound an egg makes as it is fried is very different from the sound a boiling egg makes. Even so, this type of learning is different. It requires parents and teachers to become more efficient at using experiences which emphasize use of the child's hearing and touch, smell and taste.

Early intervention is important for children with visual impairment because through instruction and modeling, children (and their parents) can learn how to best interact with the world using all of their senses—thus minimizing delays in learning.

Early intervention programs not only help the child, but also the family. Parents learn about their child's eye condition and about the services available in the community. Teachers and therapists show them ways to help their child develop. In addition, counseling support may be available to help parents and other family members cope with emotional issues related to having a child with visual impairment.

Getting Started

Eligibility for early intervention and special education differs with each state's interpretation of the federal law. In general, however, your child is probably eligible for services if she needs special materials (such as braille or large print textbooks), or help learning special skills needed to compensate for her loss of vision (such as developing concepts, orientation and mobility skills, or listening skills).

As you get to know other parents, you will find that there are many different ways to enter into "the system" of early intervention or special education services. Children with more noticeable disabilities may be identified at birth or shortly after. In such cases, parents may be referred for services by a physician or health care professional. For other parents, the process is a little more complicated, and they may need to take the initiative in finding helpful services for their child.

A good starting place in your quest to obtain early intervention or special education services is with a call to your state department of education, your state department of health, your state school for the blind, or a local disability organization such as Easter Seals. Addresses and phone numbers for the schools for the blind for each state can be found in the resource section at the back of this book. If you live in a state that does not have a school for the blind, do not hesitate to call a school in a neighboring state, since they may have a regional program. This first phone call may lead to many others before you find the specific local resources that can help your family.

Once you are connected with professionals in early intervention or special education, your child will go through assessment procedures to determine her eligibility for services. At the very least, you will be asked to provide documentation from an ophthalmologist or optometrist about your child's visual impairment. Your child may also be given a variety of tests by teachers, therapists, and other professionals. The purpose of any assessments should be to determine your child's strengths and weaknesses so that an education program can be developed to help meet her needs while capitalizing on her abilities.

Your Child's Education Program

After your child is found to be eligible for special education or early intervention, the next step is to plan her educational program. That is, this if the next step if you consent to have your child placed in early intervention or special education. As a parent, you cast the deciding vote as to whether—or when—your child should receive specialized services.

Assuming that you agree to your child's placement in early intervention or special education, a document will be drawn up describing educational goals for your child, as well as what will be done to help her reach her goals. If your child is receiving early intervention services, this document will be called an Individualized Family Services Plan (IFSP). If she is receiving special education, it will be called an Individualized Education Program (IEP).

If your child is in a special education or early intervention program, you will become very familiar with the process of developing an IFSP or IEP. Basically, both the IEP and IFSP serve as written documentation of the yearly plan for your child. Both contain long-term goals and short-term objectives for your child's education, as well as a statement of your child's current level of functioning. They also include decisions about the setting where your child is to receive services (in a regular classroom, at home, in the school for the blind). Chapter 9 provides a more comprehensive discussion about the elements of an IEP/IFSP.

The actual writing of your child's IEP/IFSP will occur at an annual meeting. You are a very important part of this process, so the special education or early intervention personnel should make sure that the meeting is scheduled at a convenient time for you to fully participate. In order to feel comfortable and on an equal footing with the professionals present, you may wish to ask a family member, friend, or other professional to attend with you for advice and moral support. It is your right to bring such supporters to these meetings, and you will probably be encouraged to do so.

To help you take an informed role in planning your child's education, the next sections discuss the three most important elements covered in an IEP or IFSP: educational goals; services that can help a child reach her goals; and educational settings where services can be provided.

What Will Your Child Learn?

What your child is taught in her early intervention or special education program depends on the goals in her IFSP or IEP. As explained above, these goals are ideally set *jointly* by educators and parents. Teachers and therapists will have one picture of your child's unique strengths and needs. This picture will be based on their assessment of your child and on any experience they have had working

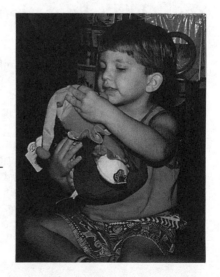

with her. You will also have a picture of her abilities and disabilities, based on your parenting experiences with her. If you and the educators can pool your ideas about what your child can and should learn next, your child is more likely to end up with appropriate, attainable goals.

The specific goals for each child with a visual impairment vary greatly depending on readiness levels and whether there are additional disabilities. In general, however, three types of goals may be set for children with visual impairments: academic, functional, and adaptive.

Academic goals are set for skills related to educational areas such as pre-reading, reading, writing, and mathematics. Your child may have specific needs in any academic area where mastering concepts is dependent upon vision. For example, without good vision, it is difficult to tell the difference between a cow and a horse; grasp the difference in height between a tree and a skyscraper; or even understand what a bumper on a car is. Most children with sight learn these concepts by using their vision instead of exploring the objects by touch.

Functional goals address skills that your child needs to live as independently as possible. These might include eating skills, dressing skills, and toilet training. As your child grows, her goals for functional skills may become more and more complex, reflecting her increased abilities and her increased need for independence. For example, in the area of dressing, a very young child might work on putting on a coat or pulling up socks, while later goals may focus on tying shoes or buttoning a shirt. Still later goals may be to use make-up and learn hair care skills.

Adaptive goals cover specialized skills needed by your child because of her visual impairment. These include orientation and mobility skills, as well as tactual and auditory readiness skills. These skills will help your child use her other senses to gather information in school.

Your child's IFSP/IEP will probably list long-term goals with short-term objectives associated with each goal. Typically, goals are broad statements about areas that will be focused on. Goals might be phrased like this:

- Tony will explore his environment with all of his senses.
- Jennifer will become more independent in dressing herself.
- Justin will feed himself independently.
- Stacy will play with other children.

In contrast, objectives are usually more short-term and specific than goals. They are measurable (your child's accomplishment of the objective can be measured) and observable (you can watch your child's activity and know whether she has accomplished the objective). Usually, several objectives are associated with each goal. For instance, these objectives might be set for Jennifer to help her reach the goal in the example above:

- Jennifer will be able to zip the zipper on her jacket up and down ten times in a row.
- Jennifer will be able to tie her tennis shoes without assistance five days in a row.
- Jennifer will put and take off mittens independently ten times in a row.

Of course, the objectives for each child will be different because they will depend on each child's individual needs and abilities. You will not be able to look at any other child's IEP/IFSP and predict what your child will be working on. But objectives should be written in such a way that everyone understands not just what the child *should* be able to accomplish, but also *how* everyone will know if she has met the objectives.

For every objective set for your child, a timeline for reaching that objective should also be set. For example, the IFSP might specify that your child is expected to learn to zip her jacket in one month, or to learn to put on her mittens in three months.

As mentioned earlier, goals must be reevaluated every year at an IEP meeting. If your child has met old goals, then new ones will be set. If your child has not met goals or objectives set for her, they may be restated, modified, or just carried over to the new year to give her more time to work on the skill. You must be invited to attend this meeting and will be encouraged to actively participate.

Who Will Work with Your Child?

Depending on their needs, children with visual impairment may receive special instruction or therapy from a variety of professionals. Some of these professionals are trained to work exclusively on problems related to visual impairment, while others have a broader background in working with children with disabilities in general. Both types of professionals will tailor their teaching methods and materials to best meet your child's needs and goals.

Described below are professionals who might work with your child at some point. Titles may vary somewhat from state to state, but areas of expertise should be the same.

Vision Specialist

A vision specialist (also called vision teacher, VI teacher, teacher of the visually impaired, vision itinerant teacher) is a certified teacher who has received specialized training in meeting the educational needs of children with visual impairment. He or she may work directly with your child in such areas as:

- encouraging movement by introducing toys that are visually or tactually interesting;
- stimulating the use of all your child's senses;
- teaching pre-reading skills such as tracking and finger positioning;
- teaching braille reading;
- helping with daily living skills such as eating and dressing.

The vision specialist will have a major role in planning and implementing an educational program for your child. In some cases, the vision specialist might be your child's primary teacher. More often, the vision specialist will help your child indirectly, by advising others about ways of enhancing your child's learning. He or she might consult with the regular classroom teacher about ways to adapt activities and materials to your child's abilities. For example, the vision specialist might suggest to the regular classroom teacher that when the weather for the day is discussed during circle time, the children dress up in appropriate clothes instead of using a paper "weather doll" and pretend clothes.

Vision specialists are also great resources for parents because they can share their knowledge and understanding of how a visual impairment may affect many areas of learning and daily life. Generally, vision specialists have experience working with many children with visual impairments and can therefore share how other families cope with the challenges of a visual impairment. A vision specialist might help you by suggesting ways to organize your child's toys or books so that she can locate them independently. Or he or she might recommend appropriate chores for your child to do around the house. By working together, parents and a vision specialist can create an environment that encourages independence.

Vision Consultant

Your child might also encounter a vision consultant. A vision consultant is a teacher who travels from school to school, providing technical assistance or support to educators. This consultant may help the teacher choose appropriate toys and educational materials, may brainstorm with teachers and parents about effective adaptations, and may bring the newest instructional innovations to teachers for use with their students. Usually a vision consultant doesn't work directly with students with visual impairments, but provides suggestions to regular classroom teachers, program administrators, and families.

Orientation and Mobility (O & M) Specialist

The O & M Specialist (also called O & M teacher, travel instructor, mobility specialist, peripatologist) is a certified instructor who has received specialized training in teaching people with visual impairment to travel safely and efficiently. Usually the O & M specialist works with children individually. At first, instruction time is spent learning basic concepts relating to space and direction (over and under, left and right). Later, the O & M specialist

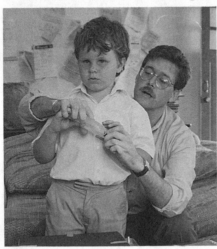

begins work on independent travel skills (from room to room, to the cafeteria and bathrooms, to the playground). The O & M specialist will teach your child when it is appropriate to use a sighted guide, when to use a cane, and, when your child is much older, when and if a guide dog might be useful.

Eventually, your child will master the skills that allow her to travel safely through her environment. With the assistance of an O & M specialist, it's possible and likely that a child who is totally blind will learn to cross busy streets, catch a bus, and locate new travel destinations independently.

See Chapter 11 for more information on orientation and mobility.

Clinical Low Vision Specialist

A clinical low vision specialist may be an optometrist, an ophthalmologist, or a university-trained professional. He or she specializes in helping children with limited visual ability optimize their remaining vision. The clinical low vision specialist will work with your child to find the best way to enhance her vision—whether through hand-held magnifiers, monoculars (telescopes), special high-powered glasses for reading, or closed circuit televisions which enlarge print onto a TV screen.

Children typically see this specialist when someone (a parent, vision specialist, classroom teacher, the orientation and mobility specialist) determines that a low vision device might be helpful. If your child's vision or her educational needs or performance have changed, then she may be referred for a visit (or follow-up visit) to the clinical low vision specialist.

The clinical low vision specialist is not usually the child's primary eye care specialist. He or she will generally work with the vision specialist and orientation and mobility specialist to determine which low-vision devices are effective for a child. The vision specialist and orientation and mobility specialist will then help the child learn to use low vision devices.

It may be difficult to find a low vision clinic in your area. Some residential schools for the blind, state departments of health, rehabilitation facilities, and local hospitals or clinics operate low vision clinics. Some states also have readily available "for profit" clinics operated by trained low vision eye care specialists, while others do not. The cost of such services varies widely. While some clinics offer low vision evaluations free of charge or at a nominal rate, others are very expensive. In addition to the above resources, you may wish to contact the American Foundation for the Blind for a listing of low vision clinics in your state.

Case Manager

The case manager is the person with the primary responsibility for planning your child's preschool education program. He or she also usually coordinates all the services your child needs. The case manager can assist with a wide variety of issues, from scheduling your child's therapists to arranging for an appointment with an eye care specialist. Federal law mandates that all children who qualify for early intervention programs be assigned a case manager.

Other Specialists

If your child has additional disabilities, other therapists or specialists may work with her. These special therapists could include: an occupational therapist (for help with fine motor skills such as holding a pencil or fork or fastening buttons); a physical therapist (for help with gross motor skills such as holding up the head, sitting, and walking); a speech and language therapist (for help with comprehending and expressing communication); a special education teacher or infant education specialist (for help with pre-academic and academic skills such as shape recognition, reading, and math). If a visual impairment is your child's only disability, it is unlikely that these professionals will work directly with her. Her vision specialist or O & M specialist, however, may consult with them if your child is having difficulty in a particular area.

Where Will Your Child Go to School?

The professionals described above work with children in both early intervention and special education programs. Where your child sees these professionals, however, may depend on her age. Infants and very young children often receive educational services in different kinds of settings than school-aged children. The sections below discuss some of the many options that may be available in your community.

Early Intervention and Preschool Settings

Early intervention and preschool programs are usually held in one of two locations: either in your home, or in a "center"—a school, clinic, hospital, day care center, or other building with classroom space. Some children receive a combination of home- and center-based intervention. Other children may go to an early intervention program several days of the week, and to a regular day care center or nursery the rest of the week. It all depends on the programs available in your community and the educational setting specified in your child's IFSP or IEP.

Home Intervention. Home intervention services are generally provided when a child is very young or when medical conditions prevent the child from participating in a program outside the home. In this type of program, parents receive scheduled visits in their home by a qualified preschool specialist. A qualified preschool specialist may be a teacher with training in early childhood/special education who receives help from a vision specialist, or he or she may be a vision specialist with experience or training in early childhood issues. The specialist assesses the child's developmental problems and then works with the child on activities to overcome them. The specialist also educates parents about the ways visual impairment may affect their child's development and their family life, and refers them to other appropriate services.

As mentioned earlier, if your child has other disabilities in addition to a visual impairment, she may need services from a variety of therapists and educators. Your case manager may help coordinate these visits, or the specialists may call you directly and make appointments to visit you and your child.

The scheduling of visits will depend on the type of services your child needs, as well as on her unique goals. You may see one therapist once a week, while another may visit less often.

Having therapists/specialists visit you at home can have many benefits. Your child is in a comfortable, familiar environment, surrounded by many of her own toys. Your child's teachers can demonstrate activities to you in your own home. They can offer specific suggestions about how to make your child safer and more comfortable in your home, perhaps by suggesting changes in lighting or the way furniture is arranged.

There are also disadvantages to home intervention, aside from the obvious inconvenience of having strangers in your home. Probably the biggest disadvantage is the isolation. Your child needs to learn how to socialize with other children, to play, and to share. You, as a parent, can also benefit from time around parents of other children. It is often comforting to know that other parents (of children with and without visual impairments) have the same questions, concerns, and dreams for their children that you have for your child.

Center-Based Programs. No two center-based programs are exactly alike, so it is difficult to generalize about their charac-

teristics. Some center-based programs serve children with visual impairment exclusively; others serve children with a wide range of disabilities; and still others serve children both with and without disabilities. Some programs are run independently by churches or private companies, some by federal agencies such as Head Start, some by state or county agencies, and some by the school district or state residential school for the blind. And, as mentioned above, programs can be housed in many different places, ranging from schools, to churches, to day care centers, to hospitals.

Center-based programs are usually offered in a centralized place where therapists can come to provide therapy and instruction. Because center-based programs have a concentrated number of students, they can sometimes hire or train specialized personnel and obtain specialized equipment. The center may also use the services of consultants in the area of visual impairment or other special needs. If your child's IFSP specifies that she is to receive consultation or direct services from a vision specialist, the specialist will usually travel to the center and provide instruction there.

Your child may go to the center all or a portion of every day, every other day, or just once a week. How much time your child spends at the center will depend on the plans developed by you and your child's team. How much you are involved will likewise depend on the program developed for your child. At times, the center's staff may be very interested in your input and assistance, and at other times your child will need to show her independence by having a little distance from you. Participating in a center-based program will help your child learn to interact with other children and adults. This does not necessarily mean your child won't also need some home intervention activities, but her home activities may be supplemented by center-based activities.

Settings for School-Aged Children

By the time your child graduates from preschool, she may already have been in special education for several years. Still, beginning kindergarten or first grade will mean many changes for her, and taking steps to ease the transition will be crucial. She will probably have new teachers and therapists, meet many new friends, and have new goals added to her IEP. One of the biggest changes, though, may be in where she goes to school. In many communities, there are more placement options for school-aged children than for preschoolers, so deciding what is best for your child may be more complicated. Below are some educational settings frequently available for school-aged children.

Homebound Instruction. This type of program is usually a temporary program designed to provide services for students who cannot attend regular classes. Medical problems are the most common reasons for homebound instruction. Children in this kind of program receive instruction in all academic subjects in the home. A qualified teacher and therapists travel to the home on a scheduled basis to meet the child's individual educational goals. The scheduling of visits by the teacher(s) depend, of course, on the child's needs as well as her health concerns. Often, parents need to take on some teaching responsibilities when the teacher(s) are not in their home.

Hospital Program. If your child has health problems that require hospitalization, a qualified teacher and therapists can provide instruction in the hospital. This is usually a temporary measure until your child is discharged from the hospital.

Residential Schools. A residential school may be a state-supported or private school for children with specific disabilities (vision or hearing impairment, for example). Here students attend classes and may live there during school terms. Children often attend such schools to gain important adaptive skills such as orientation and mobility, braille reading and writing, daily living skills, and use of adaptive technology (speech synthesis for a word processor, braille notetaker, etc.) Sometimes these skills are easier to learn in a residential program because intense specialized instruction is more likely to be available there than in a public school. Students at residential schools may also have more opportunities to practice the special skills they are learning under the watchful eyes of trained professionals.

Another advantage of residential schools is the numerous opportunities they provide for socializing with other children with visual impairment. Many offer a wide range of extracurricular activities, including scouts, sports, and special interest clubs. Especially for children who live in rural areas, a residential school may provide the only opportunity for such social interaction.

After they have picked up the needed skills, many students return to their home school. Sometimes students return to a residential school for short stays as their needs require throughout their school careers.

Often, residential schools act as resource centers to the state's local schools, providing valuable consultation, information, and educational materials.

Special Day Service Facility. This is a community-based public or private school that serves children with disabilities exclusively. Some of these facilities serve children with a mixture of disabilities, while others serve children with only one type of disability. Usually specially trained teachers and therapists provide intense, individualized services throughout the school day.

Self-Contained Classroom. A self-contained classroom is a room in a "regular" or neighborhood school. The primary purpose of these classes is to provide specialized instruction to students with disabilities. These classes usually have a smaller teacher-student ratio than classes for students without disabilities in the same school. Teachers in self-contained classrooms are usually qualified in both general and special education.

Students enrolled in a self-contained classroom usually complete at least half of their classroom work there. Students may leave the self-contained classroom throughout the day to receive special instruction (such as orientation and mobility or speech therapy) or to participate in activities in the regular classroom. Some students participate in regular classroom activities to benefit from social opportunities with children who do not have disabilities. Others participate in regular classrooms to work on academic skills.

Self-contained classrooms for children with visual impairments are rare, except in large cities where there are enough students to fill a class. Children who have other disabilities besides visual impairments may be placed in self-contained classrooms for students with multiple disabilities, where they can receive additional support.

Resource Room. A resource room is a classroom where specific skills are learned or reinforced. For example, a child might receive specialized instruction here in academic areas that are difficult for her. Or she might receive instruction in special skill areas such as braille reading, use of technology such as computers and braille printers, or concept development. No more than 50 percent of classroom work should take place in the resource room. The majority of the day should be spent in the regular classroom, receiving instruction from the regular classroom teacher.

Resource rooms may serve students with several different disabilities (noncategorical classrooms) or serve only students with a specific disability (categorical classrooms). Any resource teacher who provides services to children with visual impairments should have special training and certification in visual impairment.

Regular Classroom with Additional Direct Instruction. In this setting, a student receives most of her instruction in the regular classroom alongside students without disabilities. On a daily or weekly basis, she receives supplemental instruction within the classroom or in a special classroom from a vision specialist, orientation and mobility specialist, or other specialists, as needed. Besides providing instruction to the child, the vision specialist provides technical assistance to school staff. For instance, he or she may hold workshops to help teachers learn to work with children with visual impairments or consult on specific questions from regular classroom teachers. Sometimes this teacher is called an itinerant vision teacher if she travels from school to school.

Regular Classroom with Indirect Services. In this setting, a student receives all of her instruction in the regular classroom. Occasionally, one or more vision consultants visit to observe the student and to make suggestions to the instructional staff. For example, the vision consultant may help the regular classroom teacher determine which materials should be transcribed into braille and which should be transferred to tape or read to the student. The consultant might also suggest special adaptations for classroom activities and field trips.

Regular Classroom. Some students with visual impairment are able to succeed in the regular classroom with no outside consultative assistance. They may use adaptive equipment such as a word processor with speech output, but do not need assistance to maintain grade-level performance.

Although independence is a goal that is very important for children with visual impairments, the need for special assistance inside or outside of a regular classroom should, in no way, be considered a failure. In fact, some children who are successfully educated in the regular classroom for years may need assistance from a vision specialist or O & M specialist during transition times—when moving from preschool to kindergarten, from elementary to junior high school or middle school, or from high school into college, vocational training, or the world of work.

Choosing the Right Educational Setting

Depending on the options available in your community, there could be anywhere from a few to a bewildering number of settings in which your child *could* be educated. The challenge is to pick the

setting where your child is likely to make the best progress. Fortunately, federal education laws have set some guidelines that make choosing an appropriate setting a little easier. The most important of these guidelines is the requirement that children with disabilities be educated in the "least restrictive environment" (LRE).

The least restrictive environment is the setting which allows each child the most freedom and opportunity for educational progress. There are many issues related to LRE. You and your child's educators must consider the following questions when making decisions about placement:

- What setting will give your child the best chance of experiencing educational success and of accomplishing the goals and objectives on her IEP?
- What setting will best prepare your child to meet future educational, vocational, and social demands?
- What setting will best prepare your child to be fully integrated in society?

These questions are not easily answered. The LRE for one student is not necessarily the LRE for another student. In determining the most appropriate educational setting, each child's specific needs and abilities should be taken into account. It is also important to remember that needs and abilities may change throughout a student's educational career. Therefore, the least restrictive environment for a particular student may change throughout the years.

Any given placement option is sometimes the least restrictive environment, sometimes the most restrictive environment, and sometimes somewhere in between. It all depends on the student. The resource room may be a more restrictive environment for one student; a less restrictive environment for another. For this reason, professionals often refer to the ideal setting as the "most appropriate placement," rather than the "least restrictive environment." You may also hear the term "most inclusive environment," which means placement with children who do not have disabilities (mainstreaming).

The variety of placement options is often referred to as the "continuum of services." Teachers and parents must consider this continuum as they determine the best possible match of educational services and individual needs. For example, the resource room might be the best place for your child to learn braille skills. But that doesn't mean that academic subjects must or should be taught in that setting. In other words, sometimes there isn't just one "right" setting for a child; rather, there is a combination of "right" settings.

As your child progresses, her settings will be constantly monitored and changed. Federal laws require that your child's setting be reviewed at least once a year to make sure that she is not spending time in the wrong setting. You may also request reviews of your child's placement at any time. See Chapter 9 for information on changing a placement.

To Mainstream or Not to Mainstream?

Today, more and more efforts are being made to ensure that all children with disabilities have the chance to interact at school with children who don't have disabilities. But where individual children are concerned, there is no one answer to the question of whether mainstreaming or inclusion is the best option. For children who have a visual impairment, the answer probably lies in a balancing act. You and your child's teachers must balance her needs for social interactions with her educational needs and requirements for special education.

Below are some unique issues that must be considered when thinking about the mainstreaming question for children with visual impairments.

Social. Placing children with visual impairments in a regular classroom provides an opportunity for them to interact with children who are sighted. This is certainly important. We live in a sighted world and children who are blind or visually impaired must be able to feel successful in social interactions with sighted people.

On the other hand, children with visual impairments—especially those who live in rural areas—may have limited contact with other people with visual impairments. We all like to know that we "are not alone," and that some of our concerns are shared by others. Children also benefit from interaction with other children (and adults) who have had similar experiences and concerns.

Academic. The number one purpose of schools is to teach "academics" to students. For children with visual impairments to succeed and compete with their classmates, two things must occur. First, they must have access to adapted materials. If your child reads braille, for example, she must be given braille textbooks and classroom materials. Ideally, she will have creative teachers who will find ways to modify other types of class materials, including workbooks, handouts, tests, maps, and bulletin boards. Your child must be included in all classroom activities in order to benefit from them.

Second, children with visual impairments need to know how to skillfully use adapted equipment and skills. Using a talking calculator or an abacus might help your child complete her mathematics assignment more efficiently; using a computer with speech output might help her express her ideas in writing more independently. Merely having adapted equipment is not enough, however. Your child must know which equipment would be helpful and feel comfortable using it.

When considering a placement for your child, ask yourself whether she is prepared to succeed academically. Does she need special equipment to handle the academics? Does she need intense special instruction to learn to use the equipment? Some students do better if they are placed for a short time in a program designed to teach how to use special equipment before they enter a classroom where they need to use the equipment.

Special Skills. Children with visual impairments typically receive instruction in special skills that sighted classmates do not. These skills may include orientation and mobility, braille reading and writing, daily living skills, listening skills, and adaptive physical education and recreation skills. When deciding which placement is best for your child, it is important to consider her strengths and weaknesses in these special skills, and determine which placement will best help her build on her skills.

You should have a great deal to say about whether—and to what extent—your child is mainstreamed. For many parents, finding the most inclusive setting for their child is THE most important factor in choosing a placement. But there are also other factors that you may want to consider in determining the most appropriate setting for your child. Factors to consider for school-aged children are summarized in Figure 1; for preschool children, in Figure 2. Some factors that you may want to give extra weight to include:

- Are there sufficient numbers of staff per child? Do children in the class receive the assistance they need to accomplish their educational goals?
- Is the staff trained to work with children with visual impairments? If not, is there a vision specialist or other expert that staff members are willing and able to consult? Are staff members willing to seek out in-service training opportunities to learn more about visual impairment?
- Does the staff seem comfortable with your child, and vice versa? Sometimes teachers ask children to attempt tasks which might be a little frightening at first (walking up and down steps, reaching for something). Your child may be

more likely to try unfamiliar activities, movements, etc. if she likes and trusts the teacher or therapist.

- Do you agree with staff about the educational goals that are important for your child? Minor differences of opinion such as about classroom routines can usually be worked out at the meeting to plan your child's IEP. But if you have major disagreements such as about the introduction of braille reading and writing, you might want to seek a program where you are more likely to see eye to eye with the staff.

Figure 1
Questions to Consider in Selecting a School Program

- What is the teacher-student ratio? Are there sufficient personnel (for example, paraprofessionals, parent volunteers, etc.) to support the teacher in providing individualized attention when necessary?
- What are the qualifications of the teaching staff and administration? Have they had experience with including students with disabilities in their school?
- What opportunities are available to teachers for inservice training or workshops on new teaching techniques (including techniques useful for the education of students with visual impairments)?
- Do the teachers and administrators seem to accept and respect differences in students? Are they open to the opportunity of working with a student who is visually impaired?
- Are there opportunities for students with disabilities to participate fully in extracurricular activities in school?
- Is a trained vision specialist available to provide appropriate instruction to your child and consultation to your child's classroom teacher?
- Are there opportunities for alternative, short-term placements? Are teachers and administrators flexible in providing placement options?
- Are adaptive equipment and materials (including large print and/or braille textbooks) readily available?
- Are physical facilities safe, clean, and accessible?

Figure 2
Questions to Consider in Selecting a Preschool Program

- Are there sufficient numbers of staff per child?
- Is the facility licensed by the state with a good reputation?
- Are the workers trained to work with children with visual impairment, or do they have a resource to assist them? Do they seem willing to seek out in-service training opportunities to learn more about visual impairments?
- Does the staff seem to accept children with visual impairments?
- Are other parents satisfied with this program?
- Does the program allow open, unscheduled visits by parents?
- Are motivating toys and materials (high contrast, interesting texture, bright colors) used with the children?
- Are written materials available that describe safety and emergency procedures?
- Do staff members provide a safe environment while encouraging independence?
- Are physical facilities safe, clean, and accessible?

Becoming an Active Member of Your Child's Educational Team

So far, this chapter has touched on several ways that parents are typically involved in their child's education program: they help teachers and therapists set appropriate goals; they have a voice in choosing the right educational setting; they may help their child work on educational or therapeutic goals at home. But if you choose, you can play an even more important role on your child's educational team. You can have a say in virtually every decision made about your child's education. To do so, you need only decide to become your child's advocate.

The idea of becoming an advocate may sound intimidating to you if you have only heard the word used in a legal context before. But to advocate simply means to speak up on someone else's behalf. This is something you have likely been doing for your child, wittingly or unwittingly, since her birth. For example, every time you take your child to the grocery store, the shopping mall, or Sunday School, you are advocating for her right to be fully involved in the community. When you answer questions from other children, parents, or professionals, you are also being an advocate.

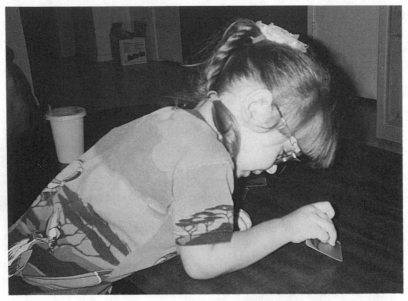

To be an educational advocate for your child means, in simplest terms, figuring out how she can get the maximum benefit possible from her educational program. And it means doing whatever it takes to ensure that she gets that benefit. Some of the many ways you might advocate may therefore include: talking informally to teachers and therapists about your child's strengths and needs; requesting specific educational services at an IEP meeting; investigating different placement options and then asking for the one you think would be best for your child; joining other parents in requesting that your school system offer more and better services for children with visual impairments.

You don't need any formal training to advocate for your child. But here are some pointers that can help you get started on the right foot:

- Review assessment results prior to educational meetings. This way you will be able to ask appropriate questions and make informed recommendations.
- Gather as much information as possible relating to your child's needs. Read books and articles such as those recommended by organizations for the blind and in the Reading List of this book. Watch educational films. Talk with other parents about their experiences with the school system and services that have helped their child. As you gather in-

formation from other parents, it may be helpful to ask open-ended questions: What has been most helpful to you? What books would you recommend?

Ask doctors to clearly explain all medical conditions. Don't hesitate to keep asking questions until you understand every term relating to your child's condition. Keep in mind, however, that medical doctors are rarely educational specialists. Although their suggestions are well intentioned, you should rely primarily upon qualified educators to assist you with educational decisions. Remember, if a doctor expresses a personal opinion about the use of braille, large print, or regular print materials, it is just that: a personal opinion. Be sure to get other opinions, especially from experienced vision specialists.

- Consider compiling a one- to two-page summary of information pertinent to your child's needs which you could distribute to new teachers and other appropriate educational staff. (See the next page for a sample summary.) This preliminary information will help staff members feel more comfortable with your child. Of course, they will continue to gather more information on their own so that they will get to know your child better.

- Keep a resource file to share with educators. This file might include names and phone numbers of helpful people and organizations, catalogs of adaptive materials, and copies of helpful articles.

- Cultivate a relationship of mutual respect with your child's teachers and therapists. Be accessible to teachers if they want to communicate with you about your child. Show your concern by periodically visiting the classroom or becoming involved in parent activities when possible. If your schedule permits, volunteer to grade papers or assist teachers in other ways. If you and your child's teachers learn to treat one another as equals, negotiations will go more smoothly when disagreements arise.

- Document formal and informal contacts with school personnel. If you jot a note to yourself about each meeting and what happened during the meeting, you will not have to rely on your memory when you have questions.

- Try to remain objective in meetings with your child's teachers and administrators. Listen carefully to what others have to say and consider their point of view. While you

MARIA GONZALEZ
Fact Sheet

Name: Maria Teresa Gonzalez
Birth Date: October 2, 1989

Mother: Lydia Gonzalez
office phone number: 555–7404

Father: Richard Gonzalez
office phone number: 555–0229

Home Phone: 555–2742

Siblings:
Catherine, 14 years
Stephen, 8 years

Visual Impairment:
Cataracts
Secondary Glaucoma

   Maria was born with cataracts (this is sometimes called "congenital cata-racts" because it was present at birth). She had surgery to remove the cata-racts when she was less than a year old. The surgery was successful, but because they removed the lens of her eye she wears glasses to replace the lens.

   Maria has developed glaucoma as a secondary result of her congenital cataracts but she takes special eye drops, so her glaucoma is controlled at this time.

   Maria's visual acuity with her glasses on has been measured as 20/200. She does not appear to have difficulty seeing things which are near to her.

Additional Disabilities:
   Maria has no additional disabilities.

Concerns:
   Maria should be able to participate in all activites along with other chil-dren. She must wear her glasses at all times. We are beginning to look into the possibility of contact lenses for Maria.

   We are most concerned about the secondary condition of glaucoma. As Maria continues to grow, we will have to watch her carefully to make sure that her medication is correct. Please notify us immediately if she begins to complain about headaches, becomes nauseated, or complains of feeling sick to her stomach. If you notice any other behaviors which would indicate that she isn't seeing as well as usual (such as rubbing her eyes, squinting, watery eyes) please let us know as soon as possible.

Strengths:
   Maria is a curious child. She makes friends easily and enjoys exploring new places and activites. She will let you know if she has difficulty seeing something.

may not change your mind, you will at least come to a better understanding of the views of the other people on your child's educational team.

- Try to learn the meaning of common educational terminology to facilitate communication with school personnel. Whenever a teacher or therapist uses unfamiliar jargon, ask for clarification.

- Know your rights and the rights of your child. Find out about the laws, regulations, and school policies that affect her. Chapter 9 provides an overview of the most important federal laws you should know about. If you know what you and your child are entitled to, you will feel confident in asserting your rights and in requesting appropriate educational assistance.

- Find out about advocates and organizations that can assist your efforts in the educational process. A list of national organizations can be found in the back of this book. Some of these organizations publish newsletters that keep parents abreast of new and pending federal legislation and other issues relevant to parents. Local organizations may be able to help you more directly. For example, they may be able to refer you to people (lay advocates, parents, lawyers) in your area who can give you advice or help you advocate for something. On a smaller scale, you may simply want to find an experienced parent who will help you talk to your child's teachers, or go with you to IEP meetings to lend moral support. Ask your doctor about support groups for parents of children who have visual impairments, or whether he or she knows of other families that you might contact. You can also call your state residential school, state department of education, state department of human services, state health department, or state rehabilitation agency for the blind.

Remember, although the school professionals who work with your child have good intentions, *you* will remain the best advocate for your child. School personnel will come and go, but you will be the constant in your child's life; you will be *the* expert on her strengths and needs. It will be great if others help you advocate, but even so, it will always be important for you to directly oversee your child's education. Keep in mind that the more you know, the less frightening the process will be. Compile and store information in your memory banks and a kitchen drawer for the time that you will need it. If you forget or don't know a crucial piece of information, don't be shy—ask for help . . . from an advocacy group . . . a fellow parent . . . your spouse . . . a neighbor . . . or an interested friend. Don't try to take the world on alone; there's usually help if you look for it.

Conclusion

For most parents, early intervention and special education are uncharted territories at first. The terminology, assessment and eligibility procedures, special services, classroom settings, even the subjects taught all seem very different from what they encountered during their own school years. Over time, however, most parents come to see that there are very good reasons for these differences. Good early intervention and special education programs give many children with visual impairments the best shot at mastering the knowledge and skills they need to become productive members of their community.

As you become more familiar with the worlds of early intervention and special education, you will begin to see how all the parts fit together. You will begin to see the importance of setting appropriate goals for your child's IFSP or IEP. You will also begin to see which professionals can help your child and how. And perhaps most importantly, you will begin to see how you can work with these professionals to ensure that your child makes the optimum progress. It might seem like a tall order at first, but if you take things a step at a time, you can learn to use the special education system to your child's best advantage.

Parent Statements

It's great when the special education system works.

◄○►

I've learned that when someone (a doctor or teacher) uses an acronym I don't understand I just ask what it means. I don't even hesitate.

◄○►

We really couldn't have made it without Laura, our early intervention case manager. Not only did she answer our questions, she anticipated most of our needs.

—◄o►—

Our first meeting with the early intervention team was a nightmare. I feel like I had to prove that I was a good parent. I don't think it has to be that way.

—◄o►—

It seems as if our son is constantly being tested. I know they have to know where he stands so they will know what to work on, but sometimes it seems as if they do more testing than teaching.

—◄o►—

Sometimes I feel outnumbered by all of the special education experts with long titles.

—◄o►—

In our county, the early intervention team comes to your house. I hate having to tidy up all the time so they won't think I'm a bad housekeeper. But I think it's good that they can see our son in his natural environment and make suggestions about adapting our household to his needs. They also show us fresh ways to play with his toys.

—◄o►—

We've gotten support from the School for the Blind all along. Even though my child is not going to school there, they still have time to answer questions and even sent some people to help my child's teachers out when everything was new to them.

—◄o►—

In some IEP meetings, teachers seem to think my comments are unimportant.

—◄o►—

I'm just afraid that Sara will be made fun of by the other kids in the regular third grade class.

—<o>—

Our school district does not have a vision specialist. The special education supervisor says that Caitlin will go to the resource room, but I know that teacher doesn't know braille. I'm afraid Caitlin will fall through the cracks.

—<o>—

I get real confused in special education meetings. I hate having to sign all those forms that I do not understand.

—<o>—

The special education teacher doesn't know as much about blindness as I do.

—<o>—

I've discovered that how much our daughter learns is directly related to the quality of the professionals who are teaching her. Some of them are so much more knowledgeable and skilled at getting and keeping our daughter's interest in the task at hand. Others of them seem kind of burnt out or apathetic.

—<o>—

I think Sue Ellen has learned so much more by being around other kids from the neighborhood than she would have in a special class.

Chapter Nine

◄○►

Legal Issues

Kathy Balkman, M.Ed., and Tom E.C. Smith, Ed.D.*

In the past, people with visual impairments or other disabilities were often left out of the mainstream of daily life. Children were sent to special schools or classrooms for students with disabilities, or to no schools at all. There were no braille labels on elevator buttons, no braille labels for building room numbers. Consequently, people with disabilities were frequently told, "I'm sorry; you can't participate" or "We'll tell you when you get to the floor you want." But, of course, these traditional ways of dealing with people's disabilities didn't allow for independence *or* for civil rights. Parents, people with disabilities themselves, educators, and other strong advocates worked diligently to change this form of discrimination through legislation. Because of their efforts, the world will be very different for your child than it was for children a generation ago.

It is important for you to have current information and an understanding about the major laws that provide basic rights, protec-

---

* Kathy Balkman is currently Special Education Director of Greenwood Public Schools in Greenwood, Arkansas. She has had many years of experience working directly with parents and children with disabilities and has a long-term interest in the needs of children with visual impairments.

  Tom Smith is a professor of Special Education at The University of Arkansas at Little Rock, where he coordinates the graduate program in severe and profound disabilities. He has written many books and articles related to the special needs of children with disabilities and their parents. He has recently co-authored the special education textbook, *Teaching Children with Special Needs in Inclusive Settings*.

tions, and benefits for you and your child. Unless you know about these laws, you cannot ensure that your child is receiving all the services and benefits that he needs and is entitled to. This chapter covers information about these laws and offers guidance in using them. It also provides information on other legal issues such as taxes, governmental assistance programs, and becoming an advocate for your child.

In reading through this chapter, remember that each state has its own interpretation and guidelines for implementing federal laws. Check with your own State Department of Education to find out the guidelines for your state's early intervention and special education programs. An attorney or other professional specializing in this area can also give you more detailed information on a variety of disability laws.

It is also important to remember that federal laws must be reauthorized from time to time. It is entirely possible that Congress may weaken or do away with some of the important disability laws described in this chapter. To keep informed about any proposed changes to the law, you may want to subscribe to a parent advocacy newsletter such as the *Pacesetter*, which is listed in the Reading List.

Education Laws

The Individuals with Disabilities Education Act (IDEA)

The Individuals with Disabilities Education Act (IDEA, Public Law 101–467) is perhaps *the* most important law for you to know about now. This law, which was formerly known as The Education of All Handicapped Children Act of 1975 or Public Law 94–142, guarantees all children with disabilities the right to a free and appropriate education provided at public expense. This section explains the most important provisions of this vital law.

Coverage. The IDEA applies to all children who have a disability that has an adverse effect on their education—that is, a condition that interferes with their ability to learn. Children with qualifying disabilities are covered by Part H of the IDEA from birth through age 2, and by Part B of the IDEA from age 3 through 18 (or through 21, if the state provides a public education for students without disabilities through that age). To determine if your child qualifies for special education services, he will be evaluated by a team of professionals, including an eye care specialist (an ophthalmologist or optometrist) and a vision specialist. Depending on your child's needs, a school psychologist and one or more therapists may also be involved. These professionals will determine whether your child meets your state's "cut-off" for visual acuity or visual field to qualify for special education on the basis of a visual impairment. These "cut-off" measurements vary from state to state. Some states provide services to children with an acuity of 20/70 with best correction. Some states require a visual acuity of 20/200 or worse with best correction. Most states will consider a child as eligible for special services even if his visual acuity does not meet a "cut-off" if his vision is expected to get worse over time.

Generally, your child will be eligible for special education services if: 1) his loss of vision has or can be expected to have an adverse effect on his educational performance; and/or 2) educational goals need to be set to enable your child to compensate for his visual impairment.

If your child has additional disabilities besides a visual impairment, the professionals on the evaluation team will determine to what extent these disabilities affect your child's development and ability to learn. For example, if your child has cerebral palsy, physical and occupational therapists will determine whether he needs special exercises or equipment to help him master the fine and gross motor skills needed in the classroom. Or if your child has mental retardation, it will be important to determine the degree of cognitive impairment so teachers will know what instructional materials and strategies might work best with your child.

Free and Appropriate Education. By law, all students who qualify for coverage under the IDEA must receive a free and appropriate public education. The "free" part of this phrase means exactly what it sounds like. Your child has the right to receive an education at public expense, without any cost to you. "Appropriate" means that he must receive an education that meets his unique learning needs. He cannot simply receive the same education as other children his age, or even other children with visual impairments his age. He must receive specially designed instruction tailored to *his* individual learning needs. He must also receive all needed *related services*—developmental, corrective, and supportive services necessary for your child to benefit from his education pro-

gram. Specialized transportation, physical therapy, occupational therapy, and orientation and mobility instruction are examples of related services that might be scheduled for your child. All related services must be provided by trained and qualified personnel.

It is important to recognize that "appropriate" does not necessarily mean "best." Sometimes there may be many different devices, systems, curricula, or programs that *could* meet your child's educational needs. Your child's school or early intervention program is not required to choose the method that you think would be best, so long as the one they choose is appropriate for his needs.

Least Restrictive Environment. Under the IDEA, students must receive their special education services in the least restrictive environment (LRE). The least restrictive environment is the setting that allows your child the most opportunities to work and play with students who do not have disabilities *and* to receive the special education services he needs. As Chapter 8 explains, there are a wide variety of settings that might be considered the least restrictive environment, depending on your child's needs. For some children with visual impairments, the LRE might be a regular classroom where none of the other students have disabilities; for others, it might be a residential school for the blind; for still others, it might be something between these two extremes.

Individualized Education Program/Individualized Family Service Plan. For your child's educational program to be appropriate, it must be individualized to his strengths and needs. To ensure that a child's program is individualized, the IDEA requires that a written plan be developed, outlining exactly how that child's unique needs will be met. For children aged three and older, that plan is called the Individualized Education Program (IEP). For children aged two and younger, the plan is called an Individualized Family Service Plan (IFSP).

There are six areas that the IEP is required to address:

1. A description of your child's level of performance, or what your child is currently able to do. This will include a description of skills in all developmental areas.
2. The annual goals and short-term objectives for your child. See Chapter 8 for examples of goals and objectives.
3. The specific special education services that will be provided to your child. These might include Orientation and Mobility services and direct instruction from a vision specialist.
4. The date these special education services are expected to begin and a projected date when they will conclude.
5. The method(s) that will be used to determine whether goals are being achieved. For example, progress might be monitored using standardized tests, teacher-made tests, and classroom observations.
6. The ways in which your child will participate in regular school programs and activities.

The required elements for an IFSP are basically the same. One major difference, however, is that the IFSP does not just list services intended to benefit the child with a visual impairment. The IFSP must focus on the entire family's needs, and therefore must also list services that will be provided to help parents and siblings. For example, a goal on the IFSP might be for the parents to learn braille either through correspondence courses, a class, or independent work with a teacher. Or the IFSP might specify that brothers or sisters will be involved in a sibling support group to help them with coping skills. In addition, the IFSP must indicate who your child's service coordinator (case manager) will be.

Your child's IEP or IFSP will generally be developed in joint meetings between you, the teachers, and other school or program representatives. At the meetings, you will work together to iden-

tify your child's needs and to determine what goals and services are appropriate. The IEP must be written and agreed upon before special education services begin, and must be reviewed at least annually to make sure that it continues to meet your child's needs. The IFSP must be reviewed every six months. You, as a parent, have the right to request a meeting to review or reconsider your child's IEP or IFSP at any time.

It is extremely important for you to take part in the IEP/IFSP process. You will recognize needs of your child that the professionals may not see. For example, when your child is young you will probably have a much better idea of the difficulties he is having with dressing or feeding, and you may have some very good suggestions for activities that are reinforcing for your child. Your role is to make sure these unique needs are identified and included in the IEP or IFSP.

When you first begin attending planning meetings, you may feel reticent about speaking up about your child's needs and how you would like to see them met. Eventually you will learn, however, that teachers and professionals really do value your input. This is especially true if you do your homework before you come to a meeting and show that you have put some thought into your child's IEP/IFSP.

To prepare for an IEP or IFSP meeting, first gather as much information about the educational programs available in your community and state as you can. This will enable you to go into meetings with knowledge and opinions of what might be best for your child. Observe classes in a variety of programs, such as public schools, state schools, and residential schools. Talk with administrators and officials in your school system and other community agencies about the programs and support systems available. Parent groups and other organizations can help by putting you in touch with other parents who may already know a great deal about the pros and cons of different programs. The Resource Guide lists organizations that may be able to help.

Second, put together a file that includes all evaluations and any educational and medical reports and records that pertain to your child. This should include copies of letters that you write as well as those you receive, teacher's notes, and records of telephone calls. Keep this file updated with any new information, such as the current IFSP or IEP. This will help you remember the events, issues, and solutions that occur throughout your child's education. It will also provide you with a record of who said what, which can be helpful if you ever become involved in a due process hearing or other litigation.

Third, decide before the meeting what goals and services you feel are necessary for your child and in what setting you think he should receive them. If you are unsure about appropriate goals, feel free to consult with other parents or professionals who are familiar with your child's strengths and needs.

Write down questions and concerns that you would like to have addressed during the meeting. Then, during the meeting, be sure to take notes, including the answers to your specific questions. Also be sure to ask for clarification of any unfamiliar terms or puzzling comments that come up during the meeting.

Fourth, consider asking others to attend the IEP/IFSP meeting with you. You might ask a friend to come along for moral support or to help you remember everything you want to say. Or you might ask a doctor or private therapist to give their professional advice about your child's need for a particular service. Then again, you might ask an advocate or attorney to attend if you think you will have trouble persuading the school or program staff to see things your way. Finally, it is quite likely that you will want your child to attend meetings as he grows older. As time goes by, you can encourage him to take more and more responsibility for his education by including him in the development of his IEP and the placement decision.

You can think of your child's IFSP or IEP as a roadmap or guide to make sure your child receives necessary services. There is no guarantee, however, that the goals on the IFSP or IEP will be accomplished. It will take hard work and energy from you, from your child, and from the educators who work with him for him to progress toward the goals set in his IFSP or IEP.

Procedural Safeguards. The requirement that every child in special education have a written IEP is one of the ways that the IDEA protects the right of children with disabilities to a free, appropriate education. The IDEA also includes a number of other *procedural safeguards*—or rules that are aimed at upholding the rights of you and your child. Under the IDEA, every state must abide by these safeguards if they want the federal government to provide them with money to finance special education programs and services (and every state does). Table 1 summarizes nine of the procedural safeguards most important for you to know about.

Resolving Disputes. Despite the safeguards outlined above, disputes sometimes arise between parents and the school or early intervention personnel working with their child. Here are some examples of possible disputes:

- Parents feel that their child needs weekly instruction in orientation and mobility skills, while the school thinks one O&M lesson per month is sufficient.
- The school system thinks a child would be best served in a class solely for children with visual impairments, while his parents think he would make better progress if he received most of his instruction in a regular classroom.
- Parents feel that their child requires a fulltime paraprofessional to work solely with their child in the classroom, but the school feels that this is not necessary.
- Parents want their child to learn braille, while the school wants to provide only large print materials.

If possible, it is best to work through any disagreements informally, during the IEP or IFSP process. Although the IDEA includes formal dispute resolution procedures, it is usually easier, quicker, and less expensive to settle disagreements through informal discussions.

A good first step in trying to resolve a dispute is simply to try to be persuasive and tactful in explaining why you disagree. If this tactic does not work, you might talk with school administrators about your concerns. For instance, if you have a disagreement with a teacher, talk to that teacher's supervisor first, then consult with the principal if you are still dissatisfied. Ask other parents who have worked successfully with the school for advice. You can also

TABLE 1
MAJOR PROCEDURAL SAFEGUARDS UNDER IDEA

1. *NOTICE*—You must be given written notice when the school district begins, changes, or stops the special education and related services for your child, including the schedule or the location of services.

2. *CONSENT*—You must give give written permission or consent for the school district to: 1) initially evalute your child to determine if he is eligible for special services; 2) initially place your child in a special education program; 3) release any confidential or personnally indentifiable information to anyone not authorized by law to be able to review it.

3. *CONFIDENTIALITY OF RECORDS*—You can have access to review any records the school district keeps on your child. Specific school personnel who are working with your child can review these records. Your written consent, though, is necessary to release the information to others who are not authorized by law.

4. *PROTECTION IN EVALUATION PROCEDURES*—Your child must be given a variety of tests or a multidisciplinary evaluation by qualified personnel, both during the initial eligibility evaluation and during later evaluations, to gather information needed to develop an IEP/IFSP. This is to ensure that the educational programming decisions for your child are made on the most current, accurate, and complete information available. The tests used must not discriminate in terms of race or culture. Testing must also be arranged so that the results are not affected by your child's disability.

5. *INDEPENDENT EDUCATIONAL EVALUATION*—You have the right to have an evaluation of your child done by persons of your choice. If you disagree with the results of the school district's evaluation, you may ask the school district to conduct another evaluation using professionals not employed by the school system. You might want to seek an independent evaluation, for example, if the school district refuses to provide special education services because they did not find that your child's visual impairment has an adverse effect on his educational performance. Or you might seek another evaluation if the school is willing to provide services for problems related to your child's mental retardation, but not for problems related to his visual impairment. Sometimes the school district may be obligated to pay for this evaluation, but only if you request it from the school district itself. If you go out on your **(own and personally put together an evaluation team, then you will have to pay for it.)**

6. *INDIVIDUALIZED EDUCATION PROGRAM (IEP)*—This is a written plan that describes the special education and related services that will be given to your child. This plan is based on the needs of your child identified in his evaluation and the goals and objectives that are designed to meet those needs.

7. **SURROGATE PARENT**—If a child is a ward of the state or the parents cannot be located or identified, the school district must appoint a surrogate parent to protect the child's rights. This surrogate parent must receive training so that he or she can make appropriate educactional decisions for the child.

8. **MAINTENANCE OF PLACEMENT**—During any dispute between you and the school district regarding evaluation, programming, placement, or services, your child has the right to remain in the setting or program he was in when the dispute arose. This is called "stay put." Your child has the right to remain in this setting until the dispute is resolved.

9. **ATTORNEY FEES**—If you "substantially prevail" (win your case) in any hearing or lawsuit regarding a special education issue for your child and you are represented by an attorney, you may be able to recover your attorney fees from the school district.

ask the school for *mediation services*—discussions before one or more neutral individuals aimed at resolving the dispute without going to a due process hearing. Many states actually require mediation efforts before a due process hearing can occur. In fact, studies have shown that mediation is successful more often than not.

If you cannot resolve the disagreement informally, the IDEA gives you the right to request a *due process hearing*. A due process hearing may be requested by a parent, surrogate parent, or a child, if he is at least eighteen but younger than twenty-two. School or early intervention personnel may also request a due process hearing.

You may ask for a due process hearing because of a disagreement about any aspect of your child's educational program. Possible reasons for requesting a hearing include:

1. you disagree with the results of the evaluation of your child;
2. you disagree with a proposed IEP;
3. you disagree that your child should stop receiving special education services;
4. you disagree with the proposed placement for your child, or believe it is not in the least restrictive environment;
5. you object to a proposed change of placement;
6. you refuse to consent to a requested evaluation of your child;
7. you refuse to give consent for initial placement.

To request a due process hearing, you must first write a letter to the school administrator in charge of the special education program or to the coordinator of early intervention services at the agency responsible for administering those services. In your letter, you should explain the nature of the dispute, as well as how you would like to see it resolved.

You should then be granted a due process hearing conducted by an "impartial hearing officer." This hearing officer will be knowledgeable about special education and special education laws, and have training in how to conduct a due process hearing. At the hearing, you will have an opportunity to explain your disagreement or complaint. You should come prepared to present facts, testimony, expert evaluations, and other information to show why the school's decision is wrong and will not provide a free and appropriate public education to your child in the least restrictive environment. You may be represented by an attorney or advocate, if you wish.

The hearing officer will consider all the evidence presented by you and the school and make an impartial decision. If either you or the school does not agree with the decision, an appeal may be made to state or federal court. At this stage of appeal, you should present expert evidence to support your position and hire an attorney to represent you. The court will then determine whether the decision made at the district level was proper for your child.

During the due process hearing and any appeals, the IDEA requires that your child stay in his present educational placement. This is known as the "stay put" provision. This is something to bear in mind if your very reason for requesting a due process hearing is to change your child's placement. On the other hand, if you like your child's current placement and are fighting the school's decision to change it, the provision can work in your favor. In any case, if you decide on your own to transfer your child to another school or program without the school district's approval, you will have to pay any costs involved unless you ultimately win the dispute.

After all the hearings are over, you may be able to be reimbursed for any attorney's fees. Under an amendment to the IDEA, parents can sometimes recover these fees if they were found in the hearing or lawsuit to have "substantially prevailed"—that is, that the school district or agency had to alter its behavior as a result of the parents taking action. The court, though, can limit or refuse the awarding of attorney's fees if parents reject a settlement offer from the school district or early intervention agency and then do not obtain a better outcome.

As mentioned earlier, a due process hearing can be time-consuming and emotionally draining, as well as expensive. Consequently, experts usually recommend that you request one only as a last resort. If other means of resolving a conflict fail, however, don't hesitate to assert your rights. Remember, your child's educational welfare is what is most important.

Family Educational Rights and Privacy Act (FERPA)

The Family Educational Rights and Privacy Act (FERPA) is a law that applies to all families with children. However, it has special significance for families who have a child with a disability. FERPA was passed to guarantee the confidentiality of personally identifiable information in educational records. ("Personally identifiable" means attaching something that would reveal who the child is, such as his name or his parents' name, to information—such as IQ scores or behavioral data—that should not be available to people who do not have a need to have it.) FERPA also guarantees that parents have access to their child's records. It is especially important for you to know about this law because of the many evaluations, reports, IFSP/IEP documents, and so forth that will be gathered and maintained throughout your child's school career.

Under FERPA, you have several rights regarding your child's educational records. They are:

- *The right to know your rights*—You have the right to be told your rights under FERPA.
- *The right to examine records*—You have the right to see the education records the school or early intervention program keeps on your child. You also have the right to see a list of all others who have seen your child's education records. The early intervention coordinator or school building administrator should be able to share that list with you.
- *The right to consent to release information*—You must give written consent before the school can release personally identifiable information to individuals who are usually not entitled to see it. For instance, you must give consent before a medical doctor, vocational rehabilitation counselor, or school consultant you have hired can see your child's records.
- You have the right to request that information you believe is incorrect or violates your child's privacy rights be cor-

rected or removed from the records. Usually, you would make this request to the special education supervisor or early intervention coordinator. If your request is rejected, you have the right to ask for a hearing where you can present your concerns.

Anti-Discrimination Laws

The Americans with Disabilities Act of 1990 (ADA)

The Americans with Disabilities Act of 1990 (ADA) is a sweeping piece of legislation that should open doors and provide opportunities for your child to participate equally in society. Some of its provisions will benefit your child from birth on; others will not become important until he reaches adulthood. Becoming familiar with the law now can help ensure that your child is an active participant in his community at all ages.

The ADA prohibits discrimination against people with disabilities in three major areas: public accommodations, public services, and employment. Here is how these provisions might help your child now and in the future:

Public Accommodations. The ADA requires that any place open to the public be accessible to people with disabilities unless this is not physically or financially feasible. Restaurants, motels, office buildings, parks, zoos, stores, libraries, movie theaters, day care centers, schools, stadiums, airports and bus terminals—anyplace where people without disabilities can go—are all affected by this part of the ADA. By law, these places must all make changes to their programs and facilities so that persons with disabilities can participate fully.

For individuals with visual impairments, this provision means that there should be many more braille and speech output materials available, making it possible for them to participate in community activities. Restaurants must have braille menus or be prepared to have staff read them aloud to patrons; state and local government services such as courthouses, post offices, and licensing offices will have easily available personal readers, cassette recordings, and braille materials. Amusement parks, too, will have braille markings, and museums and historical sites will have braille descriptions of exhibits, or perhaps tape recorded tours.

Under the ADA, it is also against the law for individuals with disabilities to only be offered opportunities to participate that are different and separate than the opportunities for individuals without disabilities. That is, your child cannot be relegated to a program, facility, or activity that is only for children with disabilities if he would rather be mainstreamed into a regular program. For example, a county recreation program could not stipulate that children with visual impairments could enroll in some activities, but not others. Or the skating rink could not require that children with visual impairments only skate at a certain time, when other children with visual impairments are skating. In rare cases, your child could still be excluded from participation if he was found to "pose a direct threat to the health and safety of others."

Public Services. The section of the ADA that addresses public services requires that architectural barriers found in local or state government buildings or facilities be removed to the "maximum extent feasible." New buildings and facilities must be constructed without barriers. This section also requires that buses, trains, and other transportation services be accessible to individuals with disabilities. In fact, it is a violation of the ADA for state and local governments to purchase vehicles or transportation equipment that is not accessible. Although the majority of these requirements are aimed at increased accessibility for people with physical disabilities, your child will also benefit. Transportation schedules should be available in braille, and elevators, room numbers, and restrooms will have braille markings.

Employment. All parents think and dream about what their child will be when he "grows up." In the past, parents of children with disabilities have had special concerns about their child's future because of the possibility that employers would discriminate against their child, regardless of his abilities. The ADA prohibits discrimination against a qualified worker on the basis of disability. Specifically, the law prohibits an employer from refusing to hire, train, or promote an employee just because he has a disability. In fact, an employer cannot even ask a prospective employee if he has a disability.

Employers must make modification within the workplace that will enable an otherwise qualified worker to perform the job—provided these modifications can be made without "undue cost." Examples of modifications an employer might be expected to make for a worker with visual impairments include providing magnifying mechanisms for a worker to use various types of machinery, providing a part-time driver if the job required limited travel, providing special lighting, or modifying the layout of furniture or equipment in an office. This section of the ADA applies to employers with fifteen or more employees.

What should you do if you think your child is being discriminated against and you believe that the ADA prohibits such discrimination? The first step is to try to resolve your complaint informally. Talk to the person in charge about what you think the problem is and how you would like to see it resolved. Perhaps they do not even know that they are violating the ADA and will be happy to work with you to mend their discriminatory practices.

If complaining informally does not work, your next step depends on the nature of your complaint. If you believe the school system is discriminating against your child, you should contact the ADA coordinator for the school. Under the ADA, all schools must develop procedures for families to file complaints about discrimination under the ADA. If you have a complaint against a state or local government agency or a private company or organization, you should contact the U.S. Department of Justice (U.S. Dept. of Justice, Civil Rights Division, Office on the ADA, P.O. Box 66118, Washington, DC 20035. 202–514–0301). If you have a complaint against an employer, you should contact the Equal Employment Opportunity Commission (EOC, 1801 L St., NW, Washington, DC 20507. 800–669–EEOC).

The Rehabilitation Act of 1973, Section 504

Before the Americans with Disabilities Act was passed in 1990, no federal law categorically prohibited discrimination against individuals with disabilities. The strongest anti-discrimination law was the Rehabilitation Act of 1973. Section 504 of this act prohibits discrimination against people with disabilities by programs and activities that receive federal funds.

Specifically, Section 504 states that "no otherwise qualified individual shall, solely by reason of his handicap, be excluded from the participation in, be denied benefits of, or be subjected to discrimination under any program or activity receiving Federal financial assistance." Section 504 also requires that reasonable modifications be made so that individuals with disabilities can participate in programs which receive any funding from the federal government.

Almost all schools or early intervention programs receive some funding from the government, so this is one place where you should definitely notice some effects of Section 504. To enable your child to fully participate in educational activities, there might be braille or large print materials and adapted toys and games (such as balls with a beeper or bell inside and board games with tactual markings and textures). The classroom environment should also be modified according to the orientation and mobility needs of your child. For example, there might be a space free from obstacles or items placed so they can be used as landmarks.

Another area where your child may see benefits from Section 504 is in parks and recreation facilities that receive federal funding. For example, children with visual impairments cannot be excluded from participating in classes or sporting events sponsored by a federally funded recreation program. Parks and the buildings on them must be physically accessible to children with visual impairments.

Section 504 will probably be most important to your child if his

visual impairment is not considered to be severe enough to qualify for special education services under the IDEA. This is because the definition of a "handicapped individual" is somewhat broader under Section 504 than it is under the IDEA. According to Section 504, a handicapped individual is anyone who has a physical or mental impairment that substantially limits one or more of that person's "major life activities" "caring for one's self, performing manual tasks, walking, seeing, hearing, speaking, breathing, learning, and working." So, even though your child's visual impairment may be above the "cut-off" measurement your school uses to determine who qualifies for IDEA assistance, he might still qualify for assistance under 504.

Children who qualify for educational assistance under Section 504 are entitled to receive a free appropriate education in the least restrictive environment. Schools are required to provide modifications to materials, the classroom, or instructional methods that will enable eligible students to receive an education "comparable" to the education that non-disabled students receive. Under Section 504, schools are not *required* to have a written plan describing adaptations that will be provided (similar to an IEP), but they can if they choose to. If you believe that your child might qualify for educational assistance under Section 504, you should ask to speak to the school system's 504 coordinator.

Government Benefits

A number of federal programs offer financial assistance for people with disabilities. Children with visual impairments may qualify for some or all of these programs, providing they meet eligibility requirements.

Supplemental Security Income (SSI)

Supplemental Security Income (SSI) is a program administered by the Social Security Administration. Its purpose is to provide cash benefits to children and adults with disabilities to "supplement" their family's income. As of 1995, the maximum monthly SSI payment was $458 for an individual and $687 for an eligible married couple.

To qualify for SSI, an individual must satisfy two requirements. First, his disability must be so severe that he cannot engage in "substantial gainful activity"—that is, he cannot work for a living. Because children do not generally work for a living anyway, the Social Security Administration considers whether their disability is as severe as one that would keep an adult from holding a job. The second requirement is that the individual's income and assets must fall below a certain level. When the applicant is a child under eighteen who lives at home, his family's income and assets are counted toward the limit. Currently, an individual cannot qualify for SSI if his assets exceed $2000. The rules for determining what assets do and do not count toward that limit are rather complicated, however.

To determine whether you and your child may meet the financial need requirements for SSI, visit your local Social Security office or call the national Social Security Administration information line at 1–800–772–1213. If the Social Security office determines that your child is financially eligible for SSI, you will be referred to an office called Disability Determination Services to determine whether your child's disability is considered severe enough for benefits. The application process usually takes several months. If your child is determined to be eligible, however, he will receive SSI payments from the day you began your application.

Medicaid

Medicaid is a government-sponsored health insurance program. It can be used to pay for medically related services such as physical therapy, speech therapy, occupational therapy, and some medical examinations and treatment. At present, orientation and mobility instruction is not covered, although that may change in the future.

Eligibility for Medicaid is based on income. Income guidelines vary from state to state, but children who are eligible for SSI are also often eligible for Medicaid. To apply for Medicaid, contact the Department of Human Services.

TEFRA

There is an alternative to Medicaid for families whose income is too high to qualify for Medicaid. Under a program called TEFRA (Tax Equity and Fiscal Responsibility Act of 1982), families in some states can qualify for medical assistance (MA) based on the severity of their child's disability. The family's income is *not* counted when determining eligibility for this assistance.

To be eligible for TEFRA assistance, a child must be under nineteen and require a certain level of home health care comparable to care that would be provided in a hospital, nursing home, or an intermediate care facility for persons with mental retardation. It is up to the State Medical Review Team to determine whether a child needs that level of care, based on information they receive about the child from doctors, hosptals, and schools.

Under the TEFRA option, all services medically necessary to care for your child at home are covered, up to your state's payment limits. These include therapy, prescription drugs, medical supplies and equipment, and private duty nursing.

This is an optional program for states; currently fewer than half of the states participate. Contact your Department of Human Services or local social service department for more information on this program.

Free Matter for the Blind

If your child is legally blind, he is entitled to send and receive certain materials through the mail postage free. Materials such as textbooks, educational materials, braille letters, talking books (books on tape from The Library for the Blind or other services) may be mailed without postage. These materials must have the words "free matter for the blind" stamped or handwritten on them. It is important to remember that these materials must be for the use of someone who is legally blind, not simply related to visual impairments in some way. For example, the service is not available for parent groups to mail newsletters to their members, but can be used for a grandmother to mail a braille letter to her grandchild who reads braille.

Conclusion

If we lived in a perfect world, you would not have to learn about disability law on top of all the other new information related to your child's special needs. No one would ever do anything that violated your child's rights, and he would automatically receive all the benefits he was entitled to without you having to lift a finger. Unfortunately, that is not how the world works. Although laws guarantee your child some very valuable rights and benefits, he will not necessarily receive them unless you make sure that he does. This does not mean that you need to become a lawyer or even an expert on disability laws. But you do need to be informed about your child's basic rights and keep abreast of any changes or challenges to them. Eventually, you, your child, and your family will all benefit immeasureably from this knowledge.

Parent Statements

Sometimes it seems as if things aren't the way they should be, but I don't know whether I should call a lawyer or not.

━◀○▶━

I hear people talking about "due process." I don't know what due process is.

━◀○▶━

Who gets to make the final decision about where Mike should be educated, us or the school? That's what I'd like to know.

━◀○▶━

Sometimes I go to meetings and I don't know whether to sign something or not. But everyone is sitting around waiting for me and I feel so much pressure.

━◀○▶━

I just don't believe them. The schools have *their* best interests at heart, not my child's.

━◀○▶━

The laws that we have now have made such a wonderful difference in Bennie's education. I can't imagine going through this 50 years ago.

━◀○▶━

I think that the law requires the school to do a lot more for my child than they are doing but I don't really know the best way to challenge them. I wish I knew more about what is really best for my child.

━◀○▶━

"Appropriate" is such a tricky word. The school can interpret it one way, and parents can interpret it another. The school gets to have the final say, though, unless you're prepared to challenge them.

━◀○▶━

I live in a small town and I've known the superintendent of schools since I was little. He lives right down the street from me. When I try to question anything the school is doing or not doing, I feel like I am destroying my relationship with the people who work at the school. Even more important, I'm afraid of the repercussions that would have for my son.

—◀◉▶—

I think that the school wants me to be there for the meetings, but really doesn't want to hear what I have to say.

—◀◉▶—

My husband and I both went to Jessie's IEP meeting. It wasn't easy because we both had to take off from work and we had to arrange for a babysitter for the kids, but it was worth it because we both heard the school's recommendations, and we were both able to have input.

—◀◉▶—

Once when I was a freshman in college, I helped a blind student find her way through the cafeteria line. We ate supper together and had a really lively, interesting conversation. I hate to admit it, but I didn't go on to make friends with her, and never even talked to her again. I guess this was mainly because I felt a little uncomfortable around her—didn't know where to look when I was talking to her, and so on. With today's laws encouraging community inclusion, kids without disabilities will hopefully grow up to have a much more enlightened attitude about kids with disabilities than I had.

—◀◉▶—

I find myself spending a lot of time thinking about what kinds of jobs my child might be able to do when he grows up. I know the ADA prevents job discrimination, but I still can't help worrying that he may have a tough time finding a decent job.

—◀◉▶—

I want my child to be in the "real world." I hope the Americans with Diasabilities Act will help us achieve that goal.

Chapter Ten

◄○►

Growing into Literacy

Alan J. Koenig, Ed.D.*

Literacy is highly valued in our society, so parents may be concerned about how their child with a visual impairment will learn to read and write. While the way in which children with visual impairments learn reading and writing will be much the same as for children with normal vision, there are differences that will need attention. You can provide a wealth of simple, valuable early literacy experiences in the home that will build the foundation for reading and writing for your child. With guidance and assistance from a teacher of students with visual impairments, the early home experiences you provide will help prepare your child to achieve literacy to the greatest extent of her ability.

Literacy is the ability to use written language—reading and writing—to accomplish a variety of important tasks in our daily lives. Early literacy, sometimes called "emergent" literacy, refers to children's early experiences with, and attempts at, reading and writing. During this stage, children develop an awareness that letters and words have meaning, and that we use them to communicate our ideas. The early literacy period lasts until a child enters a formal reading and writing program, generally in late kindergarten or first grade.

The foundation for literacy actually begins at birth. When an infant begins to understand that crying will get Mom or Dad to

---

* Alan Koenig is currently an Associate Professor in the college of Education at Texas Tech University. He taught children with visual impairments for several years in Iowa and Illinois. He has published articles, book chapters, and books about teaching reading to children who have visual impairments and is co-author of the book *Foundations of Braille Literacy*.

come into the room or that "go bye-bye" means a ride in the car, she is developing language skills that will be essential in learning to read and write. As a preschooler begins to master basic skills in understanding and producing oral language, she acquires the foundation needed for developing literacy.

Children demonstrate early literacy skills when they scribble a message and then "read" it back to someone or when they look at a book and tell the story from the pictures. Children also show early literacy skills when they recognize that the "golden arches" mean "a place to eat hamburgers" or that an outline picture of a man or woman on a door means a restroom. Children pick up these early literacy skills because they see print being used around them, and they learn to associate certain literacy events with meaningful things in their lives.

Children who have visual impairments also learn through association, but they must rely less or not at all on visually observing events in their environment. For example, a child with a visual impairment may associate the sound of the garage door opening with Mother coming home from work. Or she may pick up a book with a fuzzy patch on the front and associate it with her favorite story, *Pat the Bunny*. Because a child with a visual impairment cannot rely on her vision to imitate others, it is important to take more direct steps to assure that early literacy develops. This chapter will suggest some ways you can help your child gain important early reading and writing experiences. But first, to give you an idea of where your child is heading, the chapter discusses options for reading and writing for people with visual impairments.

Options for Reading and Writing

A visual impairment does not prevent literacy from developing, nor does it necessarily make it more difficult to learn to read and write. With appropriate intervention, children with visual impairments can arrive in a formal school program well prepared to learn to read and write. But a child with visual impairments may need to learn an alternative to reading and writing standard print, depending on her learning characteristics, abilities, and needs.

There are a variety of options for reading and writing, and one or more of them will be appropriate for your child. This section describes the various options; a later section explains how the choice among options will be made.

Print

Many children with visual im pairments read and write in print. But because a visual impairment may affect the resolution (or clarity) of printed words, the image must be enlarged so the child can read efficiently. There are a variety of ways to enlarge the visual image that the eye receives. One way is to actually make the print larger. When a book is enlarged, however, the pictures lose their color and become less interesting to children. Fortunately, books for young children are already in large print, so it is usually unnecessary to enlarge them even more.

If a child cannot read ordinary print in children's books, there are various ways of improving resolution. One way is simply getting closer to the book! For example, a child can essentially double the size of print by bringing a book from ten inches away to five inches. Despite common fears that reading at a close distance will harm a child's eyes, this is not true. Increasing the contrast, or sharpness of the words, may also help. Adjusting lighting or using acetate filters may help to increase the contrast. A vision specialist (a teacher who is specially trained to teach students with visual impairments) and your child's eye care specialist can advise you about the types of modifications that will be most helpful for your child.

Yet another option for reading print is to use a magnifying glass. A magnifying glass increases the size of letters and allows a child to read more easily. Generally, low vision devices such as magnifying glasses are not prescribed for very young children because they can use other simple modifications to explore books. Also, some children—such as children with restrictions in their peripheral vision (tunnel vision)—may not benefit from a magnifying device. This decision, however, must be made individually for each child. If your child needs a low vision device, an eye care specialist who has special training in low vision will help to choose the most helpful one.

There are a variety of ways to write print. Some children with visual impairments are able to use a regular pencil, but others use a black felt-tip pen to provide additional contrast. For many children just learning to write, a soft-lead artist's pencil works best, since it produces a very dark line, but can also be erased. Most children with visual impairments learn typing or keyboarding, usually earlier than children with normal vision.

Braille

Reading in Braille. Children who use their touch and hearing, rather than their vision, as their primary senses generally will learn to read braille. Braille is a system of reading and writing in which letters and words are formed by patterns of raised dots that are felt with the fingers. Children usually learn to read braille with the index fingers of both hands, although some people use all fingers except their thumbs.

Braille was invented by Louis Braille in the early 1800s when he was a student at a Paris school for children who were blind. Louis was intrigued by a system used in the military to read by touch at night. This system had twelve dots that were arranged in a grid that was two dots across and six dots down. Louis felt that twelve dots were too many, so he developed a six-dot "cell" with two across and three down. (See Figure 1.) He assigned different shapes to each of the letters. Louis's system of reading was used by the students at the school in Paris, but was not formally adopted or even called "braille" until after his death.

The braille code used in the United States today is based on the alphabet invented by Louis Braille. A "w" had to be added, however, since the French alphabet does not have this letter. Figure 2 presents the braille alphabet, numbers, and some punctuation marks, as well as a short poem.

In addition to having shapes for each letter of the alphabet, the braille system used in the U.S. also has a series of contractions. There are a number of ways contractions are made in braille. For example, one or more letters from a word can be used to stand for the whole word, when used in a sentence. Thus, in the braille version of "Twinkle, Twinkle, Little Star" in Figure 2, the letter "s" written by itself stands for the word "so," while the letters "ll" stand for "little" and "abv" stands for "above." Sometimes a special configuration stands for a word or part of a word. For example, Figure 1 shows the configuration that stands for

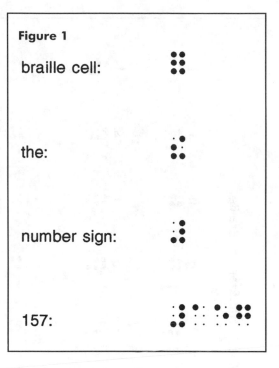

Figure 1

braille cell:

the:

number sign:

157:

the word "the" and can also be used as part of a word such as "then." Notice that there is a single lower dot in front of each word at the beginning of the lines and the word "I." This is called the "capital dot" and means that the next letter is capitalized. In braille there are no unique shapes for capital letters, as there are in print, so capitals are indicated with the capital dot.

As with capital letters, there are no unique shapes for numbers. Numbers are indicated with a "number sign," as shown in Figure 1. When the letters a through j have a number sign before them, they are the numbers 1, 2, 3, 4, 5, 6, 7, 8, 9, 0, as shown in Figure 2. For example, Figure 1 shows how 157 is written.

Altogether, there are 189 contractions in the braille code. When something is written using all possible contractions, it is called "grade 2" braille. If something is in "grade 1" braille, it means that no contractions are used. In the United States, grade 2 braille is almost always used. Children begin to use grade 2 braille in reading and writing instruction from the very beginning.

You might think that with all those contractions, learning to read in braille must be very difficult. But it really is no more diffi-

Figure 2
The Alphabet, Numbers, and "Twinkle, Twinkle, Little Star" in Braille

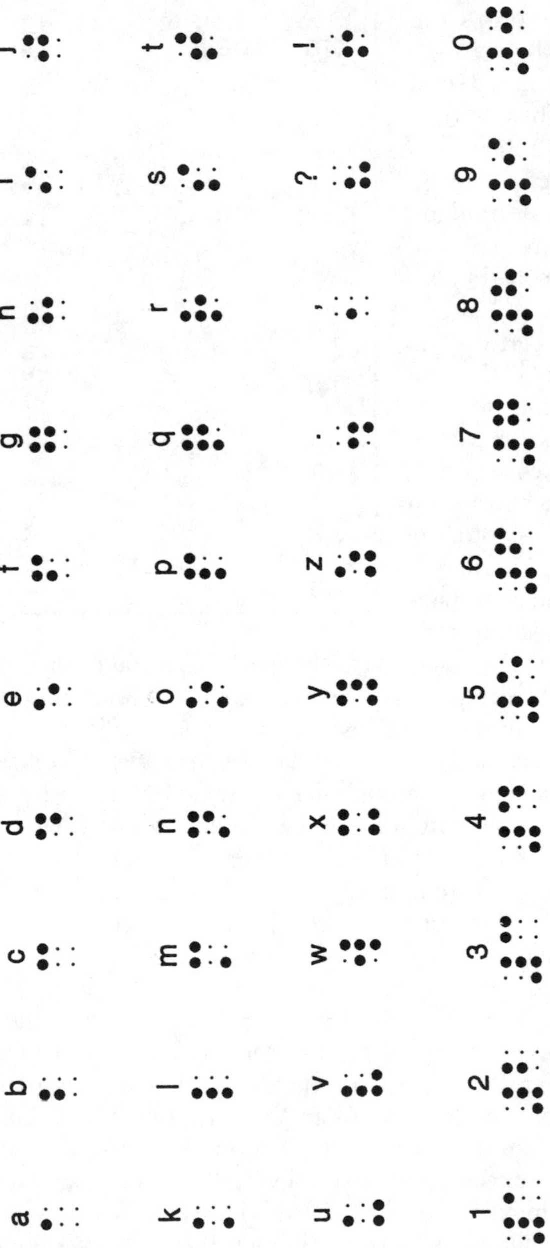

Twinkle, twinkle, little star,

How I wonder what you are!

Up above the world so high,

Like a diamond in the sky.

cult, or easy, than learning to read in print. True, some people claim that the braille code is more *complex* than the print code because more symbols are used. But if a child receives good reading instruction and has a rich variety of background experiences, learning to read braille should not be "difficult." If a child says that braille is difficult to read, it is probably because she has heard an adult say so. So it is very important to share positive experiences with young children as they begin to encounter braille reading, rather than focusing on its perceived complexities.

Using a Perkins Braillewriter.

Writing in Braille. When young children begin to write braille, they usually use a machine called a Perkins Braillewriter. This is a mechanical device somewhat like a typewriter, but it has only six basic keys—one for each of the dots in the braille cell. To write the word "little" (which is "ll" in braille), all of the keys for the left hand are depressed twice, once for the first "l" and once for the second "l." To write the letter "a," just one key is pushed. The brailler also has a space key, a back-space key, and a line-advance key.

Another way to write braille is with a slate and stylus. The slate is a template of several rows of braille cells, and the stylus is a device with a blunt metal tip that is used to punch each dot individually. The slate and stylus is a portable way to write braille and is very handy for tasks such as jotting lists, taking notes in class, and writing down addresses and phone numbers.

Usually children master the use of the braillewriter before learning to use a slate and stylus. Learning the slate and stylus usually occurs sometime in the late primary grades or early in junior high school, but when your child learns will be a decision made by the team working with your child in school—including you.

Typing is another very important skill for children who read and write in braille. Since it allows them to communicate directly with people who read print, it is very helpful in school and later for employment. Typing is a rather easy skill for a child to learn when good instruction is provided. This skill is generally introduced after a child has learned to write with a brailler,

Using a slate and stylus.

usually around third or fourth grade. With so many computers now in schools, however, some children learn "keyboarding" even earlier than third grade. When to introduce typing or keyboarding is another important decision that will be made by the educational team working with your child.

How Can Parents Learn Braille? If your child will be learning to read and write in braille, you probably will want to learn braille yourself. As your child goes through school, this will allow you to assist with homework, as well as write messages and letters to her. Also, as your child comes to realize that you value and respect braille as a way to read and write, she will develop this same value and respect.

Table 1 outlines some good programs that can help you learn braille. *Just Enough to Know Better* is perhaps one of the best, because it was designed especially for parents. This guide introduces the alphabet, punctuation marks, some special symbols such as italics, and all of the contractions. Other programs are valuable as well, although they are generally geared to future teachers or braille transcribers, and therefore go into extensive detail about the rules governing use of various braille contractions. Whichever program you use, your child's teacher should be able to give you valuable help.

Listening

For children with visual impairments, listening is a very important way of gathering information from the environment. Your child will learn to rely more on her listening skills than children who have normal vision. It is a myth, however, that children with

Table 1
Instructional Materials on Braille for Adults

TITLE AND SOURCE	DESCRIPTION
Just Enough to Know Better The National Braille Press 88 Saint Stephen St. Boston, MA 02115	This friendly book was written specifically for parents to introduce the Grade 2 braille code. It is written in both print and braille and contains a handy guide to all the braille contractions. It even has flash cards to help you practice!
New Programmed Instruction in Braille, Second Edition SCALARS Publishing P.O. Box 158123 Nashville, TN 37215	This book uses programmed learning to introduce small sections of the grade 2 braille code and allows ample practice before going on. It is written in print and facsimile braille. It covers all letters, contractions, and rules. A supplementary book provides reading practice in real braille.
Instruction Manual for Learning to Read Braille by Sight American Printing House for the Blind P.O. Box 6085 Louisville, KY 40206–0085	This is a thorough instructional series that will introduce all the letters and contractions in the braille code, as well as all of the rules. It is printed in both print and braille, and has practice exercises and answer keys.
Instruction for Braille Transcribing American Printing House for the Blind P.O. Box 6085 Louisville, KY 40206–0085 Library of Congress 1291 Taylor St., NW Washington, DC 20542	This instructional manual was written for individuals who wish to become braille transcribers. It introduces all letters and contractions in grade 2 braille and the rules that govern them. It also contains information on basic format techniques for braille materials. The manual can be purchased through APH. Or if you want to become a certified braille transcriber, you can take a free correspondence course from the Library of Congress/National Library Service for the Blind and Physically Handicapped.

visual impairments have "better" hearing. It is more accurate to say that they learn "more efficient use" of hearing.

During the preschool years, your child will learn to associate different sounds with certain activities. For example, she will learn that the refrigerator door opening may mean it is time for a snack! Likewise, most of the information she receives while watching television will be through listening to conversation and sound effects.

When your child enters school, listening will become critical to her progress. She will need to listen for and remember things that other children can readily see, such as assignments or other information written on the chalkboard. Later in elementary school or junior high, your child will learn to "read" books that have been recorded on cassette tapes by listening to them. This is called "aural reading" and will be very important when your child is in high school and college. Many textbooks are not available in braille at the high school level, and almost none are available in college. All books, on the other hand, can be received on cassette tapes through a nonprofit organization called Recording for the Blind & Dyslexic (RFB&D). (See the Resource Guide for the Address.) As your child enters high school, she will need to learn to order books from RFB&D.

Although listening will be extremely important for your child, it is not a substitute for learning to read and write in print or braille. Listening will be a valuable *supplement* to reading, but will not replace it. Your child will need to learn to use both reading and listening, and then later decide when it would be best to use one or the other for completing certain tasks. For example, if your child is working on a report and needs to read several books in a short amount of time, it may be more efficient to use books on tape rather than to read all the books. If, however, she is making a list of friends to invite to her birthday party, she will probably choose to use braille or print to compile her list.

Computers and Other Technology

Computers and other technological devices will also be valuable supplements to your child's primary reading and writing medium. These devices can enable your child to compete more equitably in the classroom with peers who have normal vision.

There are many different ways for children with visual impairments to use computers. One of the most important ways is

through word processing programs. A word processing program allows you to write documents, revise them, and then print out a final product. There are word processors that can provide large print on the screen, braille on a special display, or speech sounds through a synthesizer.

Because there are so many useful computerized devices, most children today learn to type on a computer keyboard rather than on a typewriter. However, it is still important to know how to use a typewriter for some tasks. For example, it may be easier to address envelopes with a typewriter than with a computer system. Also, technology may break down sometimes or a computer may not be available, so there may be a need to have an alternative, such as a typewriter, for writing print documents.

Here are some ways technology may be useful to your child:

- A closed-circuit television (CCTV) operates like a small television station. The student moves a regular print book on a moving table under the camera, and the CCTV presents enlarged print on the monitor.
- Some devices, such as the Kurzweil Reading Machine, convert printed words to spoken words. The speech is "synthesized" by a computer, so it sounds somewhat like a robot.
- There are a number of programs that enlarge print on a computer screen or convert words on a computer screen into synthesized speech.
- There are some devices that can be attached to a computer and allow the user to have a braille display of what is on the computer screen.
- Portable braille note-taking devices allow individuals to braille information into the device and retrieve it later.

The devices can be hooked up either to a computer or directly to a printer.

- One type of device allows a child to braille on a Perkins Brailler in contracted braille, then produce a print copy for the teacher via an attached inkprint printer.

New devices are being developed so quickly that there is currently a technology explosion. Since any list printed in this book would soon be outdated, the best source of information on available technology will be your child's teacher. He or she will discuss the various options with you and help you decide which might be best for your child.

Technology for children with visual impairments ranges in price from a few hundred dollars to over a thousand dollars. If the educational team agrees that certain technology is needed and this is placed in the IEP, the school district is responsible for providing the recommended technology, for use at school, at no cost to the parents. Technology used in the home often becomes the financial responsibility of the parents. Sometimes state social services can help families with the purchase of technology for home use, although this varies widely among the states. Another source to explore may be local community service clubs, such as the Lions or Kiwanis.

While technology will likely be a valuable tool for your child in school and in adult life, it still will not replace reading and writing in print or braille.

Building the Foundation for Literacy

Now that you have an idea where your child is heading, you can begin to think about ways to help her get there. In other words, what can you do to help foster her literacy?

We know through research that the essential building blocks for literacy come from early experiences and exposure to reading and writing activities in the home. So parents play an important role in preparing their child for the type of literacy that is taught in school programs. As the parent of a child with visual impairments, you may have to be somewhat more aware of your role in readying your child to read and write. But in general, your child will pick up literacy skills in much the same way as any other child. Early home activities that will help prepare your child to read and write include actively engaging her in first-hand experiences, exposing her to literacy activities in the home and community, reading to her, and encouraging her early explorations in reading and writing.

Providing Experiences

The foundation for literacy—as for all learning—comes from first-hand, common experiences, such as going to a friend's birthday party, helping to clean out the garage, and riding a tricycle. It is through these early experiences that your child will be able to bring meaning to a story or a book. If your child has experienced first-hand the activity or event portrayed in a story, then she will be able to understand the story as it is being read. The meaning of a story doesn't come from the print or braille itself, but from your child's previous experiences.

To understand the importance of early experiences, you might think of words as capsules that are stored in your child's brain. If your child can say a word but does not have any actual experience to back it up, the capsule will be nearly empty. For example, your child may be able to say the word "sheep" because she has heard you talk about sheep on the farm, has heard a story about sheep on *Sesame Street*, or has heard the "baa" from a "See and Say" toy. All of these things provide a little bit of information, so there is a little bit in your child's "sheep" capsule. However, the capsule is not filled until you child has had an actual, first-hand experience with a sheep, ideally on a real farm. If your child has an opportunity to pet a real sheep, smell a sheep in its natural habitat, hear a live sheep "baa," and so forth, then the "sheep" capsule will be adequately filled.

If your child has low vision, her use of vision will provide some information for the capsule as well. But again, the actual experience is needed to fill the capsule with rich and accurate meaning. In some cases, visual information from pictures in a book or on television will be incomplete or, perhaps, inaccurate. Pairing visual images with information from other senses is accomplished through first-hand experiences. While pictures or TV shows can provide some information, it is nothing like the real thing!

In providing experiences for your child, try to concentrate on common occurrences in the home and the community. To be useful and valuable to your child, an experience does not have to be a major family undertaking such as a five-day cruise on an ocean liner. While this would be a wonderful experience for any child, it is not necessary for developing an essential base of early experiences. (Taking a ride in a paddle boat or row boat would be more valuable as a basic experience!)

When your child has an opportunity to actively experience things in the world around her, meaningful language will develop. This can occur when your child associates what she is experiencing with a word that already exists but which she has not experienced before. For example, your child may say "boat" without ever riding in a boat. But after you ride in a boat, she will have a real experience to make the word "boat" meaningful. Or it can occur when you provide a new label as part of a new experience. For example, your child may not know the word "silo." But as part of a trip to the farm, she is able to explore outside of the silo, crawl up the ladder, and play around in the grain inside the silo. As part of this experience, she is told that this thing is a "silo." So your child not only adds a new word to her vocabulary, but also has the background experiences to make it meaningful. Again, the most meaningful way to learn things is through actual, hands-on learning. For example, it is more valuable for your child to learn that most tree trunks are rough and most leaves are smooth during a family outing to a forest than it is to learn to sort rough and smooth blocks.

Here are some types of activities in the home that provide rich experiences:

- helping prepare a snack or bake cookies;
- picking up the morning paper;
- helping stack dishes in the dishwasher;
- helping rake leaves or plant flowers;
- picking up clothes or toys;
- getting the mail from the mail carrier;
- playing with siblings or friends in the backyard;
- calling Grandma and Grandpa on the telephone.

Early in your child's life, these home experiences will likely be the focus for many of your activities. But you should expand your child's experiences outside the home as well. Some common community activities might include experiences such as:

- playing at the city park with siblings and friends;
- splashing in the "baby pool" at the public swimming pool;
- exploring the grocery store and stores at the mall;
- visiting a farm with animals and machinery;

- eating at a fast-food hamburger stand and a "sit-down" restaurant;
- visiting a petting zoo;
- visiting public places such as the post office, fire station, and library.

To assure that your child is gaining the maximum benefit from experiences you provide, keep these important points in mind:

- Make sure your child is an active participant in the experience. She should use all her senses, since the more information that is received, the more accurately she will understand and fill her literacy capsules. If your child is a passive participant (for example, by going to a farm but not going into the animals' pens), capsules will not be sufficiently filled with quality information.
- If your child has vision, visual information should be paired with other types of sensory information during experiences. Visual information is valuable to store in capsules, but generally should not be the only source of information. Again, the more senses that can be used to learn things, the better.
- If the experience includes several steps, make sure your child participates in all steps from the beginning to the end of the process. For example, if you are baking cookies, the first step would be gathering all the ingredients from the cabinets (although you could even make the first step a trip to the grocery store!). And the final step before eating them might be to wash the dishes. Your child needs to experience the whole process, rather than isolated and fragmented bits. For example, if your child only stirred the ingredients when making cookies, then she would think that to get cookies you stir the batter and then eat the cookies. She may not be aware of all the other steps that go into making cookies unless she actually participates in each step.
- Throughout the experience, be sure to provide your child with the vocabulary associated with it. For example, a trip to the farm would include names for the various animals as they are being explored, as well as "farm," "barn," "pen," "tractor," and so forth. Then later, when your child hears you read these words, or reads them herself, the previous experience will provide a basis for understanding the story.

- When you have a chance for some special experiences that might not be so "common" (such as that five-day trip on a cruise liner), take advantage of the opportunity! It will be a valuable enrichment to your child's life and yours.

Obviously, there are certain first-hand experiences that your child will not likely be able to have. For example, most children will not have an opportunity to visit the Great Wall of China. But if your child has climbed on a fence, opened and closed gates, and compared different types of fences, she can use these experiences—perhaps along with a three-dimensional model—to develop a general understanding of the Great Wall. Without the basic experiences, this would not be possible. So the focus should remain on developing a core of common experiences that will be the foundation for everything your child learns.

Exposure to Literacy in the Home and Community

Children become aware of written language and the way it is used by observing adults and others use it as part of daily life. Children who have normal vision are constantly seeing reading and writing happening around them throughout the day, and, as is often the case, they want to imitate what they see. For example, a child might see Mom looking at the newspaper and hear her say, "Oh, there's a concert tonight at the park—let's go." So the child might pick up a newspaper (maybe even upside-down) and say, "Oh, free pizza tonight—let's go!" Or when the child sees a parent writing something, she might take a crayon and scribble a message (sometimes on the refrigerator). It is through these constant interactions with print that children begin to understand that written language has meaning, and that we use reading and writing to accomplish important tasks in our lives.

Children with visual impairments miss some or all of these incidental exposures to literacy activities, so learning through imitation is greatly restricted. Therefore, you will need to make literacy activities overtly obvious to your child. In your home, you can have your child sit in your lap and help to hold things as you read the morning paper or the mail, "talking your way" through the process. You might say, "Oh! Here's a letter from Grandma. Let's see what she has to say." After opening the letter, you can read it aloud and then encourage your child to react to it in some way. You might say to your child, "Grandma asked if we would like to visit next week-end. Would you like to go to Grandma's? Let's write a letter and tell her!"

In the community, you will need to take time to explore signs and printed materials. If your child has low vision, getting closer to things, coupled with tactual exploration, will be a good strategy. If your child is blind, making direct contact with the materials works best. For example, you might lift up your child so she can explore street signs or signs in stores—many have raised letters. Also, most elevators are now marked in braille, so you can show your child the braille number of the floor you wish to visit and say, "We're going to the third floor, so let's push this button." A growing number of restaurants offer braille menus, so ask your waiter if your child can hold and explore one while you are reading the choices.

Literacy is used almost constantly throughout the day, and your child needs to know this! A child with a visual impairment needs to know the range and variety of reading materials in the home and community, including telephone books, magazines, newspapers, cookbooks, signs, brochures, and church bulletins. At first, you will need to make yourself super-conscious of the literacy tasks you do, because these tasks are generally done so automatically. The key thing to remember is to take active steps to make your child aware of these materials and the ways reading and writing are used.

Reading to Your Child

One of the best ways to build a solid foundation for literacy is to read aloud to your child on a regular basis starting early in life. In many homes, reading to a child during the evening or at bedtime is one of the most cherished activities of the day, and—for developing early literacy skills—one of the most important. As children hear their parents read stories on a regular basis, they begin to understand that ideas can be written down and kept forever in a book.

The first thing you will need is reading material. If your child has low vision, you will find an ample supply of wonderful children's books at the public library or local bookstore. Beginning in infancy and during the preschool years, it will be important to select motivating books that are brightly illustrated but contain relatively simple pictures or drawings. Too much clutter in the pictures may overwhelm your child at first. Be sure also to consider your child's background experiences and the age-appropriateness of the reading materials. For example, if your child has visited a farm, you may choose stories and books about farms and farm animals. Because of the prior experience with a farm, your child will understand and enjoy the story and be motivated to hear more. Also, farms and farm animals are likely to interest young children, while things such as mountain climbing and homecoming dances are not likely to provide the same interest until they grow older. You want your child to be able to understand and enjoy the story and to be motivated to hear more.

If your child is blind, there are a wide variety of reading materials in braille, although the selection is not as abundant as for books in print. Some braille books, called "twin-vision books," contain both print and braille. These are ideal if you do not know how to read braille yet, since they expose your child to braille *and* provide print for you to read. Twin-vision books are also good if you are not sure whether your child will later read in print or braille. Table 2 lists sources of twin-vision books, some available for purchase and others for loan. While it is vitally important for your child to have exposure to braille books, do not feel as if you should *only* use braille materials. Other books can be quite motivating to your child, especially if you add some real objects for your child to hold and explore while you are reading. For example, if you are reading "The Three Little Pigs," you could have some straw, sticks, and a brick for your child to explore as you read each section of this delightful book.

After you have found appropriate reading materials, then it is simply a matter of starting! Here are some suggestions for reading aloud to your child*:

- Start reading to your child as soon as possible. It is never *too* early.
- Read from twin-vision books or books with simple, colorful pictures. Be sure your child is sitting in your lap or right next to you so she can see or feel the book.
- For infants, use Mother Goose rhymes, repetitive stories, and simple songs. These stimulate an infant's curiosity and attention. You might include finger plays to actively engage your child in the event. For example, if you are singing "The Itsy Bitsy Spider," you might show your child

---

* Suggestions adapted from (and added to): Jim Trelease, *The New Read-Aloud Handbook* (New York: Penguin Books, 1989).

Table 2
Where to Get Twin-Vision Books

SOURCE	DESCRIPTION
The National Braille Press 88 Saint Stephen St. Boston, MA 02115 617–266–6160	This company offers a *Braille Book of the Month Club* for children. For the cost of any print book in their collection, you can receive the twin vision version. These books contain the original print book with braille either on the print pages or inserted on clear plastic sheets. These books are for purchase only.
Seedlings P.O. Box 2395 Livonia, MI 48151–0395 1–800–777–8552	Two types of books are produced. The first has braille labels placed on print books for preschoolers—some with sound buttons! Other twin-vision books are rewritten onto braille paper with print typed above the braille lines (although not necessarily word by word); these books contain no pictures. These books are for purchase only.
American Action Fund for Blind Children and Adults 18440 Oxnard St. Tarzana, CA 91356	This organization offers a variety of twin-vision books for preschoolers through 4th graders on loan at no cost. Write to them for an application. You will provide your child's age and interests, and they will send you books via free matter for the blind. When you finish, you return them the same way, so there is no cost for postage. They also provide free braille calendars!
National Library Service for the Blind and Physically Handicapped Library of Congress 1291 Taylor St., NW Washington, DC 20542 1–800–424–8567	The Library of Congress offers twin-vision books on loan through their various regional libraries. If you are unsure of how to contact your regional library, just ask the librarian at your local public library. Your child will need to be registered with the regional library in your area. All books are sent via free matter for the blind. You can also obtain children's books and some magazines in recorded formats and braille through the Library of Congress.

how to use the index and middle finger of one of her hands to "crawl" on her other hand.

- Set a specific time every day to read a story to your child. You may find that reading just before bedtime will become part of an enjoyable night-time routine and an important social event for you and your child.

- Start with simple picture books, then move to longer stories and perhaps even short novels. Before reading, be sure to describe pictures to your child or help her interpret the pictures. Take time to enjoy the pictures on each page!

- When you have advanced to longer stories and books that cannot be completed in one reading session, be sure to finish the story the next time or over several successive readings.

- Before you begin a story, read the title and ask your child what the story might be about. Take some time to recall similar experiences that you and your child have had that relate to the story.

- Read with plenty of expression, especially the dialog. Remember not to read too fast, and adjust your rate of reading to match what is happening in the story. During a chase scene, for example, it is OK to read faster to stimulate your child's excitement.

- Reading aloud is something that takes practice. You can help yourself by reviewing the book beforehand and maybe even reading it aloud to yourself or to your spouse.

- Try to add a real object or objects to the story whenever possible. If you are reading "Jack and the Beanstalk," you may want to have some beans in their pods or some actual beanstalks ready to show your child. It would be ideal to have visited a garden and taken some time to work in it prior to reading the story. Also, scratch and sniff books and pop-up books are interesting and motivating to many young children. Again, it is important that your child have real-life experiences with the activities in the story. For example, if you are reading a scratch and sniff book to your child that has common food smells, you want to make sure that she has had previous experiences with helping in the kitchen.

- If you find that your child is simply not interested in a book (regardless of whether it interests you), find another

book that will bring excitement and enjoyment to your
reading sessions.

- If your child is becoming acquainted with braille, it would
be ideal to have someone who is blind read to your child.
This modeling of true braille reading is as important to a
child who will read braille as modeling of print reading is
to a child who will read print.

- Learn more about reading aloud. Borrow *The New Read-
Aloud Handbook* by Jim Trelease from your public library or
buy it from Penguin Books.

- Most of all, have fun! This is an important social time for
you and your child, and you want it to be a special time.

As you read aloud to your child, you can help her develop a
sense of "book behavior." These behaviors are things like holding a
book right-side-up, turning one page at a time, reading from top to
bottom and left to right, using page numbers, and taking care of
books. These are important behaviors your child will use the rest of
her life.

Early Reading and Writing Experiences

In addition to reading to your child, there are a variety of early
reading and writing experiences that you can use to foster development of literacy. Generally during the preschool years or kindergarten, your child will begin experimenting with reading and writing,
so it is important for you to encourage and respond to what she is
doing in a nurturing and reinforcing manner. Here are some suggestions for activities you might use with your child:

- After reading a story with your child, act it out using family
members as various characters. Be sure to use some real objects that were used in the story to make it even more
meaningful.

- Labeling objects that are important to your child is a good
early reading experience. You can label objects according
to what they are (toy box, bedroom), or just label them
with your child's name. If you are unsure whether your
child will read in print or braille, label objects in both. Ask
a vision specialist or an adult who is blind to help you
make labels in braille using plastic labeling tape. It's a
good idea to make a few extra labels for special things that

get a lot of use because labels tend to come off after awhile.

- After your child has an experience, have her tell you a story about what happened so you can write it down in print or braille. (You may need to ask a teacher or an adult who is blind to help you with the braille version.) Then make it into a book and put in on the shelf with other books. Reread this story with your child whenever she would like. Since your child told you the story, she will likely be able to say some of the words that are coming up.

- After some experiences, you may want to record an account of your adventures onto cassette tape. These can be kept on the bookshelf and listened to whenever your child chooses.
- Create book bags or book boxes to accompany stories and books. Fill the bags or boxes with some of the items from the story. Or if the story was based on an actual experience, fill the bag with items you picked up along the way. For example, if you took a trip to the zoo and later wrote a story about it, the book bag or box might contain a model of a giraffe, a popsicle stick from one of your snacks, and a snake skin you found.
- Keep plenty of paper, crayons, pencils, and paints around the house for your child to use. You may want to have a screen on which your child can draw. Just wrap a small piece of window screen around a piece of stiff cardboard or board and secure it. Then when your child draws or writes on it, she will receive tactual feedback. If your child is blind, you might want to get a Sewell Raised-Line Drawing Kit from the American Printing House for the Blind. This simple kit has a clipboard with a rubberized surface,

sheets of thin plastic, and a drawing device like an ink pen, but without ink. When the drawing device moves across a plastic sheet, it creates a bumped-up or raised line.

- Encourage her to "write" messages using her own spellings or pictures. If your child is blind, if possible have a braille writer with paper in it so she can practice "scribbling" as well. After your child "writes" something, have her read it back to you. After drawing, have her tell you about the picture. Be sure to post these creations on the refrigerator so she will know you value her work.

- When you are going to the store, have your child make a list of things she needs. She can do this with invented spellings or pictures, or you can write the list together. You might also make a list of "things to do" or write a message to another family member.

- Your child might want to keep a diary or journal of the important events during the day (or on some special days). You can write down the events as your child dictates them to you. Your child will notice you writing as she dictates the events, helping her make the connection between what is being said and what is being written.

- If your child is blind, be sure her fingers are in contact with the braille as you read things together. Encourage her to "track" along the lines with the pads of the fingers on both hands as you read. It is not necessary for her fingers to be on the same words as you are reading—this will come later with more formal instruction. As your child gets older and more experienced with books, you may want to read only when she is tracking. This way she will begin to understand that to read braille, you must keep your hands moving!

- If your child has low vision, move your finger under the words as you read. Let her fill in words she knows or can guess from the context of the story. Also take time to interpret pictures. Your child may need help in picking out the most important things in the pictures and in moving her eyes around the page in a systematic manner.

These are just a few of many early reading and writing experiences you can use with your child. For more ideas, talk to the vision specialist who is working with your child. Above all, have fun with your child as you begin to explore early experiences with reading and writing. If these experiences become a chore, then neither you nor your child will benefit.

As your child enters kindergarten, she will receive formal instruction in reading and writing. If your child has low vision, the vision specialist will make sure that she is learning the efficient visual skills needed for reading and writing. Also, the teacher will make sure that appropriate materials and other adaptations, as were mentioned earlier, are made. If your child is blind, it is most likely that the vision specialist will be the primary teacher of reading and writing. The teacher will provide instruction in tactual discrimination and efficient hand movements so your child can quickly identify braille words and concentrate on the meaning in the story. You will work closely with your child's teachers by helping with reading and writing assignments and activities as they request, as well as by continuing to read aloud to your child and expand her background experiences. The foundation you provide before your child enters formal schooling and your continued cooperation throughout her school career will help assure that she has the literacy skills needed for living and working after graduation.

Making Decisions about Print or Braille

During the preschool years, it may or may not be evident whether your child will be a braille reader or a print reader. If it is not clear whether your child should begin formal reading instruction in print or braille, the decision will be made about the time she enters kindergarten. As Chapter 8 explains, this decision will be made by a team of individuals, including you, who are involved in your child's  education. The educational team will systematically assess your child to determine which reading medium will be most appropriate.

To make a decision on the best reading medium, the team will gather a lot of information about how your child uses sensory information, and then select an appropriate reading medium to match. If your child is most efficient in using visual information, especially for completing detailed tasks twelve to fourteen inches from her eyes or closer, then she may use print for reading. If she is most efficient in using tactual information to accomplish such tasks, then she may use braille for reading. In the meantime, if there is any question at all, you should present both braille and print to your child and observe how she responds to each.

Because you see your child more often than anyone else does, you will have an important role in helping to gather information on the best medium for your child. Here are some questions to keep in mind:

- When people enter the room, does your child recognize them by listening to them talk, touching them, or seeing them?

- When reaching for a toy, is your child attracted to it visually, or does she use other clues such as bumping into it or hearing a sound from it?

- When exploring toys or other objects, does your child use touch or vision?

- Does your child tell likenesses and differences in toys or other objects by touch or by sight? For example, does your child tell her shoes from someone else's shoes by looking at both pairs or by touching them?

- Does your child accurately identify objects at near distances (within twelve to sixteen inches of the eyes) using vision or using other clues such as touch or sound? At intermediate distances (between sixteen and twenty-four inches)? At far distances (beyond twenty-four inches)?

- Does your child accurately identify large objects (like a chair or a bed) by touch or sight? Medium-size objects (like a teddy bear or toy)? Small objects (like a paper clip, coins, or marbles)?

- When your child uses fine motor skills (such as stacking blocks or cutting with scissors), does she use vision or touch?

- When reading from a print book, does your child show interest in the pictures or does she prefer to examine some real object that is associated with the story?

- When reading from a twin-vision book, does your child attend more to the braille or to the print?

- Does your child scribble, write, and draw using her touch or her vision?
- If your child is recognizing her name or other simple words, is she doing this in print or in braille?

For any of these tasks, your child might not show a preference for use of vision or touch, so you should note that she uses both senses. It is also important to keep a record of the distances from objects at which your child responds, as well as any observations related to the lighting conditions or the level of contrast that is preferred.

Besides gathering information about how your child uses sensory information, the team will want to consider whether your child's eye condition is stable. If your child has a stable eye condition and makes efficient use of her vision, the educational team may decide that print is the best option for reading and writing. If your child has an unstable eye condition that is likely to get worse, then the team may choose braille as the best option. They will also take into account any additional handicapping conditions that will influence development of reading and writing skills. For example, if your child has a motor impairment that affects the way she moves her hands and fingers, then braille reading may not be the best option. Or if your child has a cognitive disability, reading in either print or braille may not be possible or the most important skill to teach. The team may decide to emphasize important daily living and work skills rather than reading skills. See the next section for more information about how additional disabilities may affect literacy skills.

Based on all this information, a decision will be made about which medium your child will use in beginning reading instruction. Some children might enter a formal reading and writing program in kindergarten or first grade without a clear preference for one medium having been established. Therefore, the team might decide to begin reading instruction in both print and braille and decide which is the most efficient medium later. Children actually continue to read in both print and braille throughout the school years. Remember, any decision on reading medium can be changed as your child's needs change.

Literacy Skills for Children with Additional Disabilities

If your child has additional disabilities, the attention given to developing literacy skills may be different. A cognitive disability in addition to a visual impairment will probably make learning to read and write more difficult. In particular, a severe or profound cognitive disability may make developing literacy skills an unlikely achievement. A motor impairment, if not accompanied by a cognitive disability, may require changes in the mode of reading (such as use of taped materials rather than braille). Other disabilities, such as a hearing impairment or learning disability, may also influence the development of literacy skills. A thorough assessment of your child's abilities and skills will be needed to determine the emphasis that should be placed on developing literacy skills.

In developing an IEP, the educational team will consider all of your child's needs, and then prioritize the skills to address those needs. For children with additional disabilities, social skills, daily living skills, and vocational skills are often considered essential to living as independently as possible. These skills may therefore be considered more important than academic skills, such as reading and writing. Even though reading books and writing papers may not be emphasized, functional uses of literacy may still be taught to increase independence in daily living or vocational tasks. For example, being able to read labels on food products helps in preparing meals, and identifying one's name helps in punching a time card at work.

If the focus of your child's program is functional literacy, then the educational team will need your help to decide which tasks in the home would be easier if your child could use reading or writing. Using literacy in real-life situations is one of the primary keys in developing functional literacy. Also, regardless of the severity of your child's additional disabilities, she will probably still enjoy listening to a story being read aloud. Reading aloud is a form of communication, and communication skills are very important for everyone.

Conclusion

Fostering growth in early literacy might seem somewhat complicated at first, and you might occasionally wonder whether you are going in the right direction. But really, there are just four things to remember. First, actively involve your child in a rich background of common first-hand experiences. Second, read to your child on a regular basis. Third, give your child opportunities to interact with a wide variety of literacy materials and tasks. Fourth, when your child experiments with early reading and writing, support her enthusiastically. When you have any questions, feel free to ask a vision specialist. Above all, enjoy this time! It will be mutually rewarding for both you and your child.

References

Henderson, F.M. "Communication Skills." In *The Visually Handicapped Child in School,* edited by B. Lowenfeld. New York: John Day Company, 1973.

Koenig, A.J. and M.C. Holbrook. "Determining the Reading Medium for Students with Visual Impairments: A Diagnostic Teaching Approach." *Journal of Vision Impairment and Blindness* 83: 296–302.

Lowenfeld, B. *The Visually Handicapped Child in School.* New York: John Day Company, 1973.

Lyenberger, E. "Reaching for Literacy." In *Realities and Opportunities: Early Intervention with Visually Handicapped Infants and Children,* edited by S.A. Aitken, M. Buultjens & S.J. Spungin. New York: American Foundation for the Blind, 1990.

Miller, D.D. "Reading Comes Naturally: A Mother and Her Blind Child's Experiences." *Journal of Vision Impairment and Blindness* 79: 1–4.

Olson, M.R. and S. Mangold. *Guidelines and Games for Teaching Efficient Braille Reading.* New York: American Foundation for the Blind, 1981.

"Prebraille Readiness." *Future Reflections* 10: 13–16.

Roberts, F.K. "Education for the Visually Handicapped: A Social and Educational History." In *Foundations of Education for Blind and Visually Handicapped Children,* edited by G.T. Scholl. New York: American Foundation for the Blind, 1986.

Stratton, J.M. and S. Wright. "On the Way to Literacy: Early Experiences for Young Visually Impaired Children." *RE:view* 23, 55–63.

Sulzby, E. and W. Teale. "Emergent Literacy." In *Handbook of Reading Research: Volume II,* 727–57. New York: Longman, 1991.

Trelease, J. *The New Read-Aloud Handbook.* New York: Penguin Books, 1989.

Parent Statements

I'm learning braille now. It's not as difficult as I thought but it takes a lot of time to learn.

—◄o►—

I've wondered if I should learn braille myself. I've tried to figure out the numbers on the elevator at work and it seems like it would be hard. I don't know how anybody ever does it.

—◄o►—

I'm not sure whether braille will be important for my daughter but I want her to have the opportunity to learn it.

—◄o►—

Will has to hold books real close to his eyes to see the pictures or the words.

—◄o►—

Katherine loves books! She loves to be read to and she's begining to recognize letters and words. I think she'll be a good reader.

—◄o►—

My child is two and a half years old. At our local parent group meetings I hear lots of arguments about braille. Frankly, I don't care right now. We have other problems to solve first.

—◄o►—

It seems important for Joe to learn braille in case his eyes get worse.

—◄o►—

I get sad sometimes when I realize that I can't just walk in any bookstore and buy books for Tyler. My sister's kids have hundreds of books but Tyler only has a handful.

—◄o►—

I don't see the point of reading to my son. He can't see the words or the pictures.

—◄o►—

I wonder how my child will know what's in the newspaper or in magazines or other things that aren't in braille.

—◄o►—

I am learning braille through Hadley School for the Blind. My oldest son, Scott (who is not visually impaired), loves it! I can hardly get to the braillewriter for practice because Scott is always doing "his" braille.

—◄o►—

We put Janie's braille papers up on the refrigerator just like her sister's schoolwork.

Chapter 11

◄○►

Orientation and Mobility

Everett W. Hill, Ed.D., and
Mary-Maureen Snook-Hill, Ed.D.*

Most parents have many questions and concerns about their child's ability to get around independently. Will he be able to travel to and from school by himself? What about to a friend's house or the neighborhood grocery store? How will he find his way around an unfamiliar area without getting lost? How will he know when it is safe to cross the street? Will he need to use a cane? How early should he begin receiving training to learn to do these things?

Although you may not realize it, what you are really concerned about is your child's orientation and mobility (O&M). Orientation involves knowing where you are, where you are going, and how to get where you want to be by interpreting information available in your environment. Mobility involves moving safely through your environment. Although the two processes are complementary, they are not the same. For example, someone can be very mobile but frequently get lost or disoriented. Likewise, someone can always

---

* Everett W. Hill (deceased) was Professor of Special Education, George Peabody College for Teachers, Vanderbilt University, Nashville, Tennessee. He was the author of several books, including the most widely used textbook for Orientation and Mobility, and *An Orientation and Mobility Primer for Families and Young Children*. He is well known for advocating early training in orientation and mobility.

Mary-Maureen Snook-Hill is currently Professor and Coordinator of the Orientation and Mobility and Rehabilitation Teaching programs at Mohawk College in Brantford, Ontario, Canada. She has had extensive international experience and has been active in training O&M specialists to work with individuals with visual impairments. She has a distinguished publishing record in the area of orientation and mobility.

This chapter is dedicated to the memory of "Butch" Hill.

know where he is, but not have the capacity or ability to move safely in the environment. Children need both O&M skills in order to travel as independently as possible in any environment.

This chapter discusses the O&M skills that allow people with visual impairment to move safely and efficiently in their environment. It explains how these skills are formally taught at school, as well as what you can do at home to lay the groundwork for learning.

Orientation and Mobility Training

Children with visual impairment are often eligible to receive training in O&M skills through their early intervention or special education program. There is no set age at which O&M instruction should begin, but services should generally begin as soon as possible. During the course of this training, young infants develop environmental and sensory awareness which helps them acquire O&M skills later on. Children in preschool and elementary school learn how to travel around their school building, playground, and neighborhood by themselves. Elementary school children also learn about more complex environmental concepts, including topography (slope, hilly) and textures (concrete, bumpy), and about positional concepts (in front of, in back of). Middle and high school children generally learn how to cross streets at busy intersections, ride city buses, use distance visual devices that can help them see street signs or addresses, use compass directions, plan a route of travel, shop in malls, and travel in unfamiliar areas independently.

In general, O&M training promotes safe, efficient, graceful, and independent movement through any environment, indoor and outdoor, familiar and unfamiliar. In turn, independent travel helps build self-esteem and self-confidence as your child learns to move freely about. Independent travel gives your child more control over his environments, enabling him to travel when and wherever he wishes (within his capabilities), without having to always rely on others to take him where he wants to go. If your child learns good O&M skills as a child, he is more likely to develop into a responsible, confident, and independent adult traveler.

Orientation and mobility services are provided by O&M instructors, professionals who are trained to teach travel concepts and techniques to enhance the independent travel skills of persons with visual impairments. The O&M instructor might work directly with your child, or he might work with your child's primary teacher, showing the teacher how to incorporate O&M into the daily classroom routine and monitoring the correct use of O&M skills. After determining your child's O&M needs, the O&M instructor will consult with the teacher. Together they will determine how to incorporate O&M instruction into your child's educational program. An O&M instructor can also help a day care provider or preschool teacher learn how to work best with your child.

The orientation and mobility skills your child may learn can be divided into three general categories: 1) skills that build a foundation for O&M; 2) formal mobility skills; and 3) formal orientation skills.

Foundation Skills

Generally, before a child can learn formal O&M skills, he needs to have acquired certain developmental and sensory skills and to have a basic understanding and awareness of his environment. For example, he needs to be able to move, to understand the meaning of prepositions such as behind and under, and to use his senses to tell where he is. As a parent, you probably work on many of these skills with your child during the course of your daily routine. Therapists and educators involved in your child's early intervention or preschool program may also be working on related skills, but not necessarily with the goal of helping with O&M skills. For example, the occupational therapist might work with your child on grasping objects such as a fork or pencil, but not a cane. The O&M instructor will work with your child on the specific developmental and sensory skills your child needs in order to learn O&M skills. The major areas on which the instructor might work are discussed below.

Concept Development. Concept development involves learning about the nature (size, shape, function) and location of objects in the environment. Concepts include body image concepts such as body planes (front, back) and body parts (hand, fingers); spatial concepts such as size (big, little); position (up, down, behind, under) and measurement (near, far); and environmental concepts (floor, bedroom, high chair).

A young child needs to understand these concepts in order to understand his movement in space, his relationship to objects in space, and the relationship of objects to other objects in space. For example, positional concepts such as in front of, behind, over, and under deal with the relationship between the locations of several objects to one another. These same concepts are also used to describe the relationship of your child to an object (in front of the couch, behind the chair). Mastering these concepts helps your child gradually learn more advanced travel skills and techniques, promoting increased independent travel.

Sensory Skill Development. Sensory skill development helps children to better use their senses of vision, hearing, touch, and smell to take in information about the environment. Accessing and interpreting this sensory information helps children understand their world, as well as their location in that world. For example, a child without any useful vision may identify the kitchen by the smell of food cooking in the oven or the hum of the refrigerator, whereas a child with low vision may recognize the kitchen by the shape or color of the oven or refrigerator.

Motor Development. Motor development includes the development of both gross motor and fine motor skills. Gross motor skills involve large muscle movement and balance, and include such skills as walking and running. Fine motor skills involve using smaller muscles such as those in the hand and wrist for intricate movement and manipulation. The development of motor skills is an important prerequisite to learning many of the advanced O&M skills. For example, to learn cane skills, a child needs the gross motor skills of balance and walking and the fine motor skills of holding and manipulating the cane with the hand and wrist.

Environmental and Community Awareness. Children with normal vision learn about their environment and community incidentally as they travel with parents and teachers on errands, field trips, and daily activities. Children with visual impairment, however, often miss out on opportunities for such incidental learning because they cannot casually observe their surroundings. For children with visual impairment, direct instruction and systematic exposure to the world around them is therefore critical. These experiences not only help children learn important concepts, but also build a foundation for purposeful O&M when they are older and can function in the community independently. First, these experiences help children learn to orient themselves in the environment and become mobile. Second, by allowing efficient and independent movement within various environments, they enhance self-esteem and self-confidence, and encourage further independent exploration.

The O&M instructor will teach and reinforce these concepts throughout the O&M training program. There are also many ways parents can help their child learn concepts by letting him actively participate in community experiences. For example, take your child shopping and let him help select items through shape, texture, weight, size, and smell, instead of just putting the item in the cart or basket. If appropriate, have him shake the item to see if it makes a sound. If your child has some vision, he can identify objects by color.

Formal Mobility Skills

Formal mobility skills allow a child with a visual impairment to move about in his environment, generally through independent walking. These skills include self-protective skills that enable the child to travel safely and independently throughout a familiar environment by positioning his hands, arms, or objects in front of his body to provide protection. They also include skills involved in using a *mobility system*—a guide or device that permits independent movement through the environment. Probably the best-known mobility system is the use of a cane to move about independently, but there are other systems that may be appropriate, depending on your child's age, abilities, amount of vision, motivation, and the nature of his current and future travel environments. Self-protective skills are generally learned before a particular mobility system is introduced, but they may be used concurrently. The pros and cons of different mobility systems are discussed later in the chapter.

Upper Hand and Forearm. (See Figure 1.) The purpose of this skill is to detect objects that may be encountered in the upper region of the body. With young children, this technique may be referred to as the "upper bumper." To form the "upper bumper," the child bends his forearm at the elbow, forming an angle of approximately 120 degrees. He holds his arm in front of his body at shoulder level, parallel to the floor, with the hand aligned in front of the opposite shoulder, palm facing away from the body and fingers relaxed and close together.

Lower Hand and Forearm. (See Figure 2.) The purpose of this skill is to locate and provide protection from objects at waist level. With young children, this technique may be referred to as

Figure 2

Figure 1

the "lower bumper." To form the "lower bumper," the child extends his hand downward approximately six to eight inches from the midline of his body. His fingers are positioned close together and relaxed. For maximum protection, children sometimes use the upper and lower bumpers in combination.

Using Objects and Toys as Bumpers. Often it is possible for children to protect themselves by carrying or pushing toys or objects in front of their bodies. For example, in Figure 3, the child is carrying a tray out in front of himself while moving. In Figure 4, the child is pushing a grocery cart. Using toys and objects this way can make it easier to make the transition to using a cane or one of the alternative mobility devices described below.

Figure 3   Figure 4

Orientation Skills

Orientation skills include the cognitive and perceptual skills that enable a child to determine his position and relationship to significant objects in his environment. To establish his orientation, the child must first have a concept of self, or body image—he must understand his body parts, including the function of each part and how they move in relationship to each other (self-to-self awareness). He must also understand the environment and his relation-

ship to the environment (self-to-object relationships). Finally, he must be able to understand how different aspects of the environment relate to each other—such as where the bathroom is located in relationship to his bedroom (object-to-object relationships). Because orientation skills are very closely related to mobility skills, the two are generally taught at the same time.

Orientation skills your child may learn include Trailing, Systematic Search Patterns, Measurement, and Body Image.

Trailing. (See Figure 5.) The purposes of trailing are to establish and maintain a straight line of travel by following along a "trailing surface" such as a wall or the edge of a table, and to locate specific objectives such as the third doorway or a book on or along the trailing surface. The child extends his arm at an angle of approximately 45 de-

Figure 5

grees out in front and to the side of his body. With the fingers relaxed and slightly cupped, he maintains light contact with the trailing surface with the side of his pinkie finger.

Systematic Search Patterns. (See Figure 6.) Systematic search patterns are used to locate objects and/or to explore a space. There are two basic types of patterns. The first type involves using the hand(s) and arm(s) to find a nearby object such as a toy or an item on a high chair tray, or to retrieve a dropped object. Using this type of search pattern, the child establishes a starting point and then can use a variety of patterns (fan, circular, etc.) to locate the object. (See Figure 6.)

The second type of search pattern is used to search larger

Figure 6

spaces. It is done while walking and uses the whole body. One whole-body search pattern called the "perimeter" search method involves establishing a starting point for the search and then walking around the border of the area back to the starting point. The perimeter method provides information about the size and shape of the area, and about objects along the border. A second whole-body search pattern called the "gridline" search method involves establishing a starting point and then moving in straight lines back and forth within the perimeter of the area to locate objects within the perimeter.

Measurement. Measurement skills your child may learn include: a) using paces or steps to estimate distances; b) discriminating short and long time periods when walking in a straight line at a constant rate; and c) discriminating shorter and longer time periods when traveling routes that include turns and when walking at various rates in a familiar environment. For a preschooler, these skills are essential to avoid objects and hazards. They also lay the groundwork for formal O&M skills such as negotiating stairs or doors with a sighted guide or a cane.

Body Image. In developing body image, your child becomes aware of and understands his body and its relationship to people, objects, and the environment. This involves identifying basic body parts, understanding the relationship of body parts to one another, and understanding what occurs with the body and its parts during movement and as a result of movement. Body image is important in mastering formal mobility skills such as upper hand and forearm ("upper bumper") and cane skills.

Common Mobility Systems

There are many ways that children and adults with visual impairment can travel safely and efficiently through their environments. Being proficient in one or more of these mobility systems will greatly increase your child's flexibility and independence. Since each system has different pros and cons, however, you and your child should carefully evaluate the possibilities before choosing one. The section below provides information about the strengths and weaknesses of common mobility systems. Your child's O&M instructor will also provide information that can help you and your child choose the system that is best for him.

Sighted Guide

This is often the first formal system that a child uses to move about in his environment. Using this system, the child holds on to another person's arm or wrist and walks slightly behind him or her. When the child is first learning the system, the guide verbally describes obstacles and features they are approaching. As the child gains more experience with a guide, he takes on a more responsible and active role. Rather than relying on the guide's verbal instructions to know what to do, he learns to pay attention to the guide's body movements and information from the environment.

As a preschooler, your child needs to learn sighted guide skills so that he can travel comfortably in unfamiliar and outdoor settings with you. Consequently, the O&M instructor will probably work on sighted guide skills with you and your child together, showing you how to monitor correct sighted guide skills. As your child's guide, you will have the opportunity to describe the environments through which you are traveling with him. As your child's skills increase, he will be able to teach siblings, classmates, and friends how to be good guides.

Figure 7

Most of the sighted guide skills taught to young children are the same skills traditionally taught to school-age children and adults, with some modifications. These skills include basic sighted guide, narrow passageways, and stairways.

Basic Sighted Guide. (See Figure 7.) The child grasps the guide's wrist, positioning the thumb to the outside and the four fingers to the inside of the guide's wrist. The grip should be secure, but comfortable for the guide. The child holds his upper arm parallel and close to the side of his body, forming approximately a 90–degree angle with his lower arm so that he is positioned approximately one-half step behind the guide. This grip and position allow the guide to encounter obstacles and changes in terrain first and to provide maximum safety and reaction time for the child. Sometimes the child may grasp the guide's index finger or pinkie finger instead of the wrist. If the child is being guided by someone his own height, he would grasp the guide's arm just above the elbow.

If your young child is learning basic sighted guide skills, that does *not* mean that you cannot sometimes just hold hands with him. Whenever possible, however, you should encourage your child to use the proper grip when using the basic sighted guide procedure. Using the proper grip reinforces and develops fine motor ability and encourages active participation, while holding hands does not.

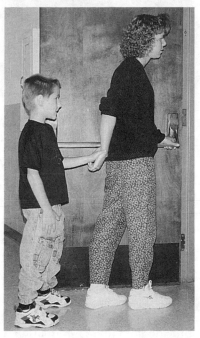

Figure 8

Narrow Passageways. (See Figure 8.) Narrow passageway technique allows for safe and efficient passage through a restricted space that cannot be negotiated using the basic sighted guide procedure. Before entering the narrow space, the guide moves his guiding arm behind and toward the small of his back. The child straightens his arm and moves directly behind the guide without stepping on his heels. After leaving the narrow space, the guide returns his arm to a normal guiding position and the child resumes the basic sighted guide procedure.

Stairways. (See Figure 9.) The guide approaches the edge of the steps squarely and pauses. The child comes up beside the guide. The guide takes the first step and the child follows at the guide's pace, remaining one step behind the guide. The guide pauses after completing the stairs, indicating to the child that he has one more step to negotiate.

Figure 9

Advantages of the Sighted Guide System. There are several advantages to using sighted guide as a mobility system. First, when used correctly and with a knowledgeable guide, it provides maximum safety to the child during movement. Second, the sighted guide provides companionship as well as information about the surrounding environment. Sighted guide is also an excellent system for introducing orientation skills such as determining time and distance relationships. Your child can, for example, focus on how long it takes to walk from the classroom to the cafeteria without having to worry about running into any obstacles along the way.

Disadvantages of the Sighted Guide System. There are also several disadvantages to using a sighted guide. First, if the sighted guide is the child's only system of mobility, his independence is limited. Because a guide might not always be available, the child will not always be able to travel where and when he wants to, which could have significant consequences for school, work, etc. Second, the child's safety might be jeopardized if the guide is inexperienced. In addition, inexperienced guides might provide inaccurate information, too much information, or too much assistance instead of expecting the child to take an active role. The child may then "latch on" to the guide and tune out incoming environmental information, letting the guide do all the work.

The Long Cane

The long cane is the mobility system most commonly used by persons with visual impairments. In the past, children did not receive instruction in cane usage until their early teens. Recently, however, cane instruction has begun to be introduced to children much earlier, frequently during the preschool years.

There are several types of canes. Two of the more common varieties are the long, straight cane with or without a crook, and the folding cane. (See Figure 10.) Long canes can be made of many materials, including aluminum and fiberglass. Most of the shaft is usually covered with a white reflective material, while a small portion of the lower shaft is covered with a red reflective material. The tips of both long and folding canes can be made of nylon or metal.

Several different cane techniques and modifications may be used, depending on the environment. For example, the diagonal technique is used primarily in familiar indoor environments to detect low objects such as chairs or coffee tables. The cane, held in either hand, is positioned diagonally across the body like a "bumper," with the tip either resting on the ground or about one inch above the ground and extending one to two inches beyond the widest part of the body (hips or shoulders).

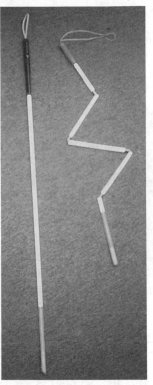

Figure 10

Another technique, the touch technique, is used in any environment, indoors or outdoors, familiar or unfamiliar. The cane, held in the dominant hand, is positioned at the center of the body, while the tip swings from side to side, contacting the walking surface about one inch beyond the widest part of the body. The cane swings in a low, flat arc with the tip touching the surface on the side opposite the forward foot, enabling the child to detect changes in the walking surface such as steps or curbs.

Touch technique trailing, a modification of basic touch technique, is used to maintain a straight line of travel along a parallel surface such as a wall, locate a specific objective such as the third doorway, and maintain contact with the wall. The child walks parallel to the wall and alternately contacts the wall and the floor with his cane tip. Shorelining, another modification of basic touch technique, is used to locate an intersecting sidewalk. The child walks parallel to the shoreline (the line between the grass and the sidewalk). As he walks, he increases the arc on the side of the body closest to the shoreline, alternately touching the shoreline and the walking surface until the intersecting sidewalk is located.

The O&M instructor introduces these different techniques over a period of time. He does not just provide a child with a cane and expect him to begin traveling independently. The O&M instructor also helps children and their families select the most appropriate cane type and length.

Before deciding whether your child needs to use a cane, several factors should be considered. These include your child's amount of vision, need for a cane (actual and perceived), maturity level, and ability to manipulate a cane while walking. You should also consider whether your child needs to get around better in his current travel environment or needs to travel to new places on his own.

There are varying philosophies as to the best age for a child to learn cane skills. Some O&M instructors think cane skills should be introduced at the earliest possible age. Others prefer to wait until the child has developed appropriate fine motor and conceptual skills such as the ability to correctly grip the cane and the ability to follow instructions using basic spatial concepts (in front, behind, over, under). Your child may benefit from cane instruction now, or he may not need a cane until he is ready to go places himself. You should ask your O&M instructor to help you decide when and if your child should use a cane.

Advantages. The ability to use a cane proficiently allows a child to move through the environment safely and efficiently. The cane provides auditory information (such as the tip tapping more loudly on a tile surface than on the carpet) and tactual information (such as the tip sticking in the carpet but gliding smoothly over the tiles) which can help the child maintain his orientation. The cane provides adequate protection from most obstacles in the travel path and identifies the child with a visual impairment to others.

Disadvantages. Although the cane provides adequate protection from most obstacles, it cannot detect suspended or overhanging obstacles such as a tree branch at head level. Fortunately, there are not many of these types of hazards on well-traveled pedestrian walkways. Some young children with low vision may consider the long cane a disadvantage because it identifies them as having a visual impairment.

Alternative Mobility Devices

Alternative mobility devices (AMDs) are becoming increasingly popular for use with preschool children. These devices are pushable protective devices made of plastic tubing (PVC pipe). They are lightweight and inexpensive to make. Some AMDs have rollers or casters, while others slide across the walking surface as they are pushed. Two of the more common AMDs, are the Connecticut Precane and the Walkalone. An AMD provides the same kind of protection as the long cane, but does not require the conceptual or motor skills needed for the long cane. The child is protected from obstacles in his travel path as he pushes the AMD in front of himself. Depending on the child's cognitive abilities, he may be able to interpret both auditory and tactual information to discriminate between walking surfaces such as carpet or tile.

Some children may start with an AMD and then use a long cane. Other children may always use some type of AMD, because they never develop the motor control, kinesthetic (movement) awareness, maturity, or cognitive ability to adequately use a long cane.

Advantages. An AMD increases a child's ability to move about independently early in the O&M instructional process. Most AMDs are simple to use, can detect curbs and other drop-offs, and provide information about the walking surface. Compared with the long cane, they require relatively brief instructional periods. An AMD does not require as much fine motor control to use as a long cane, as a child just uses both hands to push it in front.

Disadvantages. An AMD can be difficult to use when ascending or descending stairs and when passing through doorways. When used frequently on outdoor walking surfaces such as concrete, some AMDs "wear out" and need to be replaced frequently. In addition, some young children may use the device as a weapon or toy instead of as a functional tool.

Dog Guides

Dog guides have been used in the United States since the late 1920s. Dog guides may be German shepherds, golden retrievers, labradors, or other breeds.

The dogs are trained extensively before they are matched with a person with a visual impairment. They are trained to help the person with a visual impairment safely and efficiently locate familiar landmarks and negotiate obstacles, doorways, and congested areas. The dogs are also trained to understand verbal commands paired with gestures. (For example, the dog guide user says "forward" while making a quick, forward sweep with the arm.) After the initial one-on-one training is completed, the dog guide is matched with a suitable person. The one-on-one training continues until the two become an efficient working unit, usually within four weeks. Contrary to popular myth, the dog guide user must have good orientation skills and cannot simply expect the dog guide to know where they are going.

Less than 2 percent of the population with visual disabilities use a dog guide. There are several reasons for this. First, the majority of people with visual impairments are over sixty-five years of age and cannot maintain the three to four miles per hour walking speed of the dog guide. Second, many people with visual impairments have too much functional vision to effectively use a dog guide. (They have enough vision to detect obstacles or overhangs along the travel path, thereby "second guessing" the dog guide and interfering with its ability to do its job.) Third, most dog guide schools require users to be at least sixteen years of age, eliminating children as potential users. Fourth, some people dislike dogs or do not want to deal with the ongoing care and maintenance of a dog guide. Finally, many people with visual impairment have additional disabilities which prevent them from assuming responsibility for a dog guide.

Those who wish to use a dog guide must complete an application and meet specific eligibility requirements. In general, to qualify for a dog guide, the person must be in reasonably good health, be able to walk at a good, brisk pace, have sufficient reason to use a dog guide, provide ample opportunity to use the dog on a regular basis, and, usually, be at least sixteen years of age. Applicants are also required to go to a dog guide training school for approximately one month of intensive training. A complete list of Dog Guide Schools can be found in the Resource Guide.

Advantages. A dog guide allows someone with a visual impairment to move quickly in a straight line along the travel path. A well-trained dog guide provides maximum safety by moving around obstacles in the travel path and avoiding overhangs and drop-offs. Safety is also increased through "intelligent disobedience." For example, if the guide dog user attempts to cross a street into the path of an oncoming car, the dog guide has been trained to refuse to continue moving forward. The dog guide also provides companionship and can open doors to socialization with others who strike up conversations about the dog guide. In addition, dog guides are relatively inexpensive. Some schools ask the individual to purchase the dog for a nominal fee of up to $150, while others give the dog outright to the person.

Disadvantages. A dog must be active and continually worked in order to remain effective. The user must also be willing to provide continued maintenance, obedience training, and care. A dog guide should not be selected as a mobility system primarily for protection, socialization, or companionship. Some dog guide schools have waiting lists for students, which can be a significant inconvenience for a dog guide user who must wait for a replacement dog and additional training. Most schools, however, give priority to returning students. Also, some guide dog users have trouble adjusting to a new dog guide if they were attached to one who died, but time and experience generally eliminate any problems.

Electronic Travel Aids

The majority of electronic travel aids (ETAs) operate on the principle of ultrasound or infrared light. In general, these ETAs work by providing advance detection of obstacles through auditory and/or tactile feedback. This allows the user to move around the obstacle without making physical contact. One ETA, the Sonicguide™, also provides information about the environment through its signals, which enable the user to: 1) estimate how far he is from an object through changes in pitch (i.e., the pitch drops as the user moves closer to the object); 2) decide in which direction an object is located through amplitude differences in each ear (i.e., the sound of an object on the left side is louder in the left ear); and 3) distinguish characteristics of an object's surface through tonal characteristics (i.e., a plate glass window and a wooden crate will reflect echoes of different tone qualities). Other commonly used ETAs include the Laser Cane, Mowat Sensor, Pathsounder, Polaron, and Sensory 6.

An ETA is typically used in combination with another mobility system such as the long cane or dog guide. People in wheelchairs, however, may use ETAs as their primary mobility system. An ETA such as the Pathsounder or Step Detector can be mounted on a wheelchair to detect obstacles or drop-offs, or wheelchair users can hold the Mowat Sensor (provided they have the use of their hands). Sometimes ETAs are used to help infants and young children with visual impairments develop environmental awareness and learn spatial concepts such as near, far, long, and short, and specific measurement concepts such as inch, foot, and mile.

Advantages. There are several advantages to using an ETA. Of particular relevance to children, ETAs make it easier to learn spatial and environmental concepts and may encourage movement and exploration. Not only does the user receive advance warning of obstacles, but he is also able to detect objects away from the travel path. Many ETAs may also be used for alignment and maintenance of a straight line while walking.

Disadvantages. Cost is a major drawback of ETAs. Prices vary from about $400 for the Mowat Sensor to $4,000 for the Sonicguide™. Maintenance and repairs can also be costly and inconvenient. The appearance of the devices deters many potential users, and the size and weight of some makes them cumbersome or awkward for young children.

Choosing the Best Mobility System for Your Child

There is no one best mobility system for children with visual impairments. What will work best for your child depends on several factors, including your child's specific needs, the complexity of the environments through which he travels, his physical and cognitive capabilities, and his motivation and attitude toward O&M. Some children may use several different mobility systems at different stages of their educational careers. For example, a young infant may start off with a walker and then progress to using push toys and then to a specific AMD or the long cane. Another child may use the cane exclusively as his main mobility system, once he is able to walk. There are many options. The O&M instructor can provide useful information and help with this decision based upon your child's needs and capabilities.

Who Needs O&M Training?

If your child does not bump into objects at home or school, you may wonder whether he really needs O&M training. The fact is, most children with visual impairments learn to get around familiar places quite well. However, this does not necessarily mean that they could not benefit from O&M services.

A child capable of good mobility in familiar places may still have some orientation needs, such as learning to travel in unfamiliar places and understanding environmental concepts such as neighborhood, street corner, intersection, etc. Even children with low vision can often profit from training in concept development, sensory skills, and orientation. For example, a child with some vision may not automatically understand what he is seeing, and may therefore have trouble understanding concepts such as four-way stop intersections. Allowing the child to experience concepts in a variety of ways involving all the senses helps him to better understand what he sees. This same child could probably improve his orientation skills by learning what, when, where, and how to look for important landmarks and features of the environment. For example, he might be taught how to systematically scan and visually search for the swing set in his backyard. Additionally, learning how to use optical devices such as telescopes to locate important objects and landmarks is helpful for some young children with low vision.

In short, regardless of how much vision your child has, he could probably benefit from some O&M training. A comprehensive O&M assessment will help determine the nature and extent of need for O&M services. This assessment might take place when your child is being assessed for early intervention or special education services for the first time. Or, it might be conducted after your child has been receiving services for some time. This may be the case if his eye condition has deteriorated, affecting his ability to travel safely and independently. As a parent, you may also request an O&M assessment at any time.

The O&M instructor takes the lead role in assessing formal orientation skills and formal mobility skills; determining the appropriate mobility system (a particular AMD, the long cane, etc.); and analyzing the home and school environment to determine what assistance parents and teachers will need in teaching safe and efficient O&M skills. The O&M instructor also works with the teacher of children with visual impairments to assess a child's needs and abilities in concept development, motor development, and sensory skills development. Other professionals such as the regular classroom teacher and occupational and physical therapists should also be consulted and involved in the assessment if the child also has a physical disability or other special needs.

If your child is found to need O&M services, he will be periodically reevaluated to find out whether he still needs the services or whether his need for services has changed. Often, a child receives O&M instruction over his entire educational career. Sometimes O&M instruction is short-term to meet specific needs, is terminated, and then reactivated as the child's needs change. For example, a child in a kindergarten classroom may need formal O&M instruction to learn basic sighted guide skills, self-protective skills such as trailing, or how to use an AMD to travel with his classmates from his classroom to the cafeteria and the playground. Once he has successfully learned the routes, the teacher can be responsible for monitoring correct skills. As the child gets older and changes schools, the O&M instructor would resume training and introduce more advanced skills such as diagonal cane techniques.

When a child is very young or has multiple disabilities, the O&M instructor often works directly with family members and other professionals most of the time, rather than with the child. For example, the O&M instructor might spend time at home with the family, observing the daily routine and suggesting and demonstrating ways the family could incorporate O&M skills into daily activities. During playtime, parents or siblings could place a favorite, noise-producing toy just out of the child's reach and encourage him to grab for it. Or, parents could hang a musical mobile over their child's crib to encourage reaching and eye-hand coordination.

Working on O&M at Home

When your child is young, there are a number of ways you can help him develop O&M skills. Many of these strategies are simply common sense, and you may already have adopted them without even realizing that you were enhancing your child's O&M skills. Others can be easily incorporated into your daily routine, once you become aware of what helps children acquire O&M skills. What follows are some general suggestions for helping a child develop O&M skills. Your child's O&M instructor will give you specific suggestions tailored to your child's unique needs and capabilities.

Modifying Your Home

How your home is arranged can greatly affect the development of O&M skills. Usually families do not need to go to a great deal of time and expense to modify the home environment for their children. In most cases, common sense changes which benefit all family members can be made. The following factors should be considered when making modifications.

Safety. Families should decide on the amount and nature of "child-proofing" to be done in the home. Many safety considerations for children with visual impairment are the same, as those for children with normal vision. For example, most babies love to mouth objects, so make sure your child does not get a hold of objects or toys that are small enough to swallow. Provide optimum natural lighting without glare at critical locations throughout your home. For example, avoid sudden changes in lighting as your child moves from the hallway to the family room by partly drawing the blinds when the sun is brightly shining through the window. A landmark such as a low-hanging picture can be placed at the end of the hallway to indicate the presence of a staircase. Protect your child from hurting himself on table corners by using padding or corner buffers and keep closet and cabinet doors fully open or fully closed. Keep all electrical cords out of main travel paths to prevent tripping accidents. Use non-slip guards under area rugs and runners to prevent your child from slipping or tripping over curled corners.

Spatial Arrangement. How organized, complex, and consistent is your home environment? Sometimes rearranging furniture to create accessible travel pathways for a young child makes it much easier for him to move about the house and develop confidence. For example, when your child is first learning to travel from his bedroom to the kitchen, he may need to travel through the family room. Instead of expecting him to travel through a large, empty space, you could initially arrange the furniture along the walls so that he could travel along the furniture without having to move out into open space.

As your child becomes more motivated and proficient, you could rearrange the furniture and provide landmarks. For example, when your child contacts the coffee table, instead of continuing in the same direction along the wall, he would turn left, trail the edge of the coffee table to the end, continue across two feet of open space to the big chair, walk around the chair to the wall, and turn the corner into the kitchen. As your child becomes still more proficient, you can challenge him to continue to use his O&M skills by creating a more complex environment. That is, increase or decrease the amount of furniture or rearrange it to encourage him to problem solve how to safely and efficiently make his way through the environment.

Accessibility to Items. Your child's clothes, toys, personal belongings, and other personal objects such as a potty chair should be placed within easy reach. Making items accessible will encourage your child to explore his surroundings and enhance early movement.

Familiarity/Novelty. It *is* important to establish some consistency in the environment so that your child becomes familiar with the spatial arrangement and develops confidence in his mobility. Sometimes, however, children do not use proper O&M skills because they are "too familiar" with the environment. For example, if your child knows where all the furniture is, he may stop using self-protective techniques. Therefore, you should continually assess and adapt the environment to provide appropriate novelty and stimulation. For example, you might move the toy chest to a different corner of the room so your child has to use his self-protective techniques to travel the new route from the doorway to the toy chest.

Taking Advantage of Community Resources

Most communities offer a rich array of opportunities for enhancing O&M concepts and skills. For example, taking your child grocery shopping is an excellent opportunity to teach many new concepts. If your child is sitting in the grocery cart, hand him the items you select and let him explore them and make comparisons. Talk about their size (big, little), weight (heavy, light), texture (rough, smooth), temperature (cool, very cold), shape, etc. For example, as your child is examining a package of bacon, you could talk about it being cold, shaped like a rectangle, packaged in a smooth covering, etc. Upon arriving home, have your child help you unpack the grocery items and place them in their appropriate places. This, again, is an excellent opportunity to teach spatial arrangement and concepts in the home. When it is time to cook the bacon, let your child get the bacon out of the fridge, locate the appropriate size frying pan, and help to place the bacon in the pan, noting the texture, smell, and shape of the bacon.

Spending time at a neighborhood park is another excellent activity for introducing and reinforcing many O&M concepts and skills as well as language skills. When pushing your child in the swing, you can tell him he is going high or low, up or down, fast or slow. You might also take your child to a slide and have him experience those same concepts in a different manner (going up and down the slide).

Riding in the car provides an opportunity for you to develop environmental awareness in your child and to teach specific spatial concepts. For example, you can play games with your child by having him keep track of left turns, right turns, and full stops. When taking trips in the community, you can have your child make comparisons about the time and distance it takes to get to different places. For example, going to the post office from home is a shorter trip than going to the bank.

Motivating Your Child to Explore

Children need a reason to move. Infants with sight may pick their heads up to look at someone's face or crawl across the room to get an appealing, colorful toy. Children with visual impairments, however, may not be aware of all the exciting objects they would find if they moved about. Use sounds your child likes, such as your voice or a musical toy, to encourage him to move across the room. Instead of placing a rattle in your child's hand, shake it to one side of him and help him reach for it. Stand a few feet from your child and have him move toward you when you approach him. Help him explore the cupboards, crawl up and down steps, and get up on a stool to see what is higher than his reach.

Encourage your child to be as mobile as other children his age. Most infants are allowed to crawl about on the floor, so be sure not to keep your child confined to the playpen. Leaving a "good" baby content for a long period of time in the crib or playpen is not always the best thing for him. If the children in the neighborhood are riding tricycles, help your child learn how to do this, too. You can select a smooth surface for him to ride on or fasten his feet to the pedals with straps. If he cannot seem to get the hang of it, ask his teacher for suggestions on how to teach him. Like all children, your child will fall, bump into things, and cry. These experiences are a normal part of growing up, and your child should be allowed to have them.

Focusing on Everyday Learning Opportunities

You can help lay the foundation for your child's O&M skills by involving him in everyday activities that help him learn about environmental and sensory information. It is especially important to help him learn about sounds. Talk about the way things sound (loud, soft, high, low). Also help him learn about the sources of sounds. Tell him what or who is making the noise when the phone rings, when someone comes into your home, or when the water is running. If possible, allow him to touch the source of the sound. Recognizing the source of sounds will be critical later for such activities as crossing the street, when it is essential to know the position of passing cars. It is helpful if all family members become aware of the importance of discussing sounds and incorporate this discussion into the daily routine.

Help your child learn about other sensations just as you help him learn about sounds. Talk about how things feel (hard, soft, smooth, bumpy, wet, dry), look (dark, light, what color), and smell (strong, sweet, dangerous). When your child is in a new place or gets a new toy, describe the way it looks, sounds, feels, and smells. During bath time, talk about the smell of the soap and powder and have your child help rub lotion onto his body. Point out and name the textures on the walking surface (carpet, wood, tile, grass, dirt, sidewalk) and connect these textures to a specific location or activity. For example, tell your child that the bathroom has a tile floor and that the grass is in the backyard.

Remember that your child depends on you and others to show him what he might not learn naturally on his own. Children without visual impairments learn a great deal by watching their parents. For instance, young children learn how clothes become clean by seeing their mother or father take the dirty clothes from the hamper, put them in the washing machine, move them to the dryer, and then fold them and place them in drawers. A child with a visual impairment may only be aware that every morning he is handed his clothes from mid-air and that at night when he takes them off, his mother or father takes them away. By having your child help with the laundry, you can teach him where dirty and clean clothes come from and go to, what the concepts of wet and dry mean, and how to identify clothes by touch. Think of all the things you can teach your child while shopping at the grocery store, planting flowers in the yard, housecleaning, or washing the car.

Teaching about Spatial Relationships

It is important to teach your child position words that will enable him to understand his relationship to objects or other people in the environment. Tell your child where he is as he moves or is carried from place to place. For example, tell him that he is *in* the living room, *in front of* the couch, his blocks are *behind* his back, and you are sitting *on* the rocking chair. Have him touch the couch, blocks, and you to reinforce what these position words mean. Help him learn that his bed is *next* to the wall and that the bathtub is *in* the bathroom. When he drops a toy or is looking for something, tell him it is to his *left*, *under* his foot, or *in front of* him. Help him reach *to his left* to find the toy. Ask him questions about where objects are located.

When your child is just learning to use a new position word such as *behind*, be sure to use this word every time you describe an object in that particular location. Once he knows what it means, you can tell him that other words, such as *in back of*, mean the same thing. Remember that verbal directions are not enough. Hands-on experiences will reinforce your child's learning of all these position words.

It is also important to teach your child to look for or explore objects in an organized way. If he drops a toy, he should listen for the sound of it hitting the floor and look for it in that particular direction, first searching closer to him, then further away. At lunchtime, he can figure out what kind of food he has by systematically exploring his tray and the tabletop surrounding it. If his cup is always placed in the same location, he will learn to anticipate this and can reach the same distance in the same direction each time. This can help him avoid accidental spills as well as frustration.

Working with the O&M Instructor

Although the O&M instructor will provide suggestions, information, and ideas about your child's development and O&M needs, family members are a child's best teachers. You, the child's family, have the most love, concern for your child's best interests, and time to teach and reinforce O&M skills. This means you can really help your child learn and grow by forming a partnership with your child's O&M instructor.

As a parent, you can work with the O&M instructor in several ways. First, you can help the instructor and other educational team members develop short- and long-term goals, as well as reasonable time limits for completing the goals. An example of a long-term goal might be that your child will demonstrate that he knows right from left (the concept of *laterality*). Short-term goals that might help your child reach this larger goal could include that he will identify his right and left hands, roll a ball with his right or left hand, and turn right or left upon request with 100 percent accuracy 100 percent of the time. These goals should be written into your child's IFSP or IEP.

Second, you can expect the O&M instructor to work with you to develop specific activities that you and other family members can do at home to make sure there is continuity of instruction. These activities should be designed so that you can incorporate them into everyday and recreational activities. For example, at the supper table, you can ask your child to pass you the butter with his right hand and pass the peas with his left hand. In your back yard, you can ask your child to kick the ball with his left foot and pet the cat with his right hand.

You should expect the O&M instructor to keep you informed about your child's progress, possibly through a notebook, regular (bi-weekly or possibly monthly) phone calls, or written progress reports (perhaps every six or eight weeks). In addition, you should feel free to observe O&M lessons whenever possible. Showing confidence in your child's travel abilities both at lessons and out in the community can help give him the assurance he needs to develop his skills to the utmost.

As your child grows older, the O&M instructor can let you know when your child has the skills to go places by himself or with friends and how you can encourage him to use his O&M skills. It is understandable that you might be concerned about his safety when using O&M skills. Remember, though, there is a certain amount of risk for all of us in moving about the environment. Orientation and mobility instructors are specifically trained to monitor the safety of children with visual impairments and to intervene when necessary.

Conclusion

Early O&M instruction is critical to enabling your child to successfully move about his environment. Your involvement in your child's O&M program is equally important. The O&M instructor is responsible for providing you with an ongoing parent education program which will help you actively participate in your child's O&M instructional program and reinforce important O&M concepts and skills on a daily basis. It is important for the O&M instructor to teach you to understand your child's strengths and needs and to provide you with the skills necessary to reinforce his strengths and compensate for his needs. At the same time, the O&M instructor should encourage you to participate in the decision-making process regarding your child's O&M program and should respect your wishes or suggestions for instruction. Ultimately, the focus of the O&M program should be on providing your child with appropriate O&M instruction at the earliest possible age through an ongoing partnership between you and the O&M instructor.

Parent Statements

When the orientation and mobility specialist brought Nakisha's cane to her, I thought she was too young but she really took to it easier than I thought.

◄o►

I know I should encourage my son to use his cane but it is so much easier just to hold his hand as we walk. If he uses his cane we walk so slowly.

◄o►

I'm just getting used to my son using a cane. At first I didn't know how much information I should give him and how much I should allow him to discover on his own.

◄o►

There is a blind person in our town who takes the bus everywhere. He shops by himself and goes to work. He visits friends and goes to church. All on a city bus. I know I should be encouraged by this but it really scares me to think of Matthew using public transportation.

◄o►

I hate when somebody "pulls" my child. I know they don't understand but it still makes me mad.

◄○►

How will my child get around in school? Will he have trouble in the lunchroom?

◄○►

My child has great mobility. He runs around outside and plays with the other kids just fine. He has trouble when he tries to look at things close up, but he doesn't have trouble walking around. Sometimes that is confusing for people—they doubt that he has a visual impairment.

◄○►

I've asked the vision specialist about guide dogs. It seems like a good option for the future.

◄○►

I have been stopped at the mall or at the grocery store by people who think I am being mean to Beth by making her walk by herself with a cane. They just don't understand.

◄○►

I know that a big part of independence for Joey will be his ability to get around by himself. So, even though it is hard sometimes, we try to encourage him to be independent now. It would be so much easier and faster to take his hand or guide him, but that won't really help him.

Chapter Twelve

◄○►

Children with Multiple and Visual Disabilities

Jane Erin, Ph.D.*

It was time for breakfast! Eric knew this because he could hear the coffeepot dripping and the clatter of the bowls as his sister got them out of the cupboard. As his mother lifted him into his special chair and buckled the strap around him, he began to chuckle with anticipation. "Time to eat, champ," his father commented from across the table.

Mr. Harris thought about how much had changed since Eric was born four years ago. Then, doctors had said that his son might not live: he was three months premature, and so tiny that his father could have held him in one hand if they had been allowed to hold him at all.

They knew from the beginning that Eric might have some disabilities. But they were so happy that he had survived that it was a long time before they considered how Eric's differences might affect the family's life. Doctors had talked about the possibility that he might have cerebral palsy and mental retardation, but no one had mentioned blindness. Mrs. Harris had been the first to notice that Eric's eyes didn't seem to follow people walking in front of

---

* Jane Erin is an associate professor at The University of Arizona, where she
   coordinates the program in Visual Disabilities. She has been a teacher of
   students with visual and multiple disabilities as well as a program
   supervisor at the Western Pennsylvania School for Blind Children. She has
   written many articles related to the education of children with multiple and
   visual impairments, and co-authored the third edition of the book *Visual
   Handicaps and Learning* with Dr. Natalie Barraga.

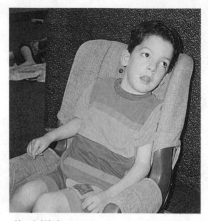

him. When they took him back to the doctor and learned that Eric could only see light, it seemed like the ultimate irony. After all of the medical crises that Eric had survived, it was difficult for his family to accept that he would never enjoy the visual beauty of the world that he had struggled to enter.

During the first two years, there were times that the Harrises wondered whether Eric's disabilities were more than they could handle. He had difficulty eating, was often ill, and needed frequent hospitalizations. It became apparent that he had cerebral palsy and that he would learn very slowly. But after the second year, things began to change. Gradually, Eric was becoming a member of the family. His laugh was contagious, and his brother and sister learned that he enjoyed roughhousing and listening to music. And it was obvious that he could learn: in the last year he had started sitting up by himself and searching for toys when they disappeared. He could imitate sounds that others made, and now used special sounds for "cup" and for rides in the car. Although Eric was very different from what the Harrises expected their third child to be, they were often glad that he had introduced them to an unknown world.

There are many children like Eric who have a visual disability in combination with one or more other disabilities. Disabilities commonly associated with visual impairment include cerebral palsy and other movement disorders, mental retardation, and hearing impairment. As many as 40 percent of children who have these physical and mental handicaps may also have some visual impairment. Conversely, as many as 50 to 60 percent of children with visual impairments have other disabilities.

Most children who have a visual impairment in combination with another disability have low vision. Although their vision may not provide as much detail or information as it does for others, they can still use vision as a means of learning. A smaller number of children are functionally blind and learn mainly through touch and hearing. They may be aware of light or the location of lighting, but cannot see detail and form well enough to use sight to learn about the world around them.

The term "multiply handicapped" is frequently used to describe a child who has more than one condition that affects learning. Under the IDEA (formerly Public Law 94–142), a child is considered multiply handicapped if she has two or more handicapping conditions that require educational attention. According to this definition, a child who has cerebral palsy which makes it impossible for her to write with a pencil and who also has low vision which makes enlarged print necessary for reading would be considered multiply handicapped. A child with the same visual condition whose reading skills are delayed for no identifiable reason would not be considered to have multiple disabilities. Some states define multiply handicapped a little differently. For instance, some specify that a child must have major delays in several developmental areas in order to qualify for educational services as multiply handicapped. (Although many people today prefer the term "disability" to "handicapped," you will probably still hear the term "handicapped" if your child is identified as having multiple disabilities. This is because some legal and legislative documents use the term "multiply handicapped" to refer to children who may receive certain specialized services.)

Each child with multiple disabilities is unique. Each child has her own temperament and her own set of experiences and may be affected in different ways by a medical condition or physical disability. This makes it almost impossible to predict how much any child will learn and what she will be able to do as an adult. For parents of children with multiple disabilities, facing this uncertainty may be the greatest challenge. No doctor, therapist, or educator can predict just what to expect for the future, and coordinating information and experiences from many sources may sometimes seem overwhelming. Ultimately, you will become the expert on your own child.

This chapter discusses the types of disabilities that sometimes accompany a visual impairment. It also examines the effects these conditions can have on a child with a visual impairment, as well as some ways to help minimize these effects on learning and growing.

Visual Conditions That Often Occur with Other Disabilities

Any of the visual conditions described in Chapter 2 can occur with or without additional disabilities. Several visual conditions, however, almost always occur with another disability. These visual conditions are discussed in this chapter to help you understand why.

Cortical Visual Impairments. Cortical visual impairments are caused by an abnormality in the brain. The eyeball and other optical structures are often normal, but for some reason, the brain has difficulty processing and interpreting visual information. The damage that causes the visual impairment may result from loss of oxygen to the brain, bleeding in the brain, or other types of trauma. This same injury to the brain may also result in cerebral palsy, mental retardation, seizures, or language difficulties.

Although some children with this condition are totally blind, most have some vision, and their use of vision often improves over time. Children with cortical impairments may behave in puzzling ways. For example, their vision may seem to change at different times of the day, they may seem to stare straight ahead or "through" things, and they may seem to use vision to confirm information discovered through other senses rather than as their primary sense. Many children with this condition pay more attention to colorful or moving objects.

Optic Nerve Atrophy and Optic Nerve Hypoplasia. These conditions affect the optic nerve, the bundle of fibers that transmits signals from the retina to the brain. In optic nerve atrophy, the optic nerve has been damaged in some way; in optic nerve hypoplasia the nerve has not developed. This may mean that the child may have some vision or may be blind, depending on how much of the optic nerve is intact.

These conditions often occur in children whose brains are impaired in other ways. A child's optic nerve may fail to develop properly because of something that has occurred early in pregnancy. These events, such as a mother's exposure to a toxic substance or an accidental change in the genes, can result in damage to other parts of the brain. Children with optic nerve hypoplasia may have other disabilities such as cerbral palsy or growth problems, since the optic nerve is located close to the pituitary gland.

Some children with optic nerve atrophy or hypoplasia have a loss of peripheral vision and can only see objects that are straight ahead of them; others lose central vision and may notice objects to the sides more easily. If your child has either diagnosis, it is important to observe her carefully to discover whether her central or peripheral vision is better and whether she prefers using one eye over the other. This is important so you can teach your child to pay attention to things on the side where the visual field is not as wide. In addition, children who mainly use one eye do not see depth as easily as other children, and may have particular difficulty walking down stairs or catching a ball.

Other Conditions. Various other conditions can also affect both the brain and the visual system. Cytomegalovirus is a common virus that can damage a child's brain before birth, resulting in such disabilities as mental retardation, hearing impairment, and visual impairment. Toxoplasmosis is a parasite commonly transmitted by cats which can invade the brain and eyes. The resulting brain damage can cause mental retardation, seizures, cerebral palsy, and visual impairment, alone or in combination. Rubella, or German measles, can affect the developing fetus if the mother has the illness early in her pregnancy. Depending upon when in the pregnancy the illness occurs, the baby may be born with conditions such as mental retardation, cerebral palsy, seizures, heart defects, and visual impairment. A very common cause of visual and multiple disabilities is a loss of oxygen to the brain (anoxia), either during delivery or as a result of an accident later in childhood. Again, loss of oxygen can lead to brain damage and a wide variety of disabilities, including learning disabilities, mental retardation, cerebral palsy, and visual impairment.

The vision loss caused by these conditions can range from a mild impairment to complete blindness. Most students do have some vision and should be encouraged to use it. However, children with visual disabilities and brain damage may seem to use their vision differently at different times of day. In addition, these children often have trouble with perceptual responses such as perceiving depth, remembering visual information, reaching for objects they see, and identifying important visual information.

While it is helpful to know the cause and implications of your child's visual condition, it is important to keep in mind that the amount of functional vision varies greatly among children with most conditions. It is impossible to predict how a child will function based on a medical diagnosis. Even the information provided by complex medical tests cannot describe exactly the amount and nature of a vision loss for a child with multiple disabilities. This is because parts of the brain have different purposes in different people. The amount of vision that a child has depends on how old she was when the brain damage occurred, as well as on other factors such as the child's maturity and learning experiences.

Most of the methods of assessing vision in children require the child to speak or to match pictures. When a child cannot do these things because of a physical or other disability, it is important to watch the way she acts when there are things to see. Careful observation of your child in many different situations will provide the best information about your child's vision.

Common Conditions Associated with Visual Impairments

Several disabilities frequently occur with visual impairments. They include mental retardation, cerebral palsy, spina bifida, physical impairments resulting from trauma, speech and communication disorders, and hearing impairments.

In combination with a visual difference, these conditions can affect the rate or characteristics of your child's development. First, they may change the rate of learning. For example, if your child has mental retardation, she will require more time to learn most skills than she would if her only disability was a visual impairment. Second, they may change the form of learning. For example, if your child has a hearing impairment, she may need to rely more on touch than on hearing to learn. Third, they may change the content of learning. If your child has a physical disability and a visual impairment, learning the rules of football are not as important as learning how to operate a tape recorder.

Generally, the most important skills for children with multiple disabilities to learn are functional skills. These are the skills that enable your child to do ordinary daily tasks. They may be as simple as grasping a spoon or as complex as traveling to a job independently. But in any case, the skill is something that will require assistance from another person if your child cannot learn to do it on her own. In planning for your child's future, the questions that are important to ask are: What does she need to do now in our household? What might she need to do soon . . . next month or next year? What does our family really want her to learn? The sections below will help you understand the challenges that face children with various types of multiple disabilities so that you can begin to answer these questions for your family.

Mental Retardation

Children with visual impairments often show delayed development during the preschool years because of the learning challenges posed by their vision differences. For example, they may be slow to crawl or walk because they are not aware of interesting things around them to be explored, or they may repeat the words of others more frequently than most children because the sounds of speech are more available to them than information about the meaning of language. But these developmental lags often disappear as language becomes more meaningful to them and as they begin to explore and understand their environment. When a child's slowness in learning is only the result of visual impairment she is said to have "developmental delays."

Other children with visual impairments experience a true limitation in the rate and quality of learning. They do not ever "catch up" with other children their age. Their skills in all areas of development—cognition, language, movement, self-help, and social skills—usually remain significantly below average all their lives. In addition, they have more difficulty learning adaptive behaviors. These are the skills that enable people to independently meet the expectations of their world, such as dressing and feeding themselves, managing money, or talking appropriately with other people. Children with these limitations in learning are said to have mental retardation. About 3 percent of all children in the United States have mental retardation, but the percentage among children with visual disabilities is much greater—possibly as high as 40 percent.

Mental retardation is not caused by visual impairment, although either condition can increase the delays normally caused by one of the conditions. That is, children with mental retardation would have significant learning delays even if they did not have visual impairments, but learning may take still longer if they also have a visual impairment. As the preceding section explained, often what causes a child's visual impairment also causes her mental retardation. For example, lack of oxygen (anoxia) can result in both mental retardation and visual impairment. Less often, the two conditions result from entirely different causes. For example, a child may have mental retardation from bleeding in the brain at birth and may be blind as a result of retinopathy of prematurity, a retinal problem that may occur in premature infants. Frequently, the cause of mental retardation cannot be pinpointed, even though over 350 causes of mental retardation have been identified.

It can be very frustrating for parents to see that their child is not progressing rapidly and to wonder whether this delay is only the result of a visual impairment. Your frustration may be compounded because mental retardation can be especially difficult to diagnose in children with visual impairments. Often, the evaluation procedures used by schools do not take a child's visual differences into consideration. This may result in a child being diagnosed with mental retardation when her delays result from a lack of experience due to a visual impairment. Or a child's mental retardation may not be diagnosed as mental retardation because learning delays are attributed only to a visual impairment.

Because it is more difficult to assess the true cognitive abilities of children with visual impairments, a professional who is knowledgeable about children with these impairments should be involved in the evaluation of your child's intellectual function. If the psychologist or diagnostician who evaluates your child is not experienced in working with students with visual handicaps, a certified vision specialist should help decide what tests and procedures will give the most accurate picture of your child's abilities. And if the way a test is given is modified because of your child's disabilities, this information should be written in the report. It is also important to gather information about your child's abilities using other methods besides tests and planned activities. For example, observations of your child and interviews with you and other family members can help to provide a more accurate picture of your child's behaviors. As Chapter 9 explains, if you are concerned that an assessment may not be accurate, you have the right to request a second evaluation by a qualified person of your own choice.

If your child is diagnosed as having mental retardation, you may also be told that she has a specific degree of mental retardation. That is, you may hear that her mental retardation is mild, moderate, severe, or profound. Or, if the professional who diagnoses your child is using more recent terminology, you may hear that your child needs intermittent, limited, extensive, or pervasive support. These degrees of mental retardation have been identified because children with mental retardation, like all children, have a wide range of intellectual abilities. Although their development is delayed, some children with mental retardation learn more quickly and easily than other children with mental retardation.

Children who have mild mental retardation (or need intermittent support) may not look or act much differently from others of their age and often learn to read and write beyond the sixth grade level. However, they may have difficulty with complex thinking and reasoning, and as adults may need occasional assistance to live independently. Children who have moderate mental retardation (or need limited support) usually can speak and understand full sentences. They may learn to read the words they need to know to function semi-independently as adults, and with assistance can usually learn most daily living skills such as dressing, grooming, and meal preparation. Children who have severe mental retardation (or need extensive support) have more difficulty with all skills, but with help can often learn to communicate their wants and needs and can learn community survival skills, such as signing their name and behaving appropriately in a variety of situations. Children who have profound mental retardation (or need pervasive support) can sometimes learn some self-help and communication skills with intensive training, and may communicate using manual signs or gestures, or simply through voice sounds. Children with severe or profound mental retardation need a responsible person to care for them throughout their lives, but can participate in and enjoy many routines and activities with friends and family members.

The world can be a confusing place for children who have mental retardation in addition to a visual handicap. One reason is because it is very difficult for them to make sense of the abstract cues and symbols, such as speech or pictures, that give order and meaning to events around them. An example is understanding the significance of putting on a coat. Although a child with a visual impairment may not see others do this, she learns to associate her own experience of putting on a coat and the conversation of others with the experience of going outdoors. A child who has mental retardation but no other disability will also learn this by noticing others put on their coats, although it may take her longer to make this association. A child with both mental retardation and blindness does not have visual cues (seeing her own and others' coats) and may not understand spoken cues. It may therefore take this child even longer to learn that when she is dressed in a coat she is going outdoors, and she may not learn it at all unless it happens frequently.

If your child has both mental retardation and a visual impairment, it is important to carefully structure her world to help her anticipate events and objects, through touch and sound as well as through sight. For example, using a timer with a bell to signal the end of playtime provides a cue that your child can understand and learn to associate with the change of an activity. Always using the same materials, such as a familiar plastic mug for drinking, provides the best chance for your child to recall the cue, understand its meaning, and learn the related skill.

Children with visual and cognitive disabilities may have extra difficulty understanding the concept of time, including past and future events, since they do not see the visual cues to coming events such as mother getting out a paintbrush to paint or father carrying a book and walking toward his chair. If they do not understand speech, others cannot convey information to them about events as they might with a child who has a visual impairment but no additional disabilities. They need to participate directly in an activity to learn from it, and they need many more repetitions of a new skill in order to master it. The sections below describe some ways that mental retardation can complicate learning in specific developmental areas and offer suggestions for helping children with mental retardation learn. Some organizations that can be helpful to parents of children with mental retardation are the ARC and the Association for Persons with Severe Handicaps (TASH). Information on how to contact these organizations is provided in the Resource Guide.

Communication Disorders. People usually expect communication to be easy for a child with visual impairments to learn. This is not always the case, however, especially if the child also has other disabilities.

To communicate effectively, your child must understand that she can receive a response from others if she expresses a message or feeling. She must also have a form of communication that she can use and respond to. That form of communication may be gestures, picture symbols, object symbols, sign language, speech, braille, or print. Children with multiple disabilities can have more trouble than usual with either of these elements of effective communication. That is, they may have extra difficulty understanding how language works or remembering specific elements such as words or signs.

All children with mental retardation have more difficulty than usual learning how to understand and use language. This is because mental retardation causes delays in all areas of development, including communication skills. When a child with mental retardation also has a visual impairment, the difficulties are compounded. One reason is that the development of language depends on the child's awareness of *referents*—the objects, events, and people to be talked about. If a child cannot see what others are talking about, it is harder to learn that a specific word refers to a specific object or event. If the child also has cognitive delays, figuring out the relationships between words and objects or events becomes still harder. Using the same words and phrases to refer to familiar routines and events will give the child the best opportunity to match language with its referents, especially if language is used while an activity is taking place.

Echolalia, or the word-for-word repetition of other's speech, is another communication problem common to children with visual impairments, especially those with mental retardation. Children with visual impairments are likely to use echolalia for a longer period of time than other children. This can range from meaningless repetition, in which a child repeats the words, but doesn't understand them, to the meaningful use of echolalia in an interactive situation. For example, when someone asks, "Do you want a cookie?" and five-year-old Mary holds out her hands, smiles, and says, "Do you want a cookie," she is clearly responding, "Yes, I want one!" When a child has mental retardation in addition to a visual impairment, she is even more likely to persist in using echolalia. This may be because the child's ability to speak has outdistanced her understanding of words and concepts.

If your child often uses echolalic speech, it is best to respond as if she has made an appropriate attempt to communicate. For example, when Mary responds to the questions about a cookie using the same words, handing her a cookie and saying, "You do want a cookie!" is one way to let her know that her message is understood. Ignoring echolalia or correcting it may make your child feel that her communication is not effective, and she may try to speak less often. Only if your child has proven that she is a competent speaker should you suggest, "Try it again," when she uses echolalia.

Some children may speak infrequently, or, in some cases, not at all. This may result from a lack of understanding of the function of language or from the inability to take part in interactive situations. Specific drill or practice is not as important as establishing a meaningful, motivating language environment in the natural setting of home or classroom. This is especially true for children whose language is in the early stages of development. Speaking to your child in short, simple sentences about things happening around her will provide opportunities for her to build bridges between words and experiences.

Movement Skills. Most children with mental retardation—with and without visual impairments—have motor delays. As a rule, they learn to sit up, stand, walk, climb stairs, draw with a crayon, cut with scissors, throw a ball, ride a bike, and so forth later than normally developing children do. Depending on their level of mental retardation, they may never learn to do some of these things at all, or may never be able to do them as proficiently as someone who doesn't have mental retardation. This is because mental retardation impedes learning in all areas, not just intellectual development.

Having a visual impairment on top of mental retardation can cause even greater delays in motor skills. For example, many children with mental retardation are slow in learning to crawl or walk. When a child also has a visual impairment, she may be less motivated to learn these skills, because she may not know what objects are available to be explored or may not be curious about something she hears which is out of reach. It also may be more difficult for her to recall an experience or activity that has brought her pleasure in the past, so she may not make the effort to begin it again. For example, it may take many repetitions of hitting a mobile to ring a bell before a child understands that the sound is the result of her own movement.

You can encourage your child to move by positioning objects or people just out of reach. A music box or the voice of her grandmother will remind your child that there is someone or something interesting out there to be discovered. At first, the sound should be constant: the music box or grandmother's voice singing or talking motivates your child to move forward. Later, just calling your child's name once or twice will require her to remember where the sound came from as she moves.

Play activities can also encourage different movements and positions. Physical play on the floor with pillows and on hard and soft surfaces, as well as body contact with others, will teach your child how it feels to push and move against gravity. The feeling of physical contact is pleasurable for many children and should be introduced according to your child's preference. Many children prefer firm touches to light ones. Physical play with familiar people provides a chance to discover how others move their bodies and that others have body parts similar to your child's own. This can help extend your child's understanding of the world beyond her own body and discourage the repetitive behaviors that some children develop because their own body is the most available source of stimulation. These repetitive motions, such as rocking or head banging, may occur in part because children do not know what else to do with their bodies.

Social and Emotional Skills. Because vision brings us information about how others act and react, a visual disability can make it more challenging to learn social skills. If your child also has mental retardation, it may take longer to understand information that is available through nonvisual means. Identifying a person who is speaking or remembering names requires memory of voice sounds, and understanding social rules such as when to shake hands means that a child must know when this is appropriate.

It is important for you to describe and model social behaviors so that your child can learn about them: "I shook hands with Mr. Green because he is my friend. Let's try shaking hands the way I did with Mr. Green." Another way you can help your child develop social skills is to make sure she learns that other people are enjoyable and can make interesting things happen. So as not to overwhelm or confuse her, it is best to start out with a few familiar people in her circle of acquaintances. These people should be reminded to let her know when they are approaching, especially if your child does not have enough vision to see them coming. If your child cannot understand words, you may want to think of a consistent way to help her identify familiar individuals by touch. For instance, placing your child's hand on her sister's long ponytail or on grandmother's ring will help her learn to expect the voice and manner of that person.

Later, you can arrange for play activities with groups of other children. It may be helpful to explain to other children what your child can and cannot do: "Sharon doesn't see with her eyes, but if you put the clay in her hand, she likes the cold feeling on her fingers." You can help choose materials that will interest your own child as well as other children of the same age, even though their interests and capabilities are different.

It can be particularly challenging to teach children with visual and mental disabilities how to protect themselves and follow safety rules. Skills such as walking on sidewalks rather than in streets or not going away with strangers can be learned through role-playing and practice. To be sure that your child remembers what you have taught her, provide frequent opportunities to repeat the role playing. Because children with disabilities interact with many different adults and may become very trusting, also be sure to explain to your child when others should *not* be trusted.

Although some children will not be able to interact with others using speech, they should be encouraged to develop their communication skills in normal social situations. Attending parties and social events, going to the grocery store, attending religious services, and visiting friends can be very satisfying to children and can give them practice with social routines that will make them more pleasant companions and family members.

Like other children, your child must also learn that there are limits and rules that apply to daily routines. Your approach to discipline should be as similar as possible to the approach you take with other children in the family. Sometimes you may need to provide extra opportunities to practice a rule so that you can be sure your child understands it. Then you can give your child praise and occasional rewards when she behaves appropriately.

Occasionally you may need to discipline your child by withdrawing a privilege. When you do this, be sure that your child understands why you are taking something away, and make the punishment fit the misbehavior. For example, if your child does not put a toy away, you might tell her that she may not use the toy for a week. Show her where the toy will be stored, and each time she asks to use it, remind her that she will be able to use it again on Monday. Then be sure that you praise her for putting the toy away until that becomes a habit. Many children with mental retardation do not understand complex reasoning, and scolding or lecturing will not change their behavior. It is more effective to arrange their world so that good things happen when they behave appropriately.

PHYSICAL AND MOTOR IMPAIRMENTS

For a child with a visual impairment, the ability to move out into the world, to explore with hands and feet, and to experience changes in temperatures and texture are important in building concepts about what the world is like. If a child also has a physical disorder that limits her ability to move and explore, she may have trouble learning directly through discovery. A child with "normal" intelligence who has both a physical and visual handicap may learn

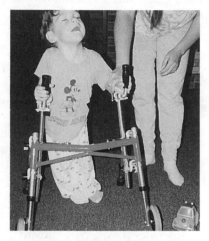

to rely excessively on words and sounds for information and stimulation. She may play with rhyming words or may prefer listening to the radio to any other activity. A child with mental retardation may withdraw into a world that does not extend beyond her own body and physical needs. Because she does not know that there are other people and objects to be explored, she may repeat behaviors like rocking or making interesting sounds that have no meaning.

Several types of physical disabilities, including cerebral palsy and spina bifida, often accompany visual impairment. The sections below discuss how these conditions can further complicate learning and development in children with visual impairments.

Cerebral Palsy

Cerebral palsy is the name for a variety of disorders that affect a child's motor abilities, including movement, balance, and posture. The condition results from a difference in the early development of the brain or from an injury to the brain before birth, during birth, or shortly after birth. Types of injuries that can result in cerebral palsy include: infections; head trauma during or after birth; toxic injuries from maternal drug or alcohol use; too little oxygen before, during, or after birth; bleeding in the brain. Cerebral palsy is not a disease. It does not become worse with time, and it is not contagious.

How cerebral palsy affects a child's motor skills depends on the location and extent of the brain injury. But all children with cerebral palsy have problems with *muscle tone,* or the amount of resistance to movement in a muscle. Types of muscle tone problems that may be present include:

- High tone (*hypertonia, spasticity*). Children with high tone have muscles that are "tighter" or more resistant to movement than usual. As a result, their movements are stiff and awkward.
- Low tone (*hypotonia, floppiness*). Children with low tone have muscles that are "floppier" and less resistant to movement than usual. Consequently, it requires a great deal of effort for them to move and to maintain a position.
- Fluctuating (variable) tone. Children with fluctuating tone sometimes have low tone and sometimes have high tone.

Besides having problems with muscle tone, some children with cerebral palsy also have involuntary movements. Involuntary movements are uncontrolled movements in the face, arms, legs, or elsewhere in the body. Cerebral palsy is also frequently associated with mental retardation and seizures.

A child with cerebral palsy may have motor problems throughout her entire body. That is, she may have involuntary movements or high or low tone in her head, trunk, arms, and legs. This is known as *quadriplegia.* Then again, motor problems may affect only the upper extremities, the lower extremities, or one side of the body.

As mentioned earlier, some children with cerebral palsy have cortical visual impairments. In addition, about 50 percent of children with cerebral palsy have difficulty controlling the muscles of the eyes. This lack of muscle control usually results in *strabismus.* In this condition, the eyes are misaligned so that one or both eyes turns inward or outward. The eyes may be misaligned all the time, or only when the child looks in a particular direction. *Amblyopia,* or loss of vision in one eye due to disuse, may occur as a result of strabismus. Both of these conditions are described in greater detail in Chapter 2.

To correct strabismus, sometimes the doctor will try surgery to tighten the eye muscles or put a patch over the stronger eye. For many children with cerebral palsy, however, the problem is never completely corrected. Instead, these children learn to use their eyes selectively in order to get the most visual information. Many children with strabismus rely mainly on one eye for visual information. This means that they may have difficulty judging depth. They may, for example, have trouble anticipating a ball rolled toward them or difficulty inserting coins into a piggy bank. They also have a small field loss on the side of the less useful eye. This means they may turn their head slightly toward that side to make up for the missing information. Some children learn to use one eye for near tasks and the other for distance tasks. Watching your child carefully when she is using her eyes will help you decide what she is seeing and whether she is using one eye more than the other.

United Cerebral Palsy (UCP) and its many local affiliates can provide helpful information and support to parents of children with cerebral palsy. See the Resource Guide for contact information.

Other Physical and Motor Impairments

Although cerebral palsy is the most common cause of visual and motor difficulties in children, there are other reasons why a child with a visual impairment may also have a physical disability. Spina bifida, for example, is a physical disability that can indirectly cause a visual disability. In this condition, a child is born with open vertebrae in the spinal column and sometimes with hydrocephalus, or excess fluid in the brain. The exact cause of spina bifida is still unknown. Children with spina bifida may be unable to walk or experience sensations, often in the lower part of the body. They often have optic nerve atrophy or cortical visual impairment as a result of extra pressure within the brain. This can cause a visual impairment or complete blindness.

Occasionally children are injured in accidents which result in visual disabilities. Very often, this is due to a head injury, and children may experience a cortical visual loss as well as physical disabilities in various parts of the body. Some children who acquire physical and visual disabilities as the result of accidents rapidly recover their visual and physical abilities during the first year or two after the accident. Others improve more gradually for years after the accident occurred. And some never fully recover.

How Physical Disabilities Affect Learning

Most young children do a great deal of learning by watching and doing. For example, they learn about the concept of cause and effect by smacking a tower of blocks and then watching it fall over. They learn about the concept of object permanence by watching a ball roll under the couch and then retrieving it. They learn the difference between hard and soft by touching or chewing on a variety of different objects.

Obviously, when a child has both visual and motor handicaps, she may have trouble learning by watching and doing. And yet, she still needs immediate and concrete opportunities for learning, with plenty of emphasis on doing rather than just listening. As a parent, there are many ways you can provide these opportunities to your child. For example, if your child cannot see a toy or reach forward to get it, you can make her aware of its presence some other way. Although technology has expanded the options for children with combinations of disabilities, the best solutions to problems such as retrieving a toy are not always technologically complex. Your child's cue to an object's existence may be a ticking timer or her brother's voice calling; her means of getting the object may be a string or a stick with a T hook. What is important is that your child experiences the result of her own actions.

If your child has some vision, it is important for her to be positioned in a way that will help her to see efficiently. Sometimes the positions that promote good physical development do not provide the best visual information. For example, a child positioned on her stomach with a wedge for support may see only objects directly in front of her and may not be able to raise or turn her head to see other parts of the room. Your child's physical or occupational therapist should work closely with the vision specialist to help you decide what positions are best for your child. They can also help you decide how much time your child should spend in different positions.

If your child cannot walk or crawl, there are many ways you can help her experience movement through space. When she is young, you can carry her in a sling or backpack as you move around the house. This way, she can experience the immediate sensations that go along with routine activities. She can hear and feel water coming out of the faucet or the breeze blowing in when you open a window.

As your child gets older, physical and occupational therapists can work with your family to obtain an appropriate travel chair or wheelchair. There are wheelchairs that require very little movement and control to operate, and children with severe physical disabilities can often learn to control their own movement using a mechanical wheelchair. Your child's wheelchair should provide comfortable, symmetrical positioning which allows her maximum control over the position and the movement of the chair. If your child has vision, take care that the side panels on the head support of the chair do not restrict head movement or reduce visual field.

If your child does not have enough vision to anticipate landmarks in a route of travel, devices can be attached to her wheelchair or travel chair to provide feedback. For example, an antenna attached to the right wheel can act as a trailing device and provide an auditory cue about your child's distance from the wall. Some children are able to use devices such as the Mowat sensor™, a small box which is held in the traveler's hand and vibrates to tell her that she is approaching an object. The orientation and mobility instructor can work with the physical and occupational therapist to devise the most effective adaptations for your child. See Chapter 11 for more information on orientation and mobility.

The following sections describe some ways that having a physical disability can affect specific areas of development. They also include suggestions to help your child learn and grow in these areas.

Communication Skills. Children who have cerebral palsy in addition to a visual impairment also have added problems in learning to use speech and understand language. The physical process of producing speech may be affected by the child's difficulty controlling muscles of the face, mouth, throat, and chest. Some children may produce speech that is difficult to understand, partly because they cannot close their lips to produce clear consonant sounds. A child who also has a visual impairment may not see the lips of others moving, so imitating the movements that produce specific sounds may be difficult.

Physical disabilities can also affect a child's ability to understand language. Movement limitations may reduce opportunities for new experiences and for interaction with others. Others may assume that the child understands a word or idea which relates to something the child has never done. For example, words that refer to a farm, a circus, or to forest animals may have little meaning to a child who lives in a city and spends most of her time indoors, especially if she does not have enough vision to learn from pictures.

Obviously, it can be very frustrating if your child can understand others' speech but has great difficulty making herself understood. To help your child communicate, an augmentative device may therefore be recommended. As the term implies, an augmentative device is one that is meant to *augment*, not replace, a child's speech abilities. Although parents sometimes worry that using an augmentative device will prevent their child from learning to speak, this is not the case. Most studies show that using an augmentative device encourages a child to use other forms of expression, such as speech.

Your child's augmentative device will be selected based on her communication needs, developmental level, and useful vision. For a young child who has some vision, picture symbols or photographs might be arranged on a language board. The child could then point to or touch pictures of objects and actions to express her thoughts and needs. Contrast, color, background, and size should be considered in choosing pictures or symbols that the child could best see. Pictures can be too large as well as too small for a child to view comfortably. For most children with visual impairments, pictures of three inches or smaller are large enough.

For young children with little or no vision, language boards often use real objects or parts of real objects as cues to meaning. For example, a small cup may represent drinking or a bell may represent music time. Later, the handle of the cup or the clapper from the bell could be used to represent the whole object.

Some children eventually learn to use language boards on which words are indicated with braille or with a symbol that has no relationship to the real object. There are also a variety of computerized devices available, including some that can produce a mechanical voice.

If your child uses augmentative communication or a gesture or sign system, remember that she may not see when others are looking at the device or at the signs she makes. Consequently, she needs to learn ways of establishing the presence of others, such as touching others' arms before beginning to communicate. Your child also needs to receive a response whenever she makes an attempt to communicate.

Whatever system your child uses to communicate, it is important that you don't just communicate with her in commands or questions. Your child needs to learn to take an active role in conversations—to initiate them, as well as to participate in them. She needs to learn that through communication, she can gain more control over her world. For example, she may not be able to walk over to the stereo and turn it on herself, but she can ask somebody to do it for her. Likewise, she may not be able to open the refrigerator and pour herself a glass of juice, but if she asks appropriately, you may do it for her.

You can encourage active communication by presenting choices whenever possible. In addition, you can be sure that your child has enough time to express ideas and a communication method that does not just limit her to answering questions. Pausing when talking is important because it lets your child know when it is her turn to speak. Responding to any movement or behavior that seems to communicate will help your child understand that communication includes at least two people.

Movement Skills. Motor dysfunctions such as cerebral palsy or spina bifida can put some real limits on how well and how quickly a child is able to master motor skills. For example, depending on the location of nerve damage, a child with spina bifida may have trouble learning to roll over and sit up, and may never be able to stand or walk unaided. Depending on the location and severity of brain injury, a child with cerebral palsy might have these same problems, as well as difficulty using her arms and hands to reach and grasp. Like other children, however, children with motor disabilities can develop the physical abilities they have to the utmost. With the right kinds of encouragement and help, they can improve their strength, coordination, and endurance, and can master many important motor skills.

As Chapters 8 and 11 explain, your child can receive a great deal of assistance in learning movement skills from physical therapists, occupational therapists, and orientation and mobility specialists at school. As a parent, you can encourage movement by positioning playthings so that your child must move to reach for them, and by making sure your child participates in daily routines that involve movement.

Social and Emotional Skills. For a variety of reasons, children with multiple disabilities may make slower progress than usual in social and emotional development. Physical, mental, or hearing impairments may make it harder for them to hone their social skills by initiating interactions with others. And others may interpret their lack of interaction to mean that they do not want to have social contact, and therefore leave them alone. Compounding the problem, parents may not correct inappropriate behavior because they feel sorry for their child or think she cannot understand what is expected of her. To get along in society, however, all children need to understand social conventions and safety rules. Your child, like all children, can pick up much of this understanding in the home.

One way you can help with your child's social skills is to discourage any repetitive behaviors such as eye poking, rocking, finger chewing, or head banging. Children with multiple disabilities may sometimes have these mannerisms because they are not aware that there are things to be explored beyond their own bodies. If a child is blind, she may not be aware that others do not have the same habits. You can discourage these behaviors by a gentle reminder or a signal such as a tap on the shoulder. You can also offer your child toys or other objects to draw her attention away from the repetitive behavior.

Another way to boost your child's social skills is to prepare her for visits and social events. If your child understands words, this may mean talking to her about what she will do and who will be there. If your child does not understand words, it may help to show her pictures of people she will see or to give her an object to remind her of a special event to come. For example, she may hold an

inflated toy as you drive to the swimming pool or an overnight bag with her pajamas on the way to her grandparents' house. This will help her to be aware of the people and objects around her and to feel good about being with other people.

Deaf-Blindness

Less than 5 percent of all children with visual disabilities also have hearing disabilities. Although these children are often called "deaf-blind," most of them do have usable vision, hearing, or both. In some areas of the country, the term "dual sensory impairment" is used to describe a reduction in both vision and hearing.

Deaf-blindness in children can be caused by several conditions: neurological complications that accompany premature birth; infections and viruses such as toxoplasmosis, meningitis, or cytomegalovirus; and maternal rubella are among the most common causes.

There are two types of hearing losses: sensorineural and conductive. A sensorineural loss means that the nerves which receive sound and carry it into the brain are damaged or have not developed. This kind of loss can result from any condition that damages the brain, such as infection before the baby is born, premature birth, or the effects of drugs or medication. Some sensorineural hearing loss is inherited. Sensorineural losses are often more severe than conductive losses. Sometimes hearing can be improved through use of a hearing aid, but other times hearing aids are not helpful.

A conductive loss occurs when something interferes with the passage of sound through the ear canal or the structures of the middle and inner ear. This can be a permanent condition, and may be caused by something like a growth of tissue in the ear, or it may be temporary and caused by a cold or a middle ear infection. Often this type of hearing loss can be improved by surgery or by the use of a hearing aid.

Children with hearing losses may hear some frequencies of sound better than others. Frequency refers to how high- or low-pitched sound is, and is measured in hertz. The loudness or volume of a sound, measured in decibels, can also affect how well it can be heard. When your child's hearing is tested, the degree of hearing loss she has at each frequency will be measured. A reading of 0 to 15 decibels at any given frequency means your child has normal hearing at that frequency; anything higher than 15 generally means she has a hearing loss.

A variety of tests can assess hearing, but finding one that is appropriate for a child with both a hearing and vision impairment can be difficult. You may need to work with professionals to teach your child an action such as dropping a block in a can to signal that she hears a sound. There are also medical tests that can provide general information about whether your child is receiving sound in the brain, even if she is too young or otherwise unable to signal what she hears. In an auditory brain stem response (ABR), for example, clicks or other sounds are produced and a computer recording made that tells whether the brain has received the sound signals. This test does not provide information about the quality of sounds that a child hears, but it does tell whether the brain has received the sounds. If she is given an ABR, your child may need to be sedated.

You can also learn about your child's hearing on an informal basis by watching her reactions around the house. Does she pay attention to the stereo but ignore water running? Does she notice her father's voice more than her mother's? Her use of hearing in everyday situations is often the best way to learn whether sounds and voices will be meaningful to her.

Some children with hearing losses can be assisted by hearing aids, which increase the loudness of the sounds they hear. Sometimes children initially reject the hearing aid, because louder sounds may be unpleasant at first and they may not know what the sounds mean. In the beginning, it may therefore be better for the child to use the hearing aid for short periods of time. The speech/language therapist or vision specialist can also help the child become accustomed to the hearing aid. Some children do not benefit from the use of a hearing aid, and will be encouraged to make sense of sound in other ways if they have some hearing. For example, games in which the child listens to one sound at a time and then learns to recognize that same sound with other noises in the background can help a child tell important sounds from unimportant sounds.

If your child is deaf-blind, her senses bring her limited information about the world around her. This makes it easy for her to become withdrawn and to be most interested in her body or in inanimate objects that are readily accessible. For example, she may prefer to bang two blocks together again and again because they make a loud sound she can hear. She may not know that blocks can be stacked, placed in containers, or used to create structures.

With appropriate instruction, most children who are deaf-blind can make steady progress in all areas of development. Children with deaf-blindness usually learn best when they have immediate contact with a few familiar caregivers in a predictable environment. Educational programs that use methods such as the Van Dijk procedures are especially effective with some deaf-blind children. This program emphasizes learning language through movement and the use of predictable routines. For example, a child can be taught to imitate the movements of an adult by moving with her along a mat or balance beam. Later, the child learns to anticipate events of the day through the use of a "calendar box," a sectioned box which contains objects representing each activity of a child's day.

Sometimes children become deaf-blind as the result of an accident or illness later in childhood. Educational programs for these children focus on retaining their current communication skills while developing additional ones. For example, speech therapists will work on helping the child continue speaking clearly, but professionals may also introduce sign language so that she can easily receive information from others.

It is crucial that all children with deaf-blindness be encouraged to communicate and to socialize. Having regular opportunities to interact with others is vitally important, both at school and at home. The next sections offer some strategies that can enhance development of communication, social, and motor skills in children with deaf-blindness. There are also several organizations, including the Deaf Blind Coaltion, based at Perkins School for the Blind, that you can contact for more information on deaf-blindness. See the Resource Guide for addresses.

Communication Skills. How well a deaf-blind child is able to communicate depends on several factors, including how much vision and hearing she has. How she communicates is also influenced by her mental ability, including her memory and ability to apply words and ideas in different situations. In addition, a child's motivation has a big impact on learning to communicate. Some deaf-blind children are very motivated to communicate, but others are not very interested in other people. If your child is deaf-blind, an important step in building the foundation for communication skills is to make the environment more meaningful. For example, you can make a habit of tapping her on the palm of the hand to let her know that you are there and that you will respond to her efforts to communicate. You can also work out cues to help her recognize familiar people. For instance, you could place your child's hand on Dad's beard or Mom's curly hair to aid in identification. You could hand her a spoon before you guide her to the table to eat, or place the same cap on her head each time you take her outdoors. When using signals like these, make sure that the event happens immediately after your child is aware of the object, especially if she is young or has a short memory.

If your child is not very motivated to communicate, it is important to help her see how others are involved in her favorite activities. For example, if your child enjoys eating or swinging on a
swing, help her understand that these good things happen because
another person is there to provide the things she likes.

Some deaf-blind children learn to use gestures, body movements, or sign language as their primary form of communication.
Your child may begin communicating through natural gestures.
These are gestures she chooses for herself to stand for people and
events in her world. For example, she may touch her mouth when
she is hungry or tug at her socks when she wants to walk in bare
feet. You should accept and respond to these gestures until she is
ready to move on to a more complex sign language system. At that
time, you should plan to learn sign language yourself so that you
can begin to show her some of the accepted signs when they are
needed. Some children will learn formal signs as toddlers, but
many deaf-blind children take years to reach that point, and others
use natural gestures all of their lives.

If your child is blind as well as hearing impaired, she may learn
"covered" sign. That is, she will lightly cover the hand of the signer
with her own hand. If she has sufficient vision to see signs, you will
need to take her visual differences into account when presenting
signs. It is helpful to present the signs against a background that
contrasts with your hand, and at the most appropriate distances for
her visual field and acuity. Although the classroom teacher and
speech/language therapist may be the team members who instruct
your child in sign, it is important for all family and team members
to learn sign language so that your child has plenty of opportunities
for real communication.

However your child learns to communicate, it is important that
everybody at home and school provide her with consistent input in
the chosen form of communication. Using words and signs related
to activities like dressing, eating, and using the toilet are especially
important since these are things that your child will do every day.

Movement Skills. Children who are deaf-blind can learn the
same movement skills as other children. However, many learn
more slowly. Because their hearing and visual impairments make it
difficult for them to know what is around them to be explored,
they may not have the motivation to move through space. And like
children with visual impairments alone, they cannot imitate the
movements of others around them. You will need to keep your

child close to you as you move so that she can notice your movements. You may need to guide her as she moves from one position to another, such as sitting to standing, so that she will feel secure while doing this. Many deaf-blind children enjoy repeated movement activities such as rocking or swinging. You can encourage these for short periods of time, but help your child find ways to add variety to them and to use movement to explore, not just stimulate.

It is also important to give your child cues to help her understand where she is going when she moves. For example, using an object that stands for an activity, such as a cake of soap to be carried to the bathroom, will help your child understand that she is moving toward the same room where she took a bath the day before.

Social and Emotional Skills. Children who are deaf-blind may have more difficulty learning social skills because they cannot easily perceive others' responses or imitate others' behavior in social situations. Some social skills will be learned gradually. For example, waiting in a store line or taking turns with a toy may be difficult if your child cannot understand the reason, so you will need to start by providing a reward for just a little cooperation. In other situations, you may decide that the skill is too difficult for your child and that it is not important to learn right now. For example, you may take your child along for a meal at a fast-food restaurant, but leave her with a family member or babysitter while the family goes out to a more formal restaurant.

Some deaf-blind children have behaviors that are difficult to deal with at times. This may be because they cannot communicate their real feelings and thoughts, but it can also be because their brains have been affected by the same condition that caused their hearing and vision impairment. To deal with a difficult behavior, you can begin by writing down what happens just before the behavior usually occurs. For example, if your child always cries and throws toys at mealtime, then you can begin to explore the cause. Does she dislike a food? Does she dislike having her hand held with a spoon in it? Once you know why your child behaves as she does, you can try rewarding her during or immediately after the difficult time if she controls her behavior. For example, if your child does not like riding in the car but plays quietly with a toy during a car ride, you could reward her with a favorite activity like rocking in the rocking chair or watering plants right after the car ride. This helps your child learn that good things happen when she works to control her behavior. If your child regularly does things that hurt herself or other people, request that her educational team include someone who is knowledgeable in managing difficult behaviors.

The Importance of Routine

For all children with multiple disabilities, it is important to have regular routines that provide opportunities to repeat and apply new skills and to learn to anticipate events. Otherwise, a child with multiple disabilities may not realize that there are connections between what happens at different times or at different places. For example, she may not understand that putting on a coat has any connection with the cold outdoors unless she always puts her coat on right before going out.

Your child should have routines for functional activities such as eating or preparing for bed, as well as routines for recreation or play. Routines should always occur in the same place using the same materials. And they should require that your child and at least one other person take roles understood by each. For example, at mealtime someone should always give your child a signal that helps her understand what will take place next. Handing her a bib or a place mat to carry to the kitchen or showing her a picture of a plate of food are examples of such signals. When your child understands what will happen next, she is more likely to cooperate in a routine.

You can establish routines around interactive play to help your child learn communication and social skills. For example, if you rock your child to a song and then pause, your child can learn to use a gesture or word to ask to continue. If you hide a toy in a box with a latch, your child can tap on the box to signal you to open it. The success of such activities depends on your child's interest in achieving the result, and your ability to read the response and elaborate on it.

For most children with multiple handicaps and major learning delays, routines must be repeated frequently and consistently in order to be effective. They should occur daily or several times a day until they are well established. After your child has learned her role in the routine, you can vary it somewhat and make the routine more elaborate. The routine can then act as a framework for presenting new information and for teaching your child to deal with novel occurrences, as well as expected ones. For example, if your child bounces on your knee as a signal that she wants to be bounced up and down, then you can encourage her to use new signals to indicate that she wants to rock, swing, or do other movements she enjoys. When your child has thoroughly learned a routine, you may introduce an unexpected object to encourage her to communicate. For example, you may give her a comb instead of a spoon at breakfast so that your child will notice the difference and request the appropriate item for her routine.

Conclusion

If your child has multiple disabilities, she may learn many skills at a slower rate than she would otherwise, and she may need to learn about the world through a different medium. She will also need more support from a wider range of people to make progress at home, school, work, and play. There are, however, many things that you, as a parent, can do to make learning easier for your child. The key is to establish predictable routines that provide the framework to expand learning and give your child a sense of control over events around her.

Regardless of your child's strengths and needs, she should receive the message that she can make things happen. Lifting a spoon, calling out to a friend, protesting about a wet diaper, or moving her own wheelchair are everyday events that may help her understand that she can take action. With the support of an effective, consistent educational team, your child can make steady progress toward becoming a participating member of her family and her community.

Parent Statements

Our daughter's grandparents just could not understand why she was born this way, but they have grown to love and care for her in spite of the problems she goes through.

◄○►

Her sister tries to help and sometimes has to stick up for her in front of other children.

─◄o►─

Our daughter wishes that she did not have both blindness and cerebral palsy. The cerebral palsy has been much harder for our family to understand and accept.

─◄o►─

Having more than one disability really seems to complicate matters, especially with the school. I never know which problems they should be focusing on the most.

─◄o►─

It has been a real battle to get David to wear his hearing aid and in the process we seem to have lost the battle with his eyeglasses. But we haven't given up yet.

─◄o►─

At first I was very angry and bitter, and I blamed God. I have since learned to adjust to my son's disabilities. Never will I accept them, but I will continually adjust.

─◄o►─

Nicky has so many problems, blindness is the least of our worries at present.

─◄o►─

I hate to admit it, but I sometimes resent parents of children who have only one disability.

─◄o►─

From my child, I have learned to love unconditionally. My life has been opened up to include experiences I never would have considered.

Chapter 13

◄○►

The Years Ahead

LaRhea Sanford Ed.D., and Rebecca Burnett, Ed.D.*

Even though your child is young now, you probably already have many questions about his future. Will he be able to finish high school and go to college? Will he date? How will he be able to get to work when he is living on his own? What about grocery shopping and laundry and balancing his checkbook? All parents have questions and concerns about their children's future. Your questions and concerns are more complicated, however, because you don't know how your child's vision loss will affect his future.

It may be frightening for you to think of your child (who may now be four years old) ironing his own clothes. But by the time he is a young adult, he will be ready to learn to do such things with adaptations. You and his teachers will make sure that he will have learned the prerequisite skills to make these activities much eas-

---

* LaRhea Sanford is currently director of vision services for Metro Nashville Public Schools. She has worked extensively with children who have visual impairments in public school and residential school settings. She has also taught university classes for pre-service teachers at Peabody College of Vanderbilt University, where she received her doctorate in special education. She is co-author of an assessment of functional vision and reading media.

   Rebecca Burnett is currently a vision specialist with Metro Nashville Public Schools. She received her doctorate from Peabody College of Vanderbilt University and has worked with children who have multiple disabilities, children who have visual impairments, and their parents both in public school settings and at special summer programs. She recently co-authored an assessment of functional vision and reading media for students with visual impairments.

ier. Taking time now to think about some of your concerns and questions can help you identify ways to help your child accomplish future goals.

Educational Issues

As Chapter 8 explained, you will probably be actively involved in your child's schooling when he is young. You will be consulted about what you think is important for your child to learn, how you think he would learn it best, and where you think the learning should take place. You may be asked to help your child work on educational goals at home, and you may have direct contact with teachers and other educators fairly frequently. As your child grows older, the intensity of your involvement may diminish. One reason, of course, is that your child will learn skills that enable him to be more independent. Another reason is that your child will probably take on more responsibility for his own education. He should have increasing involvement in the IEP process and decisions as he gets older and becomes more independent.

Despite all the gains your child will make, you will still probably be more involved in his education than you would be if he did not have a visual impairment. If he continues to need special education services, you will continue to help plan his IEP every year. You will also want to make sure: 1) that he is placed in, and remains in, the most appropriate educational setting; 2) that all adaptations necessary to help him learn are made; and 3) that there is the right balance between academics and compensatory or special skills in his curriculum.

Placement Decisions

Throughout your child's elementary and high school years, a wide variety of placement options will be available. These range from full integration into a regular classroom with consultation services from a vision teacher to placement in a residential school for the blind, with a variety of options and combinations of options between the two extremes. (See Chapter 8 for a description of these options.)

Often, children with visual impairments do not stay in the same type of placement from kindergarten through high school. They may need more intensive and specialized services in the early years when basic skills and concepts are being developed. So, they may start out in a self-contained classroom or residential school that provides intense specialized services. Then, once they have acquired skills and learned to compensate for their visual impairment, they may move to a placement that requires more independence. It is also possible that a child may periodically need more intense specialized services at various times in his educational career. This may be the case if he has a sudden loss of vision or a change in his educational needs.

To make sure that your child's needs are being properly met by his educational placement, his needs must be re-evaluated at least once a year at the annual IEP meeting. His placement can also be reviewed any other time you request it. Some questions you may want to ask are:

- Is my child making progress as expected—academically, socially, and physically?
- Is he challenged academically?
- Is he learning the compensatory skills he needs? (See below.)
- Are his vocational needs being met?
- Are services available in all the areas needed? (For example, orientation and mobility, speech, occupational therapy)
- Are adapted materials available in a timely manner? (Your child's textbooks and classroom materials should be available at the beginning of each school year and as needed throughout the school year.)
- Do my child's teachers receive appropriate and timely consultation with the vision specialist about his special needs? This may be essential to providing effective instruction.

Successful placement depends on the flexible use of a variety of placement options for different periods of time. The length of time your child spends in a particular setting may vary from as little as six to twelve weeks to as much as several years, depending on your child's needs and how well they are being met. For example, your child might be in a public school program during the school year. In the summer, however, he may attend a residential program for a specified period of specialized and intensive training in orientation and mobility, adaptive technology, or self-help skills. Or a child placed at a residential school may attend public school for certain classes. This might give him more opportunities for social interactions as well as academic variety.

If you believe that your child's needs are not being met or that his placement should be changed, you should request an IEP meeting to discuss your concerns. Putting your request in writing and sending it to the special education teacher (vision specialist) and district special education administrator should help you get results.

Classroom Adaptations

Whatever your child's placement, he will likely need at least some specialized materials, equipment, techniques, or curricula to benefit fully from his education. For example, Chapter 10 describes adaptations that can enable people with all kinds of visual impairments to read and write.

As your child grows older, he may need additional adaptations, or he may learn to use more sophisticated equipment. For instance, in the primary grades, your child might be able to read the print in regular textbooks. But in about fourth grade, when the print becomes smaller, he may require large print. Print size in handouts and class materials might be increased by actually making the print larger with a copier or a word processor, or by using a magnifying device, such as a closed circuit television.

Your child may also need to have assignments modified so that he is not inadvertently penalized for having a visual impairment. One common reason for modifications is that students who are visually impaired and blind usually read at a slower rate than their sighted classmates. Some students' eyes tire more easily and may require brief rest periods or alternating periods of near and distant visual tasks. Students can be given extra time to complete assignments or standardized tests, they may be allowed to use adaptive equipment such as a talking calculator, or, rarely, their assignments might be shortened.

If your child's visual impairment prevents him from reading print efficiently, he will learn to use the braille code, as Chapter 10 discusses. As he grows older, he will also learn to use other types of technology that will open up the world of communication for him. Most likely, he will learn to type so that he can communicate in print with sighted readers. He may also learn to use *access technology*—adaptive equipment that allows your child to type information into a computer and make braille and print copies. Many students use taped books to read their assignments and a tape player to take notes in class. They may also use specially designed machines that scan and read a book using computerized speech output. Books such as encyclopedias are also available on computer software to use with voice output.

The vision specialist is responsible for adapting and ordering any special materials and equipment your child needs, as well as for informing teachers about appropriate techniques to meet your child's needs. The vision specialist will observe your child in the classroom, and talk with you, your child, and his classroom teachers to determine appropriate adaptations. This process is continuous throughout the school years and changes are made as needed.

Not all school systems are as able and willing as others to provide expensive adaptive equipment. Generally, however, schools are responsible for providing the technology necessary to meet a student's needs at school. Federal court cases have upheld that school systems must provide needed equipment and materials, but are not required to provide "Cadillac" (very expensive and advanced) services or equipment. However, energetic teachers and parents can often find funding sources to provide more equipment and materials. See the section on "Computers and Other Technology" in Chapter 10 for suggestions of funding sources.

CURRICULA

Most students with visual impairment receive instruction not only in the usual academic subjects, but also in *compensatory ("special") skills*—skills that are needed specifically to help compensate for poor vision or the loss of vision. Because students with visual impairments have more to learn than other students, they should not be pushed through the grades just so they can graduate with others their age. Under federal law, students with disabilities are eligible for educational services through their twenty-first birthday.

You and your child should take advantage of this provision, if necessary. The additional skills your child needs to learn because of his visual impairment may require additional time in school.

Academic Skills

A visual impairment, per se, does not affect a child's ability to learn academic skills. But a visual impairment usually does affect how a child is taught academic skills, to a certain extent. Often, textbooks and other instructional materials designed for normally

sighted children are transcribed into braille or large type or recorded on tape. Sometimes instructional methods and materials need to be adapted in other ways. The sections below describe some typical differences in the ways academic subjects are taught.

Language Arts. Your child will most likely learn to read using reading programs designed for sighted students. How materials and teaching techniques are adapted will depend on your child's need and age. After he has developed his skills and is a proficient reader, taped books may be provided for extensive reading assignments, especially at the high school level. CD Rom and computer software with voice, large print, and braille output capabilities will help your child conduct research. Technologies of today and the future will put your child on the Information Super Highway.

The American Printing House for the Blind has developed a special reading curriculum called *Patterns* for students who learn to read braille in kindergarten through third grade. The series is designed to eliminate or minimize braille reading problems for beginners. This basal-type reading series takes into consideration such factors as the sequence of difficulty of the braille code and the frequency of occurrence of specific braille characters. The texts emphasize acquisition of experiences through senses other than vision. After completing the program, students are provided with the same reading materials that sighted students use, but transcribed into braille.

Spelling books are transcribed into braille with no changes in format or content, except that words are first presented in contracted form (Grade II braille), then spelled out letter by letter (Grade I braille). Keyboarding may be taught as early as first grade. Keyboarding helps strengthen spelling skills because each word must be spelled letter by letter, instead of using braille contractions. See Chapter 10 for a description of the writing methods a child with visual impairments might learn.

Mathematics. Your child will learn mathematics using the same curriculum designed for sighted students. Adapted materials and manipulatives (concrete objects that can be handled) will help him learn mathematical concepts.

The primary adaptation used to teach mathematics to braille readers is the Nemeth Code, the braille symbol system for mathematical and science notations. Students usually learn the Nemeth Code at the same time other students are learning the symbols for addition, multiplication, etc. To help your child make calculations, he may use several aids and devices. These include the braille writer, which is used to write numbers and math problems; the abacus; and the talking calculator. Talking calculators are relatively inexpensive and are quite helpful in solving complex problems in advanced classes, especially after the student has memorized the basic facts in mathematics and understands computational processes.

Science. Students with visual impairments can learn the concepts underlying all sciences through adapted reading materials. And they can learn about most sciences through hands-on experiments. Your child will be able to conduct experiments using specialized and adapted equipment, materials, and techniques. The classroom teacher should incorporate a hands-on approach utilizing all the senses—sight, hearing, touch, and smell. For example, your child may plant a bean seed in a container filled with water instead of soil so he can touch and feel the root system as it grows.

A science activity program has been developed for elementary level students with and without visual impairments working together in a mainstreamed setting—SAVI/SELPH (Science Activities for the Visually Impaired/Science Enrichment for Learners with Physical Handicaps). The SAVI/SELPH materials include teacher guides for forty science activities, student materials, and other print resources. These activities are designed to teach the same concepts that sighted students typically learn.

Social Studies. Much of social studies is verbal in nature, so students with visual impairments can easily learn the information and participate in discussions. The main difficulty that arises is using pictures, maps, globes, graphs, and diagrams. The vision specialist will make sure that your child understands the concepts and acquires the skills needed to interpret maps and other materials, and that materials are available in bold line or tactile form. The classroom teacher will provide verbal descriptions of adapted materials and of pictures and diagrams that have not been adapted.

Physical Education. There are several reasons why it is important for children with visual impairments to participate in physical education. First, they often lag behind in developing mobility skills and tend to be less physically active than other children. This may be due to fear of the unknown and an inability to observe and imitate motor skills. Second, poor posture is sometimes a problem for children with disabilities. Sometimes students must hold their heads or bodies in unusual positions in order to use their vision most efficiently.

Adapted techniques and materials must be used for your child to participate safely in physical education. One or more of the following modifications might be required: 1) adapted methods (for instance, maintaining physical contact at all times when wrestling); 2) adapted equipment and materials (such as the use of a rail during bowling to help students with balance and directionality, or a beeping or brightly colored ball and bold boundary markers for certain kinds of ball games); 3) deletion of activities such as ping pong which require good vision; and 4) modified versions of activities, such as having a sighted student run with a blind student.

Generally, your child will be able to participate more easily in individual activities than in group sports. He may need special instruction in some skills such as gymnastics, especially if he cannot observe and imitate these skills. Many different people may help your child during physical activities, including teacher assistants, adult volunteers, and other students.

The vision specialist should consult with the physical education teacher and let him know about your child's visual needs and concerns. For example, if your child is extremely sensitive to sunlight, the P.E. teacher should advise you when to provide protective clothing, a sun visor, and sun glasses for outside activities.

Foreign Languages. Most students with visual impairments do not have any more trouble than usual learning to *speak* a foreign language. But learning to *read and write* a foreign language can be somewhat more difficult for children with severe visual impairments. This is because not all foreign languages use exactly the same braille code as is used in English. Although the symbols for most letters are the same as in English, there may be symbols for accents and other symbols not present in English. The vision specialist will need to refer to the Code of Braille Textbook Formats and Techniques (1977) to teach your child the braille code used in reading and writing the language. To add to the difficulties, foreign languages are usually written in Grade I braille, which takes much longer to read and write. And obtaining the textbook in braille or large print can be hard. Again, the vision teacher should be able to help obtain the needed materials, including, ideally, a recorded copy of the book for listening.

Art and Music. Which art activities your child is able to participate in will depend on how much residual vision he has. Students who are totally blind may need to use materials such as clay that can be manipulated solely through touch. Many art activities, however, can be easily adapted into tactual experiences through the use of textures and shapes. Students with low vision may enjoy working with bold primary colors or highly contrasting materials.

Children with visual impairments can usually participate fully in vocal music activities. Lyrics to songs may need to be provided in large print or braille. If your child sings in a chorus, he may need to be given some kind of cue (an introduction played on the piano or a nudge from another student) so he knows when to begin singing, if he can't see the director. Students who are interested in learning to play a musical instrument should be encouraged to do so. Children with visual impairments usually have all the motor skills necessary to play any instrument in the band or orchestra, as well as piano. Blind students, however, need to learn a special braille music code if they wish to read music. They must also be prepared to memorize their music prior to performing it.

Compensatory Skills

Compensatory skills is the umbrella term for a variety of specialized skills that can help individuals with visual impairments lead satisfying lives and get along as independently as possible in the

real world. These skills are taught in addition to the regular academic curriculum. The kind and amount of specialized instruction your child receives in these skills will depend on his abilities and needs. Usually students who are totally blind require more specialized training and teaching than do students with mild visual impairments.

The members of your child's education team must evaluate his needs for compensatory skills at least once a year. To document your child's progress and identify future needs, checklists and task analyses (breaking a skill down into small steps) may be used. The vision teacher is then responsible for either teaching your child these skills or for coordinating the services and activities your child needs.

When scheduling instruction, you, your child, and his education team members should not underestimate the importance of compensatory skills. Academics are important, but the compensatory skills are also a necessity.

Following is a list of areas that can help children compensate for a visual loss and develop their skills and concepts more completely. Training in any of these skills should be available to your child if he needs them, no matter what his educational placement.

- Sensory development (visual, auditory, tactile, olfactory)
- Concept development (such as directionality, size, positions, time)
- Prevocational skills (such as on-task behavior, task completion)
- Visual efficiency training (learning to use vision to the greatest extent possible to identify and discriminate objects)
- Listening skills
- Braille reading and writing (See Chapter 10)
- Nemeth code (the braille math and science code)

- Mathematical devices (such as an abacus or talking calculator)
- Orientation and mobility (such as protective technique, sighted guide and cane travel); See Chapter 12
- Handwriting (such as learning to sign checks and other documents in cursive, even if the child is totally blind; using adaptive writing materials and equipment such as raised line paper and writing guides)
- Keyboarding
- Study skills (such as using reference materials, notetaking)
- Organization skills (such as keeping an assignment notebook or organizing and packing a school bag)
- Activities of daily living (such as personal grooming, eating, and meal preparation)
- Using technology such as a tape player or computer
- Low vision devices (such as hand-held magnifiers and closed circuit televisions)
- Using resources (such as Recording for the Blind & Dyslexic, Library for the Blind, the local public library)
- Social skills training
- Counseling (such as in dealing with unwanted attention in public or changes in vision due to a deteriorating eye condition)
- Sex education
- Leisure activities
- Career education
- Vocational education
- Use of sighted readers

Vocational Education

As your child grows older, you may become more concerned with the question "What will he be when he grows up?" The job options available to people with visual impairments are numerous and should not be limited by misconceptions, misinformation, and low expectations of others. However, your child must be prepared to take advantage of these opportunities.

Whether or not they are aware of it, all children receive vocational education throughout their school years. They learn how to follow directions, how to organize their work, and how to be on time. Students with visual impairments need to learn these skills, too, but they may require adaptations to help them acquire these skills. For example, they might use a braille Dymotape (dynamo tape) labeler to help them organize their materials, or use a talking watch to help them be on time.

It is sometimes hard to separate vocational skills from those skills that will help your child be a good student. Under IDEA, however, his IEP must include objectives that will help him make the transition from school to the next phase in his life, whether that is work or college. These objectives should be written into his IEP by the time he is sixteen years old, and ideally sooner.

Social and Emotional Concerns

As your child grows older, his social and emotional well-being will increasingly depend on his feelings about his own worth. These feelings, in turn, will be influenced by whether or not he feels that others value him. Generally, if your child feels good about himself he will get along better with others and have an easier time fitting in with a sighted society. The reverse is also true. If his relationships with others are good and he is well integrated into society, he will feel good about himself. The following sections discuss some important social and emotional concerns that can help or hinder your child's ability to relate to others and get along in society.

Fitting In

In later childhood and adolescence, most young people want to dress like, talk like, act like—*be* like—everybody else. Being part of the crowd will probably be equally important to your child. And so it should be: social acceptance is essential to successful integration into sighted society.

Fitting in is sometimes difficult for children with visual impairments. Merely having a visual impairment—being physically different—can make your child stand out from the crowd. Your child may also appear different if he has not learned social behaviors such as head movements, facial expressions, gestures, and use of body space that most children learn through visual imitation. And if your child has any mannerisms such as eye poking or rubbing, rocking, or hand or object flipping, he can draw even more attention to his differences. Delayed communication skills can also impede your child's social acceptance. Because they have trouble reading facial expressions and other social cues, some children with visual impairments have difficulty staying on topic, knowing how and when to interrupt in a conversation, taking turns, and resolving conflicts.

Because of these common obstacles to social acceptance, children with visual impairments often need formal training in social skills. This training should be included in your child's IEP as a compensatory skill for as long as he needs it. This is true whether or not your child is mainstreamed in a class with sighted students. Just being placed with sighted children does not necessarily mean that your child will develop and learn appropriate social behaviors.

At school, teachers should help your child develop social skills. For example, they might train sighted classmates to initiate and reinforce interactions with your child; use role playing; give your child assertiveness training; model appropriate behavior; and give your child feedback about appropriate and inappropriate behaviors. The techniques teachers use will depend on your child's age and abilities. When your child is in fifth grade, for instance, a sighted classmate might be taught to initiate interactions with your child and to reinforce him with fun, meaningful conversation when he responds and initiates interactions himself. In high school, role playing might be used to help your child learn to develop confidence to ask someone to go on a date.

At home, there are many techniques you can use to help your child develop appropriate social behaviors. The following is not an all-inclusive list, but some suggestions you can use beginning before your child enters school and continuing through the school years.

1. Be aware that your child's openness and comfort level about his visual impairment will go a long way in helping others feel comfortable around him. Help your child to accept and understand his visual impairment without overemphasizing it. Encourage the attitude that your child can do the same things as sighted peers, but may do them in a different way. If your child has albinism or other obvious physical differences, he may need special support and counseling from the teacher and the vision specialist to help him deal with any problems he has being accepted by other children.

2. Talk with your child on his level and tell him what is and is not socially appropriate. For example, a fourth grader may

need to be reminded to clean his prosthetic eye daily and a high school girl may need to be reminded to check her feminine hygiene more often. To prevent your child from being set apart from others even more, it is essential that he be well groomed. Make sure he presents a neat and clean appearance, and, as he grows older, let him know what is "in style." It is also important to emphasize good eating habits—most people feel uncomfortable with someone who has poor table manners. As your child gets older, encourage him to find a special friend who can give honest feedback about social appearances and behaviors.

3. Use verbal and physical prompts to show your child how to make certain gestures, how to use utensils correctly, and procedures for proper table manners. Provide as many opportunities as possible for hands-on experiences with games, sports, and audio and video equipment while explaining and demonstrating proper use.

4. Provide opportunities for your child to be involved with other children in a variety of activities such as clubs, the YMCA, and Boy Scouts. Do not constantly hover over him, but give him room to explore. Overprotectiveness will make your child more dependent and will prevent interactions that allow healthy growth and development.

5. Praise your child for behaving, or attempting to behave, in socially acceptable ways. Give him gentle reminders when necessary. For example, say, "If you face me when you talk, I can hear you better." Remember: you must consistently expect him to behave appropriately if you want him to develop good social skills.

6. Help and encourage your child to know when and how to request assistance and when and how to decline it. No one likes to be around someone who is rude. Well-meaning people will sometimes offer unneeded assistance and it is important that your child respond in a polite and mannerly fashion.

7. Continue to discourage or prevent mannerisms, as described in Chapter 5. Not only can mannerisms physically harm your child, but they can also make him appear even more different from "normal" children. And the more self-stimulation your child engages in, the less he can interact with others.

Recreation and Leisure

Having opportunities for recreation and leisure-time pursuits is just as important, if not more so, for your child as it is for other children. Recreational activities help children grow up to be well-balanced and well-adjusted human beings by helping them hone gross and fine motor skills, learn about social rules such as turn taking, stay fit and healthy, make friends with similar interests, express themselves, make decisions, and last, but not least—have fun.

Sighted children often develop recreation and leisure interests and skills naturally and effortlessly. Children with visual impairments, however, may not be able to observe and imitate others participating in recreational activities. This can make it harder for them to cultivate such interests and skills. Parents and teachers may need to provide encouragement, inspiration, deliberate exposure, direct teaching, and modeling to help children with visual impairments learn to make good use of leisure time. The eventual goal is to enable your child to make informed, voluntary choices about recreational activities and how to spend his leisure time, as well as to fully participate in the activities he chooses.

Your child, like other children, will probably first learn about leisure-time activities from his family. He will begin to lay the foundation for the development of recreational skills during infancy and early childhood by playing with toys and other children. As time goes by, you can help him develop interests in hobbies, games, and passive leisure activities. Your child's passive leisure activities will probably be very similar to other children's, and may include listening to radios, records, tapes, and compact discs; reading books and magazines; watching television and going to movies; and attending sporting events. A variety of adaptations can make these activities more enjoyable. For example, a family member or friend can sit beside your child to describe the action of movies and television shows. Or your child might prefer using descriptive video—a spoken, pre-recorded description of actions on the screen that can be heard through a special simultaneous radio broadcast or directly from video. Descriptive video is becoming more available for television shows and movies. Your child may get more out of sporting events if he listens to the play-by-play action on a portable TV or radio.

With modifications and adaptations, your child can also play many table games and ball games. A number of table games are available in tactile and enlarged formats. Examples include Monopoly, cards, checkers, and dominoes. Ball games can be adapted by using beeping balls and other modifications described under the section on Physical Education. Your child can also pursue a wide range of hobbies—with or without adaptations—ranging from indoor activities such as arts and crafts, pet care, and collecting, to outdoor activities such as gardening, hiking, and biking.

When introducing a new activity to your child, there are several ways you can make learning easier. First, help your child become oriented to the environment of the activity. For example, allow him to explore game boundaries, game pieces, equipment, or other materials with his hands, and verbally explain the object of the game, the rules, equipment, and procedures. If necessary, provide a hand-over-hand demonstration. For some activities, you may need to develop signs and cues to tell your child when to start, stop, change directions or actions. During a kickball game, for instance, the basemen might provide sound cues so your child can find the bases. Some activities lend themselves to buddy systems, which should be used as appropriate. For example, during the same kickball game, your child might prefer to have a sighted player run the bases with him. Activities may also need some minor environmental modifications (a bright red or yellow kickball) for your child to successfully participate. For guidance in adapting rules, procedures, or equipment for your child, consult his vision specialist.

You may also want to inquire about recreational activities in your community (*not* what activities are available for a child with visual impairments). As Chapter 9 explains, your child should be allowed to participate in any activity that can be adapted to his needs, thanks to the Americans with Disabilities Act (ADA). If your child is old enough, let him choose an activity to try. After you enroll him in the chosen activity, make sure that he receives appropriate support from you or someone familiar with visual impairments, so that he and the other participants have positive and successful experiences.

Special groups, organizations, and agencies in your community might also offer activities specifically for children who have disabilities. Groups such as those organized for blind skiers can provide role models and tremendous opportunities for your child. You can find out about recreational opportunities for children with disabilities from the vision specialist, parent groups, or community organizations such as the ARC or Easter Seals.

Whatever modifications or adaptations your child needs, he should be involved in a variety of activities. This will prepare him to make choices of leisure-time activities based on knowledge and experience rather than on ignorance and feelings of inadequacy. Eventually, your child should choose his own activities based on his enjoyment, satisfaction, and pleasure.

Sex Education

People with visual impairments have the same desires for intimacy and love and the same sexual urges as other people. Children with visual impairments therefore need the same information about sex as any sighted child.

Ordinarily, even very young children pick up basic information about sex through visual observation. But because your child may use the sense of touch to gather much information, and touch is often discouraged in learning about sex, access to information may be more limited. Your child may ask fewer questions about sexual matters because he sees fewer things to ask questions about. And what he does see he may misunderstand or misinterpret.

With your direction, your child can learn much about sex, even with limited or no vision. When he is young, you can point out gender differences during normal family interactions and activities, such as bathing, dressing, and diaper changing. Later on, you can give your child factual information about gender differences, body changes and processes, and sexual behaviors, habits, and diseases. You should provide this information in the way that seems most comfortable to you—just as you would with any other child. To help your child understand, you might let him tactually examine anatomically correct dolls, personal hygiene items, and birth control devices. Commercially available books and tapes may also be useful in helping you with the how-to and what-to of your child's sex education. In addition, some agencies serving individuals with visual impairments have developed and adapted sex education materials.

Just as other students do, your child will participate in class discussions and activities regarding sex education. The education team may also determine that your child would benefit from additional instruction. If so, this should be included in his IEP.

As you would with any child, you should share your own value system and standards for moral conduct, discuss the consequences of behaviors, guide your child in making good choices, and make sure he understands the impact of his choices on his own and others' lives.

Especially as your child grows older, he needs to have someone—a family member, relative, or close friend—that he can confide in about personal matters. Being able to ask personal questions, accept feedback about personal and social matters, and discuss and share feelings, doubts, and experiences all contribute to the development of a healthy, well-adjusted human being.

Of course, all parents worry about their children's safety. Children with visual impairments may be more vulnerable to exploitation. You will need to talk openly with your child about dangers and how to protect himself. This may be uncomfortable and difficult for you, but the more openly you discuss these matters, the more aware your child will be and the more willing he will be to share concerns and fears.

Dating

The adolescent years are both exciting and troubling for most children, in part because this is when they enter the world of dating. Like other teenagers, your child will likely have mixed feelings about dating at first. He may want to date because he feels attracted to the opposite sex, because he feels social pressure to do so, and because dating is often essential to peer approval. At the same time, however, he may have fears and anxieties about his own physical attractiveness, sexuality, or the process of dating.

Your child will need to resolve many of these fears and anxieties himself, simply by taking the plunge into dating and confronting his feelings head on. But you can also help prepare your child by helping him acquire the basic building blocks needed for successful socializing. These include conversational skills, good grooming habits, appropriate table manners, and interests and abilities in activities that others enjoy talking about or doing. Helping your child develop a healthy sense of self-esteem, as described in Chapter 7, is also critical. In addition, you may want to ensure that your teenager has the opportunity to meet, interact with, and share experiences with peers and successful adults who are also visually impaired. This will allow him to talk about problems and concerns and to hear how others have handled difficult situations.

When your child is just beginning to date, you may want to suggest that he start with group boy/girl activities and dates in familiar environments (for example, parties in your own home). Your child may find these types of dates more comfortable at first. Group activities and double dating with sighted friends can also solve your child's transportation needs. Few teenagers—sighted or not—find that being chauffeured around by a parent is conducive to romance! In these situations, your child can help out with travel expenses by paying for gas.

Unfortunately, even if your child has good social skills, he may sometimes run into dating difficulties due to ignorance, prejudice, or fear. You may need to help him realize that he will encounter rude and insensitive people and that he should not let this affect the way he feels about himself. Ultimately, you and others who care about your child will help him realize his self-worth. These types of problems seem to decrease after the adolescent years, possibly because older people are more mature and better educated, or because there are often opportunities to get to know others on a deeper level before dating.

The Transition to Independence

When your child is young, you should proceed on the assumption that he will grow up to be independent. The potential for children with visual impairments to be independent depends a great deal on expectations, family and community support, and education and training. These factors help children to compensate and become independent, no matter how severe their visual impairment. In addition, advances in technology are opening up more opportunities for independence.
Thanks to technology, adults with visual impairments can participate in more activities than ever before and have an increasing number of career opportunities.

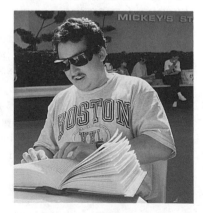

To be as independent as possible as an adult, your child needs to acquire self-help skills in many areas, including travel, personal grooming, housekeeping, food preparation, money management, and shopping. He also needs to learn good work habits and specific job skills and become informed about possible living arrangements. Your child can receive training in all of these areas at school if his education team agrees that it is necessary. But it is also important for you, other family members, and other significant adults to work *together* to help your child develop the skills needed for independence. You should make sure that training toward independence begins when your child is very young and that he has plenty of opportunities to practice and form good habits early on.

Travel

In many states, some people with low vision are able to obtain driver's licenses, with or without the use of low vision devices. However, for most people with visual impairments, driving is not a reality. This can be very difficult to accept. Other methods of transportation may not always be as convenient, and driving is often regarded as a critical step in making the transition to independence.

If your child will be unable to drive, he will need to learn that independence is possible without a driver's license. With training and experience, he can learn to use a variety of transportation modes. While he is still in high school, transportation needs can be met through group activities, double dating, or having a sighted friend, date, or relative drive, with the understanding that he will help defray expenses by paying for gas. In adulthood, he can achieve true independence in transportation by using a car pool (paying instead of driving), a paid driver, or a bus, taxi, subway, train, or other forms of public transportation.

Personal Grooming

Chapter 5 covers personal grooming for parents of younger children. As your child grows older, he will become more independent with his personal grooming skills. Following are some questions you may ask:

1. *How can my child distinguish personal care items?* Items such as perfume, lotion, and shampoo can be distinguished by their weight, size, odor, and shape of container. Similar objects can be labelled or placed in separate locations so they can be distinguished. Bits of tape and rubber bands can be used to identify items. For example, shampoo and cream rinse

can by distinguished by placing a rubber band around one container, and a piece of tape on a lipstick tube can help distinguish it from another similar tube.

2. *How can clothing be distinguished?* Some clothing can be identified by texture, seams, pockets, buttons, and shapes. Knots of thread can be sewn inside matching pieces of clothing. For example, a matching suit coat, pants, shirt, and tie may all have three knots. In general, learning which colors, types of patterns, and fabrics match requires input from a relative or friend.

3. *How does my child know whether his hair needs brushing, combing, or cutting?* Are there any special considerations in choosing hairstyles? Teach your child to wash his hair frequently. Have a friend, family member, or hairdresser help select an easy-to-care-for, attractive hairstyle. Morning hair care should generally suffice, although you should teach your child to brush or comb his hair more often in bad weather. He should also learn to ask a friend for feedback.

4. *How does a girl learn to use cosmetics?* Department stores often offer free advice and training about selection and use of make-up. Daily practice and feedback from a friend will increase skill and competence in make-up application. Your child can learn that when in doubt, neutral colors are often best.

5. *How will my child handle shaving?* Encourage your child to delay this activity if possible. When he starts shaving, it will be easier to use an electric razor at first. Mustaches and beards may need to be trimmed by a friend or a hairdresser.

6. *How does my child know whether his clothes are wrinkled, stained, worn, or dirty?* Teach your child to launder his clothes after he wears them. Wrinkle-free fabrics make laundering easier. Dials on washers and dryers can be easily marked for use by a person who is blind. Most likely, your child will be aware of spills which cause stains on clothes. Teach him to either send stained clothes to the laundry or to ask for help in treating the stain. Your child can learn to iron his own clothes by first beginning with a simple garment and a cool iron. To prevent burns when a hot iron is used, your child can purchase a specially made guard for the iron.

Specific grooming skills can and must be taught to children with visual impairments. However, there is no substitute for the honest feedback of a family member or a good friend where personal grooming is concerned.

Housekeeping

Children with visual impairments are usually able to do most housekeeping chores with minor adaptations. You can introduce your child to these chores at the same age you would if he did not have a visual impairment. Giving your child these responsibilities will not only prepare him to be independent, but they will also increase his sense of self-worth.

When teaching your child to clean surfaces such as a countertop or floor, it is helpful to show him how to follow a systematic pattern. For instance, have him wipe a countertop length-wise across the entire surface and then width-wise. Using a systematic pattern also works for vacuuming and dusting and prevents spots from being missed. Also teach your child to clean spots and spills immediately to prevent slipping or staining. As with toiletries, cleaning products may need special labels or markings so they can be distinguished if your child cannot identify them by weight, size, odor, or shape.

Tidying up should also be done methodically. Your child should learn to put items back where they belong as soon as he is through with them. Otherwise, he may not be able to find them again or he may trip over them.

Food Preparation

Like any child, your child should be actively involved in food preparation at an early age—pouring a drink, getting a bowl of cereal, making a snack. As with all children, safety is an issue in the kitchen. Some precautions to keep in mind include:

1. Teach your child the location and purpose of kitchen equipment, food items, and cleaning supplies, and keep a well-organized kitchen.
2. Keep items in the same location and label them with brailled dynamo tape to help your child identify them.
3. Make sure pot handles point inward over the stove and not out where they can be bumped into.

4. Use heavy pots and pans and teach your child to approach handles slowly and cautiously when stirring or attempting to remove pots from the stove.
5. When pouring liquids into glasses, measuring cups, etc., teach your child to place an index finger slightly inside the top of the container to determine when it is full. This can be tricky when the liquids are very hot. A better method would be to measure the amount of liquid needed and then use the microwave to heat it.

Labeling dials and controls with raised lines or dots can enable your child to use kitchen appliances. You can file notches, make braille dots on dynamo tape, or use drops of glue or paint to mark items. Usually at least one reference point is placed on a dial and one on the background. For example, on the stove, marks may be placed at the off position, 300 degrees, and 500 degrees. To avoid confusion, it is usually best to use a minimum of marks. Before using any unfamiliar appliances or equipment, your child should examine them to become familiar with the way they are constructed and the way they operate.

With minor adaptations to equipment, your child should be able to participate in the standard curriculum in a high school Home Economics class. To help your child succeed in class, the vision specialist should: 1) demonstrate adaptive techniques to your child and the teacher; 2) provide books and recipes in large print, braille, or recorded form; 3) advise or assist in labeling equipment and packaged food; 4) assist during certain activities such as sewing; 5) order or obtain adaptive devices needed in the kitchen; 6) recommend safety precautions such as keeping doors open flat or closed; 7) suggest ways of storing utensils and food for ease in locating. (Before your child is in high school, the vision specialist can advise you about adaptations in the home or sources of adapted cooking equipment.)

It is advisable that *all* students, male and female, take Home Economics. The Home Economics curriculum is usually extremely useful in helping students develop independent living skills.

Money Management and Shopping

Most adults who are blind need to rely on someone else to help them when shopping in a store. You can, however, acquaint your child with the basics of shopping at an early age. Take him along on shopping trips to grocery, clothing, drug, and other stores and describe the environment, the products, and the process of buying to him.

Once your child begins to shop and make his own selections, he can decide whether he would like a friend, relative, or store employee to help him. Federal law requires that stores provide assistance upon request to people with disabilities. Often, however, it is wise to call ahead or shop during less busy times when using a store employee for assistance. Teach your child how to politely request and refuse assistance, and how to be assertive in getting his shopping needs met.

Ordering by telephone, home shopping from the television, and using a computer to shop electronically can be helpful and convenient. To shop using these methods, your child should know specifically what items he needs when ordering by phone; listen to detailed descriptions given on television; and have a computer with voice output.

With a few adaptations, your child should be able to pay for his purchases himself. If he cannot identify coins by sight, he can identify them by feel. He can identify them by their size, thickness, and their smooth or ridged edges—pennies and nickels have smooth edges, while dimes, quarters, and half dollars have ridged edges. If your child cannot visually identify paper money, he can learn to fold different denominations different ways. For example, dollars can be left unfolded, fives can be folded in half, and tens can be folded lengthwise. Or he can place different denominations in different places in his billfold.

Writing and signing checks is a necessary activity for most adults. Your child will need to learn to sign his name, using a signature guide if needed. This is a small cardboard or plastic card, about the size of a credit card, with a rectangular slot cut out. The card is placed on the paper with the slot over the space where the signature is required. A trusted sighted friend might help prepare checks for your child by filling in the date, payee, and amount ahead of time. Your child can also fill out the information himself on a raised-line check, or he can use a computer program that fills out checks after he types in the information.

Career Opportunities

Unfortunately, there is a high rate of unemployment among adults with visual impairments at present. However, there are good reasons to believe that the job outlook will brighten in the near future. Career opportunities for workers with visual impairments have grown tremendously in recent years. These expanded opportunities are due in part to new technology, such as computers with speech output, portable electronic braillers, and print-enlarging devices. The Americans with Disabilities Act, which prohibits discrimination on the basis of disability, is also opening the door to more and better job opportunities. Today, career opportunities should no longer be limited by misconceptions, misinformation, and negative attitudes of family members and the general public.

Some adults with visual impairments are fully capable of working on their own along with nondisabled employees in "blue collar" or "white collar" positions. This is known as competitive employment. Sometimes before an adult can be competitively employed, he needs to work in a supported employment setting. During supported employment, a job coach accompanies the worker to his job and helps him adapt to the environment and learn skills needed to work independently. Adults who have visual impairments and additional disabilities may work in sheltered workshops. Here they work alongside other employees with disabilities and receive supervision and training in job-related skills. Some adults with visual impairments may work in sheltered workshops throughout their working career, but others learn skills that enable them to move on to supported or competitive employment.

Living Arrangements

Where your child lives as an adult depends on many factors. These include the level of his personal, social, and financial independence; personal preference; safety; options available in your community; and community resources and support. Many adults with visual impairments are able to live on their own, with a roommate, or with a spouse in an apartment or house. But even those who need more support or supervision can usually move out of their parents' home and into the community. Residential options generally available include: semi-independent living; group home; family home; and residential facility.

Semi-independent Living. This option includes living in a boarding-house type situation in which meals are provided for residents. It could also involve living in a house or apartment with a roommate/assistant. This roommate could be a family member, friend, or someone who is paid to help with certain activities.

Group Home. Group homes for adults with disabilities are operated by state and community agencies. Trained employees provide supervision and involve residents in housekeeping and meal preparation to the degree possible. Costs vary, but are usually very expensive.

Family Home. Some adults with visual impairments and their families may choose to continue to live together. Living arrangements, individual responsibilities, and so forth naturally vary from family to family.

Residential Facility. Some adults with severe multiple disabilities may live in a residential facility where supervision, housekeeping, meal preparation, and other types of care are provided by the staff. Generally, states are phasing out these facilities. This option is very expensive and usually funded by the state.

For information about residential options in your community, contact the local ARC, Easter Seals, or other community agencies serving people with disabilities. You can also contact Rehabilitation Services for the Blind, a federal and state agency, for information. (See the Resource Guide.) These federal, state, and community resources can advise you about financial assistance in providing residential options.

Working with Other Parents

Because visual impairments are relatively rare, the resources and support your child needs in order to maximize his independence may not be readily available in your community. As a result, you may need to help develop some of your own resources. For example, you may want to help develop better living arrangements, or educate prospective employers about the abilities of persons with visual impairments. Often, the best way to accomplish these types of goals is to work together with other parents. Finding other parents to join with is easy if there is already a parent group in your community. You will often find parents who share your concerns in the state and local chapters of organizations such as the National Association for Parents of the Visually Impaired (NAPVI).

NAPVI hosts conferences and regular meetings that provide parents with pertinent information and opportunities for sharing.

If there is no local chapter in your community, you may want to help form your own group. Your child's vision teacher or other vision professional may be able to give you the names of parents who might be interested in starting a group. Your group can then receive guidance in advocacy and the important issues confronting adolescents and adults with visual impairments from such national organizations as NAPVI, The Council for Exceptional Children (CEC), The American Foundation for the Blind (AFB), The American Printing House for the Blind (APH), and The National Federation of the Blind (NFB). All provide helpful publications for parents, and are listed in the Resource Guide at the back of this book.

Conclusion

Many parents of young children have their hands full just taking care of their family's day-to-day needs. And when your child is young, most of your efforts probably *should* go toward taking care of his current needs. It is also important, however, to remember that someday your child will grow up. And because his transition to independence may be more complicated than most children's, you will probably be more directly involved in helping him make the transition.

Taking the time now to get an idea of your child's needs later can help you anticipate where and when trouble spots may arise. This will help prepare you to deal with potential difficulties and to plan ways around them.

Parent Statements

Hope is a key word for me. Even though my child is having difficulty now, I have to believe that everything will turn out alright for him.

◄o►

If we do not work on things now, Janie won't be ready for her future.

—◄o►—

Evan has a bright future. He can do anything he sets his mind to do.

—◄o►—

My child is almost four years old and I am just now beginning to look to the future. Before now it has just seemed too overwhelming.

—◄o►—

I know it sounds crazy but I have spent a lot of time since Paul was born worrying about what his life will be like in high school. I focus a lot on driving, I guess because I like to drive and I can't imagine a life in which driving wasn't possible. Will he date? Will he have friends? My wife thinks I should stop thinking about that and just concentrate on today but I have trouble doing that. I want some answers to the bigger picture.

—◄o►—

We visited a summer program at the School for the Blind and saw lots of kids. They were laughing and joking around at lunch just like any school-aged children will do. It helped me a lot to see that things were so "normal" for them.

—◄o►—

When my child grows up, I just want him to be happy.

—◄o►—

I hate thinking that there are doors that will be closed for my child because of his blindness. It's hard for me to accept that there are things that he won't be able to do. I mean, what if he wanted to be a major league baseball player. . .?

—◄o►—

My daughter is pretty stubborn. That is difficult to deal with now, but I think it will help her in the future.

Before Donna was born I never noticed anything about blindness. Now it seems that every time I turn around there is something in the paper or on the news or a magazine article about someone who is blind. Now I know that there are many more successful blind adults than Stevie Wonder and Ronnie Milsap.

Glossary

Academic goals: the overall plan for increasing skills related to educational areas such as reading, math, and science.

ADA: The Americans with Disabilities Act of 1990. It prohibits discrimination against individuals with disabilities in the areas of employment, public services, and public accommodations.

Accommodation: the focusing ability of the eyes.

Adaptive behavior: the ability to take care of personal needs independently and to act appropriately in social situations.

Adaptive goals: the overall plan for learning specialized skills (such as orientation and mobility) needed because of a child's visual impairment.

Advocate: to speak up on someone else's behalf.

Albinism: an inherited condition which causes decreased pigment either in the skin, hair, and eyes or in the eyes alone.

Amblyopia: ("lazy eye") a visual impairment which is the result of a child not using her eyesight in one eye during the developmental period (until the child is about 9 years old).

Americans with Disabilities Act. *See ADA.*

Aniridia: congenital absence of an iris of the eye, resulting in some degree of visual impairment.

Anisometropia: a significant difference in the refractive power of the right and left eye.

Anoxia: lack of oxygen to tissues (including the brain), which causes cell death or damage. May be a complication of a difficult birth.

Anterior chamber: the space between the cornea and the iris.

Apert syndrome: an inherited disorder in which skull bones fuse prematurely and there is underdevelopment of facial bones, wide-spaced and bulging eyes, and webbed fingers and toes.

Aphakia: an eye with no lens.

Aqueous: the fluid which fills the anterior chamber of the eye.

Astigmatism: blurry vision caused by abnormal curvature of the cornea.

Attachment: the process by which infants and parents learn to care for and love one another and form a human bond.

Augmentative communication: the use of non-speech techniques such as signs, gestures, or pictures to supplement a child's speech abilities.

Avascular: without blood vessels.

Bilateral: related to or affecting both sides of the body—for example, both eyes.

Binocular vision: the ability of the eyes to fuse their separate images into one single three-dimensional image.

Blindisms: movements or behaviors that are repetitive and not purposeful. Examples include body rocking, head swaying, and eye rubbing.

Blindness. *See* **Total blindness.**

Book behaviors: behaviors which children use as they read books, such as turning pages of the book, holding the book right-side up, reading from left to right.

Braille: a system of reading and writing in which letters and words are formed by patterns of raised dots that are felt with the fingers.

Braille, Louis: the inventor of the braille system.

Calendar box: a sectioned box which contains objects representing each activity of a child's day.

Cataract: a cloudiness of the lens of the eye.

Categorization: the ability to organize objects according to characteristics such as color, size, group, function, etc.

Cause and effect: the understanding that certain actions can make certain things happen (for example, stacking too many blocks in a tower will cause it to tumble down).

Cell: the unit in braille which consists of six dots, two across and three down.

Center-based program: special instruction provided in any of a variety of centers (schools, offices, hospitals) for preschoolers.

Central nervous system: the brain and the nerves which travel along the spinal cord to and from the brain.

Cerebral palsy: a disorder of movement, balance, and coordination resulting from damage to the brain before the age of three.

Chromosomes: the microscopic rod-shaped bodies that contain genetic material and are located in every cell of the body.

Clinical low vision specialist: an optometrist, ophthalmologist, or university-trained professional specializing in helping children with limited visual ability optimize their remaining vision.

CF: counts fingers.

Choroid: the second layer of the eye that is rich in blood vessels and carries nourishment to the eye.

Cognitive development: the acquisition of the ability to think, reason, and problem-solve.

Conductive hearing loss: a temporary or permanent hearing loss which occurs when something (such as fluid) interferes with the passage of sound through the ear canal or middle ear.

Cones: located in the center of the retina, these cells enable us to see detail and color.

Continuum of services: the variety of placement options available in special education (from placement in a typical classroom with no extra support to placement in a school solely for children with disabilities).

Contractions: words or letters represented by one cell in the braille code.

Cornea: the clear dome on the front of the eye.

Cortical visual impairment: a visual loss due to damage to the part of the brain that interprets visual information.

Counts fingers: a measurement indicating that a person can determine how many fingers are being held in front of him.

Crouzon syndrome: an inherited condition in which the sutures between the bones of the skull close prematurely. Other characteristics include bulging eyes due to shallow orbits, hearing loss, and underdevelopment of the upper jaw bone.

CV: color vision.

D: diopter.

Deaf-blind: sometimes called dual sensory impairment, this term refers to a combination of hearing and vision problems that require educational modification.

Development: the process by which children grow physically and mentally and learn increasingly complex skills.

Developmental disability: a lifelong condition that begins before adulthood and prevents a child from developing normally. Often used to refer to conditions that result in mental retardation or autism.

Developmental pediatrician: a physician who has specialized training in assessing and treating disorders that affect development.

Dilate: to widen.

Diopter: the unit of measurement of the strength or refractive power of lenses.

Dog guides: dogs that receive extensive training and then are matched with a person with a visual impairment to help the person safely and efficiently locate familiar landmarks and negotiate obstacles.

Domains of growth: the areas of cognitive, communication, motor, self-help, sensory, and social development.

Due process hearing: one of the procedures established to protect the rights of families during disputes under IDEA. The hearing is held before an impartial person to resolve disagreements about a child's identification, evaluation, placement, or special educational services.

Early intervention: individualized programs of instruction and therapy developed for children two years old or younger to help minimize the effects of conditions that can delay development and learning.

EC: eyes closed.

Echolalia: word-for-word repetition of other's speech.

Emergent literacy: early literacy.

Enucleation: removal of the eyeball.

Epilepsy: A condition that causes recurrent episodes of seizures—abnormal electrical discharges in the brain that result in involuntary movement and/or changes in consciousness.

Esotropia: A type of strabismus in which one or both eyes turn inward.

Etiol: etiology (cause).

Exorbitism: a condition in which the eyes appear to bulge because the bony areas around the eyes (orbits) are too small and shallow to contain them.

Exotropia: a type of strabismus in which one or both eyes turn outward.

Expressive language: the ability to use gestures, words, and written symbols to communicate.

Extraocular: outside the eye.

Farsightedness: a condition in which objects are focused at a point behind, rather than on, the retina. As a result, the child must strain excessively to focus, especially on nearby objects.

FC: finger counting.

Fine motor skills: the ability to use small muscles such as those in the hands and face (for example, drawing, using a fork, drinking from a straw).

Fixates: focuses.

Fluctuating tone: muscle tone that is sometimes high, sometimes low.

Fluctuating vision: visual functioning that is different at different times of the day.

Functional goals: educational goals related to increasing skills for living independently (for example, cooking, handling money, using public transportation).

Functional vision: how well vision is used to function in the world.

Generalization: the ability to apply previous learning to new situations (for example, if one furry animal that has four legs, wags its tail, and barks is a "dog" so are all animals with the same characteristics).

Genes: the material in the chromosomes that contains the chemical directions that determine a person's physical, intellectual, and other traits.

Genetic: related to something that is caused by one or more of a person's genes. Genetic conditions may be inherited (due to genetic material passed on by one or both parents) or may occur due to spontaneous changes or mutations in a child's genetic material.

Glaucoma: a condition in which the pressure from fluid inside the anterior chamber of the eye is too high.

Gross motor skills: Skills that involve large muscles such as those in the arms, legs, and abdomen (for example, throwing a ball, walking, sitting up).

Hand movement: a measurement that indicates the distance at which the child can recognize the movement of a hand in front of her eyes.

Handicapping condition: one of the disabilities listed in IDEA as qualifying a child for special education services.

HM: hand movements.

Home intervention: special instruction provided at home.

Hydrocephaly: a condition in which excess fluid collects in the ventricles of the brain.

Hyperopia: farsightedness.

Hypertelorism: a condition in which there is an abnormally wide space between two paired body parts, such as the eye (orbital hypertelorism).

Hypertonia: increased tension or spasticity of the muscles; also known as high muscle tone.

Hypertropia: a condition in which the gaze of one eye is higher than the other.

Hypotonia: decreased tension of a muscle, resulting in floppiness; also known as low muscle tone.

Hypoxia: insufficient oxygen to the tissues of the body, including the brain.

IDEA: The Individuals with Disabilities Education Act—the law that guarantees children with disabilities a free, appropriate education in the least restrictive environment.

IEP: Individualized Education Program. The written plan that describes the special education program the local education agency has promised to provide a child with disabilities.

IFSP: Individualized Family Service Plan. The written document that describes the early intervention program to be provided for a child with disabilities.

Incidental learning: learning from experience.

Inclusion: an educational term that may be used to mean that a child with disabilities is mainstreamed with typically developing children for some or all activities of the school day. Increasingly, the term is being used to mean that the child does all activities with typically developing children ("fully included").

Integration: mainstreaming; including children with disabilities in the school activities of typically developing children.

Intersensory coordination: the process of taking information obtained through one sensory system and using it in another.

Intraocular lenses: artificial lenses permanently implanted after cataract surgery.

IOP: intraocular pressure (pressure inside the eye).

IQ: the score from a standardized test of intelligence indicating a person's overall level of cognitive functioning relative to other people of the same age.

Often scores between 80 and 119 are considered to be in the "average" range of intelligence; those 70 and below, to indicate mental retardation.

Iris: the colored part of the eye that regulates the amount of light that enters the eye.

Keyboarding: use of a computer or typewriter keyboard.

Laterality: knowledge of right and left.

Lazy eye: *See* Amblyopia.

Learning disability: a condition that causes a child to have more difficulty learning in one or more specific areas (such as reading or math) than would be expected based on the child's overall cognitive abilities.

Least restrictive environment (LRE): the setting which allows each child the most freedom (contact with typically developing children) while still allowing the most opportunity for educational progress.

Legal blindness: a visual acuity of 20/200 or less in the better eye after correction, and/or a visual field which is no greater than 20 degrees.

Lens: located behind the iris, the lens helps focus light on the back of the retina.

Lighthouse Flash Card Test for Children: a test for assessing visual acuity which does not depend on the ability to recognize words or letters, but uses a circle, an apple, a house, and a square.

Light perception: the ability to detect the presence or absence of light.

Light projection: the ability to tell where light is coming from.

Literacy: the ability to use written language—reading and writing—to function at an age-appropriate level in one's daily life.

Locomotion: moving independently from place to place.

Low vision: vision that is impaired, but sufficient to read print with or without magnification devices.

Lowe syndrome: a disorder that affects only males and is characterized by congenital cataracts, poor growth, mental retardation, low muscle tone, and sometimes glaucoma.

LP: light perception

LRE: *See* Least restrictive environment.

Macula: the area of sharpest vision in the retina.

Mainstreaming: *See* Integration.

Marfan syndrome: A genetic disorder characterized by tall, thin stature, long, thin limbs, loose joints, heart abnormalities, and sometimes loss of vision.

M.D.: medical doctor.

Mental retardation: cognitive functioning (thinking abilities) below the average range, resulting in difficulties and delays in learning and adaptive behavior.

Scores below 70 on IQ tests are usually considered to indicate mental retardation.

Microphthalmia: abnormally small eyes.

Mobility: the ability to move safely through the environment.

Mobility system: a guide or device (such as a cane) that permits an individual with a visual impairment to move independently through the environment.

Motor development: acquisition of the ability to move effectively and efficiently.

Muscle tone: the amount of tension or resistance to movement in a muscle.

Myopia: nearsightedness.

Nearsightedness: a condition in which images of distant objects are not focused precisely *on* the retina, but in front of it. This results in blurred vision, with distant objects usually appearing more blurred than near objects.

Nystagmus: a rhythmic oscillation or jerking of the eyes which cannot be controlled by the child.

O: eye (Latin: oculus).

Object constancy: the concept that objects that look different can still be the same thing.

Object permanence: the concept that things continue to exist even when they can no longer be seen, heard, or touched.

Occupational therapist (OT): A professional who specializes in improving the development of fine motor and adaptive skills.

O2: both eyes.

OD: right eye (Latin: oculus dexter).

O.D.: doctor of optometry.

O & M: orientation and mobility

Ophthalmologist: a medical doctor (M.D.) who has specialized training in diagnosing and treating diseases and conditions of the eye.

Optical system: the parts of the eye which receive light rays and focus them.

Optic nerve: the structure consisting of millions of nerve fibers which carries the message from the light receptors to the brain.

Optic nerve atrophy: damage to the fibers of the optic nerve which interrupts transmission of signals from the retina to the brain.

Optometrist: a doctor of optometry (O.D.) who is qualified to measure visual acuity and visual fields and to prescribe eyeglasses.

Orientation: knowing where you are, where you are going, and how to get where you want to be by interpreting information available in your environment.

Orientation and mobility specialist: a certified teacher who has received specialized training in teaching people with visual impairments to travel safely and efficiently.

OS: left eye (Latin: oculus sinister).

Osteogenesis imperfecta: a genetic disorder in which bones are unusually susceptible to fractures. Other features include hearing impairment, cataracts, blue sclera, and short stature.

OT: occupational therapy.

OU: both eyes together (Latin: oculi unitas).

Partially sighted: a term used to describe individuals who have sufficient vision to read print.

Peripheral vision: side vision.

Perseveration: continuing or repeating an activity or thought to such an extreme that it interferes with other activities.

Photophobia: sensitivity to light.

Physical therapist (PT): a professional who specializes in improving motor skills (especially gross motor skills) and posture.

Preferential looking: a technique used by eye doctors to determine an approximate visual acuity in infants or children with communication difficulties.

Ptosis: droopy eyelids.

Public Law 94–142: The Education for All Handicapped Children Act of 1975, which has been amended and renamed the Individuals with Disabilities Education Act (IDEA).

Public Law 101–467 (IDEA): The Individuals with Disabilities Education Act, reauthorization of P.L. 94–142. *See* IDEA.

Pupil: the black dot in the center of the eye created by the doughnut-shaped iris.

Receptive language: the ability to understand spoken and written communication as well as gestures.

Refraction: the process by which the cornea and lens of the eye bend light rays so that they focus on the retina.

Refractive error: an inability of the eye to sharply focus images on the back of the retina. Nearsightedness and farsightedness are types of refractive errors.

Related services: transportation and other developmental, corrective, and supportive services (such as OT, O&M, speech-language therapy) needed to enable a child to benefit from her special education program.

Residential school: a state or private school where students attend classes and live.

Resource room: a classroom where students spend part of the school day to learn or practice specific skills.

Respite care: child care services provided by workers with special training in caring for children with disabilities, designed to give parents a break from caring for their child.

Retina: the inner layer of the eye consisting of millions of specialized cells which serve as light receptors.

Retinitis Pigmentosa: a disorder which causes the retinas to degenerate and areas of abnormal pigment accumulation to develop. The disorder is usually due to genetic factors and leads to varying degrees of vision loss.

Retinoblastoma: a malignant tumor that develops in the retina of the eye and is usually diagnosed in infancy. Although the tumor can often be successfully removed, vision in the eye is usually impaired or lost.

Retinopathy of prematurity (ROP): a condition caused by damage to the retina that can cause vision loss in infants born prematurely.

Rods: the rod-shaped cells in the retina that are primarily responsible for peripheral vision and night vision.

Sclera: the outer layer (white part) of the eye.

Seizure: a temporary burst of abnormal electrical activity in the brain, resulting in involuntary changes in consciousness or behavior. *See* Epilepsy.

Self-contained classroom: a room in a "regular" or neighborhood school designed to provide specialized instruction to students with disabilities.

Self-esteem: feelings of self-worth.

Self-help development: acquisition of skills needed to take care of oneself and become more and more independent (for example, eating, dressing).

Sensorineural hearing loss: a hearing impairment that results when the inner ear or the nerves which receive sound and carry it into the brain are damaged or have not developed; usually permanent.

Sensory development: acquisition of the ability to use one's senses to gather information.

Slate and stylus: the slate is a template of several rows of braille cells, and the stylus is a device with a blunt metal tip that is used to punch each dot individually. Together, they provide a portable means of notetaking.

Snellen Chart: also known as the "E Chart" used to measure visual acuity.

Social development: acquisition of the skills needed to interact with others and build relationships.

Special day service facility: a community-based public or private school that serves children with disabilities exclusively.

Special education: tailor-made programs of instruction and other services designed to fit the unique learning strengths and needs of a child with disabilities.

Speech-language pathologist: a therapist who works to diagnose and improve difficulties with speech and language skills, as well as to improve oral motor abilities.

Spina bifida: a condition in which a child is born with open vertebrae in the spinal column and sometimes with excess fluid in the brain (hydrocephalus).

Strabismus: misaligned ("crossed") eyes.

Stereoacuity: Three-dimensional vision using both eyes together.

Structural impairments: damage to one or more parts of the eye.

Syndrome: a set of signs and symptoms that occur together due to the same cause and are therefore characteristic of a particular disorder.

Tactile defensiveness: an overreaction to or avoidance of touch.

Total blindness: no useable vision.

Twin-vision books: books with both braille and print.

Unilateral: relating to or affecting one side of the body—for example, one eye.

Usher syndrome: An inherited condition which causes sensorineural hearing loss and progressive loss of vision. Mental retardation may also be present.

VF: visual field.

Vision consultant: a teacher who travels from school to school providing technical assistance or support to educators.

Vision specialist: a certified teacher who has received specialized training in meeting the educational needs of children with visual impairment.

Visual acuity: a measurement of how clearly one sees.

Visual field: the total area that can be seen without moving the eyes or head.

Visual handicap: one of the handicapping conditions listed in the IDEA as qualifying a child for special education. The IDEA defines it as a visual impairment which, even with correction, impedes a child's ability to learn.

Visual impairment: any condition in which eyesight cannot be corrected to what is considered "normal."

Reading List

Chapter 1

Ferrell, K.A. *Parenting Preschoolers: Suggestions for Raising Young Blind and Visually Impaired Children*. New York: American Foundation for the Blind, 1984. The most common questions from parents of preschoolers who are visually impaired are answered in this booklet. Practical suggestions are offered to address some typical concerns.

American Foundation for the Blind. *Directory of Services for Blind and Visually Impaired Persons in the United States and Canada* (24th ed). New York: Author, 1993. This book contains a comprehensive list of resources for services organized by state and including national organizations.

Nousanen, D., & Robinson, L.W. *Take Charge! A Guide to Resources for Parents of the Visually Impaired*. Watertown, MA: National Association for Parents of the Visually Impaired, 1980. As its name suggests, this helpful guide provides parents with an overview of resources.

Chapter 2

Batshaw, M., M.D., & Perret, Yvonne. *Children with Disabilities: A Medical Primer*. 3rd ed. Baltimore: Paul Brookes, 1992. This easy-to-use reference includes useful explanations about the structure and development of the eye, as well as common causes of visual impairments. The information about genetic disorders and prenatal development may also be helpful to parents.

Chalkley, T., M.D. *Your Eyes* (3rd ed). Springfield, IL: Charles C. Thomas, 1982. This book was written for individuals outside of the ophthalmology profession and contains detailed but easy-to-read information about eye anatomy and physiology and common eye diseases.

Goldberg, S., M.D. *Ophthalmology Made Ridiculously Simple*. Miami: MedMaster, Inc., 1989. This book provides a brief, simplified explanation of ophthalmological terms and common eye conditions. It was written to give an overview of medical issues in layman's terms.

Harrell, L. (1984). *Touch the Baby: Blind and Visually Impaired Children as Patients - Helping Them Respond to Care*. New York: American Foundation for the Blind, 1984. This pamphlet was written to help medical professionals (doctors and nurses) care for young children who are visually impaired in a medical setting. Parents will find the practical information and suggestions useful as they communicate with physicians.

Chapter 3

Exceptional Parent, P.O. Box 3000, Dept. EP, Denville, NJ 07834–9919. 800–247–8080. This monthly magazine offers a wealth of information and support for parents of children with disabilities. It regularly features articles on coping, daily care, family life, and educational issues, as well as information on new products and resources of interest to families of children with disabilities.

Kushner, H. *When Bad Things Happen to Good People.* New York: Avon, 1981. This book was written by the author, a rabbi, following the death of his son from a rare disease. His insights will be helpful to anyone struggling to cope with strong emotions. Parents who wonder how God could have let this happen will be especially interested in Kushner's reasoning.

Marsh, J. & Boggis, C., editors. *From the Heart: On Being the Mother of a Child with Special Needs.* Bethesda, MD: Woodbine House, 1995. This book gathers together the insights, worries, hopes and dreams, and anecdotes of nine women who participated together in a support group for parents of children with disabilities. For parents of children newly diagnosed with a disability, their experiences give reassurance that life, eventually, does go on.

Meyer, D., editor. *Uncommon Fathers: Reflections on Raising a Child with a Disability.* Bethesda, MD: Woodbine House, 1995. Fathers of children with a variety of disabilities reflect on the emotions that go along with parenting a child with disabilities, as well as on the many ways such parenthood has changed their lives.

Sullivan, T. *Special Parent, Special Child.* New York: G.P. Putnam's Sons, 1995. This book is a compilation of interviews of parents conducted by Tom Sullivan, who is blind. He begins the book by discussing his mother's reaction to his blindness and then focuses on the stories of six families. The stories are inspirational accounts of families' struggles and triumphs.

Recchia, S. *Heart to Heart: Parents of Blind and Partially Sighted Children Talk about Their Feelings.* Los Angeles, CA: Blind Childrens Center (4120 Marathon St., P.O. Box 29159, Los Angeles, CA 90029–0159), 1985. This insightful booklet provides an honest look at the emotions of parents of children who are blind. Its easy-to-read format makes it helpful to a wide audience. It is also available in Spanish.

Chapter 4

Chernus-Mansfield, N., Hayashi, D., & Kekelis, L. *Talk to Me II: Common Concerns.* Los Angeles, CA: Blind Childrens Center (4120 Marathon St., P.O. Box 29159, Los Angeles, CA 90029–0159), 1985. A follow-up to *Talk to Me* (see below), this publication addresses some of the most common questions and concerns relating to language development of young blind children.

Ferrell, K.A. (1985). *Reach Out and Teach: Meeting the Training Needs of Parents of Visually/Multiply Handicapped Young Children.* New York: American Foundation for the Blind, 1985. This comprehensive program contains a guidebook, workbook, and slide/tape presentation focusing on raising a child with a visual impairment. Chapters include information on developmental areas as well as self-concept, family interactions, behavior, and parent rights.

Healy, J. *Your Child's Growing Mind: A Practical Guide to Brain Development and Learning from Birth to Adolescence.* Revised edition. New York: Doubleday, 1994. This book was written to provide all parents with answers to the questions "Where does brain power come from, and what can we do about it?" In layman's terms, it covers the most current research about how children develop language and memory, and also explores academic learning and differences in learning styles.

Kekelis, L. & Chernus-Mansfield, N. (1984). *Talk to Me: A Language Guide for Parents of Blind Children.* Los Angeles, CA: Blind Childrens Center, 1984. This 11–page pamphlet addresses the needs of parents as they communicate with their child who is visually impaired. Practical solutions for common questions are presented.

Schwartz, S. & Miller, J. *The New Language of Toys: Teaching Communication Skills to Special-Needs Children.* 2nd Ed. Bethesda, MD: Woodbine House, 1996. The authors of this guide explain how to make language learning fun by using commercial and homemade toys to teach and reinforce vocabulary, concepts, and other language skills.

Warren, D.H. *Blindness and Children: An Individual Approach.* Cambridge: Cambridge University Press, 1994. This book is often used in university courses as a textbook. It provides a summary of research findings relating to infants and children with visual impairments.

Chapter 5

Brennan, M. *Show Me How: A Manual for Parents of Preschool Visually Impaired and Blind Children.* New York: American Foundation for the Blind, 1982. A manual for parents of children who are visually impaired, this publication contains information on: growing and learning, building self-concept, moving around, playing, daily living skills, and developing sensory awareness.

Garber, S.W. *The Good Behavior Book.* New York: Villard Books, 1987. Although not written specifically for children with visual impairment, this book offers useful information on dealing with childhood stages and behavior management.

Recchia, S. *Learning to Play: Common Concerns for the Visually Impaired Preschool Child.* Los Angeles: Blind Childrens Center (4120 Marathon St., P.O. Box 29159, Los Angeles, CA 90029–0159). This booklet was written for parents and provides suggestions for helping children explore toys and materials, move from one activity to another, and play with other children.

Chapter 6

Bergman, T. *Seeing in Special Ways: Children Living with Blindness.* Milwaukee, WI: Gareth Stevens, 1988. With clear black-and-white photos and simple text, this book for elementary-school readers shows how children with severe visual impairments function at home, at school, and in the community.

Featherstone, H. *A Difference in the Family: Life with a Disabled Child.* New York: Basic Books, 1980. This book contains a personal story of a family's struggle in accepting the severe disabilities of their child.

Longuil, C. *Oh, I See!* (video produced by Shoestring Videos and available from American Foundation for the Blind, at the address in the Resource Guide).

Martin, B. & Archambault, J. *Knots on a Counting Rope.* New York: Henry Holt, 1987. In this children's picture book, an Indian grandfather tell his blind grandson about the story of the boy's birth and an exciting horse race.

McConnell, N., Cliff, D., & Duell, N. *Different & Alike.* 3rd edition. Colorado Springs: Current, 1993. This book for elementary school children explains various disabilities and makes the point that anyone can be disabled at times.

Meyer, D., Vadasy, P., & Fewell, R. *Living with a Brother or Sister with Special Needs: A Book for Sibs.* Seattle: University of Washington Press, 1985. In addition to providing factual information about disabilities, including visual impairment, this book for young readers also explores common emotions and concerns that nondisabled siblings often have.

Schleifer, M. & Klein, S., editors. *The Disabled Child and the Family: An Exceptional Parent Reader.* Brookline, MA: Exceptional Parent Press, 1985. This collection of articles from *Exceptional Parent* magazine covers a wide range of topics related to having a child with disabilities in the family.

Turnbull, A. & Turnbull, H. *Parents Speak Out: Then & Now.* 2nd ed. New York: Macmillan, 1985. In their own words, parents tell what it is like to raise a child with disabilities.

Chapter 7

Krementz, J. *How It Feels to Live with a Physical Disability.* New York: Simon & Schuster, 1992. This book for young readers contains interviews with a dozen young people with physical disabilities. Included is an interview with a thirteen-year-old blind girl whose words reflect a healthy self-esteem despite mixed emotions about her differences and the special challenges she faces.

Lindemann, J.E. & Lindemann, S.J. *Growing up Proud: A Parents' Guide to the Psychological Care of Children with Disabilities.* New York: Warner Books, 1988. The authors provide tips for nuturing self-esteem in children with a variety of disabilities.

Tuttle, D. and Tuttle, N. *Self-esteem and Adjusting with Blindness.* Springfield, IL: Charles C. Thomas, 1995. This book focuses on the adjustment process as individuals come to terms with a visual impairment. It is especially interesting to read excerpts from autobiographies written by individuals who are blind as illustrations of stages of adjustment.

Chapter 8

Anderson, W., Chitwod, S. & Hayden, D. *Negotiating the Special Education Maze: A Guide for Parents and Teachers.* 3rd Ed. Bethesda, MD: Woodbine House, 1997. This is a step-by-step guide to making the system work for your child, whether she is in early intervention or special education. Many worksheets and exercises are included to help with all the stages of the process from evaluation to development and monitoring of the IFSP/IEP.

Coleman, Jeanine. *The Early Intervention Dictionary.* Bethesda, MD: Woodbine House, 1993. This dictionary defines and clarifes terms and abbreviations used by the many different medical, therapeutic, and educational professionals who provide early intervention and special education services.

National Information Center for Children and Youth with Disabilities (NICHCY). NICHCY publishes a number of free publications on special education issues. Titles include: "Parent's Guide to Accessing Programs for Infants, Toddlers, Preschoolers with Disabilities"; "Planning for Inclusion"; "Education of Children & Youth with Special Needs: What Do the Laws Say?"; "Sexuality Education for Children and Youth with Disabilities." Contact NICHCY at 800–695–0285 to request any of these publications or a current publications list.

Torres, I. & Corn, A. *When You Have a Visually Handicapped Child in Your Classroom: Suggestions for Teachers.* New York: American Foundation for the Blind, 1990. This pamphlet was written for classroom teachers to provide basic information about including a child with a visual impairment in the regular classroom. Parents will find interesting suggestions and information that they can share with a wide variety of people about including their child in everyday life.

Chapter 9

The Americans with Disabilities Act: Questions and Answers. Available free from the U.S. Equal Employment Opportunity Commission, 1801 L St., N.W., Washington, DC 20507. 800–669–3362. In simple language, this helpful booklet explains the major provisions and limitations of the ADA, discussing such concepts as "reasonable accommodation" and "auxiliary aids and services" in detail.

Des Jardins, C. *How to Get Services by Being Assertive.* Chicago: Family Resource Center on Disabilities (20 E. Jackson Blvd., Room 900, Chicago, IL 60604. 312–939–3513), 1992. Among the topics tackled in this manual are developing advocacy and leadership skills, cutting through bureaucratic red tape, and being assertive at IEP meetings or due process hearings.

Halperin, S. (1981). *A Guide for the Powerless and Those Who Don't Know Their Own Power.* Washington, DC: The Institute for Educational Leadership. This booklet provides a simple explanation of the legislative process and the steps to take in passing legislation. It addresses advocacy on a national level.

Pacesetter Newsletter, Parent Advocacy Coalition for Educational Rights (PACER), 4826 Chicago Ave., Minneapolis, MN 55417. This quarterly newsletter focuses on helping parents obtain quality educations for children with disabilities through advocacy. It includes updates on new legislation or threats to existing legislation affecting people with disabilities.

Summary of Existing Legislation Affecting People with Disabilities. One copy available free from Clearinghouse on Disability Information, Office of Special Education and Rehabilitative Services, U.S. Dept. of Education, Room 3132 Switzer Building, Washington, DC 20202–2524. 202–205–8241. This booklet, periodically updated, covers the basics of major disability-related laws such as IDEA, The Rehabilitation Act of 1973, and ADA.

Chapter 10

Koenig, A.J. & Holbrook, M.C. *The Braille Enthusiast's Dictionary.* Nashville, TN: SCALRS Publishing, 1995. This reference book, containing approximately 30,000 words in print and contracted braille forms, was compiled for teachers and parents as a resource for braille transcription.

Miller, D. "Reading Comes Naturally: A Mother and Her Blind Child's Experiences." *Journal of Visual Impairment and Blindness,* 79, 1–4 (1985). This article tells about early literacy experiences in braille that Mrs. Miller enjoyed with her daughter, Jamaica, who was blind. Experiences such as reading from twin-vision books, keeping an auditory experience album, making book bags, and scribbling with the brailler are presented in a friendly, understandable manner.

Olson, M.R., & Mangold, S. *Guidelines and Games for Teaching Efficient Braille Reading.* New York: American Foundation for the Blind, 1981. This book was written primarily for teachers, but includes valuable information for parents as well. One chapter on preschool experiences provides suggestions on developing early concepts and gaining important early experiences that will provide a foundation for literacy. Another chapter gives suggestions for games that will help children practice braille reading skills in elementary school.

Stratton, J.M., & Wright, S. *On the Way to Literacy: Early Experiences for Visually Impaired Children.* Louisville, KY: American Printing House for the Blind, 1993. This user-friendly resource guide provides a wealth of practical information and ideas for developing early skills needed for toddlers and preschoolers with visual impairments to keep moving on the way to literacy. It was written for parents and teachers of young children who are blind and who have low vision. Several twin-vision books are included if the complete set of materials is purchased.

Trelease, J. *The New Read-Aloud Handbook.* New York: Penguin Books, 1989. This book presents information on the importance of reading aloud to children, as well as many practical suggestions on how to read aloud. It was written for a general audience, so adaptations will have to be made before using some of the suggestions. This is a valuable resource for all parents.

Chapter 11

Dodson-Burke, B., & Hill, E.W. *An Orientation and Mobility Primer for Families and Young Children.* New York: American Foundation for the Blind, 1989. Written for parents, this book provides an introduction to beginning orientation and mobility instruction for children. It contains easy-to-understand definitions of key terms used in Orientation and Mobility and then offers practical suggestions for parents to encourage movement with their children.

Raynor, S., & Drouillard, R. *Get a Wiggle On.* Lanham, MD: American Alliance Publication, 1975. Helpful suggestions for parents and others working with very young children who are visually impaired.

Raynor, S. & Drouillard, R. *Move it!* Lanham, MD: American Alliance Publications, 1977. A follow up to *Get a Wiggle On* (see above) this booklet contains more helpful suggestions for parents.

Smith, E. & Dodson, B. *A Guide Dog Goes to School: The Story of a Dog Trained to Lead the Blind.* New York: Morrow Junior Books, 1987. This book for younger children offers a look at how dog guides are trained and how they work with blind people.

Chapter 12

Baker, B., Brightman, A., Blacher, J., Heifetz, Louis, Hinshaw, S., & Murphy, D. *Steps to Independence: A Skills Training Guide for Parents & Teachers of Children with Special Needs.* 2nd ed. Baltimore: Paul Brookes, 1989. This is a step-by-step guide to teaching children with developmental disabilities the skills that are essential to independence—self-help, play, housekeeping skills. Information on behavior management is included.

Batshaw, M., M.D., & Perret, Yvonne. *Children with Disabilities: A Medical Primer.* 3rd ed. Baltimore: Paul Brookes, 1992. Included in this encyclopedic and readable book are chapters on mental retardation, hearing loss, language and communication disorders, cerebral palsy, spina bifida and other neural tube defects, brain injury, and prematurity.

Bloom, B. & Seljeskog, E. *A Parent's Guide to Spina Bifida.* Minneapolis, University of Minnesota Press, 1988. This brief parent's guide includes information on the causes and treatment of spina bifida, associated problems such as hydrocephalus, orthopedic problems, and daily care issues such as bladder and bowel control.

Bolton, S. *One Step at a Time: A Manual for Families of Children with Hearing and Vision Impairments.* Monmouth, OR: Teaching Research (345 N. Monmouth Ave., Monmouth, OR, 97361; 503–838–8391), 1990. This is a manual written for families of children who are both hearing impaired and visually impaired. It presents specific guidelines and strategies for communication, feeding and eating, play, self-care skills, toilet training, bedtime routines, and motor development. It includes a resource section with information on useful toys, hearing aids, glasses, and financial assistance.

Cipani, E. *A Guide to Developing Language Competence in Preschool Children with Severe and Moderate Handicaps.* Springfield, IL: Charles C. Thomas, 1991. Although somewhat technical, this book offers useful advice for enhancing development of language in children with moderate to severe disabilities.

Geralis, E., editor. *Children with Cerebral Palsy: A Parents' Guide.* 2nd Ed. Bethesda, MD: Woodbine House, 1998. Written by parents and professionals, this book includes chapters on the nature and treatment of cerebral palsy, daily care, development, family life, educational and legal issues, useful therapies, and advocacy.

John Tracy Clinic. *John Tracy Clinic Correspondence Learning Program for Parents of Young Deaf-Blind Children.* Los Angeles: John Tracy Clinic (806 W. Adams Blv., Los Angeles, CA 90007; 213–748–5481), 1990. This manual contains twelve lessons for parents of children and youths who are deafblind on general development, communication (including basic signs), future expectations, and appropriate activities. Additional information is included on gross and fine motor development, eating, sleeping, dressing, toilet training, and personal hygiene.

Smith, R., editor. *Children with Mental Retardation: A Parents' Guide.* Bethesda, MD: Woodbine House, 1993. Like other parents' guides in the Woodbine House special-needs series, this book covers emotional concerns, family life, daily living, development, and legal and educational issues. Also included are useful chapters about children with multiple disabilities (including visual impairment and mental retardation) and the multidisciplinary evaluation process.

Chapter 13

Kelly, J.D. (Ed.) *Recreation Programming for Visually Impaired Children and Youth.* New York: American Foundation for the Blind, 1981. This book addresses recreation for individuals with visual impairments. It contains basic information about the need for recreation and addresses some of the barriers to full participation in recreation activities.

Monat-Haller, R. *Understanding and Expressing Sexuality: Responsible Choices for Individuals with Developmental Disabilities.* Baltimore: Paul Brookes, 1992. Although written primarily for professionals, this text offers helpful information for parents interested in guiding their child with developmental disabilities to appropriate sexual behavior.

Swallow, R., & Huebner, K.M. *How to Thrive, Not Just Survive: A Guide to Independent Skills for Blind and Visually Impaired Children and Youth.* New York: American Foundation for the Blind, 1987. This book for parents and professionals focuses on teaching practical skills such as eating, toileting, grooming, etiquette, and leisure and recreation skills.

RESOURCE GUIDE

National Organizations

The national organizations listed below offer a variety of services that may be of help in meeting the needs of children with visual or multiple disabilities and their families. For more information about any of these organizations, call or write them and request an information packet.

American Academy of Ophthalmology
P.O. Box 7424
San Francisco, CA 94120–7242
(415) 561–8540
This organization promotes continuing education for ophthalmologists and quality care in ophthalmology.

American Council of the Blind
1155 15th Street, N.W., Suite 1004
Washington, DC 20005
(202) 467-5081; (800) 424-8666
The American Council of the Blind's membership consists of individuals who are blind, family members, and professionals. ACB advocates for civil rights, national health insurance, rehabilitation, eye research, technology, and other issues that concern people who are blind.

American Diabetes Association
National Center
1600 Duke St.
P.O. Box 25757
Alexandria, VA 22314
(703) 549–1500
The American Diabetes Association is a non-profit organization designed to promote knowledge of diabetes, to seek prevention and cure of diabetes, and to improve the lives of those affected by the disease. The association can inform parents about the visual implications of juvenile diabetes, as well as about how best to take care of the needs of their child to avoid vision complications, if possible.

American Foundation for the Blind
11 Penn Plaza, Suite 300
New York, NY 10001
(212) 502–7600; 800–AFB-LINE
The American Foundation for the Blind is a national organization which works to promote equality of access and opportunity to individuals who are blind or visually impaired. Regional offices and the national office provide information, publications, and a toll-free national hotline.

American Optometric Association
243 North Lindbergh
St. Louis, MO 63141
(314) 991–4100
This organization distributes information and promotes high standards, continuing education, and professional involvements in optometry.

American Printing House for the Blind
1839 Frankfort Ave.
P.O. Box 6085
Louisville, KY 40206–0085
(502) 895–2405
The American Printing House for the Blind publishes literature and textbooks in braille and large print, talking books, microcomputer software, and electronic books. Educational aids for persons with visual impairments are also provided.

The Arc
1010 Wayne Ave., Suite 650
Silver Spring, MD 20910
(301) 565-3842
A national organization of people with mental retardation and their advocates, formerly known as the Association for Retarded Citizens. It publishes information on all types of developmental delays and has an extensive network of local affiliates which offer support, information, respite care, and other services.

The Association for Persons with Severe Handicaps (TASH)
29 W. Susquehanna Ave., Suite 210
Baltimore, MD 21204
(410) 828–8274
TASH is a national membership organization for professionals and parents whose purpose is to advocate for a dignified lifestyle for all individuals with severe disabilities. It publishes a newsletter and other publications.

Association for the Education and Rehabilitation of the Blind and Visually Impaired
206 N. Washington Street, Suite 320
Alexandria, VA 22314
(703) 836–6060
This membership organization promotes all phases of education and work for blind and visually impaired persons. AER certifies orientation and mobility specialists, rehabilitation teachers, and vision specialists.

Blind Children's Fund
311 W. Broadway, Suite 1
Mt. Pleasant, MI 48858
(989) 779-9966
The mission of this organization is to promote the education and welfare of preschoolers who are blind or visually impaired by developing programs and disseminating information. They publish the *VIP Newsletter*.

Canadian Council of the Blind
396 Cooper St., Ste. 200
Ottawa, Ontario K2P 2H7
Canada
(613) 567-0311
A national consumer organization that works to improve the quality of life for Canadians who are blind through social, recreational, and advocacy programs. Sponsors over 90 local CCB clubs.

Corneal Dystrophy Foundation
1926 Hidden Creek Drive
Kingwood, TX 77339
(713) 358–4227
Corneal Dystrophy Foundation is a national organization whose mission is to promote
public education about corneal dystrophy and support ongoing research.

Council for Exceptional Children
1920 Association Dr.
Reston, VA 22091–1589
(703) 620–3660
The Council for Exceptional Children is a membership organization striving to improve
educational opportunities for individuals with exceptionalities by advocating for appropriate government policies, setting professional standards, providing continuing professional development, and assisting professionals to obtain resources necessary for
effective professional practice. The division within CEC focusing on the needs of children with visual impairments is The Division on Visual Impairment, which publishes the
Division on Visual Impairment Quarterly.

Council of Families with Visual Impairments
c/o American Council of the Blind
1155 15th St., Suite 1004
Washington, DC 20005
(202) 393-3666
This is a support group of parents of children who are blind or visually impaired within
the American Council of the Blind.

DB-Link: The National Information Clearinghouse on Children Who Are Deaf-Blind
c/o Teaching Research
Northwestern Oregon State College
345 North Monmouth Ave.
Monmouth, OR 97361
(800) 438-9376
This collaborative effort between the American Foundation for the Blind, Helen Keller
National Center for Deaf-Blind Youths and Adults, Perkins School for the Blind, and
Teaching Research seeks to provide information related to children ages 0-21 who are
deaf and blind.

Foundation for Glaucoma Research
490 Post St., Suite 830
San Francisco, CA 94102
(415) 986–3162
Through research and the dissemination of public information, the Foundation for Glaucoma Research seeks to eliminate blindness caused by glaucoma.

Hadley School for the Blind
700 Elm St.
Winnetka, IL 60093
(708) 446–8111 or (800) 323–4238
The Hadley School for the Blind offers free at-home study courses for individuals who
are blind and for parents of blind children. Courses include braille reading and writing.

Helen Keller International
90 West St.
New York, NY 10006
(212) 766-5266
Helen Keller International is a non-profit organization designed to promote programs in the prevention of eye disease and blindness, especially through working with governments in developing countries.

Helen Keller National Center for Deaf-Blind Youths and Adults
111 Middle Neck Rd.
Sands Point, NY 11050
(516) 944–8900
This non-profit national organization is designed to facilitate a national coordinated effort to meet the social, rehabilitative, and independent living needs of individuals who are deaf and blind.

Hilton/Perkins National and International Program
Perkins School for the Blind
175 North Beacon St.
Watertown, MA 02172
(617) 924–3434
Through special projects, the Hilton/Perkins National and International Program works to improve the quality of life for individuals with visual impairments (including those with multiple disabilities) though support and direct service to children, their families, and professionals.

John Tracy Clinic
806 W. Adams Blvd.
Los Angeles, CA 90007
(800) 522-4582
Parents of children who have a hearing impairment can enroll in the John Tracy Clinic's correspondence courses on deaf-blindness or sign language, or attend summer programs.

Lions Clubs International
300 22nd Street
Oak Brook, IL 60521–8842
(708) 571–5466
Lions Clubs have a major interest in issues relating to blindness and visual impairments. Sometimes funding is available through local Lions clubs for equipment or special projects.

Library of Congress
National Library Service for the Blind and Physically Handicapped
1291 Taylor St., N.W.
Washington, DC 20542
(800) 424–8567
The Library of Congress, National Library Services for the Blind and Physically Handicapped distributes reading materials of a general nature to U.S. citizens who are blind or have a physical impairment which prevents their using ordinary printed materials. The service is free of charge. See the state listings, below, for the address of your state or regional library service.

March of Dimes Birth Defects Foundation
1275 Mamaroneck Ave.
White Plains, NY 10605
(888) 663-4637
The March of Dimes Birth Defects Foundation offers information (fact sheets) on genetic counseling and prevention of birth defects.

National Association for Parents of the Visually Impaired
P.O. Box 317
Watertown, MA 02471
(800) 562-6265
This national membership organization for parents and agencies provides support to parents and families of children with visual impairments. NAPVI operates a national clearinghouse for information, education, and referral, and publishes the newsletter *Awareness*.

National Association for Visually Handicapped
22 West 21st St., 6th Floor
New York, NY 10010
(212) 889–3141
This organization offers publications, a newsletter (*In Focus*), support, and referral services for individuals with low vision, their families, and professionals.

National Camps for Blind Children
4444 South 52nd Street
Lincoln, NE 68516
(402) 488–0981
This non-profit organization operates summer camps for children and adults who are blind or visually impaired and publishes the newsletter *Campfire Light*.

National Easter Seals Society
250 W. Monroe St., Suite 1800
Chicago, IL 60606
(800) 221-6827
The National Easter Seals Society works to help people with disabilities increase their independence through advocacy, publishing and distributing information on rehabilitation, and other services. There are many local affiliates throughout the country.

National Federation of the Blind
1800 Johnson St.
Baltimore, MD 21230
(410) 659–9314
This national membership organization of and for the blind works to improve social and economic conditions of blind persons. NFB publishes *The Braille Monitor*.

National Information Center for Children and Youth with Disabilities (NICHCY)
P.O. Box 1492
Washington, DC 20013–1492
(202) 884–8200; (800) 695–0285
This non-profit organization was established to provide information on education and other special services for children and adolescents with disabilities. NICHCY offers fact

sheets on a variety of disabilities, information packets, and "State Sheets," which list each state's resources for people with disabilities. Parents can call or send in requests for free information or a publication list.

National Organization for Albinism and Hypopigmentation (NOAH)
1500 Locust St.
Suite 1816
Philadelphia, PA 19102
(215) 545–2322; (800) 473–2310
This non-profit membership organization provides information on albinism and hypopigmentation, provides peer support, sponsors conferences, and publishes a newsletter.

National Organization of Parents of Blind Children
1800 Johnson St.
Baltimore, MD 21230
(410) 659–9314
A division of the National Federation for the Blind, the National Organization of Parents of Blind Children focuses on the needs of parents and families and publishes *Future Reflections.*

PACER Center (Parent Advocacy Coalition for Educational Rights)
4826 Chicago Ave. South
Minneapolis, MN 55417–1098
(612) 827–2966
The PACER Center is dedicated to helping parents understand special education laws and obtain appropriate educations for their children. The center offers an extensive selection of publications (some free of charge), including several newsletters, and provides workshops for parents of children with disabilities.

Prevent Blindness America
500 East Remington Rd.
Schaumburg, IL 60173
(800) 331–2020
Fax: (708) 331–2020
Through public and professional education, research, and service, this organization supports local and regional efforts to promote eye care and prevention of eye disease and blindness. It was formerly known as the National Society to Prevent Blindness.

Recording for the Blind and Dyslexic (RFB&D)
20 Roszel Rd.
Princeton, NJ 08540
(800) 221–4792
Recording for the Blind and Dyslexic (RFB&D) is a non-profit agency providing recorded and computerized textbooks, library services, and other educational resources to people who cannot read standard print because of a visual, physical, or perceptual disability.

RP Foundation Fighting Blindness
(National Retinitis Pigmentosa Foundation, Inc.)
Executive Plaza 1, Suite 800
11350 McCormick Rd.

Hunt Valley, MD 21031–1014
(410) 785–1414; (800) 683–5555
Through research, the RP Foundation Fighting Blindness strives to discover the cause, prevention, and treatment of retinitis pigmentosa.

Senate Document Room
Hart Building
Washington, DC 20515
(202) 225–7860
and
House Document Room
Room B-18
House Annex #2
Washington, DC 20515
(202) 225–3456
Either of these offices can supply you with a copy of federal bills or laws such as the Americans with Disabilities Act or Individuals with Disabilities Education Act.

Spina Bifida Association of America
4590 MacArthur Blvd., N.W., Suite 250
Washington, DC 20007–4226
(202) 944–3285; (800) 621–3141
This national organization for individuals with spina bifida and their families provides information and referral, distributes a newsletter and other publications, supports research, holds conferences for parents and professionals, and advocates for individuals with spina bifida.

United Cerebral Palsy Associations
1660 L St., N.W., Suite 700
Washington, DC 20036
(202) 776–0406; (800) 872–5827
UCP is a national organization for people with cerebral palsy and their families. Through local chapters, it provides services that include information and referral, parent support, advocacy, and educational and work programs for individuals with cerebral palsy.

United States Association for Blind Athletes
33 North Institute St.
Colorado Springs, CO 80903
(719) 630–0422
This national membership organization promotes sports involvement for people who are blind.

Dog Guide Schools

Canadian Guide Dogs for the Blind
4120 Rideau Valley Dr. North
Manotick, ON K0A 2N0
CANADA
(613) 692–7777

Canine Vision Canada
c/o Lions Foundation of Canada
P.O. Box 907

Oakville, ON L6J 5E8
CANADA
(416) 842–2891

Eye Dog Foundation for the Blind, Inc.
512 N. Larchmont Blvd.
Los Angeles, CA 90004
(213) 626–3370 or (213) 468–8856

Eye of the Pacific Guide Dogs and Mobility Services, Inc.
747 Amana St., #407
Honolulu, HI 96814
(808) 941–1088

Fidelco Guide Dog Foundation, Inc.
P.O. Box 142
Bloomfield, CT 06002
(203) 243–5200

Foundation Mira
1820 Rang Nord Oest
Sainte-Madeleine, Quebec PQJOH 1SO
CANADA
(514) 795–3725

Guide Dog Foundation for the Blind, Inc.
371 E. Jericho Turnpike
Smithtown, NY 11787–2976
(516) 263–2121; (800) 548–4337

Guide Dogs for the Blind, Inc.
P.O. Box 151200
San Rafael, CA 94915–1200
(415) 499–4000

Guide Dogs of the Desert, Inc.
P.O. Box 1692
Palm Springs, CA 92263

(619) 329–6257

Guiding Eyes for the Blind, Inc.
611 Granite Springs Rd.
Yorktown Heights, NY 10598
(914) 245–4024

International Guiding Eyes, Inc.
13445 Glenoaks Blvd.
Sylmar, CA 91342
(213) 362–5834

Leader Dogs for the Blind
P.O. Box 5000
Rochester, MI 48307
(313) 651–9011

Pilot Dogs, Inc.
625 West Town St.
Columbia, OH 43215
(614) 221–6367

The Seeing Eye, Inc.
P.O. Box 375
Morristown, NJ 07960
(201) 539–4425

Southeastern Guide Dogs, Inc.
4210 77th St. East
Palmetto, FL 34221
(813) 729–5665

State Organizations

This section includes the agencies in each state that oversee special education
and early intervention programs, as well as state schools for the blind, state library
services for individuals with visual impairment, and other organizations specific to
visual impairment. For names and addresses of additional state resources, contact
the National Information Center for Children and Youth with Disabilities
(NICHCY) at the address given in the national listings, and request a "State
Sheet" for your state.

ALABAMA

Alabama State Department of Education
50 North Ripley St.
Montgomery, AL 36130
(334) 242–9708 or in Alabama (800) 392–
8020

Early Intervention System
Alabama Department of Rehabilitation
Services
2129 East South Blvd.
Montgomery, AL 36111
(334) 281–8780

Alabama School for the Blind
803 East South St.

P.O. Box 698
Talladega, AL 35160
(334) 761–3259

ALASKA

Alaska Department of Education
801 West Tenth St., #200
Goldbelt Building
Juneau, AK 99801
(907) 465–2800

Early Intervention Program
Alaska Department of Health and Social
Services
1231 Gambell St.

Anchorage, AK 99501
(907) 277–3841

Special Education Service Agency
Infant Learning Program
2217 East Tudor Road, Suite 1
Anchorage, AK 99507
(907) 562–7372

Alaska State Library Services for the Blind
and Physically Handicapped
344 West Third Ave., Suite 125
Anchorage, AK 99501
(907) 272–3033

ARIZONA

Arizona Department of Education
Division of Special Education
1535 West Jefferson St.
Phoenix, AZ 85007
(602) 542–3184

Governor's Interagency Coordinating
Council on Infants and Toddlers
Arizona Department of Economic Security
P.O. Box 6123, 801–A-6
Phoenix, AZ 85005
(602) 542–5577

Arizona State School for the Deaf and the
Blind
1200 West Speedway Boulevard
P.O. Box 5545
Tucson, AZ 85703–0545
(602) 770–3700

Foundation for Blind Children
1201 North 85th Place
Scottsdale, AZ 85257
(602) 331–1470

Arizona State Braille and Talking Book Library
1030 North 32nd St.
Phoenix, AZ 85008
(602) 255–5578 or in Arizona
(800) 255–5578

ARKANSAS

Arkansas Department of Education
Special Education Department
4 Capitol Mall
Education Building, Room 105–C
Little Rock, AR 72201
(501) 682–4221

Arkansas School for the Blind
2600 West Markham
P.O. Box 668

Little Rock, AR 72203
(501) 296–1810

Library for the Blind and Physically Handicapped
One Capitol Mall
Little Rock, AR 72201–1081
(501) 682–1155

CALIFORNIA

California Department of Education
Special Education Division
721 Capitol Mall
Sacramento, CA 95814
(916) 657–3213

Early Intervention Program
California Department of Developmental
Servicies
1600 Ninth St., Room 310
P.O. Box 944202
Sacramento, CA 95814
(916) 654–2777

California School for the Blind
500 Walnut Ave.
Fremont, CA 94536
(510) 794–3800

Foundation for the Junior Blind
5300 Angeles Vista Boulevard
Los Angeles, CA 90043
(213) 295–4555

Blind Babies Foundation
1200 Gough St.
San Francisco, CA 94109
(415) 771–5464

Blind Children's Center
4120 Marathon St.
Los Angeles, CA 90029
(213) 664–2153 or in California
(800) 222–3567

Blind Children's Learning Center
18542–B Vanderlip Ave.
Santa Ana, CA 92705
(714) 573–8888

California State Library
Braille and Talking Book Library
600 Broadway
Sacramento, CA 95818
(916) 322–4090 or in California (800) 952–
5666

COLORADO

Special Education Division
Colorado Department of Education

201 East Colfax Ave.
Room 301
Denver, CO 80203
(303) 830–6710

Colorado School for the Deaf and Blind
33 North Institute St.
Colorado Springs, CO 80903
(719) 578–2100 or (719) 578–2201

Anchor Center for Blind Children
3801 Martin Luther Boulevard
Denver, CO 80205
(303) 377–9732

Colorado Talking Book Library
180 Sheridan Boulevard
Denver, CO 80226
(303) 727–9277 or in Colorado (800) 685–2136

Parent Advocates for Visually Impaired
Children (PAVIC)
P.O. Box 461812
Aurora, CO 80046
(303) 693–0959 or (303) 699–8685

CONNECTICUT

Connecticut State Board of Education and
Services for the Blind
170 Ridge Road
Wethersfield, CT 06109
(203) 249–8525

Bureau of Early Childhood
Education and Social Services
Connecticut Department of Education
25 Industrial Park Road
Middletown, CT 06457
(203) 638–4208

Oak Hill School
Connecticut Institute for the Blind
120 Holcomb St.
Hartford, CT 06112
(203) 242–2274

Connecticut State Library
Library for the Blind and Physically Handicapped
198 West St.
Rocky Hill, CT 06067
(203) 566–2151 or in Connecticut (800) 842–4516

DELAWARE

Delaware Department of Public Instruction
John G. Townsend Building

P.O. Box 1402
Dover, DE 19903
(302) 739–5471

Divison of Planning and Research Evaluation
Delaware Health and Social Services
1901 North Dupont Highway
Newcastle, DE 19720
(302) 577–4647

Delaware Division for the Visually Impaired
305 West Eighth St.
Wilmington, DE 19801
(302) 577–3333 or (302) 577–3573

Library for the Blind and Physically Handicapped
Delaware Division of Libraries
43 South DuPont Highway
Dover, DE 19901
(302) 739–4748 or in Delaware (800) 282–8676

DISTRICT OF COLUMBIA

District of Columbia Special Education
Branch
Logan Administrative Office
215 G St., N.E.
Washington, DC 20002
(202) 724–4800

Early Intervention Program
District of Columbia Department of Human Services
609 H St.
Fourth Floor
Washington, DC 20002
(202) 727–1839

Infant and Child Development Program
Columbia Lighthouse for the Blind
1421 P St., N.W.
Washington, DC 20005
(202) 462–2900

District of Columbia Library for the Blind
and Physically Handicapped
901 G St., N.W., Room 215
Washington, DC 20001
(202) 727–2142

FLORIDA

Bureau of Education for Exceptional Students
Florida Department of Education

614 Florida Education Center
Tallahassee, FL 32399–0400
(904) 488–1570

Office of Prevention, Early Assistance and
  Childhood Development
Florida Department of Health and Reha-
  bilitative Services
1323 Winewood Boulevard
Building 1, Room 209
Tallahassee, FL 32399
(904) 488–2761

Pre-Kindergarten Early Intervention
Office of Early Intervention and School
  Readinesss
Florida Division of Public Schools/Depart-
  ment of Education
325 West Gaines St., Suite 754
Tallahassee, FL 32399–0400
(904) 488–6830

Florida School for the Deaf and the Blind
207 North San Marco Ave.
St. Augustine, FL 32084
(904) 823–4000

Division of Blind Services
Florida Department of Education
2540 Executive Center Circle West
Tallahassee, FL 32399
(904) 488–1330

Bureau of Library Services for the Blind
  and Physically Handicapped
420 Platt St.
Daytona Beach, FL 32114
(904) 254–3824 or in Florida (800) 342–
  5627

GEORGIA

Georgia State Department of Education
Division for Exceptional Students
1970 Twin Towers East
Altanta, GA 30334–5040
(404) 656–6317

Early Intervention Programs
Division of Public Health
Georgia Department of Human Resources
878 Peachtree St., N.E.
Room 203
Atlanta, GA 30309–3999
(404) 894–8940

Georgia Academy for the Blind
2895 Vineville Ave.
Macon, GA 31204
(912) 751–6083

BEGIN (Babies Early Growth Intervention Network)
Center for the Visually Impaired
763 Peachtree St., N.E.
Altanta, GA 30308
(404) 875–9011

Georgia Regional Library for the Blind and
  Physically Handicapped
1150 Murphy Ave., S.W.
Atlanta, GA 30310
(404) 756–4619

GUAM

Guam Department of Education
Division of Special Education
P.O. Box DE
Agana, GU 96910
(671) 472–8901

Guam Public Library for the Blind and
  Physically Handicapped
254 Martyr St.
Agana, GU 96910
(671) 472–6417

HAWAII

Hawaii Department of Education
Statewide Center for Students with Hearing and Visual Impairments
3440 Leahi Ave.
Honolulu, HI 96815
(808) 734–0297

Zero to 3 Hawaii Project
Pan American Building
1600 Kapiolani Boulevard
Suite 1401
Honolulu, HI 96814
(808) 957–0066

Statewide Center for Students with Hearing and Visual Impairment
3440 Leahi Ave.
Honolulu, HI 96815
(808) 734–0297

Hawaii Library for the Blind and Physcially Handicapped
402 Kapahulu Ave.
Honolulu, HI 96815
(808) 732–7767

IDAHO

Idaho State Department of Education
650 West State St.
Len B. Jordon Building, Room 150
Boise, ID 83702
(208) 334–3390

Bureau of Developmental Disabilities
Idaho Department of Health and Welfare
450 West State St.
Seventh Floor
Boise, ID 83720
(208) 334–5531

Idaho School for the Deaf and Blind
1450 Main St.
Gooding, ID 83330
(208) 934–4457

Idaho State Library Services for Blind and
Physically Handicapped
325 West State St.
Boise, ID 83702
(208) 334–2117 or in Idaho (800) 233–4931

ILLINOIS

Illinois State Board of Education
Department of Special Education
100 North First St.
Springfield, IL 62777
(217) 782–6601

Early Intervention Program Unit, S-100
Illinois State Board of Education
100 North First St.
Springfield, IL 62777
(217) 524–0203

Illinois School for the Visually Impaired
658 East State St.
Jacksonville, IL 62650
(217) 479–4400

Chicago Pubic Library
Illinois Regional Library for the Blind and
Physically Handicapped
1055 West Roosevelt Road
Chicago, IL 60608
(312) 746–9210

INDIANA

Indiana Department of Education
Division of Special Education
Room 229, State House
Indianapolis, IN 46204–2798
(317) 232–0570

First Steps
Family and Social Services Administration
402 West Washington St.
E-414
P.O. Box 7083
Indianapolis, IN 46207–7083
(317) 232–2429

Indiana School for the Blind
7725 North College Ave.
Indianapolis, IN 46240
(317) 253–1481

Indiana State Library
Special Services Division
140 North State Ave.
Indianapolis, IN 46204
(317) 232–3684 or in Indiana (800) 622–4970

IOWA

Iowa Department of Education
Grimes State Office Building
Des Moines, IA 50319–0146
(515) 281–4030

Iowa Braille and Sight Saving School
1002 G Ave.
Vinton, IA 52349
(319) 472–5221

Iowa Library for the Blind and Physically
Handicapped
Iowa Department for the Blind
524 Fourth St.
Des Moines, IA 50309–2364
(515) 281–1333 or in Iowa (800) 362–2587

KANSAS

Kansas State Board of Education
Special Education Outcomes Team
120 Southeast Tenth Ave.
Topeka, KS 66612–1182
(913) 296–3869

Kansas Department of Health and Environment
Landon State Office Building
900 S.W. Jackson
Tenth Floor
Topeka, KS 66612–1290
(913) 296–6135

Kansas State School for the Blind
1100 State Ave.
Kansas City, KS 66102
(913) 281–3308

Early Education Center
Training and Evaluation Center of
    Hutchinson
303 East Bigger
P.O. Box 399
Hutchinson, KS 67504–0399
(316) 663–2671 or (316) 663–1596

KENTUCKY

Kentucky Department of Education
Division of Exceptional Children Services
500 Mero St.
Capital Plaza Towers, Room 805
Frankfort, KY 40601
(502) 564–4970

Infant-Toddler Program
Kentucky Department of Mental Health
    and Mental Retardation Services
275 East Main St.
Frankfort, KY 40621
(502) 564–7700

Kentucky School for the Blind
1867 Frankfort Ave.
P.O. Box 6005
Louisville, KY 40206
(502) 897–1583

Kentucky Library for the Blind and Physi-
    cally Handicapped
300 Coffee Tree Road
P.O. Box 818
Frankfort, KY 40602
(502) 875–7000 or in Kentucky (800) 372–
    2968

LOUISIANA

Louisiana Learning Resources System
Louisiana State Department of Education
2758–C Brightside Lane
Baton Rouge, LA 70820–3507
(504) 765–2417

Preschool Programs
Office of Special Education Services
Louisiana Department of Education
P.O. Box 94064
Baton Rouge, LA 70804–9064
(504) 342–1837

Louisiana School for the Visually Impaired
1120 Government St.
P.O. Box 4328
Baton Rouge, LA 70821–4328
(504) 342–4727

Louisiana State Library
Section for the Blind and Physically
    Handicapped
760 Riverside North
Baton Rouge, LA 70802–5232
(504) 342–4944

MAINE

Division for the Blind and Visually Im-
    paired
Maine Department of Human Services
35 Anthony Ave.
State House Station #11
Augusta, ME 04330–0011
(207) 624–5323

Interdepartmental Coordinating Council
    on Early Intervention
Child Development Services
State House Station #146
Augusta, ME 04333
(207) 287–3272

Maine State Library for the Blind and
    Physically Handicapped
State House Station #64
Augusta, ME 04333
(207) 289–5650 or in Maine (800) 452–
    8793

MARYLAND

Maryland State Department of Education
200 West Baltimore St.
Baltimore, MD 21201
(410) 333–2200

Maryland Infants and Toddlers Program
One Market Center, Suite 304
Baltimore, MD 21201
(410) 333–8100

Maryland School for the Blind
3501 Taylor Ave.
Baltimore, MD 21236–4499
(410) 444–5000 or in Maryland (800) 400–
    4915

Maryland State Library for the Blind and
    Physically Handicapped
1715 North Charles St.
Baltimore, MD 21201
(410) 333–2668 or in Maryland (800) 492–
    5627

MASSACHUSETTS

Massachusetts Department of Education
Division of Special Education
1385 Hancock St.

Quincy, MA 02169
(617) 770–7500

Division of Early Childhood
Massachusetts Department of Public
Health
150 Tremont Ave.
Third Floor
Boston, MA 02111
(617) 727–5089

Perkins School for the Blind
175 North Beacon St.
Watertown, MA 02172
(617) 924–3434

Massachusetts Braille and Talking Book
Library
Perkins School for the Blind
175 North Beacon
Watertown, MA 02172
(617) 924–3434 or in Massachusetts (800)
852–3133

Massachusetts State Commission for the
Blind
88 Kingston St.
Boston, MA 02111–2227
(617) 727–5550 or (800) 392–6450

MICHIGAN

Michigan Department of Education
Special Education Services
P.O. Box 30008
Lansing, MI 48909
(517) 373–9433

Michigan School for the Blind
715 West Willow St.
Lansing, MI 48913
(517) 334–6624

Library of Michigan
Services for the Blind and Physically
Handicapped
P.O. Box 30007
Lansing, MI 48909
(517) 373–1590

MINNESOTA

Special Education Section
Minnesota Department of Education
550 Cedar St.
811 Capitol Square Building
St. Paul, MN 55101
(612) 296–4163

Minnesota State Academy for the Blind
Highway 298, P.O. Box 68
Faribault, MN 55021
(507) 332–3226

Minnesota Library for the Blind and
Physically Handicapped
P.O. Box 68
Faribault, MN 55021
(507) 332–3279 or in Minnesota (800)
722–0550

Minnesota State Services for the Blind
and Visually Handicapped
Communication Center
2200 University Ave. W., Suite 240
St. Paul, MN 55114–1840
(612) 642–0500

MISSISSIPPI

Mississippi Department of Education
Sillers State Office Building
Jackson, MS 39205
(601) 359–3513

Mississippi School for the Blind
1252 Eastover Dr.
Jackson, MS 39211
(601) 987–3952

Infant and Toddler Program
Mississippi Department of Health
2423 North State St.
Room 105A, P.O. Box 1700
Jackson, MS 39215–1700
(601) 960–7427 or (800) 451–3903

Mississippi Library Commission
Handicapped Services
5455 Executive Place
Jackson, MS 39206
(601) 354–7208

MISSOURI

Missouri Department of Elementary and
Secondary Education
Section of Special Education
P.O. Box 480
Jefferson City, MO 65102
(314) 751–0185

Missouri School for the Blind
3815 Magnolia Ave.
St. Louis, MO 63110
(314) 776–4320 or in Missouri (800) 622–
5672

Children's Center for the Visually Impaired
400 West 57th St.
Kansas City, MO 64113
(816) 333–3166

Delta Gamma Center for Children with Visual Impairments
8900A Manchester Road
St. Louis, MO 63144–2622
(314) 963–0376

Wolfner Library for the Blind and Physically Handicapped
600 West Main
Jefferson City, MO 65102–0387
(314) 751–8720 or in Missouri (800) 392–2614

Missouri Rehabilitation Services for the Blind
619 East Capitol Ave.
Jefferson City, MO 65101
(314) 751–4249

MONTANA

Montana Department of Curriculum
Division of Special Education
Capitol Station
Helena, MT 59620
(406) 444–4429

Montana School for the Deaf and Blind
3911 Central Ave.
Great Falls, MT 59405–1697
(406) 453–1404

Developmental Disabilities Division
Montana Department of Social and Rehabilitation Services
P.O. Box 4210
Helena, MT 59604
(406) 444–0230

Montana State Library for the Blind and Physically Handicapped
1515 East Sixth Ave.
Helena, MT 59620
(406) 444–2064 or (800) 332–3400

NEBRASKA

Nebraska Department of Education
Special Education Section
301 Centennial Mall South
P.O. Box 94987
Lincoln, NE 68509
(402) 471–2471

Nebraska School for the Visually Handicapped
824 Tenth Ave.
P.O. Box 129
Nebraska City, NE 68410
(402) 873–5513

Nebraska Library for the Blind and Physically Handicapped
1420 P St.
Lincoln, NE 68508
(402) 471–2045 or in Nebraska (800) 742–7691

NEVADA

Nevada Department of Education
400 West King St.
Carson City, NV 89710
(702) 687–3140

Early Childhood Services
Division of Child and Family Services
Nevada Department of Human Resources
480 Galletti Way
Building 1
Sparks, NV 89431
(702) 688–2284

NEW HAMPSHIRE

New Hampshire Department of Education
State Office Park South
101 Pleasant St.
Concord, NH 03301
(603) 271–3741

Infant and Toddler Project
Division of Mental Health and Developmental Services
New Hampshire Department of Health and Human Services
105 Pleasant St.
Hospital Administration Building
Concord, NH 03301
(603) 271–5144

New Hampshire Educational Services for the Sensory Impaired
117 Pleasant St.
Dolloff Building
Concord, NH 03301
(603) 226–2900

Multi-Sensory Intervention Through Consultation and Education (MICE)
Bureau of Special Medical Services
New Hampshire Division of Public Health

5 Hazen Drive
Concord, NH 03301
(603) 271–4526

NEW JERSEY

Division of Special Education
New Jersey Department of Education
225 West State St.
Trenton, NJ 08625
(609) 292–0147

Bureau of Program Review
Division of Special Education
New Jersey Department of Education
225 West State St.
CN 500
Trenton, NJ
(800) 322–8174

St. Joseph's School for the Blind
235 Baldwin Ave.
Jersey City, NJ 07306
(201) 653–0578

New Jersey Library for the Blind and
    Handicapped
2300 Stuyvesant Ave., CN 501
Trenton, NJ 08625–0501
(609) 292–6450 or in New Jersey (800)
    792–8322

New Jersey Commission for the Blind and
    Visually Impaired
153 Halsey St.
P.O. Box 47017
Newark, NJ 07101
(201) 648–3333 or in New Jersey (800)
    962–1233

NEW MEXICO

New Mexico State Department of Educa-
    tion
Special Education Office
300 Don Gaspar St.
Santa Fe, NM 87501–2786
(505) 827–6541

Developmental Disabilities Division
New Mexico Department of Health
1190 St. Francis Dr.
Room 3500 M
P.O. Box 26110
Santa Fe, NM 87502–6110
(505) 827–2575

New Mexico School for the Visually
    Handicapped
1900 North White Sands Blvd.

Alamogordo, NM 88310
(505) 437–3505

New Mexico School for the Visually
    Handicapped Preschool
230 Turman N.E.
Albuquerque, NM 87108
(505) 268–9506

New Mexico State Library for the Blind
    and Physically Handicapped
325 Don Gaspar St.
Santa Fe, NM 87503
(505) 827–3830 or in New Mexico (800)
    432–5515

NEW YORK

New York State Education Department
Office for Special Education
Education Building Annex
Room 1073
Albany, NY 12234
(518) 474–5548

Early Intervention Program
New York Department of Health
Empire State Plaza
Corning Tower, Room 208
Albany, NY 12237–0618
(518) 473–7016

New York State School for the Blind
Richmond Ave.
Batavia, NY 14020
(716) 343–5384

Child Development Center
The Lighthouse, Inc.
60–05 Woodhaven Blvd.
Elmhurst, NY 11373
(713) 899–9100

New York State Library for the Blind and
    Visually Handicapped
Cultural Education Center
Empire State Plaza
Albany, NY 12230
(518) 474–5935 or in New York (800) 342–
    3688

NORTH CAROLINA

North Carolina Department of Public In-
    struction
Division for Exceptional Children
Education Building
116 West Edenton St.
Raleigh, NC 27603–1712
(919) 733–3921

Governor Morehead School
301 Ashe Ave.
Raleigh, NC 27606
(919) 733–6381

North Carolina Department of Human Resources
Division of Services for the Blind
309 Ashe Ave.
Raleigh, NC 27606
(919) 733–9822

North Carolina Library for the Blind and Physically Handicapped
North Carolina State Library
1811 Capital Blvd.
Raleigh, NC 27635
(919) 733–4376

NORTH DAKOTA

North Dakota Department of Public Instruction
600 East Blvd.
State Capitol
Bismark, ND 58505–0440
(701) 224–2277

North Dakota School for the Blind
500 Stanford Road
Grand Forks, ND 58203–2799
(701) 795–3876

OHIO

Ohio Department of Education
Division of Special Education
933 High St.
Worthington, OH 43085–4087
(614) 466–2650

Ohio Department of Health
Early Intervention Unit
246 North High St.
Fourth Floor
P.O. Box 118
Columbus, OH 43266–0118
(614) 644–8389

Ohio State School for the Blind
5220 North High St.
Columbus, OH 43214
(614) 888–1154

OKLAHOMA

Oklahoma State Department of Education
Special Education Section
Oliver Hodge Memorial Education Building
2500 North Lincoln Boulevard

Oklahoma City, OK 73105–4599
(405) 521–3351

Interagency Coordinating Council for Early Childhood Intervention
Oklahoma Commission on Children and Youth
4545 North Lincoln Boulevard
Suite 114
Oklahoma City, OK 73105
(405) 521–4016

Parkview School (Oklahoma School for the Blind)
3300 Gibson St.
Muskogee, OK 74403
(918) 682–6641

Oklahoma Library for the Blind and Physically Handicapped
300 N.E. 18th St.
Oklahoma City, OK 73105
(405) 521–3514 or (405) 521–3833

OREGON

Early Intervention and Early Childhood Special Education Programs
Oregon Department of Education
700 Pringle Parkway, S.E.
Salem, OR 97301
(503) 378–3598

Oregon School for the Blind
700 Church St., S.E.
Salem, OR 97301
(503) 378–3820

Oregon State Library
Talking Book and Braille Services
State Library Building
Salem OR 97310–0645
(503) 378–3849 or in Oregon (800) 452–0292

PENNSYLVANIA

Pennsylvania Department of Education
Bureau of Special Education
333 Market St.
Seventh Floor
Harrisburg, PA 17126–0333
(717) 783–6913

Division of Community Program Development
Office of Mental Retardation
Pennsylvania Dept. of Public Welfare
P.O. Box 2675
Harrisburg, PA 17105–8302
(717) 783–8302

Overbrook School for the Blind
6333 Malvern Ave.
Philadelphia , PA 19151–2597
(215) 877–0313

Royer-Greaves School for Blind
118 South Valley Road
Paoli, PA 19301–1444
(215) 644–1810

St. Lucy Day School
130 Hampden Road
Upper Darby, PA 19082
(215) 352–4582

Western Pennsylvania School for Blind
Children
201 North Bellefield St.
Pittsburgh, PA 15213
(412) 621–0100

Carnegie Library of Pittsburgh
Library for the Blind and Physically Handicapped
The Leonard C. Staisey Building
4724 Baum Boulevard
Pittsburgh, PA 15213
(412) 687–2440 or in Pennsylvania (800)
242–0586

PUERTO RICO

Puerto Rico Department of Education
Special Education Program
P.O. Box 759
Hato Rey, PR 00919
(809) 759–7228

Infants and Toddlers with Handicaps
Puerto Rico Department of Health
P.O. Box 70184
San Juan, PR 00936
(809) 767–0870

Instituto Loaiza Cordero para Ninos Cie-
gos
Fernandez Juncos 1312
Santurce, PR 00910
(809) 724–0893

Puerto Rico Regional Library for the Blind
and Physically Handicapped
520 Ponce de Leon Ave.
Stop 8/12, Puerta de Tierra
San Juan, PR 00901
(809) 723–2519 or (800) 462–8008

RHODE ISLAND

Rhode Island Department of Education
22 Hayes St.

Providence, RI 02908
(401) 277–2031

Division of Family Health
Rhode Island Department of Health
3 Capitol Hill, Room 302
Providence, RI 02908–5097
(401) 277–2312

Rhode Island Regional Library for the
Blind and Physcially Handicapped
Rhode Island Department of Library Services
300 Richmond St.
Providence, RI 02903–4222
(401) 277–2726 or in Rhode Island (800)
662–5141

SOUTH CAROLINA

Office of Programs for Exceptional Children
South Carolina Department of Education
Rutledge Office Building
1429 Senate St.
Columbia, SC 29201
(803) 734–8222

Baby Net
South Carolina Department of Health and
Environmental Control
Robert Mills Building
P.O. Box 101106
Columbia, SC 29211
(803) 737–4047

South Carolina School for the Deaf and
Blind
Cedar Spring Station
Spartanburg, SC 29302
(803) 585–7711

South Carolina Commission for the Blind
1430 Confederate Ave.
Columbia, SC 29201
(803) 734–7520

South Carolina State Library
Department for the Blind and Physically
Handicapped
301 Gervais St.
P.O. Box 821
Columbia, SC 29202
(803) 737–9970 or in South Carolina
(800) 922–7818

SOUTH DAKOTA

Office of Special Education
South Dakota Division of Education
700 Governors Drive

Pierre, SD 57501–2291
(605) 773–3678

South Dakota School for the Visually
Handicapped
423 S.E. 17th Ave.
Aberdeen, SD 57401–7699
(605) 622–2580

South Dakota State Library for the Handicapped
800 Governors Drive
Pierre, SD 57501–2295
(605) 773–3131

TENNESSEE

Tennessee Department of Education
132 Cordell Hull Building
Nashville, TN 37219
(615) 741–2851

Tennessee School for the Blind
115 Stewarts Ferry Pike
Nashville, TN 37214
(615) 855–2451

Services for the Blind
Tennessee Division of Rehabilitation Services
Citizens Plaza Building, 11th Floor
400 Deaderick St.
Nashville, TN 37248–6200
(615) 741–2919

Tennessee Library for the Blind and Physically Handicapped
403 Seventh Ave. North
Nashville, TN 37243–0313
(615) 741–3915 or in Tennessee (800)
342–3308

TEXAS

Texas Education Agency
1701 North Congress Ave.
Austin, TX 78701
(512) 463–9414

Early Childhood Program
Texas Department of Health
1100 West 49th St.
Austin, TX 78756
(512) 458–7673

Texas School for the Blind and Visually
Impaired
1100 West 45th St.
Austin, TX 78756
(512) 454–8631

Texas State Library
Division for the Blind and Physically
Handicapped
Capitol Station
P.O. Box 12927
Austin, TX 78711
(512) 463–5458 or in Texas (800) 252–
9605

Texas Commission for the Blind
Administration Building
4800 North Lamar Blvd.
P.O. Box 12866
Austin, TX 78711
(512) 459–2500 or (800) 252–5204

UTAH

Utah State Office of Education
Special Education Section
250 East 500 South
Salt Lake City, UT 84111
(801) 538–7510

Early Intervention Program
Division of Family Services
Utah Department of Health
P.O. Box 16650–BCSHS
Salt Lake City, UT 84116–0650
(801) 538–6922

Utah Schools for the Deaf and the Blind
742 Harrison Blvd.
Ogden, UT 84404
(801) 399–9631

Utah State Library
Division for the Blind and Physically
Handicapped
2150 South 300 West, Suite 16
Salt Lake City, UT 84115
(801) 466–6363

VERMONT

Special Education Unit
Vermont Department of Education
State Office Building
120 State St.
Montpelier, VT 05620
(802) 828–3141

Vermont Association for the Blind and
Visually Impaired
37 Elmwood Ave.
Burlington, VT 05401
(802) 863–1358

Vermont Department of Libraries
Special Services Unit
RD #4, Box 1870

Montpelier, VT 05602
(802) 828–3273 or in Vermont (800) 479–1711

VIRGINIA

Virginia Department for the Visually
   Handicapped
Program for Infants, Children and Youth
397 Azalea Ave.
Richmond, VA 23227–3697
(804) 367–0030

Infants and Toddler Program
Virginia Department of Mental Health,
   and Substance Abuse Services
P.O. Box 1797
Richmond, VA 23219
(804) 786–3710

Virginia School for the Deaf and Blind
P.O. Box 2069
Staunton, VA 24402
(703) 332–9046

Children's Rehabilitation Center
University of Virginia Hospital
2270 Ivy Road
Charlottesville, VA 22903
(804) 924–5500

Virginia State Library for the Visually and
   Physically Handicapped
1901 Roane St.
Richmond, VA 23222
(804) 786–8016 or in Virginia (800) 552–7015

VIRGIN ISLANDS

Virgin Islands Department of Education
State Office of Special Education
44–46 Kongens Gade
Charlotte Amalie
St. Thomas, VI 00802
(809) 776–5802

WASHINGTON

Washington Office of Superintendent of
   Public Instruction
Division of Special Education Services
Old Capitol Building
Olympia, WA 98504
(206) 753–6733

Birth to Six State Planning Project
Washington Department of Social and
   Health Services
P.O. Box 45201

Olympia, WA 98504–5201
(206) 586–2810

Washington State School for the Blind
2214 East 13th St.
Vancouver, WA 98661–4120
(206) 696–6630

Washington Library for the Blind and
   Physically Handicapped
821 Lenora St.
Seattle, WA 98129
(206) 464–6930 or in Washington (800)
   542–0866

Washington State Department of Services
   for the Blind
521 East Legion Way
Mail Stop 0933
Olympia, WA 98504–0933
(206) 586–1224

WEST VIRGINIA

West Virginia Department of Education
State Capitol Building
Building #6, Room B-304/1900
Kanawha Blvd. East
Charleston, WV 25305
(304) 558–2696

Office of Maternal and Child Health
West Virginia Department of Health and
   Human Resources
1116 Quarier St.
Charleston, WV 25301
(304) 558–3071

West Virginia Schools for the Deaf and
   Blind
301 East Main St.
Romney, WV 26757
(304) 822–4800
West Virginia Library Commission
Services for the Blind and Physically
   Handicapped
Science and Cultural Center
1900 Kanawha Blvd.
Charleston, WV 25305
(304) 558–4061 or in West Virginia (800)
   642–8674

WISCONSIN

Wisconsin Bureau for Exceptional Children
Division for Handicapped Children and
   Public Services
125 South Webster St.
P.O. Box 7841

Madison, WI 53707–7841
(608) 266–3522

Birth to Three Early Intervention
Division of Community Services
Wisconsin Department of Health and So-
cial Services
P.O. Box 7851
Madison, WI 53707–7851
(608) 267–3270

Wisconsin School for the Visually Handicapped and Educational Services Center for the Visually Impaired
1700 West State St.
Janesville, WI 53546
(608) 758–6100

Wisconsin Regional Library for the Blind
and Physically Handicapped
813 West Wells St.
Milwaukee, WI 53233
(414) 278–3045 or in Wisconsin (800)
242–8822

WYOMING

Services for the Visually Handicapped
Wyoming Department of Education
2300 Capitol Ave.
Hathaway Building, Second Floor
Cheyenne, WY 82002–0050
(307) 777–6202

Division of Developmental Disabilities
Wyoming Department of Health
2020 Capitol Ave.
Cheyenne, WY 88002
(307) 777–5246

INDEX

About the editor

M. Cay Holbrook holds a doctorate in special education from Florida State University. She has educated children with visual impairments and served as an advocate and instructor for over twenty years. Currently she is Associate Professor in the Faculty of Education, Department of Education and Counselling Psychology and Special Education, at the University of British Columbia.